TRUTH ABOUT THE GOOD

Faith and Reason: Studies in Catholic Theology and Philosophy

The series aims at publishing scholarly studies that serve the project of "faith seeking understanding." We hope to assist in making available in English valuable work being done by theologians and philosophers abroad; in this regard we recognize a special place for the ongoing renaissance in French-language Thomistic theology and philosophy. In addition to translations, we intend to publish collections of essays and monographs from a range of perspectives, united by their common commitment to the ecclesial and sapiential work of "faith seeking understanding" so as to build up the Church and proclaim the Gospel afresh.

Published Volumes

Serge-Thomas Bonino, OP, ed., *Surnaturel: Reflections on Nature and Grace*
Gilles Emery, OP, *Trinity, Church, and the Human Person: Thomistic Essays*
Lawrence Feingold, *The Natural Desire to See God*
Matthew L. Lamb, *Eternity, Time, and the Life of Wisdom*
Guy Mansini, OSB, *The Word Has Dwelt Among Us*
Thomas Joseph White, OP, *Wisdom in the Face of Modernity*

Truth about the Good: Moral Norms in the Thought of John Paul II

Adrian J. Reimers

EX CORDE ECCLESIAE
VERITATIS SPLENDOR
·AVE·
MARIA
UNIVERSITY

Sapientia Press
of Ave Maria University

Sapientia Press
of Ave Maria University
5050 Ave Maria Blvd.
Ave Maria, FL 34142
888-343-8607

Cover Design: Eloise Anagnost

Photo provided by the photographic service of L'Osservatore Romano.

Printed in the United States of America.

Library of Congress Control Number: 2011927107

ISBN 978-1-932589-57-3

Dedicated to my Parents
George Irving Reimers, 1919–1974
and
Margaret Cecelia Doyle Reimers, 1920–2000
who taught me the Truth about the Good

Table of Contents

Preface

NOT LONG AFTER the publication of Pope John Paul II's encyclical *Veritatis Splendor*, the Department of Theology at the University of Notre Dame held several colloquia to discuss the encyclical, and two things about these discussions struck me as significant. The first was that, in referring to the author of the encyclical, the theologians and their graduate students habitually referred to "they" or "them," in the plural, suggesting that this work had several authors.[1] Second and complementary to the first, most of those present agreed with the comment that the unity of the encyclical was hard to discern, that it seemed to argue from divergent points of view. At the time I thought that both of these views were off the mark, although I could not then tell exactly why. Concerning the question of authorship, it seemed clear from my own knowledge of Karol Wojtyła's philosophical thought that there was one author, and it was John Paul II. As a student of his work, I thought that I could see his fingerprints all over *Veritatis Splendor*. Even if the Pope had staff to help with the writing and to draft different sections, it seemed to me that this was the work of the man who also wrote *Love and Responsibility* and *The Acting Person*. This was an impression, of course, and not an argument.

The question of the unity of the encyclical relates directly to that of its authorship. One author writing one work will (if he is any good) integrate

[1] See Richard A. McCormick, S.J., "Some Early Reactions to *Veritatis Splendor*," in *John Paul II and Moral Theology*, ed. Charles E. Curran and Richard A. McCormick, S.J., Readings in Moral Theology 10 (New York: Paulist Press, 1998), 9.

its various sections logically and guide them toward a meaningful conclusion to establish a cogent thesis. In questioning the unity of this encyclical, that theologian had raised one of the fundamental questions concerning the interpretation of John Paul II's work, both academic and pastoral. *Veritatis Splendor* starts with a reflection on a text of Scripture, the story of the rich young man (Mt 19:16–22), from which he develops a kind of meditation or reflection on the meaning of life. We see elements of the late Pope's use of phenomenology, almost a Christian existentialism. Then in chapter 2, the tone changes. John Paul II begins to use categories familiar to traditional moral theology, categories of natural law, the will, the object of the moral act, conscience, and *intrinsece malum.* The reader finds himself thrown back into St. Thomas's analysis of the will and the act in the *Prima secundae* of the *Summa theologiae.* Then the third chapter appears as a pastoral reflection on the Church, the martyrs, and the challenges of Christian witness. One may well ask what it is that ties these diverse discussions into unity. What are the principles of Pope John Paul II's analysis?

My personal concern about the comments and questions that arose from this colloquium began to find an answer in terms of a growing awareness of the phrase that forms the title of this work. As I studied the writings of Karol Wojtyła/John Paul II, I became increasingly aware of the central role played by the recurring phrase "*the truth about the good.*"[2] It is one of the central concepts in the argument of Wojtyła's main philosophical work, *Osoba i czyn*,[3] and it appears repeatedly in *Veritatis Splendor.* Finding one phrase repeatedly used suggests that perhaps that phrase expresses something

[2] "Prawda o dobru" in his Polish works, "veritas de bono" in his encyclicals, and "la verità sul bene" in Italian. I am, of course, not unique in having noticed the importance of this phrase. See, for example, Edward Kaczyński, O.P., *Verità sul bene nella morale: Alcuni temi di morale fondamentale* (Rome: Millennium Romae, 1998), 183.

[3] Karol Wojtyła, *Osoba i czyn: Oraz inne studia antropologiczne* (Lublin: Towarzystwo Naukowe KUL, 2000), 180ff. The English translation of *Osoba i czyn* is *The Acting Person* (Dordrecht: D. Riedel Publishing Company, 1979), which is, unfortunately, not simply a translation but an interpretive edition. For some of the difficulties with the translation, see Rocco Buttiglione, *Karol Wojtyla: The Thought of the Man Who Became Pope John Paul II*, trans. Paolo Guietti and Francesca Murphy (Grand Rapids: Wm. B. Eerdmans, 1997), 117n1. In this study I rely principally on the Italian translation by Giuseppe Girgenti and Patrycja Mikulska, *Persona e atto*, in *Metafisica della persona: Tutti le opera filosofiche e saggi integrative*, by Karol Wojtyła (Milan: Bompiani, 2003). In all cases (except when expressly quoting the English edition) within my text I refer to the work as *Person and Act.*

important in the author's thought. And it suggests a research project for one who would understand that author's thought. Throughout his dual career as scholar and pastor, John Paul II concerned himself with truth and goodness. Prior to his election to the papacy, Karol Wojtyła held the chair of ethics at the Catholic University of Lublin (Katolicki Uniwersytet Lubelski, or KUL), in which capacity he lectured and published regularly on questions of moral good and evil, addressing himself not only to Catholic thinkers but also to the broader intellectual community in Europe. Especially during the 1970s Cardinal Wojtyła participated frequently in the works of the International Husserl and Phenomenological Research Society.[4]

Of course, not all ethicians are prepared to affirm that there is a truth about the good or that the expression is even meaningful. In any case, the phrase does not commonly appear outside Wojtyła's work. As a Catholic bishop and eventually as Pope, Karol Wojtyła/John Paul II had to address a Church in which the objectivity and universality of moral norms was increasingly called into question. As revisionist moral theologians rejected the rigid structures and strictures of the old manualist tradition, many had difficulty accounting for these norms in the context of a more personalist account of human nature, one that adequately respected human subjectivity without thereby falling into relativism or consequentialism. As a pastor—eventually Supreme Pastor—John Paul II recognized himself as responsible for the truth, and where morality is concerned this is the truth about the good.

The Unity of John Paul II's Thought

The thesis of this present work is that in the *truth about the good* we find the unity of John Paul II's personalism, the unifying thread that runs through his writings, from the early lectures in Lublin to the encyclicals and catecheses of his papacy. To put it more precisely, an inquiry into the truth about the good will enable us to grasp both the structural unity of John Paul II's thought and its ultimate intellectual coherence, its internal teleology as it were. The reason for this is that the truth about the good is precisely what

[4] See, for example, Anna-Teresa Tymieniecka, ed., *Analecta Husserliana: The Yearbook of Phenomenological Research*, vol. 7, *The Human Being in Action* (Dordrecht: D. Reidel Publishing Company, 1978); vol. 9, *The Teleologies in Husserlian Phenomenology* (1979); and vol. 11, *The Great Chain of Being and Italian Phenomenology* (1981). The English translation of Karol Wojtyła's *Osoba i czyn*, *The Acting Person*, was published as vol. 10 of this same series.

constitutes a moral norm. If we understand what Karol Wojtyła/John Paul II understands by *truth about the good*, then we know how he connects metaphysics, philosophical anthropology, and ethics, as well as how the revealed doctrines of the faith are integrally related to its moral teaching.

The structure of our author's thought remains a topic of debate and, indeed more commonly, misunderstanding. Since his election to the papacy, it has been common to note that unlike his predecessors, who were trained in seminary Scholasticism, John Paul II was a phenomenologist.[5] One can argue, however, that John Paul II has his metaphysical roots planted firmly in Thomistic soil.[6] If he is to be taken as a phenomenologist, then his clear rejection of Scheler's phenomenology as an adequate basis for ethics and his repeated appeals in *Person and Act*, as well as other writings, to the Aristotelian-Thomistic philosophy of being should give us pause. However, his emphasis on the subjectivity of the human person, using a phenomenological analysis of the experience "a man acts" as the starting point of his principal philosophical work,[7] is, to say the least, unusual in a Thomist and disconcerting to many Thomists.[8] We have already noted that in *Veritatis Splendor* our author mingles Scriptural meditations, phenomenological analyses, and detailed Scholastic arguments. In everything he wrote, however, he was concerned about the good.[9]

[5] See, for example, Tad Szulc, *Pope John Paul II: The Biography* (New York: Scribner, 1995), 80, 182, and Robert F. Harvanek, S.J., "The Philosophical Foundations of the Thought of John Paul II," in *The Thought of Pope John Paul II: A Collection of Essays and Studies*, ed. John J. McDermott, S.J. (Rome: Editrice Pontificia Università Gregoriana, 1993), 6.

[6] See Jarosław Kupczak, O.P., *Destined for Liberty: The Human Person in the Philosophy of Karol Wojtyła/John Paul II* (Washington, DC: Catholic University of America Press, 2000), 49–57; Adrian J. Reimers, "The Thomistic Personalism of Karol Wojtyła (Pope John Paul II)," in *Atti del IX congresso tomistico internazionale*, vol. 6, *Storia del tomismo fonti e riflessi* (Vatican City: Pontificia Accademia di S. Tommaso, 1992), 364–69.

[7] Wojtyła, *Persona e atto*, 841.

[8] See, for instance, Kenneth L. Schmitz, *At the Center of the Human Drama: The Philosophical Anthropology of Karol Wojtyła/John Paul II* (Washington, DC: Catholic University of America Press, 1993), 58–89.

[9] Immediately we may note the inadequacy of Charles Curran's analysis of John Paul II's moral theology in his *Moral Theology of Pope John Paul II* (Washington, DC: Georgetown University Press, 2005), where we read such puzzling statements as this one concerning the late Pope's major encyclicals: "He is also very negative about contemporary philosophy and the use of human reason. These encyclicals

The phrase "truth about the good" has more a Thomistic than a phenomenological "ring" to it. Characteristically phenomenologists will speak in terms of *value*, which is a matter of experience, rather than of *good*.[10] The texture of the world, its constitution as the world in which we can live, is formed by values aesthetic, intellectual, moral, and religious. Values are subjectively given in experience or, to put it phenomenologically, in intentional intuition. So conceived, the life-world becomes a rich realm for human action, one filled with opportunities for personal enrichment and realization through appropriate value responses. This was, effectively, the import of Max Scheler's analyses, and it is this same nexus of insights that lends von Hildebrand's writing its winsomeness.[11] Attractive though they may be, however, phenomenological analyses of value risk falling into subjectivism and relativism. Wojtyła rejected Scheler's account of ethics based on value response, and the basis for this rejection is the failure to ground the truth of values ontologically, to find the bases of their truth, which must be the *truth about the good*. It is my hope, therefore, through this work to show both the underlying Aristotelian-Thomistic metaphysical structure of John Paul II's thought as well as his creative development of that thought by using phenomenological methods.

The debate whether John Paul II is, in the final analysis, a phenomenologist or a Thomist may matter little outside of academic circles. Much more important is the question of the coherence of his thought as a whole. What does *Person and Act* have to do with *Centesimus Annus*, or the essay "Person: Subject and Community" with the catechesis on the theology of the body? That is to say, we need to determine more precisely and concretely how Karol Wojtyła's philosophical personalism, as expressed in such works as *Person and Act* as well as its many complementary essays, informs John Paul II's pastoral corpus. The concept of the *truth about the good* is precisely such a key. The "adequate anthropology"[12] painstakingly

addressing aspects of faith never explicitly develop the ability of human reason to come to the truth" (15).

10 See John Crosby, "The Idea of Value and the Reform of the Traditional Metaphysics of *Bonum*," *Aletheia: An International Journal of Philosophy* 1, no. 2 (1977): 231–327.

11 See Dietrich von Hildebrand, *Ethics* (Chicago: Franciscan Herald Press, 1953).

12 John Paul II, *Man and Woman He Created Them: A Theology of the Body*, translated with an introduction and index by Michael Waldstein (Boston: Pauline Books and

developed in Wojtyła's philosophical writings entails a particular conception of the truth about the good, a conception that is retained throughout his writings, that plays a decisive role in his major encyclicals.

The Principle of Unity

In the introduction to his translation of Pope John Paul II's "theology of the body" audiences, Michael Waldstein offers a surprising and provocative key to the John-Pauline corpus:

> The main agenda of *The Acting Person*, however, is not dictated by Scheler, but by Wojtyła's roots in the spousal theology of St. John of the Cross, specifically by the key notion, "gift of self." In order to give oneself, one must be in responsible possession of oneself. *The Acting Person* supplies the account of the person that is presupposed by St. John of the Cross's spousal theology of self-gift.[13]

This key notion, "gift of self," is another name for love, and it is the governing concept in John Paul II's thought and activity. Love is always of the good, whether this good be real, illusory, or imagined. Whether they conceive the good to lie in pleasure, wealth, fame, friendship, achievement, scientific research and understanding, or virtue, human beings desire the good and seek to realize it in their own lives. We want to have what is good and also to be good, not always in the sense that we measure up to socially or religiously established standards of goodness, but in the sense that we realize our best dreams for or vision of ourselves. At issue, then, is what the good is. In his homily before the conclave electing him as successor to John Paul II, Joseph Cardinal Ratzinger spoke of a "dictatorship of relativism that does not recognize anything as definitive and whose

Media, 2006), 13:2. Citations from *Man and Woman He Created Them* will be according to audience number and section (13:2 represents audience 13, section 2), as developed by Michael Waldstein in that edition. The Polish term, *adekwatnej antropologii*, appears in John Paul II, *Mężczyzną i niewiastą stworzył ich: Odkupienie ciała a sakramentalność małżeństwa* [Man and woman he created them: Redemption of the body and the sacramentality of marriage] (Lublin: Wydawnictwo KUL, 2008), 44.

13 Michael Waldstein, introduction to John Paul II, *Man and Woman He Created Them*, 79.

ultimate goal consists solely of one's own ego and desires."[14] This relativism arises from the grounding of good in human subjectivity, from the denial of its foundation in the objective order of reality. This subjectivizing of good finds its roots in the Enlightenment, with the increasingly sharp division between the order of scientifically ascertainable fact and that of human values. If good arises from within human subjectivity, whether this be taken as a transcendental reality pertaining to the structure of reason itself, or as the values embraced by a particular culture, or more simply as the subjective tastes and preferences of the individual subject, there can be no "truth about the good" as such.

As we shall see, in his use of this phrase, John Paul II intends that within the real order, the objective, intersubjective order which we can know by disciplined rational inquiry, there is an order of goods. In this respect he tries to retrieve the premodern perspective of a teleologically ordered cosmos, one in which things are not value-neutral and in which there are no meaningless surds. The truth about the good is, as it were, "out there" to be found. It follows, then, that the good to be found in the natural order, the meaning of created physical structures, the significance and moral goodness of human acts, and the ends of religious devotion are all interrelated.

John Paul II works from a personalistic perspective. That is to say, instead of taking the physical or natural order as his starting point, he begins with the human person, a being that exists in the world as both subject and object. The person is a being governed not only by physical laws, those discoverable by the empirical sciences, but also by spiritual principles, by which the person transcends himself toward truth and good. Much of the present investigation will be concerned with this transcendence and its implications. What is particularly noteworthy and central to this investigation of the *truth about the good* is that to know this capacity toward transcendence requires neither an abandonment of scientific rationality nor an appeal to Revelation, but simply a careful account of ordinary human experience and careful reasoning on the basis of that experience. John Paul II does not require special insight or prior religious

[14] Joseph Ratzinger, homily for Mass "Pro eligendo romano pontifice," April 18, 2005, www.vatican.va/gpII/documents/homily-pro-eligendo-pontifice_20050418_en.html (accessed September 6, 2007).

commitment. His appeal, rather, is to what a human person is. In virtue of this personalism, the question of the truth about the good is inescapable.

Plan of the Work

In this present study, we shall consider first the notion of *good* as this concept has developed in the modern era, that is, since the Enlightenment. Then, chapter 2 will consider Karol Wojtyła's arguments concerning the locus of good in the natural order and how this relates to the empirical sciences. Having examined the bases for the general concept of *good*, we turn to the question of moral experience—our moral engagement with good—in chapter 3, followed by Wojtyła's account of the moral good, in chapter 4, which concludes with a characterization of moral norms. The theme of norms is taken up in chapter 5 with a thorough discussion of the *personalistic norm*, which is one of the two fundamental norms in John Paul II's thought. The other fundamental norm is that God is the supreme good, and as such he is the highest good for the human person. In chapter 6, I analyze the notion of *bonum honestum* ("fitting good") in relation to God as supreme good and the other goods that govern human moral life. Chapter 7 addresses John Paul II's critique of proportionalism and consequentialism in contemporary moral theology, especially in relation to the question of intrinsically evil acts. Chapter 8, titled "The Truth About the Good," applies John Paul II's analysis to two central questions: (1) the problems of legalism and "double morality," and (2) community and the common good.

• • • • •

As I send this into your hands, Good Reader, let me express my thanks on your behalf to my wife, Marie Reimers, who has served us both by diligently searching through my manuscript for typographical errors, as well as grammatical, stylistic, and—most important—conceptual infelicities and confusions. Her contributions and support, as she has listened to, questioned, and challenged my explanations of John Paul II's thought, have been invaluable to the sharpening of my argument. Along these lines, I thank John Sikorski and Luis Vera, graduate students in theology, who joined me in a close reading of *Person and Act.* Mr. Sikorski's ability to read the original text of *Osoba i czyn* was especially valuable. I also thank Christina Holmstrom, whose senior thesis I also had the privilege to supervise. She may well recognize here echoes of her own work and of our discussions. Thanks are due also to Father Grzegorz Hołub, S.B.D., of the Interfaculty Institute of Bioethics at the Pontifical Academy of Theology in Krakow for sharing his thoughts with me and particularly for his patient help as I attempted to interpret Wojtyła's Polish texts. Finally, I would like to acknowledge the editors at Sapientia Press of Ave Maria University whose contributions have served to make the text clearer at several important points.

Prologue

POPE JOHN PAUL II's encyclical on moral theology *Veritatis Splendor* begins with the story of Christ's encounter with the rich young man (Mt 19:16–22) who asks, "What must I do to inherit eternal life?"[1] At first glance the young man's question is practical and has an operational point: "What good deed must I do to possess eternal life?" The question "What good must I do?" is an ethical one, the sort of thing that ethicians and moral theologians spend much of their time analyzing. What makes an act good or evil? What are the criteria of judgment concerning moral acts? How do we judge between courses of action so as to know the correct one to take? Because John Paul II believes that such questions are not primary, he delves into the deeper implications of the young man's question. The young man has a goal in mind, "to possess eternal life." He wants to find an ultimate focus or meaning for his life. By means of this story, then, the Pope intends to put the question of moral behavior into its fundamental context. The young man's question points to his desire—his yearning—to satisfy his deepest longing. Besides considering the young man's motivation, John Paul II discusses Christ's curious response, "Why do you ask me about what is good? There is one alone who is good" (Mt 19:17). This issue—*what good is*—proves to be central for an accurate assessment not only of John Paul II's moral theology but of his entire conception of

[1] John Paul II, encyclical *Veritatis Splendor* (Boston: Pauline Books and Media, 1993), chapter 1.

human nature.[2] To put the point in other words, the Pope uses this story to direct his readers to the fundamental concept of good.

John Paul II argues that the young man is not asking simply about moral rules but about the meaning of life: "The question which the rich young man puts to Jesus of Nazareth is one which rises from the depths of his heart. It is *an essential and unavoidable question for the life of every man*, for it is about the moral good which must be done, and about eternal life. The young man senses that there is a connection between moral good and the fulfilment of his own destiny."[3] The Pope poses this same question at the beginning of his encyclical on the relationship between faith and reason, *Fides et Ratio*, where he writes:

> Moreover, a cursory glance at ancient history shows clearly how in different parts of the world, with their different cultures, there arise at the same time the fundamental questions which pervade human life: Who am I? Where have I come from and where am I going? Why is there evil? What is there after this life? . . . They are questions which have their common source in the quest for meaning which has always compelled the human heart. In fact, the answer given to these questions decides the direction which people seek to give to their lives.[4]

The thesis of *Fides et Ratio* is that the human power of reason, aided by faith, can penetrate to the truth of things to discover the meaning of human life. In virtue of this meaning, people can discern the direction for their lives. Indeed, throughout John Paul II's writings, we find a coherent, developed conception of the good, with particular reference to what is good for the human person. The human being is open to this good precisely in virtue of his power to know the truth. Truth and good hang together.

Had the young man's question been simply hypothetical—for example, "What must I do to qualify as a good postexilic Jew?"—then Christ's initial response would have sufficed; he should keep the commandments, for (pre-

---

[2] Charles Curran misses the importance of this point, writing, "The encyclical makes primary the insistence on obedience to the commandments. But morality, as portrayed throughout scripture, involves much more than just obedience to commandments." Curran, *The Moral Theology of Pope John Paul II*, 35.

[3] *Veritatis Splendor*, 8.

[4] John Paul II, encyclical *Fides et Ratio* (Boston: Pauline Books and Media, 1998), 1. Unless otherwise noted, all emphasis in quotations is in the original.

sumably) obedience to the Decalogue and observance of certain traditions would count as meeting the requirements for being a "good postexilic Jew." But Jesus addresses the core of the young man's question by adding the phrase "but if you would be perfect." We note that Jesus' words here address the condition of the young man himself as a human being, as a person. He does not speak of meeting the requirements or attaining some well-defined (and therefore limited) goal but rather of the young man's being "perfect." To put it in Kantian terms, John Paul II sees Jesus taking the young man from the hypothetical question to the categorical. The question is not simply what is "good for," the young man, nor is the answer to be in terms of "what personal goals the young man wants to attain." The significance of this becomes clear in the succeeding sections of *Veritatis Splendor.*

Ultimately, argues John Paul II, the good is found in God. Indeed, God is the Good.[5] The good is something real, objective, and outside the young man, and this good is the only end that will satisfy the young man's ultimate desire. John Paul II's intent here is not simply to interpret a text from the Bible but to interpret a fundamental human experience—or rather an aspect of all human experience. We all seek the good, an ultimate something, that gives meaning, purpose, and direction to our lives. This ultimate good is the basis for the science of ethics, but in itself it is prior to ethics.

If the good is God, then Jesus Christ, Eternal Word of God incarnate, is the truth: "I am the way, the truth and the life" (Jn 14:6). In a text that Pope John Paul II frequently quotes, the Second Vatican Council wrote:

> The truth is that only in the mystery of the incarnate Word does the mystery of man take on light. . . . Christ, the final Adam, by the revelation of the mystery of the Father and His love, fully reveals man to man himself and makes his supreme calling clear.
>
> For by His incarnation the Son of God has united Himself in some fashion with every man. He worked with human hands, He thought with a human mind, acted by human choice and loved with a human heart. Born of the Virgin Mary, He has truly been made one of us, like us in all things except sin.[6]

[5] John Paul II, general audience, September 11, 1985, 7, in *Catechesi sul Credo,* pt. 1, "Dio Padre e Creatore" (1985–1986), www.vatican.va/holy_father/john_paul_ii/audiences/alpha/index_it.html (accessed September 3, 2003).

[6] Vatican Council II, Pastoral Constitution on the Church in the Modern World *Gaudium et Spes* (Boston: Pauline Books and Media, 1965), 22. See also John Paul II, encyclical *Redemptor Hominis* (Boston: St. Paul Editions, 1979), 8–10.

The truth about the good is thus incarnate in Jesus Christ. This is the thesis of chapter 1 of *Veritatis Splendor*, that the attainment to God, who is the "One who is good," is in the following and imitation of Christ. Therefore, if the moral life is about the attainment and realization of the good, the *sequela Christi* lies at its heart: "*Following Christ is thus the essential and primordial foundation of Christian morality.*"[7] This following of Christ is accomplished by love, by the generous, disinterested gift of self. "Perfection demands maturity," writes John Paul II, "in that self-giving to which human freedom is called."[8] Here our author echoes a text from the Second Vatican Council that he was especially fond of quoting: "[M]an, who is the only creature on earth that God has willed for itself, cannot fully find himself except in sincere gift of self."[9] Just as Jesus Christ gave himself completely for the salvation of sinful humanity, each human being is called to self-sacrifice in the hope of finding himself in the disinterested love of others.[10]

And if we read John Paul II's text carefully, we see clearly that this good, which is God himself, is the good for all and not only for John Paul II's Catholic flock. The truth about the good, according to John Paul's argument, is that God is the highest good, and that this good is attainable. The moral life is formed by the human effort to realize that good, and it is in terms of that good that moral obligations arise. In some way, therefore, all human beings are called to follow Christ. And this is the argument we shall trace in the following chapters.

---

7 John Paul II, *Veritatis Splendor*, 19.

8 Ibid., 17.

9 *Gaudium et Spes*, 24.

10 Michael Waldstein observes that the two texts from *Gaudium et Spes* 22 and 24, which John Paul II frequently quotes, in fact are intimately connected in his thought. "The revelation of this mystery of love [of God in Christ] reveals that the vocation of the human being is also the gift of self." "La grazia in forma paterna e il vecchio principio metafisico dell'auto-communicazione dell'essere," in *Camminare nella Luce: Prospettive della teologia morale a partire da* Veritatis Splendor, ed. Livio Melina and José Noriega (Rome: Lateran University Press, 2004), 486.

CHAPTER 1
The Good

The Problem of "Good"

JOHN PAUL II is unabashedly theocentric. But may we not therefore question his philosophical relevance? If he holds that God is the Good, and Jesus is the Truth about the Good, has he not unduly limited his conception of *good* such that only Christians could know this good? Furthermore, even if prescinding from divine Revelation we consider God simply as Supreme Being, the metaphysical Ground of Being, it remains to be explained how this supreme good relates to the present good or evil of some existing state of affairs, or to the future good or evil of an intended act. What can be the relationship, if any, between the absolute, transcendent good and the ordinary, limited goods of our daily existence? A further apparent problem with John Paul II's conception is that one does not need to be religious, much less Christian, to understand the word "good" and to recognize good and evil. We all—whether professional philosophers or devout believers or ordinary persons in secular life—understand the predicate "good." *Good* is not primarily, much less exclusively, a religious concept. It is, as Thomas Aquinas shows, a transcendental predicate of being, applicable to anything that in any way is said to be.[1]

---

[1] Thomas Aquinas, *De veritate*, translated as *The Disputed Questions on Truth*; vol. 1, trans. Robert W. Mulligan, S.J., Ph.D.; vol. 3, trans. Robert W. Schmidt, S.J., Ph.D. (Chicago: Henry Regnery Company, 1952–1954), q. 1, a. 1. Consider also R. M. Hare's discussion of the "commending" role that "good" plays in our language in *The Language of Morals* (New York: Oxford University Press, 1969), 94–136.

Good and the Religious Sense

These difficulties notwithstanding, we must also note that the belief in a transcendent good does generally entail moral obligations and a religious response. From the earliest manifestations of distinctively human activity, the belief in superior beings, divinities, has been accompanied by responses of devotion and submission. Whether the gods are cruel or friendly, their worshipers have approached them with reverence, submission, and awe. (Of course, accompanying this reverence was often the effort to manipulate the gods through ceremonies and sacrifices.) Especially pertinent here is the experience of Plato's Socrates, who not only believed in the existence of divine beings[2] but shaped his life according to the wisdom he ascribed to them. Socrates takes Chaerephon's message to be a divine revelation that in all the world there was none wiser than Socrates.[3]

Plato and Aristotle take these reflections even further. Although Plato's Form of the Good is introduced as the ultimate metaphysical and epistemological foundation for reality, it was also the object of contemplation, the ultimate goal of the human soul's self-transcendence,[4] the admiration of which has a moral impact on the life of the philosopher.[5] In his *Metaphysics* Aristotle demonstrates the existence of a supreme being, a first mover.[6] Famously, this being—its only description can be as thought thinking itself[7]—is distant and impersonal, unconcerned with the rest of reality, which for its part is moved by desire for the first mover. Such a being is hardly the object of liturgical worship, devotion, and sacrifice. However, the very act of getting to know and reflect upon this supreme

---

2 See Plato, *Apology*, 26c–27e, 29b, 37e; *Phaedo*, 6b–c; and *Republic*, 2.377e–383c, in *The Collected Dialogues of Plato*, ed. Edith Hamilton and Huntington Cairns (Princeton: Princeton University Press, 1961).

3 *Apology*, 20d–21b and then through the remainder of the dialogue.

4 Plato, *Republic*, translated by G. M. A. Grube and revised by C. D. C. Reeve (Indianapolis: Hackett Publishing Company, 1992), 6.508d-e, 7.519c.

5 Karol Wojtyła, *Lubliner Vorlesungen*, trans. Annaliese Danka Spranger and Edda Wiener (Stuttgart-Degerloch: Seewald Verlag, 1981), 127. Of this volume, to which we will recur frequently, Jarosław Kupczak writes, "It is difficult to overstate the importance of the importance of the *Lublin Lectures* in the development of Wojtyła's own philosophy." Kupczak, *Destined for Liberty*, 37.

6 Aristotle, *Metaphysics*, in *Commentary on the* Metaphysics *of Aristotle*, by Thomas Aquinas, trans. John P. Rowan (Chicago: Henry Regnery Company, 1961), vol. 2, 12.7.

7 Ibid., 12.9.

being turns out to be an exercise in genuine religious sentiment. In book 10 of the *Nicomachean Ethics*, Aristotle characterizes the perfect happiness for a human being. Up until that point he had developed an extensive account of the moral life in terms of the moral and intellectual virtues, friendship, and pleasure, in effect the life of a virtuous Athenian active in the political, cultural, and economic milieu of the polis. The capstone and full realization of such a life, however, is attained in the godlike activity of contemplation.[8] "But such a life would be too high for man; for it is not in so far as he is man that he will live so, but in so far as something divine is present in him. . . . If reason is divine, then, in comparison with man, the life according to it is divine in comparison with human life."[9]

The Stagirite then goes on to connect this with the activity of his first mover. "Therefore the activity of God, which surpasses all others in blessedness, must be contemplative; and of human activities, therefore that which is most akin to this must be most of the nature of happiness."[10]

The culmination or full realization of the good life of the human being lies in the imitation of the divine, in admittedly limited participation in the activity of the first mover, whose beauty moves the universe. The good life is one that imitates the activity of the god. This response of awe and imitation is fundamentally religious. It shapes the life of the person who pursues it, gives him something transcendent to live for, fosters that in him that is most like the divine, and constitutes a kind of homage to the divine being. Even the impersonal "God of the philosophers," "Thought-thinking-itself," is in this respect an object of religious devotion.

The point of this brief excursus into ancient Greek philosophy is that Wojtyła's linking of the moral and natural orders with the religious is no innovation, but instead amounts to a return to the roots of the Western philosophical tradition. This is, of course, no accident, for he makes it clear in his encyclical *Fides et Ratio* that the search for the fundamental truths of philosophy is inevitably a search for the truths by which men live, for those truths that constitute the meaning of human life.[11] As a

---

[8] Aristotle, *Nicomachean Ethics*, translated with an introduction by David Ross (Oxford: Oxford University Press, 1998), 10.7. See also John M. Cooper, "Contemplation and Happiness: A Reconsideration," *Synthese* 72 (1987): 187–216.

[9] Aristotle, *Nicomachean Ethics* 10.7, 1177b14–1178a5.

[10] Ibid., 1178b21ff.

[11] *Fides et Ratio*, 2–5.

result, John Paul II is not so fastidious as most of the rest of us about maintaining sharp boundaries between philosophy and theology, between nature and grace. He is careful, as we shall see, and he respects their differences, but he does not allow these distinctions to obscure the fundamental unity that underlies the natural, moral, and religious orders.

The Enlightenment Transformation

Enlightenment philosophy removed God from the summit of being and in so doing called into question the very concept of gradations of being. With his telescope Galileo showed that the moon was rocky and the sun spotted, that neither was made of an eternal celestial matter. Newton showed that the movements of these and the "higher" heavenly bodies, the planets and the fixed stars, were determined not by governing intelligences but by the laws of gravity and motion. More dramatically, Charles Darwin and his theory of evolution by the natural selection of random inherited variations banished the notions of *good* and *end* from biology, the most evidently teleological of sciences.[12] Taken seriously with all its implications, Darwinian theory implies a universe in which the human race is nothing more than a happy (for us humans) accident, the peculiarly sophisticated and well-articulated result of a long series of fortuitous (again, for us humans) genetic changes.[13] In other words, the human race is not an end point at which the process of evolution has somehow aimed. Man is not nature's goal.

Thanks to the new sciences, philosophers saw the universe as ontologically "flat."[14] The task of reason was not to penetrate beneath the surface appearances to the essences of things, but rather to correlate experiences, in particular sense experiences, in such a way that the human mind could gain predictive and technical power. Deduction or calculation came to be seen as identical with reason. As the mathematician and scientist, rather

---

[12] See Richard Dawkins, "God's Utility Function," *Scientific American*, November 1995, 81, and Stephen Jay Gould, "The Evolution of Life on Earth," *Scientific American*, October 1994, 87.

[13] Jacques Monod, *Le hasard et la nécessité: Essai sur la philosophie naturelle de la biologie moderne* (Paris: Éditions du Seuil, 1970), 52–53 and then 195, where we read: "L'ancienne alliance est rompue; l'homme sait enfin qu'il est seul dans l'immensité de l'Univers d'où il a émergé par hasard. Non plus que son destin, son devoir n'est écrit nulle part."

[14] Schmitz, *At the Center of the Human Drama*, 131–32.

than the contemplative, provided the models for human thinking, the notion of a higher being gradually became unintelligible. If there should be a God, his superiority could consist only in his greater power to manipulate. And religion relating to such a god could only be superstitious, a matter of obeying and pleasing him simply to avoid his wrath and gain his favor. If God had a role in Enlightenment thought—we may think here of Hume and Kant, especially—it was an inspirational and ideal role. The only God Hume could accept was a kind of ideal to inspire moral sentiments and noble aspirations,[15] while Kant reduced God to a postulate of practical reason, an idealization of perfect morality.[16] Therefore Enlightenment thinkers came to separate completely questions of religion and the existence of God from those of morality.

"Good" and Modern Philosophy

With the rise of the empirical sciences and their demand for objectivity, the nature and status of the human subject as such became a distinctive philosophical problem, because the conscious subject was conceptually divorced from the physical order. Aristotle's world was populated by a variety of kinds of substance, some inert, some sentient, and some intelligent. The modern world, by contrast, was one filled with material entities having different shapes and concatenations of mass, momentum, electromagnetic charge, and other characteristics capable of mathematical representation. The self, the free and conscious human subject, became a special kind of problem. Metaphysics was abandoned in favor of empirical science and epistemology, whose task it then became to account for the experiencing self. Because of this Enlightenment shift from metaphysics to epistemology, the locus of good changed. It ceased to be objectively rooted in things, in the natural order, and was conceived to originate within the subjectivity of the human person.

John Paul II conducts his discussion consciously within the context of this discussion. His prepapal writings focus most frequently upon these modern thinkers, whose thought he sees as characteristic of the age: David Hume, Immanuel Kant, the utilitarians, and Max Scheler.

---

[15] David Hume, *Dialogues concerning Natural Religion* (Indianapolis: Bobbs-Merrill, 1947), pt. 12.

[16] Immanuel Kant, *Religion within the Limits of Reason Alone* (New York: Harper and Row, 1960), reprinted preface to the first edition, 3–6.

Hume: "Is" and "Ought"

By entirely reducing *good* to a subjective experience and evaluation, David Hume thoroughly undercut the basis of ethics, conceived as the science of moral obligation. Since Hume based his entire philosophy on experience, his account of experience is essential for understanding and evaluating his thought. And for Hume experience is nothing other than sense impressions, the *ideas* or remembered impressions derived from them, and interior sentiments. Because impressions, and only impressions, are the basis for all human knowledge, Hume established this reductionist principle:

> When we entertain, therefore, any suspicion that a philosophical term is employed without any meaning or idea . . . , we need but enquire, *from what impression is that supposed idea derived*? And if it be impossible to assign any, this will serve to confirm our suspicion. By bringing ideas in so clear a light, we may reasonably hope to remove all dispute which may arise concerning their nature and reality.[17]

All we have in our minds are the impressions received from sense and the stored images of these in memory and imagination. Knowledge and reasoning result when we connect or associate one such impression or idea with others.[18] Any "knowledge" attained by a process of reasoning that cannot be traced back directly to sense experience is unfounded and meaningless. Since experience extends only to the impressions received by the senses, beyond them the mind cannot legitimately infer, either to the underlying substance that gives rise to perceptual experience or to the causal relationships that obtain among the objects of perception. On this basis, Hume separated statements of fact from statements of value. From the fact that something is, one cannot logically deduce that something else *ought to be.*

> In every system of morality, which I have hitherto met with, I have always remark'd, that the author proceeds for some time in the ordinary way of reasoning, and established the being of a God, or makes observations concerning human affairs; when of a sudden I am surpriz'd to find, that instead

[17] David Hume, *An Inquiry concerning Human Understanding* (Indianapolis: Bobbs-Merrill, 1955), 30.

[18] Ibid., sec. 3, "Of the Association of Ideas," 31–33.

> of the usual copulations of propositions, *is*, and *is not*, I meet with no proposition that is not connected with an *ought*, or *ought not*.
>
> . . . For as this *ought*, or *ought not*, expresses some new relation or affirmation, 'tis necessary that it shou'd be observed and explain'd; and at the same time that a reason should be given, for what seems altogether inconceivable, how this new relation can be a deduction from others, which are entirely different from it.[19]

The logic is impeccable. From "*A* is *B*" and "*B* is *C*," one cannot logically infer "*A* ought *C*." From this Hume concludes that moral judgments cannot be based solely on facts but that they must be founded ultimately on desire or inclination. To illustrate this, he proposes the famous example of the parricide tree. If an observer sees a tree overshadowing another, from whose seed it had grown, depriving it of necessary sunlight and thereby killing it, he sees only a relationship among perceptions and finds no moral horror in them. But the murder of a father by his human son arouses horror, disgust, and outrage. Hume asks: Whence this moral outrage? To be sure, one can point to obvious factors distinguishing the two cases. (Indeed, Hume himself would certainly have recognized the validity of the legal distinction between accidental and deliberate homicide.) But such observations are not really to the point. Just as he grants the validity of causal inference, which derives only from "habit and custom,"[20] Hume will grant the reasonableness of distinguishing between the incidental parricide by the tree and the man's deliberate killing of his own father. At issue, however, is how we can perceive the moral values at stake. Hume's point is that the apprehension of moral values does not and cannot occur in one's experience of the facts. All that an observer can perceive are the sensible relationships among parent, offspring, physical setting, and weapons. The moral wrongness of the event is nowhere to be perceived or otherwise sensed. Therefore, argues Hume, the moral perception must come from within the observer, from his own moral sense. "There is no matter of fact in the case. The vice entirely escapes you, as long as you

---

19 David Hume, *A Treatise of Human Nature*, bk. 3, pt. 1, sec. 1, "Moral Distinctions Not Deriv'd from Reason," in *Hume's Ethical Writings*, ed. Alasdair MacIntyre (New York: Collier Books, 1965), 196.

20 *Inquiry concerning Human Understanding*, sec. 5, "Skeptical Solution of These Doubts, Part I," 54–61.

consider the object. You can never find it, till you turn your reflexion into your own breast, and find a sentiment of disapprobation, which arises in you toward this action."[21] Therefore the sentiments of wrong and right can arise only from sentiment, from the "agreeable" and the "useful."[22]

Therefore facts and values are different species of judgment, logically distinct and independent of each other. In the final analysis, there is no argument against one who insists that he wants what others dislike. Diet and exercise are of value *only* if you want to lose weight and remain healthy. In the final chapter of his *Practical Ethics*, Peter Singer addresses the awkward problem of the psychopath, "a person who is asocial, impulsive, egocentric, unemotional, lacking in feelings of remorse, shame or guilt, and apparently unable to form deep and enduring personal relationships."[23] Such people honestly and (it seems) happily feel no obligation to others, experience no sentiments of benevolence toward them, and sense no responsibility for the harms they cause. In terms of what, then, can one call such a person's behavior wrong? To be sure, the rest of us might want to restrain the psychopath when he hurts us, but in virtue of what can we say that his behavior is morally wrong *for him*? He finds no meaning in and places no value on generosity, altruism, and benevolence. This conclusion may be awkward—moral values *should* be universal—but it is inevitable. Moral values so conceived pertain only to those who value them.

The good, for Hume, is what pleases the subject or is useful for acquiring pleasure. Maintaining that the bases of morality are the *agreeable* and the *useful*, Hume presages the later development of utilitarianism. Considered in itself as sensation or feeling, a sense experience can only be pleasant or unpleasant. The emotional state of a human being can be agreeable or not. So strongly does Hume hold to the primacy of the pleasing, that he famously states: "Reason is, and ought only to be the slave of the passions, and can never pretend to any other office than to serve and obey them."[24] Good is not to be found in any independently existing state of affairs in the world.

---

21 *Treatise of Human Nature*, 195.

22 David Hume, *An Enquiry concerning the Principles of Morals*, especially sec. 9, "Conclusion," in MacIntyre, *Hume's Ethical Writings*, 109ff. See also Kaczyński, Verità sul bene *nella morale*, 185.

23 Peter Singer, *Practical Ethics*, 2nd ed. (Cambridge: Cambridge University Press, 1993), 328.

24 *Treatise of Human Nature*, 179.

The effect of Hume's theory of morals, his separation of "ought" from "is," remains to this day.[25] Whatever "good" may mean in ethics, it has no place in the physical world, in that objectively existing realm known by the sciences. Indeed, a kind of Humean phenomenalism is presupposed by contemporary philosophers reflecting on the sciences and scientific knowledge of the world. To be *good* is to be in some sense desirable, to be worthy of pursuing or attaining. Sun and rain are good for one's vegetables, because they make the plants grow. Slugs are bad; they ruin the tomatoes. However, the death of my tomato plants is bad only because *I want* tomatoes. If I were to value slugs (which I am free to), then their presence in my garden would be good (to me). But can we not argue from the plant's point of view? That is, one could surely hold that for the plant itself, sun and rain are good, while slugs are bad, because of their respective influence on the plant's natural activity of growing and bearing fruit. However, even if from a limited point of view such a manner of speaking can be defended, it is not scientifically proper. The sun and rain and plants and slugs interact in certain ways that can be known, making predictions of future events possible. However, the scientific account is held to be complete and objective without reference to purpose, goal, or good. Indeed, at the dawn of the scientific revolution, Francis Bacon called for the banishment of teleology from true science.[26] The true scientist, according to contemporary philosophical understanding, describes a structure independent of teleology, of good. Therefore, if scientific knowledge is knowledge par excellence, then "good" is only a subjective category, arising from within human consciousness and not applicable to the really existing world. In summary, we find that in Hume and subsequent empiricism the notion of "good" effectively disappears as a subject of scientific inquiry and rational knowledge.

Hume's account of morals radically undercuts the traditional notions of freedom and the human will. If what the human subject calls a "thing" is simply the nexus of varied sense impressions that he has found it useful or helpful to connect together, then, similarly, an act is simply an event or

25 See Andrzej Szostek, M.I.C., *Natur—Vernunft—Freiheit: Philosophische Analyse der Konzeption* schöpferischer Vernunft *in der zeitgenössischen Moraltheologie* (Frankfurt am Main: Peter Lang, 1992), 221.

26 Francis Bacon, *Novum Organum,* in *Great Books of the Western World,* vol. 30 (Chicago: Encyclopaedia Britannica, 1952), bk. 1, no. 65; bk. 2, no. 2.

series of events perceived in the realm of sensation. Especially relevant, for it is a point that Karol Wojtyła particularly contests, is Hume's effective denial that the acting subject experiences his own causality.

> Volition is surely an act of the mind with which we are sufficiently acquainted. Reflect upon it. Consider it on all sides. Do you find anything in it like this creative power by which it raises from nothing a new idea and, with a kind of *fiat*, imitates the omnipotence of its Maker, if I may be allowed so to speak, who called forth into existence all the various scenes of nature? So far from being conscious of this energy in the will, it requires as certain experience as that of which we are possessed to convince us that such extraordinary effects do ever result from a simple act of volition.[27]

Although one may certainly have an inner experience of volition, Hume's argument is that in itself this does not have any causal effects on the world of sense experience. All that one is entitled to is to note the connection between the repeated experience of volition with corresponding events in the world. The human subject, for Hume, is always merely an *observer*, noting the correlations between his inner and outer sentiments, but unwarranted in the further inference to causal connections between the two. We may note that contemporary philosophers continue to accept this analysis. In his discussion of freedom, for example, John Searle comments, "The characteristic experience that gives us the conviction of human freedom . . . is the experience of engaging in voluntary, intentional human actions," and further on, "[F]or reasons I don't really understand, evolution has given us a form of experience of voluntary action where the experience of freedom . . . is built into the very structure of conscious, voluntary, intentional human behaviour."[28]

The touchstone of good and evil for Hume can only be the state of the individual human being's experience, and that understood in sensationalist or phenomenalist terms. Hume's empiricism (like the scientific materialism of his contemporary philosophical heirs) severs the connection between the person's acts in the world and the intentions of his mind.

---

[27] Hume, *Inquiry concerning Human Understanding,* 80.

[28] John Searle, *Minds, Brains and Science* (Cambridge: Harvard University Press, 1984), 95, 98; Peter Van Inwagen, *Metaphysics* (Boulder: Westview Press, 1993), 192–96.

Good can only be a quality created and projected by the mind, a predicate founded on subjective experience.

Immanuel Kant and the Autonomous Legislator

Gratefully awakened by the Scot from his dogmatic slumbers, Kant corrected, sharpened, and recast Hume's phenomenalism into a transcendental idealism. Keenly aware, to an extent that Hume was not, of the scientist's need for laws that are always and everywhere true, Kant reconstructed Hume's phenomenal order in such a way that the noumenal order, the realm of Kant's *Ding an sich*, remained beyond the range of human cognition. The realm of objective knowledge is that of phenomena, and this knowledge is structured by the categories of pure reason. These categories necessarily form our reasoning. It is instructive to list them.

I. Of quantity
   - Unity
   - Plurality
   - Totality

II. Of quality
   - Reality
   - Negation
   - Limitation

III. Of relation
   - Of inherence and subsistence (substantia et accidens)
   - Of causality and dependence (cause and effect)
   - Of community (reciprocity between agent and patient)

IV. Of modality
   - Possibility—impossibility
   - Existence—nonexistence
   - Necessity—contingency[29]

[29] Immanuel Kant, *Kritik der reinen Vernunft*, in *Kant's gesammelte Schriften*, vol. 4 (Berlin: Druck und Verlag Georg Reimer, 1911), 80; Kant, *Critique of Pure Reason*, trans. Norman Kemp Smith (New York: St. Martin's Press, 1965), A 79–80, B 105–106.

With these categories, Kant hopes to have provided empirical science (in particular, Newtonian physics) with all that it needs for its work. Noteworthy for us, however, is what is not here. Kant has no category corresponding to Aristotle's final causality, no teleology, no good and evil. The significance of this is profound, for this omission means that scientific reasoning, that activity by which we acquire knowledge of the world we live in, does not operate at all through the concepts of end, purpose, teleology, or good. To be sure, Kant does not exclude these altogether, for they play a role in his ethics. However, because ethics is outside the realm of phenomena, the good does not intrude upon the realm of scientific knowledge. Situated in the realm of freedom, it is beyond sense experience, which is why it must be governed by a priori laws of reason.

"There is no possibility of thinking of anything at all in the world, or even out of it, which can be regarded as good without qualification, except a *good will*."[30] If Hume alleges logical inference from "is" to "ought" to be illegitimate, Kant effectively rejects the very possibility of meaningful discourse on the good as such. There is "no possibility of thinking," he writes, of anything that can be regarded as unqualifiedly good, except the good will. Why is this? When we contemplate the realm of phenomena, the world as studied by the sciences, we discover no relation corresponding to *good*. Given Kant's understanding of reason and the world it knows, "good" as such can clearly have no referent outside the rational subject's willing. The world, Kant's realm of phenomena, is necessarily governed by invariant laws. Whatever occurs in the realm of phenomena must obey the laws of nature.[31] The good has no power of governance in this realm. "Good" can apply only within the realm of freedom, which is treated by the science of morals and not by the empirical sciences.

Kant's deontology leaves no room for personal satisfaction in behaving morally; the moral demand flows from reason itself and not from any sat-

[30] Immanuel Kant, *Grounding for the Metaphysics of Morals*, in *Grounding for the Metaphysics of Morals* with *On a Supposed Right to Lie Because of Philanthropic Concerns*, trans. James W. Ellington, 3rd ed. (Indianapolis: Hackett, 1993), 7. "Es ist überall nichts in der Welt, ja überhaupt auch außer derselben zu denken möglich, was ohne Einschränkung für gut könnte gehalten werden, als allein ein guter Wille." Kant, *Grundlegung der Metaphysik der Sitten*, in *Kants gesammelte Schriften*, vol. 4, erster Abschnitt.

[31] Kant, *Grounding for the Metaphysics of Morals*, 1; *Critique of Pure Reason*, B 162–65, B 198.

isfaction of the body or the sentiments, which would necessarily belong to the realm of phenomena. However, Kant does find aesthetic value in the good will. He refers to the commendation of the "connoisseur"[32] regarding the good will, in which he finds a beauty deserving his admiration.[33] Kant's morally good will is to evoke a similar response to that which the saint evokes in the Christian believer's heart. The inspirational goodness of Kant's "good will" will later be reflected in Lawrence Kohlberg's six stages of moral development, the highest of which is "the universal ethical principle orientation," which Kohlberg characterizes thus: "Right is defined by the decision of conscience in accord with self-chosen ethical principles appealing to logical comprehensiveness, universality, and consistency."[34] It is this aesthetic moment that provides the subjective motivation for behaving morally, for acting in accord with duty. Thus, Karol Wojtyła will speak of respect for law as the sole emotional basis of Kant's ethics.[35]

The aspect of Kant's theory with the most significant consequences, however, is his conception of that which renders the will good. Although there may be few philosophers today who accept the theory of the categorical imperative, this governing principle remains attractive to moral theologians, that the good will (or the good person or self) is the one that is rationally and affectively consistent, coherent, and integrated.[36] The good, therefore, is not something objective, an existing reality to be attained, but rather it is conceived as a condition of the self, of one's consciousness or subjectivity. Kant envisioned a moral will that reflected the crystalline elegance of the Newtonian system, reason legislating one's behavior with the same consistent rationality as that which governs the motions of the planets. His notion of the will as dignified with its own proper autonomy and freedom has further contemporary ramifications. If

---

[32] Kant's word is *Kenner*, which translates better as "connoisseur," although Ellington renders it as "expert." Kant, *Grundlegung der Metaphysik der Sitten*, erster Abschnitt, 394.

[33] *Grundlegung der Metaphysik der Sitten*, zweiter Abschnitt, 443.

[34] Lawrence Kohlberg, *The Philosophy of Moral Development: Moral Stages and the Idea of Justice* (San Francisco: Harper and Row, 1981), 19.

[35] Karol Wojtyła, "The Separation of Experience from the Act in Ethics," in *Person and Community: Selected Essays*, trans. Theresa Sandok, O.S.M. (New York: Peter Lang, 1993), 30–31; *Lubliner Vorlesungen*, 366.

[36] See Charles E. Curran, *Directions in Fundamental Moral Theology* (Notre Dame, IN: University of Notre Dame Press, 1985), 241 and especially 247.

it is only the will that can be unqualifiedly good, then to obey another, to conform oneself to another's will, is inherently inauthentic or heteronomous. A child may obey until she is mature, but man come of age rules himself, judges for himself what is good and evil. To command is to violate what is inmost in the human self, the power to determine oneself according to one's own lights. Good must flow from within.

A final consequence of Kant's theory, one especially important for Wojtyła, is the inherent and necessary freedom, dignity, and autonomy of the rational subject. With respect to his own moral behavior, the rational being stands as supreme and (indeed) only legislator. Because the only unqualified good is the good will, no other good can stand superior to it to determine it. The rational being that recognizes another good as governing itself falls into heteronomy.[37] The will must be autonomous, subject to no laws other than the law of its own reason. The will, therefore, has the dignity of a lawgiver. Further, as the supreme lawgiver, at least for this rational being, it is free; and as the moral agent, the human will is free with respect to the laws governing the phenomenal realm. For Kant these concepts found an objective ethics, a morality of strict obligation based on the requirements of reason. The rational being is his own legislator, but the laws he imposes are those demanded by rational duty. These three concepts of *freedom*, *dignity*, and *autonomy* effectively define the Enlightenment vision of ethics and politics.

Close variants on these conceptions have survived in notions of conscience in contemporary moral theology. So, according to Richard P. McBrien, "Conscience is the *radical experience of ourselves as moral agents.*"[38] Richard Gula writes: "Conscience is the whole person's commitment to value and the judgment one makes in light of that commitment of who one ought to be and what one ought to do or not do."[39] Concomitant with this notion of conscience is that of transcendental freedom,

---

[37] See Waldstein, introduction to John Paul II, *Man and Woman He Created Them*, 50. To be sure, a rational being may choose to obey civil or domestic authority within some limited sphere, but even this obedience is governed by the autonomous judgment of that rational being. The prince is obeyed for the sake of public order, not because the prince knows what is best.

[38] Richard P. McBrien, *Catholicism*, new ed. (New York: HarperCollins, 1994), 969.

[39] Richard M. Gula, "The Moral Conscience," in *Conscience*, ed. Charles E. Curran, Readings in Moral Theology 14 (New York: Paulist Press, 2004), 53.

according to which the human person is charged primarily with the realization of his freedom as such.[40] Although not identical with Kant's notion of the rational moral agent's self-government according to the categorical imperative, such contemporary conceptions rest upon Kantian conceptions of freedom and autonomy as their ultimate foundations.[41]

Scheler and the Intuition of Value

Responding to Kant's inhuman rationalism (as he saw it), phenomenologist Max Scheler sought the root of ethics in the heart of the person rather than in the power of reason. The issue of ethics for Scheler is to respond properly to intuited values, which are "clear, palpable phenomena."[42] They are genuine objects (*Gegenstände*) that can be encountered, compared, and ranked as higher or lower.[43] This is to say, Scheler identifies in the human being a capacity to intuit and respond to values as authentically given in experience:[44] the "beautiful" and "ugly," "right" and "wrong," "holy" and "unholy." The moral status of the person is a consequence of his response to these values that are given in experience. For Scheler the intuition of these values is not cognitive, but emotional, given to our feeling.[45] The ethics built on these values is diametrically opposed to Kant's rational recognition of and response to duty. The response to value is, in a way, passive in that it is evoked by the value, whereas the Kantian ethic demands that the moral agent act independently of any incentive or experienced attraction. To put the matter simply (and a bit crudely), where Kant would have us screw up our willpower, Scheler would have us willingly drawn to beauty, truth, and nobility.

40 See Szostek, *Natur—Vernunft—Freiheit,* 110.

41 Richard Gula writes: "For moral maturity one must be one's own person. It is not enough to follow what one has been told. The morally mature person must be able to perceive, choose, and identify oneself with what one does. In short, we create our character and give our lives meaning by committing our freedom, not by submitting it to someone in authority. . . . As long as we do not direct our own activity, we are not yet free, morally mature persons." "Moral Conscience," 58.

42 Max Scheler, *Der Formalismus in der Ethik und die materiale Wertethik: Neuer Versuch der Grundlegung eines ethischen Personalismus,* 5th ed. (Bern: Franke Verlag, 1966), 38.

43 Ibid., 39; see also Waldstein, introduction to John Paul II, *Man and Woman He Created Them,* 66.

44 Wojtyła, *Lubliner Vorlesungen,* 35.

45 "Werte sind uns im *Fühlen* zunächst gegeben." *Der Formalismus,* 56.

According to Max Scheler's principal work, *Der Formalismus in der Ethik und die materiale Wertethik* (*Formalism in Ethics and Non-Formal Ethics of Values*), the central concept in ethics is *value* (*Wert*). Characteristic of the person, who is above all a loving being, is that he directly perceives values to which he is drawn, which he prefers. Values are not "out there" to be perceived in things. It is senseless to inquire about the common properties of good (or bad) things that make them good (or bad). They inhabit their own realm, as it were. "From this it follows that there are genuine and *true* value qualities, which constitute their own realm of *objects*, which have their own *distinctive* relationships and connections, and can even as value *qualities* be (e.g.) higher and lower, etc."[46] This order among values, however, is not to be deduced or derived. "Which value is 'higher' is ever anew to be grasped through the acts of preferring and pursuing. There is for this an *intuitive* '*evidence of preference*,' for which no kind of deduction can be substituted."[47]

The realm of values is, in part, constitutive of the world as experienced. The world cannot be a *world* if in it there are no values.[48] So, should Hume point to the parricide tree and challenge Scheler to compare it objectively with Smerdyakov's murder of the elder Karamazov, Scheler could say that Hume's realm of sensations and imaginings without value is not a world in which human persons live. It is not a *world.* Neither does it suffice to say with Hume that the difference between the tree killing and Smerdyakov's crime is that most of us feel within our breast a moral loathing for the latter. The essential difference is that in principle (Hume's principle, that is) one could amble through Hume's world of neutral sensations neither attracted to nor repelled by anything at all. For Scheler this is inconceivable. Values constitute the world as world. We may note, however, that these values are still rooted in the subjectivity of the person in that world. The recognition of and response to value is the same, whether

[46] Ibid., 37: "Aus dem Gesagten geht hervor, daß es echte und wahre Wertqualitäten gibt, die ein eigenes Bereich von *Gegenständen* darstellen, die ihre *besonderen* Verhältnisse und Zusammenhänge haben, und schon als *Wertqualitäten* z.B. höher und niedriger usw. sein können."

[47] Ibid., 107: "Welcher Wert der 'höher' ist, das ist immer neu zu erfassen durch den Akt des Vorziehens und Nachsetzens. Es gibt hierfür eine *intuitive* '*Vorzugsevidenz*', die durch keinerlei Deduktion zu ersetzen ist."

[48] See ibid., 170.

the events in question are real or not. The value of Antigone's filial piety is not lessened simply because her acts appear only in Sophocles's creation.

For Scheler, the concept of value holds priority over that of good. Indeed, good is itself one value, namely, that which is realized in the realization of the highest value.[49] As such it is a value of the person,[50] who becomes good (or, more precisely, realizes the good) by responding appropriately to other values. What is germane to our present investigation is that although for Scheler the world is a world in virtue of values, these values must still remain rooted in the subjectivity of the conscious, experiencing person. This is why the ethical demand cannot be rooted in some good external to the person's subjectivity, neither in obedience to command, nor in attainment of some goal or state, nor in conformity with some objective standard external to the person. If value is a constituent of the world as such, it is so because the structure of the human person demands it.

But how does the person perceive values? Although Scheler does not say it directly, it is clear from his discussion that values are perceived emotively. Indeed, Karol Wojtyła will come to refer frequently to Scheler's "emotionalism."[51] In vain do we seek from Scheler an account of the "faculty" or mechanism by which values are intuited. Values do not correlate directly with "objective" states of affairs or properties of things. Nevertheless—so may Scheler respond—values are inescapable. They are *given* in human experience; we *do* intuit them. Therefore, the valueless world of the purely physical sciences is an abstraction. The world in which the human being lives, the realm of living human experience, is full of values to which the person can and must respond. Should his critic object that such values are not real, Scheler can readily respond that their very inescapability indicates their fundamental reality.

---

49 Ibid., 47: "Der Wert '*gut*' . . . ist dann derjenige Wert, der wesensgesetzmäßig an dem *Akte* der *Realisierung* desjenigen Wertes erscheint, der (für die Erkenntnisstufe des ihn realisierenden Wesens) der *höchste* ist."

50 Ibid., 49.

51 See, for instance, Wojtyła, *Lubliner Vorlesungen*, 41, 69, 239; "The Separation of Experience from the Act in Ethics," 35; and Karol Wojtyła, *Valutazione sulla possibilità di costruire l'etica cristiana sulle base del sistema di Max Scheler*, in *Metafisica della persona*, 408.

The Missing Ontology of Good

In Hume, Kant, and Scheler, different as they are each from the other, we find this common thread: good has no independent ontological status but is rooted in the human subject. In none of these philosophies can we find warrant to assert that this or that thing is good in virtue of what it is or has. To be sure, Kant strives to establish an objective order according to which a will can be known to be good; he is not one to approve just any self-legislation that a subject may find rationally coherent according to his own lights. And Scheler does not reduce value to whatever this or that person should choose to regard as valuable. (It is, unfortunately, not possible to offer such disclaimers on Hume's behalf.) Nonetheless, with none of these thinkers can we locate the good as rooted in things as they are in themselves. Even though Scheler would have values be independent of the idiosyncrasies of the particular person who holds them, the world in which those values are rooted is one constituted in his consciousness. Values are given to feelings.[52] The value is rooted in an essence, phenomenologically regarded, and not in the being that things have in themselves. All three presuppose the Enlightenment requirement, based ultimately in scientific method, that "good" has no locus outside of human subjectivity. Kaczyński summarizes Wojtyła's position succinctly: "Therefore morality, conceived essentially as a dynamic and personal reality, cannot consist in the realization of spontaneous sensations (Hume), . . . nor in the intellectual experience of duty (Kant), nor in the emotionally given experience of value (Scheler), but consists in the realization of the true good in the act of the person and in the self-realization of the person himself by means of the moral value of the act."[53] This point and the difference it makes will become clearer if we turn to the thought of a fourth interlocutor, St. Thomas Aquinas, and his conception of good.

Aquinas: Being and Good

In his *Quaestiones de veritate* Thomas Aquinas starts from a position apparently quite similar to that of the other three thinkers. To define "truth" he considers those predicates that can be applied to every being simply insofar as it is a being.[54] He begins by specifying those predicates

[52] Scheler, *Der Formalismus*, 56.

[53] *Verità sul bene nella morale*, 220.

[54] Thomas Aquinas, *De veritate*, q. 1, a. 1.

that apply to a being considered in itself and in relation to other beings. As undivided, a being is said to be "one"; as having an essence, it is a "thing" (*res*); as distinct from other things, it is "something"; and so on. Then, noting that the rational soul stands in relation to every being, he considers the predicates that apply to a being in relation to the soul's two powers of intellect and will. Since his immediate purpose is to define "true,"[55] Thomas intends to focus on the relationship of being to intellect, in terms of which he defines the *ratio* of truth as the correspondence of a being with the intellect. In this context, he defines the *ratio* of good in terms of the correspondence of a being with the will. "Good" is the name arising from this relationship. It appears to some, then, that Aquinas also roots the good in human subjectivity. Indeed, some contemporary writers, such as John Crosby, Douglas Flippen, and Tadeusz Styczeń, have interpreted him in precisely this way, as though—to put it crudely—Aquinas defines the good as whatever the human will wants.[56] Such an interpretation, however, fails to understand the point Aquinas makes and renders impossible a coherent interpretation of the rest of what Aquinas will say about "good" in his writings. (We shall address this problem at greater length in chapter 8.) We turn now to examine the bases of Thomas Aquinas's account of the good.

Ratio boni

Ens et bonum convertuntur. Being and good are convertible insofar as they have exactly the same referent. The terms "being" and "good" differ, however, according to concept. What "good" adds to "being" is a conceptual relation, specifically that of the being to a will. This is the *ratio boni*, or "notion of good," its locus in the logical landscape, as it were. John Knasas

---

55 See Adrian J. Reimers, "St. Thomas's Intentions at *De Veritate* I, 1," *Doctor Communis* 42 (1989): 175, but also Jan Aertsen, *Medieval Philosophy and the Transcendentals: The Case of Thomas Aquinas* (Leiden: E. J. Brill, 1996), 106–7.

56 See John Crosby, "Are Being and Good Really Convertible?" *New Scholasticism* 57, no. 4 (Autumn 1983): 465–500; Crosby, "The Idea of Value and the Reform of the Traditional Metaphysics of *Bonum*"; Douglas Flippen, "On Two Meanings of Good and the Foundations of Ethics in Aristotle and St. Thomas," *Proceedings of the American Catholic Philosophical Association* 57 (1984): 56; and Tadeusz Styczeń, "Zur Frage einer unabhängigen Ethik," in *Der Streit um den Menschen*, by Karol Wojtyła, Andrzej Szostek, and Tadeusz Styczeń (Kevelaer: Butzon und Becker, 1979), 122.

sees it quite differently, effectively identifying the *ratio boni* with the *bonum* itself, so that "the *ratio boni* is the intelligible concrescence of everything real, actual—and possible."[57] Knasas goes on to remark that the *ratio boni* so conceived "ignites a firestorm in the will," because it is the will's natural object.[58] If he is right, however, then not only does the distinction between "being" and "good" collapse, but Aquinas's account of *good* falls to the critiques of Crosby, Flippen, Styczeń, and others who take the *ratio boni* to be the essence of good or the good itself.[59] Aquinas himself, however, is careful not to fall into this conceptual trap. He distinguishes the logic of the term "good" well before stating what the goodness of a substance actually consists in. At the outset of his *De veritate* he writes, "*Good* expresses the correspondence of being with the appetitive power, for, and so we note in the *Ethics*, the good is 'that which all desire.' " ("Convenientiam ergo entis ad appetitum exprimit hoc nomen bonum, ut in principio Ethic. dicitur quod *bonum est quod omnia appetunt*.")[60] This does not state that good is whatever the appetitive power desires but, more subtly, that *this word*, "*good*," expresses a correspondence with the appetitive power. In this respect, "good" is, in a way, modal; every being is good insofar as it can stand in relation to a will. A scientist studying allergies may well desire samples of common house dust, usually regarded as an evil, for he wants to examine and analyze it. For him, household dust is a good. Indeed, it is even as an evil that dust stands in relation to the will, for the housekeeper must stand in a negative relationship of desire with regard to it. This relation, then, does not tell us what is good about any particular thing or kind of thing, that is, what goodness consists in, only that it corresponds to the will.

---

[57] John F. X. Knasas, *Being and Some Twentieth-Century Thomists* (New York: Fordham University Press, 2003), 257.

[58] Ibid.

[59] Unfortunately, the Latin term *ratio boni* is not uniformly translated in the standard English editions of *Summa theologiae*. The English Dominican Fathers' translation translates the term sometimes as "goodness," other times as "the essence of good" or "formality of goodness." Similarly, Schmidt translates the term in *De veritate* sometimes as "essence of good" and other times as "note of goodness." See Thomas Aquinas, *De veritate*, translated as *Disputed Questions on Truth*, vol. 3, trans. Schmidt, q. 21, a. 4.

[60] Thomas Aquinas, *De veritate*, q. 1, a. 1.

In response to the question of what constitutes good, Aquinas replies that the *ratio* of good consists in mode, species, and order.[61] His treatment of the question in *Summa theologiae* is particularly to the point.

> Everything is said to be good so far as it is perfect; for in that way only is it desirable (as shown above). Now a thing is said to be perfect if it lacks nothing according to the mode of its perfection. But since everything is what it is by its form (and since the form presupposes certain things, and from the form certain things necessarily follow), in order for a thing to be perfect and good it must have a form, together with all that precedes and follows upon that form. . . . But the form itself is signified by the species; for everything is placed in its species by its form. . . . Hence the essence [*ratio*] of goodness, so far as it consists in perfection, consists also in mode, species and order.[62]

The desirability of a thing, that in virtue of which the *ratio boni* is expressed, is consequent on its perfection, which is rooted in its form and which is the cause of the relation of desirability, as the parallel passage in *De veritate* makes clear.[63] Now, for Thomas, Aristotelian that he was, the form is that in virtue of which a being is what it is. Indeed, a thing has its very being in virtue of its form.[64] Therefore the goodness of a thing is rooted in its innermost metaphysical core, and he will argue that, although there is indeed one Absolute Being who is Goodness itself, each being has its own intrinsic goodness insofar as it has its own form.[65]

Will as Rational Appetite

That Aquinas's account does not reduce good to subjectivism becomes even clearer when we consider his conception of the will as rational appetite. The will is ordered to whatever can be regarded in any way whatsoever as good. If there is a reason for thinking something good, then the will can desire it (and so it is possible to desire samples of household dust).

61 Thomas Aquinas, *Summa theologiae*, trans. English Dominican Fathers (Gervais, OR: Harmony Media, 1998), I, q. 5, a. 5 (henceforth cited as *ST*); *De veritate*, q. 21, a. 6.

62 *ST* I, q. 5, a. 5 *corpus*.

63 Thomas Aquinas, *De veritate*, q. 21, a. 6.

64 *ST* I, q. 76, a. 4.

65 *ST* I, q. 6, a. 4.

Abstract as this may sound, Aquinas's point is thoroughly concrete. By his animal nature, the human being is endowed with senses and internal desires, which all present their respective objects—food, drink, sex, retribution against the enemy, and so on—as good. The objects of these desires represent, as it were, a compendium of physical human goods, for their satisfaction can ensure the reasonably healthy survival of the individual human and of the species. Indeed, we might even be able to subsume these desires under the general desire "to survive as a member of the human species." Thomas's point, however, is that these desires do not constitute the will, for the will is the *rational* appetite. As such the will may recognize as good whatever reason (or the imagination governed by reason) proposes. Thus for religious reasons the hungry can turn away from food, choosing instead to fast. The inventor may envision the possibility of using silicon crystals to replace electronic vacuum tubes and set about to create the transistor and microchip. As rational appetite, the will has the capability to rule over the various appetites of sense and the goals one may have adopted, judging among them according to the criteria of reason. And what are these criteria? The intellectual power must discern rationally what it is that truly constitutes a thing as good, what it is that is the truth about the good. By implication, the truth about the good cannot therefore be constituted by the intellect; rather, it is recognized by the intellect.

This is the heart of the issue. The principle in virtue of which a thing can be known is precisely its form, in virtue of which it also has its being. The goodness of a substance and its knowability are both rooted in the form of that being. Therefore, just as truth is "objective"—that is, independent of the knowing subject's disposition—so too is goodness. Goodness is, before anything else, ontologically rooted. If certain human actions can be described as good or bad in relation to something, if there is a moral sense of "good" and "evil," this must be consequent upon the ontological sense. Furthermore, whatever may be identified as a relative good—"good for a human being," "good for me," or the like—must stand in relation to the ontologically rooted goodness of things.

Ultimately, there can be no good thing that is capable of satisfying the human will, for its orientation is toward the good in general, the universal good: "Obiectum autem voluntatis est bonum et finis in communi."[66]

[66] *ST* I, q. 82, a. 4 *corpus*; see also Thomas Aquinas, *De malo,* q. 8, a. 3 *corpus.*

This is a curious conclusion, compelled by the logic of the argument but abstract in the extreme. If Augustine's words, "You have made us for yourself, and our hearts are restless until they rest in you,"[67] stir the soul, Thomas's leave us puzzled. How is it that the flesh-and-blood human being can desire good in general? The solution to the difficulty is ultimately that both Augustine and Aquinas are saying the same thing, albeit in different ways. If the Christian convert Augustine speaks from the devotion of his grateful heart, the medieval Doctor writes systematically and theoretically. The will, an aspect or power of the human soul, desires good unrestrictedly, but within the realm of sense and reason's natural scope is found no object that fully and unrestrictedly realizes the notion of good. Therefore the will can never find within the world of goods a good that will fully satisfy its natural desire. Only God, in whom, as the Creator of all things, their perfections preexist,[68] fully realizes the notion of "good." Indeed, God is the Good; he is Goodness itself.[69] However, God cannot be given to sense, nor, in this life, can he be known in his essence by the intellectual power.[70] Paradoxically, the only object that can satisfy the will's natural desire is God, who lies beyond the range of human knowledge and experience. Consequently, the human being, by his very nature, is indeed a restless being, one who can find no satisfaction in the world in which he finds himself. We are made for something higher, something that God must reveal and carry us to, if we are to get there. The human heart, then, needs God not as simply a psychological craving or even (as Freud would suggest)[71] a salve to unfulfilled immature longings, but rather as the only good capable of fulfilling its very nature. We may say that Aquinas's rather abstract, if not indeed obscure, formulation, "Obiectum autem voluntatis est bonum et finis in communi," simply states metaphysically what Augustine's heartfelt prayer expresses. The human being is ordered by nature to an eternal good, to God himself.

---

[67] Augustine, *Confessions*, trans. John K. Ryan (Garden City, NY: Image Books, 1960), 1.1.

[68] *ST* I, q. 13, aa. 2, 6.

[69] *ST* I, q. 6, aa. 1–3.

[70] *ST* I, q. 12, aa. 2, 4.

[71] Sigmund Freud, *The Future of an Illusion*, trans. W. D. Robson-Scott (Garden City, NY: Doubleday and Company, 1964), especially 6.47–53.

The Crisis over "Good"

The difference between Aquinas's account and the modern approaches is striking. If good reduces to value known within or constituted by human consciousness, then there can be no question of God's transcendent goodness being the good for the human being. This is especially clear in Kant, who reduces religion to the ethical, as indeed his principles demand.[72] On this Waldstein writes: "Kant's God is *a God without being*, a God who is an object of human consciousness alone, and of human consciousness only in its practical form."[73] For Hume good is but a preference, and even in Scheler's thought it is hard to discern how the good can be transcendent in such a way that the human person is in any way answerable or responsible to it.[74] Religion has become subjective and private precisely because the highest good is a character of consciousness. The holy and the good find their proper locus not in objective reality, constituted metaphysically in the being of things, but rather in human subjectivity. This difference in perspectives leads to a host of related consequences, not only for religion and morality, but for political theory and life, for culture, and for the various sciences. The question is ultimately whether "good" has any intersubjectively knowable referent or whether its reference is ultimately to the subjective condition of the knowing or desiring subject. Is the expression "the truth about the good" meaningful? Before discussing Wojtyła's philosophical approach and applying it to the question at hand, we do best to sketch out the implications of this question about the good in several significant fields of human endeavor.

The Physical World

As we saw earlier, "good" has no place in scientific theory. Scientific accounts, whether in physics, chemistry, or even biology, eschew reference to purpose or goal, limiting themselves instead to the operations of well-defined mechanisms. Therefore it is scientifically illegitimate to maintain that the moon is there to cause the tides, that the earth formed 150 million kilometers from the sun so that life could develop, and that the human

[72] See *Religion within the Limits of Reason Alone.*

[73] Introduction to John Paul II, *Man and Woman He Created Them*, 47.

[74] Schmitz, *At the Center of the Human Drama*, 43–45.

species is goal or crown of the process of evolution. Indeed, strictly speaking, one may not even claim that the purpose of the heart is to keep the animal alive. All we can say is that animals without beating hearts do not live; they did not survive the cut to make evolution's team. Were the earth to have formed 130 million kilometers from the sun, then we simply would not be here to notice that we do not exist. Because we do exist, however, that happy distance is important to us and we ascribe it a purpose.

Using new mathematical formulae, diagrams, and algorithms to describe mechanisms, scientists have been able to map the physical universe to an astonishing extent. Useful as this antiteleological restriction may have been, however, it was a procedural decision and not the result of a new or deeper understanding of reality. However, to understand nature in terms of what is "fitting" or good presupposes some sort of access to the mind of nature's Maker. If the archeologist finds a strange artifact at the dig, he can determine with reasonable accuracy what it was used for, what its purpose was, for the ancient artisan and user were human like us, living in an environment we can understand. Knowing to some extent the minds of ancient human beings, the archeologist can predict with reasonable accuracy what other kinds of artifact he may discover from this population. However, we cannot so readily read off the purposes of nature's Author.

Indeed, Darwin seemed scandalized that the Creator should deliberately have created the wasteful, destructive, and cruel world his own research discovered: "I cannot persuade myself that a beneficent and omnipotent God would have designedly created the Ichneumonidae with the express intention of their feeding within the living bodies of caterpillars."[75]

Implicit in his outrage is a kind of anthropomorphism with respect both to the insects and to God. From a human perspective, to be unconsciously occupied by the young of another species who feed on one's paralyzed but living body is a terrifying prospect, the stuff of horror movies. And a human creator might well have serious misgivings about setting up so insidious a

[75] Ichneumon Wasps—Hymenoptera Family Ichneumonidae," www.cirrusimage.com/hymenoptera_ichneumonidae.htm (accessed March 1, 2010). Darwin emphasizes the importance of this in Charles Darwin, *The Origin of Species by Means of Natural Selection*, Sixth Edition (London: John Murray, 1884), 234 and 415. See also *The Cambridge Companion to the "Origin of Species"* [sic], edited by Michael Ruse and Robert J. Richards (Cambridge: Cambridge University Press, 2009), 110 and 121.

parasitic relationship. Darwin, however, provided a nonteleological mechanism, natural selection, by which the evolution of new species could be explained. This completely nonteleological mechanism, according to Darwin, suffices to account for the origin of new species from existing ones. An adaptation is neither good nor bad, only successful or unsuccessful for selection, which terms are not to be taken as evaluative. The mechanism does what the mechanism does. And with this Darwin had solved his wasp problem. This scandalously insidious predator need not be the creation of an intelligent, but morally obtuse, Creator but rather is the result of a blind evolutionary process. Just as interstellar dust gets caught up around a star and clumps into planets, the result of inexorable gravitational laws, so too does the animal world evolve new species, distinguished from the old only by a superior ability to survive and reproduce in current environmental conditions. Good plays no role in the world as known by science.

For the Aristotelian biologist, by contrast, nature is evidently full of purpose. The seed has the potency to develop into a plant and, indeed, a plant of this specific kind, and the potency of the kitten is to become an adult cat, living and reproducing the feline species. To this day, when in common speech we talk of living things, we speak in terms of purpose and perfection. The cute and cuddly tiger cubs are *destined* to grow into dangerous killers. The tree is stunted; something must have *gone wrong*. Coyotes *serve* to keep the jackrabbit population in check. The *reason* predators have strong stereoptic vision is to be able to judge accurately the distance to their prey, which for their part have the advantage of broad peripheral vision *for the sake of* detecting predators.

Darwin's achievement in biology has a twofold philosophical significance. First, he showed how purpose (or good) can be eliminated from our conception of nature. Second, in doing so, he effectively eliminated the notion of natural kinds as fundamental to the natural world. Natural kinds appear only as statistical peaks, as it were, on nature's continuum. To be sure, the difference between the fish and the chimpanzee is sharp and readily observed. However, the evolutionary line connecting both to their common evolutionary ancestor is continuous.[76] If this is the case, if the

[76] Or almost so. If, as seems likely, each stage in the evolution of a new species is determined by a variation in the organism's DNA, then the evolutionary development is not continuous in the strictly mathematical sense. Rather, a new stage is

difference between one species and another consists only in (say) the coding of their respective genetic instructions, then to distinguish them according to kinds is only of heuristic value.

The effect of Darwin's innovation on modern thought has been profound. Not only can the universe no longer be conceived as a kind of superorganism (as in Plato's *Timaeus*), it has also ceased meaningfully to be a home fit for man. Rather, it is a mechanism—indeed, a collection of more or less interconnected mechanisms—governed by laws admitting of precise mathematical expression.[77] To ask about the why of a thing is to ask no longer about purpose but about process. We find it wonderful that our human race has arisen, that our planet is so ideally situated, neither too close to nor too far from the sun, tilted at twenty-three degrees so that our seasons change and crops can grow, protected by magnetic fields from cosmic radiation and by the ozone layer from ultraviolet rays. Most of all, we find it uncanny that we are here, able not only to survive but also to reflect on our existence and the entire universe in which we find ourselves. Surely this *means something*. The worldview of scientific materialism tells us that it does not. Were the earth not situated as it is, sophisticated life-forms never would have arisen and we would not be here to wonder at our good fortune. The world as science describes it is a vast, very cold, and mostly empty and hostile place, in which all human life is but the latest and most sophisticated expression of organic development on the surface of a tiny planet orbiting one of millions of ordinary stars in the arm of a decently large galaxy, itself one of millions in the known universe. Reflecting on a photograph of earth taken from the Voyager spacecraft as it left the solar system, Carl Sagan remarked:

> Look again at that dot. . . . That's us. On it everyone you love, everyone you know, everyone you ever heard of, every human being who ever was, lived out their lives. . . .
>
> Our posturings, our imagined self-importance, the delusion that we have some privileged position in the Universe, are challenged by this point

distinguished from its predecessor by a variation of some protein in the molecule. Furthermore, an important and well-known problem in evolutionary theory is that new life-forms have apparently sprung up in fairly dramatic profusion from time to time without the long accumulation of minor changes.

[77] We keep in mind that statistics, too, admits of precise expression, even if statistical laws do not determine individual events.

> of pale light. Our planet is a lonely speck in the great enveloping cosmic dark. In our obscurity, in all this vastness, there is no hint that help will come from elsewhere to save us from ourselves.[78]

This conception of reality, according to which we are valueless beings in a pointless cosmic emptiness, constitutes a serious challenge. If teleology—purpose and value—has no place in the natural order, then in what sense can good and purpose be considered real? The usual answer, that they are simply creations of the human mind, leads inexorably to the privatization of religion, morality, and even culture.[79] Bertrand Russell wrote: "Blind to good and evil, reckless of destruction, omnipotent matter rolls on its relentless way; for Man, condemned to-day to lose his dearest, to-morrow himself to pass through the gate of darkness, it remains only to cherish, ere yet the blow falls, the lofty thoughts that ennoble his little day; disdaining the coward terrors of the slave of Fate, to worship at the shrine that his own hands have built."[80] If these conclusions, drawn from Enlightenment philosophy, sharpened by Darwinian mechanism, and driven home by the scientifically formed imagination, are correct, then the human being's place in the world is called radically into question. He is, in truth, radically *alienated* from the physical order—from the cosmos, from the earth on which he lives, from even his own body.

The Moral Order

The disappearance of "good," of end and purpose from the natural order, has ramifications for the moral order. What is the good in being "good"? What does being moral have to do with living a good life? How does a morally good will relate to the world of contingent fact? And what relation do subjective values and intentions have to the objective order of things? These are all different ways of posing what is essentially the same problem. If we may classify human behavior as "good" or "bad," then it is necessary

[78] Carl Sagan, *Pale Blue Dot: A Vision of the Human Future in Space* (New York: Random House, 1994), 6–7.

[79] If the notion of privatized culture seems counterintuitive, or even contradictory, we need only consider the do-it-yourself approach to culture so widespread in the contemporary United States of America. One's cultural expressions are more and more frequently the result of a lifestyle choice and not of heritage or religious faith.

[80] Bertrand Russell, "A Free Man's Worship," in *Selected Papers of Bertrand Russell* (New York: The Modern Library, 1927), 14–15.

to determine what criteria we have for such a classification. For Aristotle, there is no real problem. To behave morally is simply to act so as best to realize a noble, well-lived life. Even if not blessed by the gods, one who lives life as outlined by the *Nicomachean Ethics* will have lived nobly and will have flourished better than if he had lived any other way. Let us note briefly here that Karol Wojtyła's student and his successor to chair of ethics at the Catholic University of Lublin, Tadeusz Styczeń, as well as others, argues that the moral "ought" is lost in the Aristotelian eudaemonism.[81] The moral sense surely includes the notion of duty, the obligation to do what is right and just, whether one benefits from it or not. One wonders whether Aristotle has preserved the awareness of obligation that underlies authentic morality. Duty seems to be something imposed and for which the agent is answerable. Whether it leads to one's own good or ill, he is responsible for fulfilling his duty.

Moral Obligation

In any case the dawn of the modern era undercut the bases of Aristotle's integral approach. If there is no natural good, then there is no good of human nature. And Kant reasoned that ethics could not possibly be built upon a conception of happiness or human perfection, for such conceptions are empirical and nonnecessary. Therefore they are not sufficient to ground moral obligation, duty.[82] Kant recognized that the notion of duty or imposed obligation is central to moral experience. In some way the human subject stands in relation to moral demands by which she is judged. But who renders this judgment? And what is its effect? If Moses at the foot of Mount Sinai delivers Ten Commandments, their weight is palpable: the Lord God, who appeared upon the mountain in fire and smoke, will lead the obedient into the Promised Land and will punish those who do not obey. Although the ballplayer who obeys the coach to lay down a sacrifice bunt gives up his chance to get on base, he knows he has contributed to the team's chances to win. The child knows that by disobeying, he may not only suffer punishment but also "make Mommy sad." Kant has the law, but no Lord, no higher goals of the community, no loving

---

81 Styczeń, "Zur Frage einer unabhängigen Ethik," 119–20. We take up these objections in chapter 8.

82 Kant, *Grounding for the Metaphysics of Morals*, 444ff.

authority. He appeals to the objective demands of reason itself to ground duty. But reason has no sheriff. Even though duty appears as central to moral experience, the question "And what if I do not?" lurks in the background. We expect that fidelity to duty, obedience to authority will result in some good. So, when Glaucon challenges Socrates to show what good the just man's justice is to him, even if the just man should suffer humiliation, disgrace, torture, deprivation, and death,[83] Socrates must point to the higher joy of contemplation of "things that are," that is, the Forms.[84] In short, the notion of moral obligation entails a notion of accountability to some higher reality.

Teleological Ethics and Utilitarianism

For their part, Hume and his successors, Bentham, Mill, and the utilitarian school, emphasized the teleological aspect of moral reasoning and behavior. The point of acting is to do or obtain some good. From Hume's appeal to the "useful and agreeable" to Mill's doctrine of the maximization of happiness, the thrust of utilitarian accounts is not so much to account for moral obligation. Indeed, utilitarianism effectively eliminated the notion of moral obligation, because if the good is found only in moral sentiments or in the balance of pleasures and pains, then any meaningful reference to "obligation" disappears. Rather, the classical utilitarian perspective was social and political. If we are to live together in civil societies, we need to do so in a way that promotes social harmony, peace, and prosperity. Utilitarianism is an ethic for the modern liberal economy. We note, however, that utilitarianism cannot account for universal moral norms, despite Mill's effort to ground them on the general experience of the human race.[85] The teleological ethics of British empiricism and utilitarianism cannot provide a strong sense for the notion of duty.

Intuitionism

As we have seen, Max Scheler appeals to intuition as the basis for morals. In this respect, he too is heir to David Hume, who identified the "moral

---

83 Plato, *Republic* 2.360d–367b.

84 Ibid., 9.582b–586e.

85 John Stuart Mill, *Utilitarianism* (Indianapolis: Hackett Publishing Company, 2001), 24–25.

sense" as the only possible basis for moral reasoning.[86] Moral judgment can arise only from the judgment of the heart, the moral sentiments. If one lacks these moral sentiments, no instruction or process of factual reasoning can make up the lack. One may as well attempt to teach color to a blind man.[87] Hume's polemical distinction between passion and reason is well known and has already been discussed. This critique, in combination with his notion of moral sentiments, has given rise to the intuitionist and emotivist schools of ethics.[88] What these schools share in common is the notion that the moral good is something that can be grasped only by a distinctive kind of intuition unrelated to the objective or scientific knowing. Such thinkers do not deny the objectivity of moral reasoning; most would acknowledge that wanton cruelty and premeditated murder are moral evils universally to be acknowledged. They do deny that moral intuition is directly related to the factual order in such a way that intuitions can be derived, inferred, or deduced from that order. The moral intuition is, therefore, a special kind of faculty or aspect of the mind.

This intuitionist position has much to recommend it. Most evident is that in our daily lives we do not appeal to rules and principles but to our inner sense of right and wrong. The premise of the film *Indecent Proposal*,[89] that a billionaire should successfully offer a couple one million dollars for a night of sex with the wife, is precisely that potential audiences will recognize the indecency, the outrageousness of the proposal. Ordinarily one does not start moral reflection until he senses within himself a feeling, an intuition, that such an action might not be right. Furthermore, although there are morally blind individuals capable of blatant cruelty and selfishness and apparently devoid of sympathy for the effects of their actions on others, we realize that they lack something important to their humanity.

---

86 Hume, *Enquiry concerning the Principles of Morals*, sec. 1, "Of the General Principles of Morals," 23–28, and *Treatise of Human Nature*, bk. 3, sec. 2, "Moral Distinctions Deriv'd from a Moral Sense," 196–202.

87 See Hume, *Inquiry concerning Human Understanding*, sec. 2, "Of the Origin of Ideas," 28–29.

88 G. E. Moore, *Principia Ethica* (Cambridge: Cambridge University Press, 1968), chap. 1, "The Subject-Matter of Ethics," and Alasdair MacIntyre, *After Virtue: A Study in Moral Theory*, 2nd ed. (Notre Dame, IN: University of Notre Dame Press, 1984), chaps. 2 and 3.

89 *Indecent Proposal*, directed by Adrian Lyne (Paramount Pictures, 1993).

However, if moral sentiment or intuition is the *ultimate* foundation for moral judgment, then moral obligation can arise only from within one's subjectivity. The only warrant for imposing a duty upon another would be for the sake of education or training (as with children). Indeed, Scheler rejects the very notion of moral obligation as immoral, specifically as a form of Pharisaism.[90] Whoever acts according to duty acts by an extrinsic principle of goodness and not according to the values he has intuited and embraced.

The Modern Problematic

Among Scheler's intuited values, Kant's categorical imperative, Hume's moral sentiments, and Mill's greatest happiness principle we may trace connections, divergences, and aspects of authentic experience. However, considered from the perspective of the concept of good, it is not too hard to find the fundamental problematic of the modern era. We may pose the questions: In what sense (if any) can the human being as such be *good*? And in what way does the *good* relate to human actions? Aristotle believed that the human being, an existing substance, could be good or bad on the basis of its own principles. In the wake of the Enlightenment, it is no longer clear that this kind of conception is intelligible. If good, purpose, and end have been eliminated from the natural order, then the human being—one organism among many things, both living and nonliving—has no more intrinsic goodness than any other thing. In virtue of those principles by which he is the kind of being he is, the human being is neither good nor bad. At issue, then, is whether there is some objective or invariant universal good for each human being.

If there is a human good as such, it cannot lie within the physical nature of the human being, for the physical order is the realm of causal interactions but not of teleology.[91] Therefore it is necessary to find this good in human subjectivity, be that in sentiment (with Hume), reason (with Kant), the experience of pleasure and pain (with Bentham and Mill), or moral intuition (with Scheler). The problem of moral good thus reduces, in a way, to the problem of reconciling Descartes's mind and body (or Kant's *für sich* and *an sich*). This question is most dramatically illustrated by the debate over assisted suicide, in which continued physical

[90] *Der Formalismus*, 132 and especially 136.

[91] See Szostek, *Natur—Vernunft—Freiheit*, 142.

life is juxtaposed against the physical or emotional discomfort experienced in living that life. While one may indeed hold that death is bad for the physical organism, the right-to-die advocate will argue that it is not bad for the *person*, since her quality of life as experienced will be intolerable. The value of the person cannot lie simply in her physical constitution but rather is based on some subjective condition, either her own or that of some other interested person. Peter Singer relies heavily on this principle in defending both euthanasia and the parental option of infanticide of the handicapped.[92] In the former case, only the patient himself can, in the final analysis, judge the worth of his own continued life, and this on the basis of criteria of his own. In the latter, the neonatal infant has no awareness of his own existence as a distinct person, and therefore the assessment of his value falls primarily to the parents, who may, for reasons of their own, decide to preserve or to end his life.

Ultimately, the issue is to determine the locus wherein moral goodness is rooted. If the physical (or "ontic") order is without good or evil, then even human actions, regarded as physical movements interacting with the environment, lack good or evil of their own. Goodness must be a character of the subjective realm. This creates two kinds of difficult questions. First, if moral goodness is rooted in subjectivity, then must morality be subjective? Kant argues that it must not be, because human subjectivity itself, as rational, has an objective structure that every rational being is obliged to respect. Utilitarianism and consequentialism appeal to those states that most people—any reasonable and recognizably good person—would consider desirable. It is better that one person die than that the entire village be massacred (we can all agree on that); therefore it may be licit for the tourist to obey the military captain and kill one villager.[93] Such ethical approaches, which originated in Great Britain among thinkers whose concerns were primarily social and legislative, have a democratic tinge, in that they depend on common agreement. Everyone engaged in the conversation will acknowledge that the death of one villager is *ceteris paribus* preferable to the horrifying massacre of a crowd. Tacit in such a conception is not only the notion that *what most want* is a

92 *Practical Ethics*, chap. 7, and *Rethinking Life and Death: The Collapse of Our Traditional Ethics* (New York: St. Martin's Press, 1994), 32.

93 Curran, *Directions in Fundamental Moral Theology*, 177.

reliable guide to *what all should want*, but also that one is obliged to respect the intentionality of other conscious subjects. Second is the question of the status of the human being as a subject of moral rights. Singer maintains that these rights depend on that being's possessing sufficient self-consciousness and self-interest. In virtue of what does a human being deserve rights, respect, consideration, and protection?

The Social-Political Order

From the ethical we turn to the social, for, as we have already intimated, ethical concerns are closely tied with political (in the Aristotelian sense) concerns. For our principal author, Karol Wojtyła, these concerns had direct existential significance. As a young man he saw his university studies interrupted and his life almost destroyed by the Nazi invaders of his native Poland.[94] Thus he was forced to live under a regime that aggressively sought not only his personal harm and, on one occasion, death, but the destruction of his people, their culture, and their national identity. Then, after his ordination to the priesthood, he saw his country taken over by Soviet Communism, which suppressed individual and corporate freedom. As Pope, John Paul II played a major role in fostering the dismantling of Communism in central and Eastern Europe, while also presenting an insistent critique of the consumerism and materialism of the West. The central issue for this Pope's social and political thought is the relationship of the individual person to his fellows in the community.

The question of social good follows logically from that of the ethical or moral good, but with additional complications and considerations. Classically the purpose of social, legal, and governmental institutions has been to foster and preserve the common good. But what is this *common good*? Absent a conception of the good for the human being, then this common good must either be a value accepted by (or at least acceptable to) members of the society in questions or a value imposed in their name. To put the problem another way, we may ask what is the *subject* of the common good. Western democracies, following thinkers as diverse as Locke and

[94] For good accounts of Karol Wojtyła's early years, see Tad Szulc, *Pope John Paul II: The Biography* (New York: Scribner, 1995), and Darcy O'Brien, *The Hidden Pope* (New York: Rodale, 1998). For an account of his papacy, see George Weigel, *Witness to Hope: The Biography of Pope John Paul II* (New York: HarperCollins, 1999).

Rousseau, root that good in the individual. What we call the common good is that good which individuals freely embrace in some sort of consensus. This good does not, therefore, preexist the individuals making up the social unity. It is consequent upon their agreeing to it. John Locke argues that one cannot rightly be subject to law—that is, to the governance of others—without his own consent.[95] Therefore the good properly regarded inheres in the individual, who yields and shares it with others for mutually recognized advantages. By the term "properly inheres," however, I mean not that this good derives from his objective nature as a human being but simply that whatever may be regarded as the good for this person shall be counted as his good. Thus the common good is a relatively fragile thing, dependent upon the successful maintenance of a consensus among the members of the society. This fragility is especially evident when sectors of the society do not and cannot agree on important and fundamental values, in which case one or both sides may charge that the other's values are being "imposed."

Explicit in Locke and Mill, and implicit in our contemporary public life, is the understanding that this common good can be characterized in terms of property, understood as "life, liberty, and estate."[96] J. S. Mill was confident that appropriate educational and social provisions by an enlightened government of an industrialized nation could afford a good life to almost all its citizens.[97] To be sure, individuals and groups within a society may well disagree about the allocation of resources and responsibilities—does taxation fall more heavily on the farmer or the manufacturer?—but the nature of the common good is not in dispute. Members of the society are to be secure in their lives and possessions and free to dispose of them at will, provided that they not injure others. The common good for the modern liberal society is a reasonably peaceful, prosperous, and comfortable survival for all its members. So understood, the liberal common good allows us to infer standards of social morality. Theft and murder are proscribed. Parents are to care for their children. Contracts must be honored, enforced by a court when necessary. But what about pornography, prostitution, obscene language? To what extent can

---

[95] John Locke, *Second Treatise of Government* (Indianapolis: Hackett, 1980), chaps. 2 and 8.

[96] Ibid., chap. 7, §87; chap. 9, no. 131.

[97] *Utilitarianism*, 32–34.

society tolerate self-destructive personal behavior, such as drug usage and cigarette smoking? Libertarians object that if such behavior does not directly harm others, then society has no right to proscribe it as evil. That is, although the society may have certain broadly accepted standards of decency and right, standards that go beyond what can be determined by the explicit requirement not to harm what is another's, it remains to be shown what right or basis the society may have for insisting on its standards. Let us hasten to note, too, that what a society insists to be right, good, and decent may itself be corrupt. We need only look at the social attitudes toward blacks in the American South before the civil rights movement. Not only were African Americans subject to discrimination, but whites who failed to respect the segregationist values were subject to public censure. The underlying question, therefore, is whether human society can adopt values beyond those of "life, liberty, and happiness" (understood as property) as the basis of its common good.

The question of *common good* confronting contemporary civilizations and cultures is therefore the question of spiritual (or cultural) unity. As the European Union drew up its constitution, John Paul II repeatedly challenged its leaders to recognize formally the Christian roots of European civilization. At stake here is the principle by which Europe is a unity. Like the United States, the European Union seeks a unity based on economic cooperation and democratically founded governmental procedures. At this point in history, the nations of the democratic West are being challenged by a less developed and sophisticated realm of Islam. The significance of this confrontation is that the Islamic realm is relatively well unified by its values in a way that nations of the West are not. Muslims understand themselves and their lives in terms of a common good that has precedence over them—specifically submission (*islam*) to Allah. The West, on the other hand, expressly seeks for its unity in prosperity and procedure. For Americans the preeminent value is freedom. Freedom is an indeterminate right, however, one that forms an amorphous basis for unity. John Paul II's appeals for recognition of Europe's spiritual heritage constituted an implicit critique of the European Union's lack of a well-conceived understanding of its common good.

Of course, individualism has not been the only significant conception of the political order in the past two centuries. From the French Revolution to twentieth-century Communism, the notion of *class* has served as the antithetical counterpart of the autonomous individual. Under collectivism the *good* is found in the class and is independent of the individual. Indeed, the good of the class is the only good. Regardless of personal intentions, the willing servant of the aristocrat or the aide to the capitalist is counterrevolutionary. More significant, however, is that the acts and values of the individual can be judged only in terms of those of his class. The worker realizes the values of the proletariat. Modern collectivism has also this character, that in one way or another it is utopian. The good for which the society (and therefore each of its members) lives is a future state, whether this be an egalitarian republic, the dictatorship of the proletariat, or the triumphant *Deutsche Volk.*

Although the collectivists have disappeared from the West (China, however, remains a growing power), the questions raised by collectivism remain. As Nazi propaganda showed only too well, people are willing to unite around and sacrifice for a heroic ideal. The Muslim world appears to be uniting increasingly around its ideals. But as the tragedies of the twentieth century drive home, imposed and collectivized values are destructive to individuals. Too often the call to sacrifice has been a call to submit one's entire being to a vision or plan that works against the fundamental goods of individual persons. And here lies a serious problem, for it is reasonable to presume that to propose a good to the community is the work of a leader. To lead the community to its good is most certainly the leader's task. The question of the common good, then, becomes that of the legitimacy of authority. "For your own good" or "for the higher good" can be a dangerous phrase in the hands of the populist demagogue or the dictator. But the question remains whether such a good can be identified and legitimately adopted by the community and its leaders.

If there is a good for the human being as such, then it is reasonable to expect that knowledge of this good will contribute significantly to our grasp of the common good. Should there be none such, then the notion of common good must needs be a construct of human subjectivity or social convention.

Marriage and Family

A social structure of especial concern is the family, about whose good one may raise the same questions as those concerning larger societies. Certainly we may find this in Locke's writing, where he founds marriage on the explicit contract between husband and wife. Indeed, he uses this domestic relationship precisely to undermine the claims of the absolute monarch over the state.[98] The problem becomes acute, however, when we consider the nature of the relationship between the married persons. Traditionally, marriage has been understood to be a long-term—ordinarily lifelong (although, true to his principles, Locke allows for divorce after any progeny have reached their maturity)—committed relationship between a man and a woman for purposes that include the procreation and rearing of offspring. This conception, however, has come under radical scrutiny and questioning since 1930. Today the West's almost universal acceptance of contraception as a morally legitimate option, one that makes a voluntarily childless marriage possible, has called into question the traditional belief that progeny is one of the goods (a common good, if you will) of marriage. Further, liberalized divorce laws ("no-fault divorce" in the United States), along with the increasing use of prenuptial agreements specifying the division of property in the event of dissolution, have effectively rendered marriage a contract that can be terminated at will by either of the contracting parties. This conception of marriage leads to the logical conclusion that the contracting parties need not be of different sexes, that homosexual unions can qualify as marriages. To require that one party must be male and the other female is to infringe on the rights of the contracting parties to act according to their own legitimate autonomy.

This question of sexual differentiation and its significance brings into relief the more basic question of the good of the human being as such, for sex is a biological characteristic, rooted in the reproductive capacity. How does the moral good pertain to the goods represented by sexual differentiation and reproduction? These questions and developments have direct significance when considered in relation to recent developments in science and technology. Contraceptive technology makes it both possible and convenient for couples to engage in sexual intercourse without the possibility of conceiving a child, and contemporary reproductive technologies are becoming increasingly effective for achieving conception without intercourse. In other words, the natural link between sexual activity and procreation has been severed on both sides. Because the couple engaging

[98] *Second Treatise*, chap. 7, sec. 82.

in sexual activity need not be concerned that they may become mother and father, their activity need not be governed by the "natural end" of reproduction. Having pharmaceutically or technically rendered the act infertile, they may adapt it to their own purposes. Within such a framework the differentiation of the sexes becomes largely a matter of personal preference. Most men find women sexually attractive and enjoy sex with them, and so likewise are most women drawn to men. On the other hand, if sex and sexual activity can be essentially unrelated to procreation, then for those so inclined, homosexual activity is morally unobjectionable.

These facts go directly to the good of marriage. Is there such a good? Or must we say that the good of any marriage is that good which the couple themselves determine? Indeed, this is precisely the principle that forms most of our contemporary understanding of marriage. The couple themselves determine the form of their marriage according to their own values. These values may be "traditional": home and family. However, they may also found their marriage on mutual enjoyment and pleasure, pursuit of joint or complementary career goals, establishment of themselves according to a desired lifestyle, and so on. What our contemporary culture tends to prize in marriage are love (understood as strong affection and attachment), sexual intimacy, and a commitment to extended living together under sanction of law. This flexibility to adopt new values and reject the traditional goods associated with marriage result directly from the fairly recent technological advances in fertility science, which enable us so to adapt our bodies that we can avoid the consequences naturally written into human sexuality. It may be noted here that if marriage is understood in this way, then there is no reason why two persons of the same sex, who feel strongly about each other and who want to share their lives and sexual intimacy, ought to be deprived of the opportunity to marry.

An important consequence of this is that the significance of sexual differentiation is called into question. Of course, it still remains true (for now!) that only a woman can conceive and bear a child and that this conception requires the contribution of a male's semen. Nevertheless, with pharmaceutical or surgical intervention a human being can be rendered temporarily (or permanently) infertile. The self-evident responsibilities attendant upon sexual activity in earlier ages, responsibilities arising from the procreative potential, no longer need apply. It can be asked what "masculine" and "feminine" mean, if they are no longer intrinsically connected to fatherhood and motherhood. Thus we see lively debates about the bases for our cultural distinctions between male and female. Are the differences between the sexes rooted in nature, or do they result from culture? Consequent on this is the difficulty of determining what is (or might be) good for the woman as woman or what behavior is inappropriate for the man as such. If there is some good of the human being, some teleology that is "written into" our very nature, is that identical in all human beings, or does it differ according to sex? If sex is significant, then the human good is necessarily related to the biological order. Biological facts will have moral implications.

God and the Good

That God is good is, on the face of it, unexceptionable. God is the standard of goodness. And yet the question of God and his ontological status is intimately tied with the question of goodness. We may recall Kant's provocative statement opening his *Grundlegung*: "There is no possibility of thinking of anything at all in the world, or even out of it, which can be regarded as good without qualification, except a *good will.*"[99] It would follow that, as a rational being, God himself is good only insofar as his will is good. Of course, this goodness of will may be taken to follow upon his nature as a moral ideal, but such an ideal cannot be affirmed to have existence in itself. If God enjoys actual existence (an existence that Kant precludes us from knowing), then his goodness is consequent upon the goodness of his will. For Hume the situation is even sharper. To be sure, the God of the *Dialogues* is so attenuated in his being as to count as good only insofar as the idea of him might inspire appropriately elevated sentiments. But the Supreme Being himself, as an existent (should such a being exist), could hardly be considered either good or evil. He would be a center of power *sui generis*, beyond moral sentiment and accountable to none. Should he command from Mount Sinai that humans should refrain from murder, theft, and adultery, while honoring their parents, these commands would derive no warrant of goodness from his having given them. All that the divine commandment imports is that the transgressor will be punished by one stronger than he, not that his disobedience is itself immoral. If murder, theft, adultery, and filial impiety are morally wrong,

[99] *Grundlegung der Metaphysik der Sitten*, erster Abschnitt, 7.

this is to be discovered only in the sentiments of the heart. Of God all that can be said is that he has the power to reward and punish. In both cases, of course, the failure to recognize God's ontological independence renders the determination of his own goodness moot.

This subjective turn became normative in the nineteenth century, when the locus of good was decisively displaced from the divine. In Hegel the good virtually disappears, replaced by the dialectical unfolding of the Spirit in History. What is important is not good but world historical significance. In Marx's materialism this Hegelian unfolding became the revolutionary dialectic of opposed classes in economic production. Within this dialectic there is no good toward which men are to strive or that they are called to imitate but instead only the inevitable goal of history toward which they will struggle or against which they will resist, according to their own place in the structures of production. While the consciousness of the respective classes may be of the other as *enemy*, it cannot be said *sensu strictu* that the one is good and the other bad. There are no "good workers" within the proletariat.[100] This is a point that will become central in Karol Wojtyła's intellectual engagement with Polish Marxists, as Wojtyła will insistently contrast the proletarian role with the good of this individual worker who acts, not only as a member of the class but also for his own ends and to realize himself personally. Others on the Continent, influenced by Hegel, attempted to carve out room for the idea of God within the confines of consciousness. Friedrich Schleiermacher stands out as one who attempted to single out distinctively religious experience as the locus of the divinity. Feuerbach took this conception to its logical conclusion, arguing that "God" is nothing but the projection of human imagination on the basis of human need. The goodness of God, therefore, was not to be found in a transcendent divinity but within the human heart, realizing its own projects within the world governed not from above but—to the extent it may be governable—from within. Nietzsche took this principle to full nihilism, proclaiming that with the death of God, man himself can be "beyond good

---

100 To be sure, V. I. Lenin would alter this, introducing the Communist Party as vanguard of the proletariat, fostering by their efforts the revolution that Marx had foreseen developing inevitably. And in his Communist state there would be "counterrevolutionaries," "wreckers," and "enemies of the people," terms that inevitably acquired the cast of evil.

and evil." After the *Götterdämmerung* there remains but the will to power.[101] The eclipse of God issues in the disintegration of man.

This eclipse of God took a much more congenial form in England and in her daughter, the United States of America, in which the possibilities of realizing material human good in the context of industrialized production and enlightened democratic practices made possible states in which a growing, substantial middle class could enjoy comfortable, prosperous lives, where the material well-being of each generation could be better than that of the last, in which the benefits of culture and education would steadily expand even to the poorer classes, so that one could foresee the end of poverty, illiteracy, and widespread preventable disease. It is precisely in this milieu that Bentham and Mill developed utilitarian ethics, an approach that, as noted earlier, is especially apt for political and economic management. To achieve the "greatest good for the greatest number" is in the first instance a politician's maxim, and, indeed, it is valuable to one responsible for allocating existing resources, fostering growth, and maintaining public order. To the extent that politics is the "art of the possible," it is utilitarian. We may further remark that under such a conception the task of political leadership is largely commercial and economic—to manage the conditions under which wealth is created and distributed. Within this Anglo-American vision, procedures are key, with justice being constituted by the possibility of every member's having equal and ready access to the basic advantages of the society.[102] So long as the mechanisms of democratic government, reasonably free press, and free enterprise undergirded by private property and discreet public regulation function properly, material wealth will grow and become increasingly available to the populace. Since the measure of prosperity is material, God and his laws become decreasingly relevant except insofar as these govern the private lives of those who choose to recognize them. To say "God exists" is understood to be a pronouncement of one's own religious stance, not a claim about cosmology or a truth about the ultimate structure of reality.

---

[101] "If one does not acknowledge transcendent truth, then the force of power takes over, and each person tends to make full use of the means at his disposal in order to impose his own interests or his own opinion, with no regard for the rights of others." John Paul II, encyclical *Centesimus Annus*, 44, *L'Osservatore Romano*, May 6, 1991, weekly English ed.

[102] See John Rawls, *A Theory of Justice* (Cambridge, MA: Belknap Press, 1971), especially pt. 1, chap. 2, and pt. 2.

Whether Western societies can continue to thrive or even survive on a materialist foundation may well be debated by others. What we must note in this study is that with the eclipse of God, the standard of good disappears. To be sure, any society can be expected to agree on certain fundamental goods: safety from foreign enemies and domestic criminals, adequate provision of food and shelter, and reasonable social order so that life has a more or less predictable routine. Beyond the simple agreement that these are important, utilitarianism and benevolent bureaucracy falter. If God exists and is the ultimate Governor and Lord of history, then paradoxically the practical responsibility of human beings for their decisions is lessened in a critical way. By contrast, if the moral demand is to ensure the greatest happiness for the greatest number, the governor or administrator is never certain of the responsibility of his acts.[103] To do the right thing or the wisest thing is not necessarily to do the best thing. The demand on the governor is infinite and undefined; *whatever* may pertain to the happiness or well-being of the people becomes his concern. He is obliged to project accurately the outcomes of economic, social, political, legal, and military decisions he might make, for these are judged not on the basis of any law other than that of their success. By contrast, a polity under God—by which I mean one acknowledged to stand under the judgment and providence of God—need not and indeed cannot be so demanding of its leaders. In this respect we may note Abraham Lincoln's second inaugural address, in which he acknowledged that although his administration had sought a speedy end to the Civil War, its outcome could only be in God's hands, for the war itself—regardless of the intentions of the peoples and governments involved—may fulfill God's justice.

> Fondly do we hope, fervently do we pray, that this mighty scourge of war may speedily pass away. Yet, if God wills that it continue until all the wealth piled by the bondsman's two hundred and fifty years of unrequited toil shall be sunk, and until every drop of blood drawn with the lash shall be paid by another drawn with the sword, as was said three thousand years ago, so still it must be said "the judgments of the Lord are true and righteous altogether."[104]

[103] On this see Knauer's discussion of "rigorism" in Peter Knauer, S.J., "Teleologische als deontologische Normenbegründung," *Theologie und Philosophie* 55, no. 3 (1980): 327.

[104] Abraham Lincoln, second inaugural address, "The Inaugural Addresses of the Presidents," the Avalon Project, Lillian Goldman Law Library, Yale University, avalon.law.yale.edu/19th_century/lincoln2.asp (accessed January 7, 2010).

What Lincoln recognized, which a utilitarian cannot, is that the disposition of earthly affairs is subject to a judgment higher than his own, based on purposes higher even than those of the people governed. If God exists, then his will and purposes must be considered as potentially relevant to the human community. Further, his will and, as it were, his standard of goodness will be normative for the choices of values that the community may adopt as its good.

John Paul II: Thomism, Phenomenology, and Realism

This present study examines John Paul II's conception of the good in relation to truth. In it we will recognize strong affinities between his academic and scholarly writings and the thought of Thomas Aquinas. Karol Wojtyła expressly recognizes the value, adequacy, and essential correctness of the Aristotelian-Thomistic conception of the good, especially in reference to ethics: "At this point I am convinced that the ethics of Aristotle and St. Thomas Aquinas is based on a proper relation to experience and, moreover, that their view of the ethical act is the only proper and adequate description of ethical experience."[105] Repeatedly Wojtyła makes clear his stance as a philosophical realist. Although one may well characterize him as a Thomist,[106] to do so without further clarification is to risk mischaracterizing his work and his thought. He is also recognized as a phenomenologist, developing his thought in response to and often in the language of Edmund Husserl, the father of phenomenology, and especially Max Scheler. Indeed, the English translation of his main philosophical work, *The Acting Person*, first appeared as volume 10 in the *Analecta Husserliana: The Yearbook of Phenomenological Research*. In a characteristically phenomenological way, he addresses questions of consciousness in relation to reality and the formation of attitudes according to values given in experience.[107] Besides making his writings often obscure, this interweaving of two very different styles of thought can make it difficult to interpret his writings. On

---

[105] "The Separation of Experience from the Act in Ethics," in *Person and Community*, 42–43. See also 46–47, and *Lubliner Vorlesungen*, 170–202, 271ff.

[106] As Fulvio Di Blasi strongly suggests in his *God and the Natural Law: A Rereading of Thomas Aquinas* (South Bend, IN: St. Augustine's Press, 2003), 216n.

[107] The formation of values is a central theme of his *Sources of Renewal: The Implementation of the Second Vatican Council* (New York: Harper and Row, 1980).

the one hand, the reader of *The Acting Person* feels himself thrown back onto the Continent, wrestling with "consciousness," "eidetic intuition," "epochē," and so on, while on the other, some readers of *Veritatis Splendor* complain that it reads like a manual in moral theology from the 1950s.[108] This situation can give rise to debate concerning to which school he more properly belongs.[109] The most satisfactory answer is that he belongs to both, albeit in different ways to each. Following Buttiglione we can summarize his situation as follows: Wojtyła analyzes the human person's experience phenomenologically and on that basis moves into a Thomistic metaphysics of being. "To begin from the phenomenology of moral experience and to graft metaphysical reflection . . . permits one to arrive at the question of being from the question of man, through the question of the good."[110] The intellectual world we live in is not experienced as an Aristotelian realm of substance and accidents, potency and act, explained in terms of efficient, material, formal, and final causes. Karol Wojtyła wants to address the contemporary world not just in its own terms but, to the extent possible, according to its own manner of thinking. And this means to begin with human consciousness and experience.[111]

We have already indicated how the turn to the subject has affected modern conceptions of the good by situating good in human subjectivity. There appears to be an unbridgeable gulf between the demands of "objective good" and subjectively founded and embraced values. If value is constituted only in consciousness or if the reality of good is ideal and only

---

108 See, for example, Jean Porter, "The Moral Act in *Veritatis Splendor* and in Aquinas's *Summa Theologiae*," in *"Veritatis Splendor": American Responses*, ed. Michael E. Allsopp and John J. O'Keefe (Kansas City: Sheed and Ward, 1995), 278–95.

109 See Josef Seifert, "Karol Cardinal Wojtyła (Pope John Paul II) as Philosopher and the Cracow/Lublin School of Philosophy," *Aletheia: An International Journal of Philosophy* 2 (1981): 130–99; Georges Kalinowski, "La pensée philosophique de Karol Wojtyła et la faculté de l'Université catholique de Lublin," *Aletheia: An International Journal of Philosophy* 4, Epistomology and Logic (1988): 198–216; and Tadeusz Styczeń, "Reply to Kalinowski: By Way of an Addendum to the Addenda," *Aletheia: An International Journal of Philosophy* 4, Epistomology and Logic (1988): 217–25.

110 Buttiglione, *Karol Wojtyla*, 74.

111 "The great discovery of modernity concerns the consciousness of the human being." Rocco Buttiglione, "Presentazione," in *Karol Wojtyla e il pensiero europeo contemporaneo* (Bologna: CSEO Saggi, 1984), 10.

such, then the ontological foundations of the good easily become lost. Pope John Paul II has remarked that the history of modern philosophy "begins with Descartes, who split thought from existence and identified existence with reason itself: "Cogito, ergo sum" ("I think, therefore I am").[112] The philosophical challenge then is to recover the philosophy of being in relation to the philosophy of consciousness without repudiating either. The principal work in which Wojtyła addresses this is *Person and Act*, where he argues that an adequate account of the experience of acting is impossible in terms of consciousness alone. The phenomenological essence of "a human being acts"[113] requires the transcendence of the bounds of consciousness toward other things, which are to be changed by that act. The act is efficacious, and therefore it presupposes the existence of the acting person as an effective agent within the world.[114] Equally significant to his analysis of efficacy is his rejection of consciousness as epistemologically foundational. Consciousness does not found but is founded upon knowledge, especially knowledge of self.[115] Therefore the dynamism that acts—the acting subject—is conscious because intelligent and efficacious. Intellectually to grasp this reality, we must go beneath consciousness, as it were, to the *suppositum* that founds both the understanding and the dynamism that we call "will."

Good is always a standard. What is good is to be preferred to what is not good or less good. If something admits of goodness, then to the extent that one is able to affect its condition, one should—*ceteris paribus*—seek to make it good. To ask what it is that constitutes a good human person is to ask about the standards by which one judges human goodness. Aristotle's approach was to argue from analogy. We know what it means to be a good flute player or cobbler, and we know what it means to be a good eye or hand. Artisans and body parts are evaluated in terms of their various functions.[116] If we can determine the function of a human being as such, then we know what is good for him. And Aristotle concludes, on the basis of the distinctively human difference, rationality, that "human good turns out to

---

[112] John Paul II, *Crossing the Threshold of Hope* (New York: Alfred A. Knopf, 1994), 38.

[113] The project of *Person and Act* is to investigate this essence phenomenologically in order to reveal the essence of the person. Wojtyła, *Persona e atto*, 838.

[114] Wojtyła, *Persona e atto*, chap. 2, 909–23.

[115] Ibid., 872–77.

[116] Aristotle, *Nicomachean Ethics* 1.7, 1097b20–1098a10.

be activity of soul exhibiting excellence [virtue]"[117] To be a good human being is to have a well-formed, virtuous character by which one directs one's acts reasonably to noble ends, especially the contemplation of what is truly admirable.[118] As indicated above, Wojtyła accepts the Aristotelian ethics, but he does not directly trace Aristotle's analysis. Rather, he examines the intransitive aspect of every human act, its effect on the agent as a moral being. To be sure, one can well argue that the principles of such an analysis lie within the *Nicomachean Ethics*, in its analysis of habit formation; to do wrong acts is to deform one's character. Wojtyła's point and emphasis, while congenial to the Aristotelian, is sharper. He wants to argue that by choosing evil acts the will becomes evil, so that it is not simply in the formation of a vicious disposition through bad habits that one becomes evil, but that in the performance of a wicked act one becomes wicked.

The basis for this connection of personal evil with particular acts is precisely in the nexus of freedom, reason, and truth, which is, in a nutshell, the focus of this present work. Like Aristotle, Wojtyła connects good acting with rationality, but he takes the analysis one step further, locating moral goodness specifically in one's response to the truth one knows. This response is morally responsible because the human person is free. When the free, rational agent turns from the truth in his action, then not only does he do what is evil (because contrary to the truth of things), but he makes his own will evil, for it is by his own will that he has directed his acts to this evil.[119] In one sense, therefore, the standard for human good is the truth; to be good is to act according to the truth. This requires, however, that we make sense of the phrase "truth about the good," for it is truth in virtue of which we are good (or wicked). Further, if Karol Wojtyła's project is to succeed, this good must be ontologically rooted in reality independent of the individual's subjectivity. It must be "objective" good. To flesh out how Karol Wojtyła/John Paul II understands this good and the truth about it is the project of this present work.

---

[117] Ibid., 1098a18.

[118] Ibid., 10.8, 1178b23–35.

[119] See Karol Wojtyła, "The Will in the Analysis of the Ethical Act," in *Person and Community*, 3–22.

CHAPTER 2
Good and the Natural Order

ACCORDING TO THE COMMON contemporary understanding, to speak of "good" is to move out of the world of fact and into the realm of values, to move from what is objective to the subjective. In the view of most scholars and in our public discourse, we must turn to science for the truth, and in science we find not "good" but only fact. The sciences are *objective*. The realm of good may be appropriate for religious thinkers, poets, cultural leaders, and moral teachers, but whatever these may say about good cannot constitute knowledge in the strict sense, for it is not verifiable or subject to independent experimental and hence objective confirmation. The realm of "good" seems to be a realm of opinion, predilection, and personal expression, not of truth. This exclusion constitutes a real challenge for our present project, for the phrase "truth about the good" implies that good is the sort of thing about which one can have objectively ascertainable public knowledge. Since it is our conception of the natural sciences that constitutes the principal challenge to the very possibility of truth *about the good*, this chapter will examine John Paul II's conception of the natural order and the situation of good and evil within it.

"Good" and the Scientific Perspective

We begin our analysis of John Paul II's approach with a curiously brief comment in his catechesis on the theology of the body. John Paul is examining the account in Genesis 2 of the first man's experience of his initial encounter with the woman. He has already met and named the brute animals, but among them he had found no suitable partner. The woman, however, is different. She is "bone from my bones, and flesh from my flesh" (Gen 2:23). John Paul II continues:

> In the light of the earlier analysis of all the "bodies" man came in contact with and conceptually defined, giving them their names (*animalia*), the expression "flesh of my flesh" takes on precisely this meaning: the body reveals man. This concise formula already contains all that human science will ever be able to say about the structure of the body as an organism, about its vitality, its particular sexual physiology, etc.[1]

How are we to understand this text? John Paul II says that everything that human science could ever say about the structure of the body is contained in this formula "flesh of my flesh," but nothing in that phrase implies or indicates (for instance) that characteristically masculine behavior is causally related to testosterone or that a woman's fertility cycle is one lunar month. Indeed, several pages later John Paul II expressly acknowledges that the Genesis account is "pre-scientific" and "tells us relatively little about the human body in the naturalistic and contemporary sense of the word." Rather, the account of the beginning of creation presents us with the fundamental truth underlying an integral vision of the human being, and, he adds, "This truth *concerns the meaning of the human body in the structure of the personal subject.*"[2] It is in this sense, then, that we must understand how the results of the human sciences are "contained" in this formula, "flesh of my flesh."

At this juncture of his analysis of the "original unity of man and woman" (a phrase that was also the title of this series of audiences) John Paul II directs his attention to the subjectivity of that first man and its transformation as he encounters the woman for the first time.[3] This man was alone, in

---

1 *Man and Woman He Created Them*, 9:4, 164; *Mężczyzną i niewiastą stworzył ich*, 33–34.

2 *Man and Woman He Created Them*, 23:4, 231.

3 A word on method is important here. Although our author is using an authoritative text from Revelation, the book of Genesis, in this part of the analysis he is not using it theologically. Rather, he reflects on the experience of the first man and woman insofar as their experience is prototypical. The verification for this section of his argument is not found in witness to the divine testimony but in the common experience that we all share. See ibid., 11.1, 169–70.

his state of *original solitude*, which the Pope characterizes thus: "In fact, solitude also signifies man's subjectivity, which constitutes itself through self-knowledge. Man is alone because he is 'different' from the visible world, the world of living beings."[4] John Paul II here addresses a contemporary philosophical problem, that of the relationship between the facticity of the human being's presence in the world and his subjective experience. He characterizes this subjectivity as "original solitude."[5] Alone in the garden with no other visible being to talk with, as it were, the first man is alone, and, as the Scripture says, it was not good (Gen 2:18). But we may ask—as indeed many have done—whether, good or not, this solitude is inevitable. Sartre famously wrote, "Hell is—other people!"[6] And it is such because each of us is confined within his own subjectivity, unable to pass beyond the bounds of his own consciousness. From such a perspective Sartre argues that the only possible starting point for any understanding of human nature is the subjectivity, the consciousness of the individual.

> Our point of departure is, indeed, the subjectivity of the individual, and that for strictly philosophic reasons. . . . And at the point of departure there cannot be any other truth than this, *I think, therefore I am*, which is the absolute truth of consciousness as it attains to itself. Every theory which begins with man, outside of this moment of self-attainment, is a theory which thereby suppresses the truth, for outside of the Cartesian *cogito*, all objects are no more than probable, and any doctrine of probabilities which is not attached to a truth will crumble into nothing.[7]

Descartes has decreed, so Sartre would have it, that each of us can know only what is present to his own consciousness. This is similar to the position of John Paul II's Adam as he stood naming the animals in the garden. These were living things that he could know but with which he could not communicate, sharing the content of his own mind. The first man was, in a sense, the original solipsist.

---

[4] Ibid., 5.6, 150.

[5] See Schmitz, *At the Center of the Human Drama*, 100.

[6] Jean-Paul Sartre, *No Exit*, in *No Exit, and Three Other Plays* (New York: Vintage Books, 1989), 45.

[7] Jean-Paul Sartre, "Existentialism Is a Humanism," in *Existentialism from Dostoevsky to Sartre*, ed. Walter Kaufmann (New York: New American Library, 1975), 360.

Then the man encounters the woman and exclaims that she is "flesh of my flesh." In John Paul II's reading this encounter has two aspects. First, the man recognizes in her a being like himself, a person.

> Despite the diversity in constitution tied to the sexual difference, *somatic homogeneity* is so evident that the man, on waking up from genetic sleep, expresses it immediately when he says: "This time she is flesh from my flesh and bone from my bones. She will be called woman, because from man she was taken" (Genesis 2:23). In this way, for the first time, the man (male) manifests joy and even exaltation, for which he had no reason before, due to the lack of a being similar to himself. Joy for the other human being, for the second "I," dominates in the words the man (male) speaks on seeing the woman (female).[8]

The point here is so obvious as easily to be missed by one not accustomed to the puzzles of post-Cartesian anthropology. Our intellectual sophistication can mislead us, and so John Paul II here draws our attention to the significance of the man's immediate recognition of this being, the woman, as different from all the others (the animals). With the woman he has a companion, a help that is fit for him. That is to say, in his fellow human being, the man finds someone with whom he can form a true interpersonal communion. This is immediately evident to Adam at their first encounter. He did not have to examine, run tests, and reflect theoretically to determine that she is different from the animals.

The second aspect is the specifically sexual. She is woman, one with whom the man can become "one flesh" and generate offspring. The Scriptural comment that they were naked but not ashamed (Gen 2:25) is, in John Paul II's reading, evidence that they were perfectly well aware of the significance of the differences in their bodies. In virtue of this difference of sex the two were able to unite physically and to overcome the solitude that constituted the subjectivity of each. "When they unite with each other (in the conjugal act) so closely as to become 'one flesh,' man and woman rediscover every time and in a special way the mystery of creation, thus returning to the union in humanity . . . that allows them to recognize each other reciprocally and to call each other by name, as they did the first time."[9]

---

[8] *Man and Woman He Created Them,* 8.4, 161.

[9] Ibid., 10.2, 167.

This is, indeed, a key thesis for his theology of the body. The human sexual encounter is much more than the interaction of two sexually complementary organisms. It has within its very structure the possibility and indeed the proper end of uniting the two into a true *communio personarum*, a communion of persons. But of course, this phrase "communion of persons" expresses a reality that is social and psychological, a spiritual reality.

When John Paul II says, therefore, "This concise formula ["flesh of my flesh"] already contains everything that human science could ever say about the structure of the body as an organism, about its vitality and its particular sexual physiology, etc.," his point is not that somehow all the results of modern biology could be inferred from it. Rather, for Adam and for every other human being, "my flesh" is *not only* the organic system of "my body." "My flesh" is, rather, the living me.[10] My subjectivity is situated in this place and time, in this body, and is formed by the sensual experiences and efforts of this body in the world. The body reveals the man in the sense that it manifests the human being as personal subject. Eve's glance was qualitatively different from the cat's impersonal gaze. That this person is "flesh of my flesh" means that she was of a different order than the other organisms in the garden. What science can reveal is all there, but there is more besides. Therefore more than science is needed to know this being as she really is.

This brings us to the key point. Here is a being, the woman, embedded within the natural order, dependent on the resources of its environment, vulnerable to predators and natural upheavals, and subject to inner desires for food, drink, sexual activity, and comfort, but whose behavior is governed by another kind of law, the laws of persons.[11] And of course this is so, not only of the woman, but of the man and every human being. In his encyclical *Redemptor Hominis*, John Paul II wrote: "Man cannot live without love. He remains a being that is incomprehensible for himself, his life is senseless, if love is not revealed to him, if he does not encounter love, if he does not experience it and make it his own, if he does not participate intimately in it."[12]

---

[10] It is helpful to note that in his original Polish draft, the Scriptural expression "flesh of my flesh" is rendered "ciałem z mego ciała," in which the primary sense of the word *ciało* is "body." See *Mężczyzną i niewiastą stworzył ich*, 30.

[11] Karol Wojtyła, *Love and Responsibility*, trans. H. T. Willetts (San Francisco: Ignatius Press, 1993), 27, 51, 226.

[12] *Redemptor Hominis*, 10.

An inspiring exhortation, to be sure, but John Paul II intended more than only to inspire. The human being is an organism that does not get on successfully simply by surviving and reproducing, as do our animal cousins. The human person is a being with needs of a different kind and on a different level. Elsewhere, he writes, "The world of persons possesses its own laws of existence and development,"[13] and in his encyclical on the mercy of God he argues that human beings need love, that justice and equity do not suffice for meeting the needs of the human person.[14] To understand the human person, one must grasp these laws. Nevertheless, because the human person is a part of the natural order, these laws governing the world of persons must in some way be situated in the natural order.

Because the scientific method is proven to be powerful, one may well ask whether we still have the conceptual tools to surpass the scientific vision of reality. Karol Wojtyła believes that we do, and that to avail ourselves of them we must turn to metaphysics.

The Order of Existence and the Biological Order

Early in *Love and Responsibility*, Karol Wojtyła addresses the issue of the relationship between the body's sexual urges and one's conscious control of these. If *sexual morality* is to be a meaningful concept, then the expectation of self-control must be reasonable; the intelligent agent must have the resources to govern behavior that is notoriously subject to strong physical drives. If, in fact, these drives are *instincts*, which are by definition beyond rational control,[15] then the requirement that the human subject control them is unreasonable and possibly even harmful. In this context Wojtyła writes:

---

13 *Love and Responsibility*, 97.

14 John Paul II, encyclical *Dives in Misericordia* (Boston: St. Paul Editions, 1980), 12, 14.

15 Wojtyła, *Love and Responsibility*, 45: "By *instinct* . . . we mean a certain mode of action which automatically declares its origin. This is the *reflex mode of action, which is not dependent on conscious thought.*" In Polish: "Przez instynkt . . . rozumiemy pewien sposób działania, który równocześnie wskazuje na swoje źródło. Chodzi mianowicie o sposób działania spontaniczny, nie poddany reflksji." *Miłośći odpowiedzialność* (Lublin: Towarzystwo Naukowe KUL, 2001), 45–46.

> This habit of confusing the order of existence[16] with the biological order, or rather of allowing the second to obscure the first, is part of that generalized empiricism which seems to weigh so heavily on the mind of modern man, and particularly on modern intellectuals. . . . The sexual urge owes its objective importance to its connection with the divine work of creation . . . and this importance vanishes almost completely if our way of thinking is inspired only by the biological order of nature. . . . The "biological order," as a product of the human intellect which abstracts its elements from a larger reality, has man for its immediate author. The claim to autonomy in one's ethical views is a short jump from this. It is otherwise with the "order of nature," which means the totality of the cosmic relationships that arise among really existing entities. It is therefore the order of existence, and the laws which govern it have their foundation in Him, Who is the unfailing source of that existence, in God the Creator.[17]

Problems with "Generalized Empiricism"

This important paragraph will be the focus of our investigation for the next few pages, as we unfold its key points, the first of which is a turn to metaphysics, as Wojtyła distinguishes between the "order of existence" and the "biological order."[18] He ascribes the confusion of the two orders to a "generalized empiricism," one that weighs on the modern mind, "and particularly on modern intellectuals." Indeed, much of the history of modern philosophy may be fairly described as an effort to overcome and eliminate metaphysics. Certainly British empiricism and Kantian transcendental philosophy constitute significant efforts to overcome the metaphysical impulse by analyzing its conceptual roots. This antimetaphysical thrust reached its high point in the late nineteenth and early twentieth centuries with the rise of positivism. And if today philosophers are more willing than a century ago to speak of metaphysics, they are not so willing to acknowledge the existence of an object of metaphysics beyond those that

---

16 The phrase in Polish is "porzadek bytu," which may also be translated "order of being."

17 *Love and Responsibility*, 57; *Miłość i odpowiedzialność*, 55–56.

18 Birgit Schneider recognizes the importance of the metaphysical understanding of the order of being given by God, even if she disagrees with it and his application of such metaphysics to morality. See Birgit Schneider, *Wer Gott dient wird nicht krumm: Feministische Ethik im Dialog mit Karol Wojtyła und Dietmar Mieth* (Mainz: Matthias-Grünewald-Verlag, 1997), 97, 106.

are already the objects of empirical science. Kant's trio of questions, the existence of God, the immortality of the soul, and freedom of the will, must be addressed only in material or—what amounts to much the same thing—sensational terms. Metaphysics is not generally construed today to be a method of inquiry distinctively suited for investigating and answering questions about real objects of the material world. In the text just cited, however, and in his encyclical *Fides et Ratio*,[19] our author affirms the possibility and, indeed, the necessity of such metaphysical inquiry.

Although Wojtyła cites a "generalized empiricism" as the origin of the confusion between the order of existence and the biological order, he does not reject the empirical as such. Indeed, it is through the empirical that we first experience the world and our presence in it. Through the person's efficacy, his efficient causality, he participates in the objective order of being and existence. This efficacy is central to Wojtyła's concept of the *person*, because the subjective "I," which is the conscious subject of experience, is also a cause of change in the world.[20] Wojtyła relies on the efficient causality of the person as the basis of his argument with the phenomenology and philosophies of consciousness in general, for which the existence of the "external world" is a significant issue. If the foundational reality is consciousness, then it is not clear what grounds we have for asserting a reality independent of consciousness.[21] Karol Wojtyła's analysis is also important, however, for evaluating the status of empiricism. If the givenness of the empirical order in conscious sensation is foundational, then the full scope of human experience remains unexplained. An essential element of experience is that in acting, the person experiences himself as subject, as "author of the action." He experiences his own dynamism, the union of his subjectivity and objectivity. In other words, the person in act experiences himself as both belonging to the empirical order and transcending it, as it were, by reaching beyond his subjectivity into the objective order. He further transcends that order in that he freely, knowingly, and consciously intervenes in

---

19 *Fides et Ratio*, 82–83.

20 "L'esperienza vissuta dell'operatività mete in evidenza la trascendenza dell'uomo respetto al proprio agire," *Persona e atto*, 920–21; also by Karol Wojtyła, "Person: Subject and Community," in *Person and Community*, 230–31, and in that same volume, "The Will in the Analysis of the Ethical Act," 4, 8.

21 See Sartre's "Existentialism Is a Humanism."

that order.[22] This is to say that precisely in his encounter with the empirical order, the person discovers in himself an order of reality beyond the sensible. Indeed, the project of *Person and Act* is, in part at least, to analyze how the human subject makes sense of himself as an acting person, that is, as both conscious subject and efficacious agent in the world. If empiricism is truly about experience, then the experience of the self as efficacious subject of acting must count as one of the fundamental experiences.[23]

Wojtyła's response to the question of a *generalized empiricism* depends on his account of experience, a more complex account than the simple sensualism we find in Hume. For Karol Wojtyła the human person is not simply a kind of receptor and interpreter of sense experiences, but rather an efficacious agent who finds himself in a world of which he needs to make sense in order to act responsibly and effectively. Furthermore, the *generalized empiricism* he criticizes ignores the broader context of the human person's situation in the world, a context that the acting person finds himself constrained to address. The person in act simply does not go about addressing himself in an ad hoc fashion to isolated and unrelated states of affairs, but rather he fits his actions into some coherent whole.

This theme of making explicit the sense of one's place in and relation to the world comes most clearly to the fore in *Fides et Ratio*, where John Paul II attributes the origins of philosophy to the quest to discover the meaning of life. In this context he appeals to philosophers to "recover its sapiential dimension as a search for the ultimate and overarching meaning of life."[24] This task is integral to philosophy and distinguishes it from other forms of inquiry. Concerning the recovery of the sapiential dimension, John Paul II writes:

> This first requirement is in fact most helpful in stimulating philosophy to conform to its proper nature. In doing so, it will be not only the decisive critical factor which determines the foundations and limits of the different fields of scientific learning, but will also take its place as the ultimate framework of

[22] This is especially the argument of *Person and Act*, pt. 2, "Transcendence of the Person in the Act," *Persona e atto*, 963–1019. See also Karol Wojtyła, "The Degrees of Being from the Point of View of the Phenomenology of Action," in Tymieniecka, *Analecta Husserliana*, 11:126–27.

[23] "Introduzione," in *Persona e atto*, especially 832–44.

[24] *Fides et Ratio*, 81.

> the unity of human knowledge and action, leading them to converge towards a final goal and meaning. . . . A philosophy denying the possibility of an ultimate and overarching meaning would be not only ill-adapted to its task, but false.[25]

On the basis of this conception of philosophy, John Paul II can characterize specific ways in which human thought can fall short and in particular what is defective about the generalized empiricism that he has cited. He points to an inadequate conception of truth, unacceptable consequences for ethics, and nihilism.

Inadequate Conception of Truth

> Yet this sapiential function could not be performed by a philosophy which was not itself a true and authentic knowledge, addressed, that is, not only to particular and subordinate aspects of reality—functional, formal or utilitarian—but to its total and definitive truth, to the very being of the object which is known. This prompts a second requirement: that philosophy verify the human capacity to know the truth, to come to a knowledge which can reach objective truth by means of that *adaequatio rei et intellectus* to which the Scholastic Doctors referred.[26]

This requirement that philosophy verify the human capacity to know the truth means that pragmatism, relativism, and phenomenalism are inadequate. Our author expressly appeals to the Scholastic formula *adaequatio rei et intellectus* ("correspondence of thing and intellect"),[27] that is, to the notion that the aim of human understanding is to attain truth, to correspond to things as they really are. Kaczyński writes: "Knowledge cannot, therefore, be identified only with thinking, with conceptualization alone, but must be integrated above all with the grasping of truth in judgment. . . . The 'adaequatio' of the intellect with reality to be known is realized through a dynamic and continuous tendency."[28] Pragmatism of the sort popularized by William James, which holds that *truth* is nothing more than a quality we

[25] Ibid.

[26] Ibid., 82.

[27] Ibid., 56. See also *Persona e atto*, 1016.

[28] *Verità sul bene nella morale*, 198.

ascribe to ideas (or thoughts) that work for us,[29] adequately accounts only for our handling of information in matters of isolated interactions as we make our way through the world. However, the Scholastic conception indicates a deeper relationship between intellect and reality. If the human intellect can actually conform to things as they are, then the human being can share a common mind, as it were, with the rationality that underlies the order of the world.[30] The meanings of things become meanings that form the understanding of one who knows the truth. How this is actually realized is a topic for another work, but we may remark here that the realist notion of truth as correspondence implies a deeper and more intimate relationship between the human mind and the natural order than does James's pragmatism. James cannot find the meaning of life in the truth about the world and hence must construct it from within his own subjectivity.[31] We have already noted that the phenomenalism of a David Hume expressly limits knowledge to the reception and organization of sense impressions. If the person is to know the meaning of his life, the philosophy by which he does so must be able to penetrate beyond the records of his senses. What is needed, according to John Paul II, is "a philosophy of genuinely metaphysical range, capable, that is, of transcending empirical data in order to attain something absolute, ultimate and foundational in its search for truth. . . . I want only to state that reality and truth do transcend the factual and the empirical, and to vindicate the human being's capacity to know this transcendent and metaphysical dimension in a way that is true and certain, albeit imperfect and analogical."[32]

Scientism and Ethical Pragmatism

Fides et Ratio comes closest to addressing Wojtyła's "generalized empiricism in the following text:

---

[29] William James, "Pragmatism's Conception of Truth," lecture 6 in *Pragmatism* (Buffalo: Prometheus Books, 1991), especially 89–91.

[30] See John Paul II, general audience, September 10, 1986, in *Catechesi sul Credo*, pt. 2, "Gesù Figlio e Salvatore" (1986–1989), www.vatican.va/holy_father/john_paul_ii/audiences/alpha/list_7_it.html (accessed July 2, 2010).

[31] William James, "The Will to Believe," in *The Will to Believe, Human Immortality, and Other Essays on Popular Philosophy* (New York: Dover Books, 1956), 1–31.

[32] *Fides et Ratio*, 83. This is a "univocal" sense of truth that Curran finds "simplistic" and deficient in his *Moral Theology of Pope John Paul II*, 33–34.

> Another threat to be reckoned with is scientism. This is the philosophical notion which refuses to admit the validity of forms of knowledge other than those of the positive sciences; and it relegates religious, theological, ethical and aesthetic knowledge to the realm of mere fantasy. In the past, the same idea emerged in positivism and neo-positivism, which considered metaphysical statements to be meaningless. Critical epistemology has discredited such a claim, but now we see it revived in the new guise of scientism, which dismisses values as mere products of the emotions and rejects the notion of being in order to clear the way for pure and simple facticity. Science would thus be poised to dominate all aspects of human life through technological progress.
>
> Regrettably, it must be noted, scientism consigns all that has to do with the question of the meaning of life to the realm of the irrational or imaginary.[33]

This is essentially the scientific perspective outlined at the beginning of this chapter. In this context we must note that it is not simply a case of a religious leader decrying the fact that people fail to take religious values seriously. John Paul II's point is that these values are properly objects of knowledge. He thereby challenges the perspective that the only true knowledge is scientific knowledge, that which can be known through examination of the world in its facticity.

A direct consequence of this scientism is moral pragmatism, "an attitude of mind which, in making its choices, precludes theoretical considerations or judgments based on ethical principles."[34] He goes on to cite as a consequence the growing concept of democracy as a kind of mechanism with no relationship to underlying moral values.[35] The task of moral conscience is taken over more and more by institutions and their demands. It is apt here to refer also to the economic order, which increasingly functions not as a realm governed by moral considerations but rather as a kind of machine, obeying impersonal laws having no reference to human values. Whether the final determination is made by a vote count, an analysis of a balance sheet, or a strategic deployment of military force, moral pragmatism decides on the basis of the disposition of material realities and not on the basis of deeper or underlying values.

---

[33] *Fides et Ratio*, 88.

[34] Ibid., 89.

[35] See also his encyclical *Evangelium Vitae* (New York: Random House, 1995), 70.

Nihilism

When we hear of *nihilism*, our thoughts turn naturally to Nietzsche or, perhaps, Sartre, and it is certainly both easy and tempting to decry their more outrageous claims: "God is dead," and "Hell is other people." John Paul II's treatment of nihilism, however, is less dramatic and more telling. He writes:

> As a result of the crisis of rationalism, what has appeared finally is nihilism. As a philosophy of nothingness, it has a certain attraction for people of our time. Its adherents claim that the search is an end in itself, without any hope or possibility of ever attaining the goal of truth. In the nihilist interpretation, life is no more than an occasion for sensations and experiences in which the ephemeral has pride of place.[36]
>
> The positions we have examined lead in turn to a more general conception which appears today as the common framework of many philosophies which have rejected the meaningfulness of being. I am referring to the nihilist interpretation, which is at once the denial of all foundations and the negation of all objective truth. . . . It should never be forgotten that the neglect of being inevitably leads to losing touch with objective truth and therefore with the very ground of human dignity.[37]

What John Paul II identifies as "nihilism" others might define more positively. In the text from section 46, he indicates that a position according to which the journey is itself the goal reduces to nihilism, and he connects this to the attitude that life is simply an occasion for diverse experiences. One can relate this to his critique elsewhere of consumerism and materialistic cultures, in which a person is measured by possessions and the pleasant experiences he has had.[38] This is a kind of practical nihilism that, as the second quote indicates, flows from a fundamental neglect of being. Most important, however, is that the nihilist interpretation is not a simple effect of the philosophies that he has criticized, but rather it forms their common framework. John Paul II is speaking here not so much of the nihilism that boldly challenges every established truth

---

36 *Fides et Ratio*, 46.

37 Ibid., 90.

38 John Paul II, *Redemptor Hominis*, 15–16; *Dives in Misericordia*, 11; *Centesimus Annus*, 36, 41; and encyclical *Sollicitudo Rei Socialis*, www.vatican.va/edocs/ENG0223/_INDEX.HTM (accessed May 20, 2004), 28.

and hallowed institution as that which more casually dismisses the notion that any true meaning can be discovered or known, the notion that the most we can do is create our own meaning.

As the dramatic quasi-scientific nihilism of Russell and Sagan shows, science, if taken as the final standard of rationality, cannot but lead to nihilism, for not only does science make no reference to the *good*, but neither does it have any use for the *true*. With respect to the sciences, *truth* must be a metaconcept, because "truth" does not signify a physical relationship or entity. Rather, we evaluate scientific assertions and theories according to their ability to attain to and explain the truth. But, in fact, such evaluation is not at all necessary for the prosecution of science, which can be valued simply for its predictive power and its capacity for generating useful technologies. Science, to find its own value, needs to stand in relation to truth. Otherwise it is reduced to being simply another tool for the attainment and manipulation of power. This is why John Paul II proposes as a solution not so much an exposition of weaknesses and errors in pragmatism, scientism, phenomenalism, and related philosophies as a return to a robust metaphysical inquiry. To this, then, we turn as we return to our key text from *Love and Responsibility.*

The "Biological Order"

Wojtyła contrasts the "biological order" with the "order of existence," adding that the biological order is a product of human intellect and therefore an abstraction from the larger reality. If we ignore this relationship between the scientific abstraction and reality, this *biological order* can obscure the *order of existence*, which is the order of nature. This is a strong claim, one that most contemporary thinkers—especially in the scientific community!—would reject out of hand. If biology does not study the order of nature, then what science does? Biology is, after all, one of the *natural sciences.* Karol Wojtyła does not deny this. Nevertheless, he denies the biological order the fundamental importance that contemporary scholarship ascribes it. For example, many scholars (and not only biologists) now increasingly suggest that every aspect of human behavior, from mating practices to language to religion, is a result of Darwinian evolutionary mechanisms.[39] The consequence of such a

[39] See, for example, Craig Stanford, *Significant Others: The Ape-Human Continuum and the Quest for Human Nature* (New York: Basic Books, 2001); Walter Burkert,

model is that the attempt to answer the fundamental questions—such as that of the meaning of life—is cut off in advance. Ethical reflection, regarded as an enterprise concerned with truth, is rendered meaningless. These questions are not allowed, for the explanatory mechanisms of biological science allow for no explanation in terms of purpose and meaning. The ethics that characteristically arises from this generalized empiricism can only be some kind of utilitarianism, a form of ethical reasoning that is unable (as we shall see subsequently) to found moral norms.

It is precisely in these terms that we can understand Wojtyła's claim that the biological order "abstracts its elements from a larger reality." His point is not that biology (or any other natural science) is a kind of useful fiction or human construction imposed on inchoate human experience. Nor, of course, is he making the trivial point that any science—indeed, any description or representation whatever—uses abstract terms and general ideas. Using the logic of induction,[40] science abstracts from experience and thereby enables us to understand the world about us; natural science is not falsification. The problem of "generalized empiricism" is that it reduces objects studied by the sciences to *no more than* objects suitable for study by the empirical sciences. The *biological order*, as Wojtyła intends the term, consists of organic mechanisms that interact in predictable ways with other entities in their environment according to laws that (in principle) account for the entirety of their being and behavior *as organisms*. Not only the general terms used by the sciences, but the entities themselves that inhabit the biological order, are abstractions. We find further light on this in *Person and Act*, where Wojtyła writes: "[W]e can say that at this point metaphysics emerges as that field of thought where [the concepts of *potentia* and *actus*] deepen the roots of all the sciences."[41] These concepts of *potency* and *act* (or *actuality*), which were important to Aristotle's conception of science and which assumed central

Creation of the Sacred: Tracks of Biology in Early Religions (Cambridge: Harvard University Press, 1996); Joseph LeDoux, *Synaptic Self: How Our Brains Become Who We Are* (New York: Viking, 2002), 21ff.; Patrick Lee, "Human Beings Are Animals," in *Natural Law and Moral Inquiry: Ethics, Metaphysics, and Politics in the Work of Germain Grisez*, ed. Robert P. George (Washington, DC: Georgetown University Press, 1998), 136–37; and Ian Tattersall, "How We Came to Be Human," *Scientific American* 16, no. 2 (2006): 71.

40 See *Persona e atto*, "3. Tappa della comprensione e indirizzo dell'interpretazione," 845–47; also *Valutazione sulla possibilità*, 270.

41 *Persona e atto*, 915.

importance in Aquinas's metaphysics,[42] find no place in contemporary natural science. Significantly, Wojtyła finds it necessary to resuscitate *potentia* and *actus* in his examination of the human person, and the point is crucial for understanding this abstraction that he refers to in the text under consideration. Aristotle developed these concepts to account for the phenomenon of *becoming.* The acorn, which is not a tree, always or for the most part develops into a tree, just as the pup becomes an adult dog and the pupil a master. The immature organism or seed has within itself the power or potency to become what it is not yet. In virtue of this potency it is able, with appropriate help from other causes (such as nutrition and the power of the sun) to become a mature organism. This notion of becoming has disappeared from modern science, having been replaced by the concept of the law-governed mechanism, which reduces all developmental processes to complex sequences of mechanically determined changes among parts and particles. The contemporary scientist explains the generation of the mature dog by means of a self-replicating molecule, DNA, whose coding determines the development of the embryo through its successive stages of development into adulthood. This capacity for self-replication is traced to the molecule's structure, which is such that each strand can serve as a template for the formation of new, complementary molecules. By varying the coding, one can alter the final form that the organism will take; this is the basis for the expectation that gene therapy can eventually prevent or cure genetic diseases.

What is important for our present purposes is that Aristotle's unfolding of an innate potency for some ultimate state has been replaced by the operation of a sophisticated mechanism. Karol Wojtyła does not deny that such an account accurately represents the operation of living organisms as they develop. His point is that it fails to account for the full reality of the natural process. He argues in particular that the biological process cannot of itself account for the moral development of the human person.[43] This

---

[42] See, for instance, Thomas Aquinas, *Commentary on the* Metaphysics *of Aristotle*, 12.4.2483, where he writes: "[A]ctuality and potentiality are universally the principals of all things because they flow from being as being." Further, the first of the five ways to prove that God exists turns on the concepts of potency and act (*ST* I, q. 2, a. 3).

[43] There are those who argue exactly the opposite. See Nicholas Wade, "Is 'Do unto Others' Written into Our Genes?" *New York Times*, September 18, 2007, National Edition, D1–D7. Wade reports in particular on the research of Jonathan Haidt, a

conception of potency and act relates directly to the central issue of this study, for if, as Aristotle argues, the immature organism has the potency to realize itself as an adult, then we may speak of the *good* of that organism. This good is its perfection (actuality) as a member of its species.[44] Karol Wojtyła intends to argue that the human person, as a rational being, has the capacity to develop himself, to form himself by his own acts according to some standard of perfection or good, a standard that transcends his physical relationships with other entities in the visible world.

We are now able to understand more clearly what Wojtyła intends when he states that the biological order is "a product of the human intellect which abstracts its elements from a larger reality." As a product of the human intellect, this biological order is not the reality itself, which Wojtyła refers to as the "order of existence" or the "order of nature." Rather, it is an ideal representation from a restricted, if useful, point of view. This biological order is not the potential totality of knowledge about living things. Rather, it is the potential knowledge of living things considered under certain well-defined aspects. If the rules by which the biological order are defined exclude the notion of good, then whatever good may pertain to living beings is excluded from that order a priori. The biological order is constructed on materialist principles, which exclude the spiritual.

At issue in the chapter of *Love and Responsibility* where our text occurs is the relationship between sexual urges in the human being and his sexual behavior. The basis of the sexual urges is clearly biological. Our animal cousins, especially the simians, manifest urges similar to the human, and indeed, the structure of their reproductive systems is very similar to the human. The mating strategies among the higher mammals seem clearly directed toward the preservation of the strongest and healthiest specimens, which preserves their genetic line. This same mechanism, it is argued, obtains among human beings. Recent popular literature is full of articles about the genetic bases for human sexual preferences—why men are attracted to women with large breasts and ample hips, and women to men who are tall and broad-shouldered.[45] Wojtyła, then, asks whether human

---

moral psychologist at the University of Virginia. Stanford's *Significant Others* makes a similar point, especially in chapters 6 and 7.

[44] Wojtyła, *Lubliner Vorlesungen*, 172–74.

[45] Of course, human intelligence plays a role here. The intelligent woman, for example, recognizes in Bill Gates's wealth and position a source of power and protection

sexual behavior is the result of instinct, defined as "a reflex mode of action, which is not dependent on conscious thought,"[46] or is dependent on some other factor as well.

The Order of Existence

The empiricist strategy for addressing the question of the human sexual response and its consequent behavior relies on observation and controlled experimentation. One can closely observe the behavior of chimpanzees, gorillas, and other nonhuman animals to determine how they respond to various stimuli. Such studies are complemented by analyses of their organic systems, especially the reproductive and nervous systems. These results can be compared with observations of human behavior, as well as with experiments, controlled tests, and other such instruments. What such empirical methods fail to address—indeed, cannot address—are data "from within," the subjective aspects of human experience of sexual desire, and it is precisely in this subjectivity that the full nature of these urges comes to light.[47] The human being experiences humanity not only as an objective reality in the world, from the outside, as it were, but also as subject, from within.[48] Karol Wojtyła contends that the experience of acting, that is, of being an agent, reveals the depth of the person to an extent that empirical methods cannot reach. To be sure, the person may be stimulated, aroused, or excited by a sexual stimulus similar to one that would impel an animal to action, but the person is also cognizant of his own efficacy. He can indeed respond to the sexual urgings, but he knows that his doing so will have effects that can be reasonably well predicted. And in this recognition he is aware of his responsibility for the act that his desires urge upon him. Indeed, this is the insight underlying his principal philo-

---

that the former high school football player, who now sells aluminum siding, cannot match.

[46] *Love and Responsibility*, 45. See also *Persona e atto*, 1106.

[47] See *Love and Responsibility*, 267: "Looking at it from the biological point of view, sexual differences are significant only for one purpose—reproduction: sexual differentiation exists only for the sake of reproduction. The idea that procreation must base itself on love is not derivable from a biological analysis of sex, but only from the metaphysical (i.e. ultra- and supernatural) fact of being a person [metafizycznego (*tj.* "poza- i ponad-przyrodniczego") faktu byczia osobą]." *Miłość i odpowiedzialność*, 239.

[48] *Persona e atto*, 847–48.

sophical work, *Person and Act.* Hence, Wojtyła is confident that a proper examination of human subjectivity in relation to efficacy and responsibility opens the way to a fuller understanding, to a metaphysical grasp of human personhood and thereby to metaphysics itself.[49]

This appeal to subjectivity is clearly not a turn to introspection, an appeal to "what is perfectly clear to me" as I look inside my mind. Wojtyła does not allege that there is a kind of experience that philosophers can have, if they would but turn inward. Rather, he points to the kind of experiences we all have every day, the experiences of acting and being acted upon. Not only does the human subject experience things happening to him, he also experiences that he initiates his own acts. Thus, Wojtyła distinguishes "what happens in a human being" from "a human being acts."[50] Wojtyła's point, then, is not that there is some special experience to be uncovered by introspection, but that there are aspects of ordinary experience inaccessible to sensationalist empiricism.[51]

The aspect of human experience central to Wojtyła's analysis is human action. It is through the act that he hopes to grasp the richness of the person.[52] From the outset the perspective of the acting person excludes instinct as sufficient to account for human behavior. Since the question of freedom versus determinism is seriously controverted, we do well to look carefully at Wojtyła's arguments, beginning with the crucial question of perspective. Ordinarily arguments about freedom focus on predictability. The determinist can argue that preexisting causes determined (whether exactly or probabilistically) what the human subject did, how he behaved, even if not all these causes are understood. The champion of freedom will respond that the human being is too complex to be so determined and that, at any rate, he knows from his own experience that his decisions, especially the major life decisions, have been free. To which the determinist responds (in effect), "So it seemed to you." The strength of the determinist position is precisely that it proposes to explain the event after the fact. Why did the man kick the dog? The determinist is confident that by examining the man's internal structure (including brain chemistry) and the environmental pressures his

[49] Wojtyła, "Person: Subject and Community," in *Person and Community*, 223.

[50] *Persona e atto*, 893, but especially chap. 2, 924–25.

[51] Ibid., 838–39.

[52] Ibid., 841–42.

neurological system was subject to that day (angry wife, temperamental boss, dented fender in traffic), he can find a causal nexus that leads to the unfortunate kicking. And indeed, after any fact, it is not hard at all to find ample factors that can causally be connected to it. Indeed, this is precisely the task of the scientist, to discover explanatory accounts for the behavior of different classes of things, so that the future behavior of members of that class can be predicted more accurately. Therefore (so it is argued) any account in terms of freedom must be mythical, a kind of self-delusion (which may be necessary or unavoidable). If the behavior of the organism is governed by invariant physical laws, then free human behavior is impossible. Roger Wolcoll Sperry puts the issue starkly: "The common, naïve impression that we use the mind to initiate and control our physical actions has long been rejected almost universally in science, following the doctrine of scientific materialism, which predicates that a full account of brain behavior and reality is possible in terms purely physical."[53] And Daniel Dennett confirms that in contemporary thought "[m]aterialism of one sort or another is now a received opinion approaching unanimity."[54] Hence, the experience of freedom is illusory.

Wojtyła's argument is deeper than a simple contradiction of this view, for he stresses the essential function of *consciousness* as intrinsic to "a human being acts." It is a matter of experience that we think and plan, then decide and act. That we are free is also a matter of experience, expressed as "I can, but I don't have to."[55] Now, the significance of this expression lies not in a claimed introspective certainty but in its reference to the future. "I can perform this action (which I am not yet performing), but I do not have to." No matter what the neuroscientist or master actuary may predict, insofar as the action is mine to perform, no knowledge, no prediction makes it happen without my decision and choice. Looking backward, one may say, "I had no choice" or "It wasn't really my fault." One may examine his own life and the situation at hand and explain that it was all foreordained. In the moment of decision, however, there is no

[53] Roger Wolcoll Sperry, "Consciousness and Causality," in *The Oxford Companion to the Mind*, ed. R. L. Gregory (Oxford: Oxford University Press, 1987), 164.

[54] Daniel Dennett, *Consciousness Explained* (Boston: Little, Brown, and Co., 1991), 106. Dennett goes on to argue that human behavior will have to be explained ultimately in terms of blind causal interactions.

[55] *Persona e atto*, 978.

escaping the experience of freedom, the experience of "I can, but I don't have to." The chess player's castle sits on its square until he decides to pick it up and engages his own hand and arm to do so. This experience of freedom is not some sort of inner arbitrariness, a kind of uncaused inner causality to be measured by deviance from the predicted norm (so that if nine of ten thirsty subjects drink, then the freedom quotient is only ten percent). Karol Wojtyła does not affirm the position that materialism implicitly argues against, that there is within the human person a special causal power distinct from and even opposed to physical factors, a power that originates free choices. He does not say, as it were, that left to its own devices, the human organism would follow its instincts unless and until this inner spiritual power intervenes. Rather, freedom arises from the power of reason to govern human acts, from the person's ability to represent alternative values and courses of action to himself and direct his acts accordingly. An act under consideration does not occur until the subject *chooses* to act *in this way* and not in that. The determinist is not so much wrong as off the point. An acting person *cannot predict* what he will do *without deciding* to do it.

Love and Responsibility is an account of sexual morality, that is, of the rational governance of one's sexual behavior. From the text we have been considering,[56] Wojtyła goes on to propose that one need not engage in sexual activity simply for sensual satisfaction nor only for conception of progeny, arguing that a person's sexual activity can be integrated into a larger framework to realize broader or more universal goods. This is what freedom means. The rational person chooses according to a standard of good that he has recognized, comparing one value with others. Therefore, it does not argue against freedom that almost all thirsty people will accept a glass of water offered them. (Indeed, to refuse might be taken as evidence of some pathology and of diminishment of freedom.) Implicit in this and fundamental to it is the concept of *good.* Every act, as Aristotle observed at the very outset of his *Ethics,* is directed at some good.[57] *Good* is the concept that governs the acts of the person, and we cannot dispense with it unless we speak from a purely objective, descriptive standpoint, which is to say, impersonally.

---

[56] *Love and Responsibility,* 57.

[57] *Nicomachean Ethics* 1.1.

Consequent upon freedom and rationality is the concept of responsibility. If the agent is able to envision the probable outcome of his act and can freely choose the act, then he is responsible.[58] If I say to myself, *I can, but I don't have to* and then do that thing, then I experience the result as something for which I have responsibility. Had I not chosen to do the act, then the resulting situation would probably not have occurred. This ascription of responsibility arises not from feelings (such as guilt) but from a recognition of the facts that one has changed the world in a certain way for good or ill and that in so doing one has made himself the cause of good or ill. This is directly the consequence of one's objective existence in the world as a conscious efficient cause. Integral to the experience of "a human being acts" and therefore to the conception of acting is the notion of efficacy. Existing and acting in the world, the human being causally changes it, but as a personal subject, he changes it in accordance with his own choices.

With this background Wojtyła addresses the status of sexual inclinations or urges. He expressly denies that they are instincts (understanding "instinct" as "a reflex mode of action that is not dependent on human thought"). Instead of using the term "instinct," Karol Wojtyła calls sexual desire a "vector of aspiration":

> When we speak of the sexual urge in man we have in mind not an interior source of specific actions somehow "imposed in advance," but a certain orientation, a certain direction in man's life implicit in his very nature. The sexual urge in this conception is a *natural drive born in all human beings, a vector of aspiration* along which their whole existence develops and perfects itself from within.[59]

The human being, on the other hand, has the capability to decide whether or not to act on the basis of the urge. Were this not so, then morality would be meaningless.[60]

In this analysis Wojtyła closely follows Thomas Aquinas in denying that the concupiscible appetites of themselves determine human behavior. For

[58] Wojtyła, *Persona e atto*, 1044ff., 1064; also "The Teaching of the Encyclical *Humanae Vitae* on Love: An Analysis of the Text," in *Person and Community*, 309; and *Lubliner Vorlesungen*, 81–82 and especially 320, where Wojtyła shows how responsibility must disappear in Hume's analysis.

[59] *Love and Responsibility*, 46. See also *Persona e atto*, 1106.

[60] *Love and Responsibility*, 46.

Aquinas, the desires of the body and its organic systems—desires that he calls "concupiscible"—are governed by the will or *rational appetite.*[61] Indeed, Aquinas characterizes that government as "political," because the sensitive appetites have a dynamism of their own, by which they can oppose the decision of reason.[62] Concupiscence recognizes only the good given immediately to sense or emotion, whereas will is drawn to the good in its universal aspect, to the good as such.[63] Therefore, will can control and sometimes even override the stirrings of concupiscence. Given the usual negative moral connotations of the term "concupiscence," it is important to note that Aquinas attaches no sense of opprobrium to the concupiscible appetites as such.[64] The Common Doctor recognizes these appetites as aspects of our animal nature, which are to be governed by the rational principle through the *will.* And precisely this notion of will becomes centrally important to Wojtyła.

Will and **Suppositum**

In his ongoing reflections on and analyses of the will, dating from early in his career,[65] Wojtyła has frequently referred to the research of Narziss Ach (1871–1946), a German psychologist who rejected association psychology's account of human action and stressed the role of "intentional dynamics" or the will. Wojtyła finds in Ach's research a contemporary scientific confirmation of the Aristotelian-Thomistic conception of *will* in contrast to the conceptions of Kant and Scheler.[66] The questions at issue concern what it is that sets the acting person into motion (what "dynamizes" him) and what determines the structure of that act. Hume denied the will any role at all, reducing "free will" to a kind of feeling that

61 *ST* I, q. 81, aa. 1–3.

62 *ST* I, q. 81, a. 3, reply obj. 2.

63 For Karol Wojtyła's analysis and discussion of this, see "Thomas von Aquin," in *Lubliner Vorlesungen,* 170–202.

64 *ST* I–II, q. 24, a. 1.

65 See his *Lubliner Vorlesungen,* especially "Die Bedeutung der Psychologie des Willens für die Struktur des ethischen Aktes," 79–93; "The Problem of the Will in the Analysis of the Ethical Act," in *Person and Community,* 3–22; and "Person: Subject and Community," in *Person and Community,* 219–62, as well as the extensive discussion throughout *Love and Responsibility.*

66 Wojtyła, *Persona e atto,* 992; "The Problem of the Will in the Analysis of the Ethical Act," in *Person and Community,* 7–10; and especially *Lubliner Vorlesungen,* 86–90.

accompanies certain movements of the body.[67] The true cause of human actions could only be the passions.[68] We might observe that Hume's model, appropriately refined, continues to be the preferred one to this day among most scientists and philosophers. According to the Humean model, human actions are events of which the human subject is only the observer, but not in any real sense the author. Kant, for his part, located the will in the reason. "Since the derivation of actions from laws requires reason, the *will is nothing but the practical reason*."[69] Since Kant is concerned to keep the will separate from the phenomenal world of sense and contingent experience, this requirement is necessary. However, because the will *is* the practical reason, it is impossible to explain how the human subject is activated (dynamized) to perform the act selected. Take the case of a soldier, for instance. Having carefully reflected on his proposed maxim—that to preserve one's life it is appropriate to take to one's heels and flee—the soldier under fire determines that duty requires him to stand and fight. But he is still afraid. What prevents him from running? What determines that he will stay and continue fighting? Kant does not really have an explanation of the connection between the recognition of duty and the dynamization of one's own body into a particular course of action. All Kant can say is that such behavior is morally required. Wojtyła recognizes that an account must be given of the dynamization of the human person to perform the act, that Kant's intellectualism fails to account for one's actually *doing* one's duty. If, as everyday experience confirms, the person initiates his own acts, then he does so in virtue of a power lying within himself. This power is the will. The human person acts freely and of his own initiative through the will.[70]

What, then, is the status of this will? The strength of Hume's argument is that the will cannot, in fact, be observed. One can take note of his own

---

[67] *Inquiry concerning Human Understanding*, sec. 8, "Of Liberty and Necessity," especially 101–2.

[68] Hume, *Treatise of Human Nature*, 178–79.

[69] Kant, *Grounding for the Metaphysics of Morals*, 412: "Da zur Ableitung der Handlungen von Gesetzen Vernunft erfordert wird, so ist der Wille nichts anders als praktische Vernunft." Emphasis added.

[70] Particularly relevant for this paragraph are two essays from *Person and Community*: "The Problem of the Will in the Analysis of the Ethical Act" (3–22) and "The Separation of Experience from the Act in Ethics" (23–24).

inner debate as he weighs the pros and cons of a particular course of action, and he can also note that he has indeed begun to move his body appropriately to the accomplishment of one of the alternatives. But where in this is the will? In act 2 of Mozart's *Magic Flute*, Papageno decides to hang himself if he cannot have Papagena. He offers the cruel world "one last chance" and counts very slowly, "One . . . two . . . three," pausing, drawing out the count, and hesitating long enough for the Three Boys to fly in and stop him. The desperate thoughts are all there, the reflections on lost love, frustrated hopes, and a false world, but at the moment of suicide Papageno does not complete the act. He does not really *want* to die. The will is the principle in virtue of which the human person activates himself, choosing to perform the acts that will realize his wants. Karol Wojtyła writes: "[T]he essence of the will does not lie in [the contents of practical reason] but in the specific dynamism contained in the efficacy of the rational person."[71] The person performs (or, as with Papageno, does not perform) the act according to his own values. This manifests the activity of will.

Here the earlier discussion of potency and act becomes significant. Where a natural development is at stake, such as the growth of the acorn into an oak, the potency-act analysis is unproblematic. The latent potency of the acorn is realized in the oak. Where moral behavior is at stake, however, the potency-act distinction seems to imply a denial or at least diminution of moral agency. John A. McDermott asks: "Furthermore, how can the person be described in terms of a dynamism without reducing freedom to the apparent necessity of a potency-act, desire-fulfillment schema?"[72] If the wicked act arises by a dynamization of the person, does this mean that person's latent potency for evil has been realized? At stake is the mystery of the human will, the power of self-determination. According to Karol Wojtyła, the person confronted with the possibility of acting experiences the situation as one in which he can realize certain values.[73] What he does depends on which value (or values) he chooses to realize. The faculty by which he

---

[71] "The Problem of the Will in the Analysis of the Ethical Act," in *Person and Community*, 4.

[72] John A. McDermott, S.J., "The Theology of John Paul II: A Response," in *Thought of Pope John Paul II*, 67. In a footnote, McDermott cites *The Acting Person*, 33, 59, 179, 63–64, 112.

[73] Karol Wojtyła, "The Problem of the Theory of Morality," in *Person and Community*, 140; *Persona e atto*, 1003–5, 1027–28.

makes this choice is called the will, but it is a mistake to regard this will as a kind of mechanism distinct from but somehow parallel to biological mechanisms. With a mechanism, if we but know its state and the relevant "inputs," one can know what it will do. (This is why we value machines. They always act in the same way.) What the person experiences in acting, however, is that it "falls to me" to determine what will happen. Responsibility means that the acting person is the agent that realizes one value to the exclusion of another. To act means therefore to choose one state of affairs, which one can realize by one's efficacious act, over another. The act is a choice, a decision to realize something hitherto only possible. The acting person therefore experiences in himself the potentiality to realize the value he has in mind. The murderous Macbeth is haunted by the weapon with which he will kill Duncan: "Is this a dagger which I see before me the handle toward my hand? . . . [O]r art thou but a dagger of the mind, a false creation, proceeding from the heat-oppressed brain?" And then, having reflected on his illusions and the reality of the living King Duncan in his house, he concludes: "Whiles I threat he lives: Words to the heat of deeds, too cold breath gives. I go, and it is done; the bell invites me. Hear it not, Duncan; for it is a knell that summons thee to heaven or to hell."[74]

We call that in virtue of which the person acts his *will.* This will is not directly experienced or observed as an operative entity. Thinking does not produce physical acts. Indeed, as much as one tries, it is not possible to observe the cause in that moment in which the decision is effected. The issue is settled simply by acting. This was Hume's point in denying the will's causality; the causal link between the mental event and the act can never be observed. Nevertheless one does experience oneself as the agent, as the cause by which *what could be* becomes *what is,* which is the passage from potency to act. Therefore, by its very structure, the experience of acting demands a metaphysical analysis; physical considerations will not suffice to explain that spiritual power which is the will.

To account for the relationship between conscious subjectivity and the will's efficacy, Wojtyła introduces the metaphysical notion of *suppositum,* a concept that plays a significant role in his *Person and Act.*[75] It is in his

[74] William Shakespeare, *Macbeth,* act 2, scene 1.

[75] *Persona e atto,* 888–90, 924–29. This term lies at the center of the controversy over *The Acting Person,* the published English translation of *Osoba i czyn.* One of

essay "Person: Subject and Community," which was intended as a kind of companion piece to *Person and Act*, that he develops this notion most fully and explicitly. The human being experiences himself not only as a concrete self, but also as *suppositum*.[76] Wojtyła writes:

> This state of research on the human being . . . allows us to accept completely the ancient concept of *suppositum* and, at the same time, to understand it in a new way. To say that the human being—I and every other human being—is given in experience as a *suppositum* is to say that the whole experience of the human being, which reveals the human being to us as someone who exists and acts, both allows and legitimately requires us to conceive the human being as the subject of that existence and activity. And this is precisely what is contained in the concept of *suppositum*. This concept serves to express the subjectivity of the human being in the metaphysical sense.[77]

He then goes on to explain that by "metaphysical" he means not so much what is beyond the phenomenal as the "transphenomenal." "Metaphysical subjectivity, or the *suppositum* as the transphenomenal and therefore fundamental expression of the experience of the human being, is also the guarantor of the identity of this human being in existence and activity."[78] By appealing to this hoary Latin term, Karol Wojtyła expresses precisely (that is, with a technical vocabulary) that the subjective and the objective are rooted ontologically in the same entity, the human being.[79] Later in this same essay, he repudiates the phenomenological conception of consciousness as an independent subject.[80] The *suppositum* is both that which is experienced—is seen by the neighbors, aches when overworked, stands just under six feet tall, et cetera—and that which chooses and consciously acts on the basis of its own choice.

---

the editorial choices made by Anna-Teresa Tymieniecka was to render this technical term, *suppositum*, with interpretive English phrases that do not necessarily convey the full meaning of the Latin original. See Kalinowski, "La pensée philosophique de Karol Wojtyła," 202–3.

[76] "Person: Subject and Community," in *Person and Community*, 221. See also Kupczak, *Destined for Liberty*, 108.

[77] "Person: Subject and Community," in *Person and Community*, 222.

[78] Ibid., 223.

[79] *Persona e atto*, 944, 949, 956.

[80] "Person: Subject and Community," in *Person and Community*, 226.

If this *suppositum* is something "transphenomenal," then the question arises: How can it be known? In answer to this, Wojtyła appeals to another Latin phrase, *operari sequitur esse* ("operation follows [or is consequent upon] being"); the being of a thing is the root of its action.[81] In a footnote, Wojtyła explains that this philosophical adage constitutes the basis of his *Person and Act*, the thesis of which is that the person is known through his acts. The *operari*, which includes not only the physical behavior but also its subjective roots in valuing, knowing, and choosing, enables us to know the subjectivity of the human being as that which is rooted in this concretely existing thing. "If *operari* results from *esse*, then *operari* is also . . . the most proper avenue to knowledge of that *esse*."[82] In other words, it is through this *operari* that we are able to conduct a metaphysical analysis of the will.

> The *suppositum humanum* must somehow manifest itself as a human self: metaphysical subjectivity must manifest itself as personal subjectivity.
>
> This *must* is the strongest argument for the metaphysical conception of human nature. The human being is a person "by nature." The subjectivity proper to a person also belongs to the human being "by nature."[83]

Understood from the right perspective, this text can serve as the basis for a metaphysical investigation of the soul. Although Karol Wojtyła does not undertake this metaphysical investigation himself (content to point to his metaphysician forebears), his analysis of the *suppositum* comes very close to being such an investigation. In *Person and Act* he indicates the direction that such an inquiry should take.[84] Rather than analyzing the formal and therefore spiritual principle of the human substance (that is, the soul), he chooses to analyze the whole as a dynamic personal unity.

The Order of Nature

The biological order, which regards the human being only insofar as the canons of biology admit, necessarily fails adequately to account for the full

81 Ibid., 223ff. Also *Persona e atto*, 926, 938–40.

82 "Person: Subject and Community," in *Person and Community*, 223.

83 Ibid., 225.

84 "Integration of the person in the act and discovery of the relationship of the soul with the body," *Persona e atto*, 1158.

reality of the human person. Wojtyła argues that we must situate this order within the broader "order of nature" which he also calls the "order of existence [or being]." (We should note that this differs somewhat from the traditional Aristotelian-Thomist terminology, according to which the *order of nature* is but a part of the *order of existence*, which also includes intelligences or angels, separated souls, and any other immaterial beings there may be.)[85] A portion of our key text reads: "It is otherwise with the 'order of nature', which means the totality of the cosmic relationships that arise among really existing entities. It is therefore the order of existence, and the laws which govern it have their foundation in Him, Who is the unfailing source of that existence, in God the Creator."[86] In identifying the order of nature with "the totality of the cosmic relationships that arise among really existing entities," Karol Wojtyła intends to grasp the entirety of the created order as a harmonious whole. He is not concerned sharply to distinguish the natural and the supernatural orders. This is a theme to which we will return in chapter 8, where we consider the unity of the moral order.

Karol Wojtyła's distinction between the "order of nature" and the "order of existence" can be appropriately related to the fifth of Thomas Aquinas's Five Ways to prove that God exists. An examination of that text will offer us an apt entry into Wojtyła's conception.

> The fifth way is taken from the governance of the world. We see that things which lack intelligence, such as natural bodies, act for an end, and this is evident from their acting always, or nearly always, in the same way, so as to obtain the best result. Hence it is plain that not fortuitously, but designedly, do they achieve their end. Now whatever lacks intelligence cannot move towards an end, unless it be directed by some being endowed with knowledge and intelligence; as the arrow is shot to its mark by the archer. Therefore some intelligent being exists by whom all natural things are directed to their end; and this being we call God.[87]

In this argument, Aquinas makes a couple of claims that strike the modern ear as strange. First he says that "things which lack intelligence,

85 This objection was raised to me by Michael Loux in a colloquium of the University of Notre Dame Department of Philosophy, October 12, 2007.

86 *Love and Responsibility*, 57.

87 *ST* I, q. 2, a. 3.

such as natural bodies, act for an end." Second, he states that they do this "so as to obtain the best result [*id quod est optimum*]." Thomas's point, which appears repeatedly in his writings,[88] is that the totality of creation is a well-ordered and well-governed whole. It is not just the totality of things. The evidence that things act for an end is simply that they act always, or nearly so, in the same way, behaving according to more or less determinate laws, which scientific reasoning can know. This lawlike behavior of things enables the attainment of "the best result." Because things in nature behave in regular ways, there results an order within nature. The order of nature is structured, as it were, by the natural operations of natural substances. And this structure is "the best result."

Whatever else Aquinas meant, it was certainly not that the world in its natural state is the best of all possible worlds. The world is the world it is because of the kinds of things there are in it. How it is the "best" becomes clear if we consider some examples from environmental science. We now know that to introduce a new animal species into an ecosystem (or to remove a species therefrom) changes the entire system. The absence of coyotes in the American Midwest, combined with an abundance of growing corn in the summers, results in an overpopulation of deer, which trample the habitats of smaller mammals such as rabbits. The inadvertent introduction of zebra mussels into the American Great Lakes has resulted in the significant decline of native species. The bathing behavior of African elephants creates watering ponds for other species. Things in nature are interrelated in such a way that to change one structure is to affect the structure of the whole. What is for the best? Certainly, human commercial and recreational interests are harmed by zebra mussels, and abundant deer in populated areas constitute a traffic hazard. On the other hand, the clearing of forests and the plowing of the prairies rendered the American continent habitable for large numbers of people. And although medieval technologies were less advanced than ours today, Aquinas certainly knew that human behavior (e.g., building canals, farming) impacted the environment and that environmental factors could adversely affect

[88] Thomas Aquinas, *Summa contra Gentiles,* translated as *On the Truth of the Catholic Faith:* Summa contra Gentiles, bk. 2, trans. James F. Anderson (Garden City, NY: Doubleday Image Books, 1956), 24.4–7; *ST* I, q. 22, aa. 1, 2; I–II, q. 91, a. 1; *De veritate,* q. 5, a. 2; and indeed throughout his writings.

human life and intentions. But "what is for the best" need not refer primarily to human interests.

To answer more fully the question of what is for the best, we do well to consider the matter from another side. Broadly speaking, the science of structures as such is mathematics. And the curious thing about mathematics is that the introduction of a new conceptual structure leads to further ordered development and to a new order of the whole.[89] The introduction of even a new symbol into a mathematical system can have a profound impact on the science as a whole. Because the Romans had no symbol for zero, their arithmetic was crippled. (What is the solution to the problem "IV + V – IX = "?) Negative numbers and fractions made algebra possible. But what is the square root of a negative number? Of course, there is no such thing. However, Carl Friedrich Gauss proposed that we give this concept $\sqrt{-1}$ a name, *i*, and treat it as a kind of number in its own right.[90] From this proposal he developed the theory of complex numbers, which has become an essential component of modern mathematics. Indeed, it has turned out that without this theory contemporary physics would be impossible. Similarly, having recognized that Euclid's parallel postulate is not entailed by the premises of his geometry, modern geometers replaced it with their own variants and in doing so discovered rich and useful new branches of geometry.[91] Whenever a mathematical term is well defined, it finds its place in mathematics, and in terms of it further mathematical structures are developed. The crucial expression here is "well defined." The meaning of the new mathematical term must be expressed (or admit of expression) in mathematical terms so that it can be related mathematically to other terms and mathematical structures.[92]

---

[89] Wojtyła, *Lubliner Vorlesungen*, 274.

[90] Eric Temple Bell, "The Prince of Mathematicians," in *The World of Mathematics*, by James R. Newman (New York: Simon and Schuster, 1956), 1:307–9, and Bell, "The Queen of Mathematics," ibid., 1:513.

[91] Hermann von Helmholtz, "On the Origin and Significance of Geometrical Axioms," in Newman, *World of Mathematics*, 647–68.

[92] A good example of a term not well defined is "interesting." The number 2 is interesting, because it is the only even prime. Six is interesting because it is "perfect." If we seek to determine what is the lowest noninteresting number, we find ourselves caught in paradoxes and contradictions, for by the very fact of its being the lowest such number, it is interesting. This also suggests a further point, namely, that the definition of new mathematical concepts can inadvertently come a cropper if they conceal a self-contradiction.

Common to these two realms, the ecosystem and mathematics, is that the system responds to the introduction of new structures within it. New forms find their place, though possibly at the expense of some other form. The order is changed, but not destroyed. We may say that the structure of the whole interprets and is reinterpreted by the new form. The whole is recreated, as it were.

According to Aquinas, the fact that an inanimate or irrational being behaves in the same way, always or for the most part, is "for the best." If something ceases behaving in a regular way, then it creates chaos and disorder. The eruption of a normally dormant volcano is an example. Aquinas's goal here is to show that God exists. From noting that things without intelligence act (for the most part) in the same way, he goes on to argue that this regularity must have been implanted in them by an intelligent being. Leadfoot Louie obeys the traffic laws because he knows that the police will fine him for speeding, but the rock has no motivation to fall down rather than up. The rock does not want to fall toward the center of the earth, but it always does. Furthermore, this regular behavior (which we ascribe to the law of gravity) helps make possible an orderly universe in which not only can planets orbit stars and kangaroos leap without sailing into space, but galaxies and solar systems form. The regular behavior of things is "for the best" because it orders the world.

This is not all, however. Living things have regular behaviors that maintain their lives. Internal to the animal are respiratory, digestive, excretory, and regulative systems, which keep the animal's body functioning. Further, the animal performs certain kinds of acts—feeding, mating, fleeing (or fighting), and drinking—to maintain its life and existence. The failure of any of these activities results in the illness and eventual death of the animal. For example, for the pet owner to turn out a declawed domesticated cat is to condemn it to a fairly quick death, as the animal is without both the equipment (claws) and habits necessary to survive on its own. The plant's sinking its roots deep into the soil is "for the best," since without deep roots it would wither from lack of moisture. The regular behavior of a thing is a good because it helps realize the thing as the kind of thing it is. In other words, by acting in its characteristic way, a thing realizes its own perfection, a perfection that is intended by its Maker.

Developing his analysis of Aquinas's conception of the good, Wojtyła argues that Thomas's decisive development of Aristotle's doctrine of the good was to identify good with being (*ens et bonum convertuntur*). Aristotle, on Wojtyła's reading, identified the good as the end or goal. That is, one can have a theoretical knowledge of goods in teleological relationships one to another (so the grass of the savannah is good for the herds of zebra, which are in turn good for the prides of lions), and in this respect it is possible to have a purely theoretical knowledge of the good.[93] Aquinas, however, developed the notion of good further in terms of perfection, and the first perfection of any being is existence itself. "In his [Thomas's] conception of the good, existence was given priority over the end."[94] To know the good of a thing, then, is more than to know its essence.

This order of existence, considered precisely as an order, is important, because it was created. "It is therefore the order of existence, and the laws which govern it have their foundation in Him, Who is the unfailing source of that existence, in God the Creator."[95] The goodness of the creature does not consist only in its relationships with other creatures, although this does constitute an order of goodness. Here Karol Wojtyła becomes expressly metaphysical. The goodness of a thing is constituted by its perfection, and that perfection is a reflection of or participation in the divine perfection.[96] Another way to put it is that existing things, by the very fact that they exist and by their partaking in the order of creation, express the mind of their Author. The goodness of things finds its roots, therefore, in the intentions of their Author, whose own perfection the creatures reflect by their perfection. Among the creatures in the material universe, there is one, the human being, who is able to relate rationally to the Author of all things. This being can therefore know the truth about the good, relating to it by a power beyond instinct. Where other beings can know specific goods, the human being, in virtue of his rationality, can know the nature of the good as such.[97] And because he can know the good in general, the human person can—according to Karol Wojtyła—determine how he will act in accordance with the general nature of the good. In other words, knowing what good in general is, the person can ask

[93] *Lubliner Vorlesungen*, 279.

[94] Ibid., 197. See also 273.

[95] Wojtyła, *Love and Responsibility*, 57.

[96] Wojtyła, *Lubliner Vorlesungen*, 177ff., 245ff., and especially 276–77.

[97] Ibid., 193, 280. For his part, Wojtyła cites Aquinas, *ST* I–II, q. 141, a. 1; *De malo*, q. 9, a. 6.

concerning the truth about the good, and his answer to this question can affect how he acts. The human person, therefore, is the metaphysical key to Wojtyła's conception of the order of existence.

The order of nature is therefore an order of goods. Were it not so, then it could not be an order at all. This order is "the totality of the cosmic relationships that arise among really existing entities." It is not that Karol Wojtyła puts a theological superstructure on a solidly empirical scientific structure, as if to say not only that the structure is ordered but that God made it so. The point, rather, is that the order of things, the relationships among them and the laws governing them, make them intelligible not only to us, but in a way to each other. For, as we noted above, each thing by behaving in its own way helps to determine the structure of the whole, whether we are speaking of an ecosystem or a mathematical structure. Each thing within the system has what it needs to be what it is. But this order of good (and evil) is limited. First, the order among nonrational things is not a moral order, for nonrational beings are not capable of free moral choice. Second, the criterion of good is not contained within the system. We know full well that over the millennia species can become extinct, that continents move and climates change. Therefore, from the fact that a particular kind of organism has its specific good we cannot conclude that other beings somehow intend that it exist. The lion is the enemy of the lamb, caring not whether his eating habits might lead to the extinction of sheep. That there are snail darters now does not, of itself, create an obligation that there be snail darters in the future, any more than the existence of dinosaurs one hundred million years ago morally obligates their existence now. Nor can we say, on the basis of the species alive in a given era, that one is better or superior to another. The good by which the order of things can be judged is not within the order of things.

Instincts and Urges

Let us recall the context of this chapter's key text.[98] At issue was the question whether human sexual behavior is governed by instinct, and is therefore beyond rational control, or is governed by some other power. The point of the text we have been analyzing is that biological science itself can understand human sexual behavior only with biological concepts such as

[98] From *Love and Responsibility*, 57.

"instinct," which refers to an automatic or determinate reaction to some stimulus. What is governed by instinct is determined, beyond the control of will or reason. Wojtyła will argue in both his *Love and Responsibility* and later in his papal addresses on the theology of the body that the human person, as a rational subject, can form his actions according to the demands and conceptions of reason in relation to the highest good. This kind of rational control is impossible if sexual behavior is instinctive. In the next chapter of his *Love and Responsibility*, Wojtyła will argue for the importance of chastity. If materialism is true, however, then chastity is an unnatural and unreasonable expectation. If instincts are to be governed, then (by the scientific materialists' account) this government must be by some overriding physical mechanism. Recognizing the force of materialism's claims, Karol Wojtyła rejects its ultimate character. Rather, he maintains, there is a higher and more fundamental order, of which the physical order is part. This is an order accessible to metaphysical inquiry.

However, Wojtyła is careful to avoid dualism, the claim that besides the physical realm governed by physical laws, there is a spiritual realm governed by spiritual laws, such that the spiritual can override the physical. Rather, the real order is one, and it has both physical and spiritual aspects. Because its Author is an intelligent being who designed it according to his own intentions, the real order reflects and manifests his standards of good and evil, according to the natures of things in that order and their respective perfections. Although Karol Wojtyła's focus is not principally on cosmology but upon ethics and philosophical anthropology, it is here that the implications of his conception of the natural order become critical. The biological mechanisms associated with the endocrinal and reproductive systems urge the human person toward sexual interaction. This kind of urge leads human beings to mate and bear children. As we shall see in succeeding chapters, especially in discussing the theology of the body, Karol Wojtyła/John Paul II finds in this impulse toward physical union in sex the model and indeed the cause of the most perfect communion between human persons, which union is more spiritual than physical. The desires that apparently arise within the nexus of biological systems pertaining to sex have the capacity to lead the person to the ideals of the true, the good, and the beautiful.[99] Karol

[99] See *Redemptor Hominis*, 18, and *Man and Woman He Created Them*, 47.5, 318, and especially 48.1–2, 318–19.

Wojtyła first finds this integration, then, not in the cosmic order but in the human person. It is necessary for us, therefore, to turn to the question of the good for the person, the moral good.

CHAPTER 3

Acting and the Moral Consciousness

The Fundamental Question of Ethics

WHAT IS ETHICS ABOUT? What is its fundamental problematic or issue? Aristotle saw ethics as the practical science of the happy life, addressing the question of what a human being must do to live nobly and well. He answered in terms of developing excellence of character ordered to contemplation of the truth. Kant saw ethics differently, in terms of determining the morally correct acts to perform, acts that accord with the demands of rationality. Kantian morality is not concerned with one's own (or anybody else's) happiness or with the virtue of one's own character as such but rather with performing one's duty as a rational being. For utilitarians the ethical question is about the best result. What can one do to maximize happiness? If a lie brings about the most happiness for the greatest number, then (contra Aristotle) the ignobility of misrepresenting the truth in one's own mind or (contra Kant) the irrationality of undermining the universal principles of communication notwithstanding, the lie should be told. For their part, emotivists look to appropriate moral sentiments, to act according to those that are most ennobling, most fitting. For the emotivist, moral goodness therefore becomes an internal matter, a subjective state of consciousness. It is striking that these various approaches to ethics lack consensus on what ethics is about.[1] Is ethics about determining right

[1] Karol Wojtyła, *L'uomo nel campo della responsibilità,* in *Metafisica della persona,* 1236–37.

acts, developing good character, fostering social order, or realizing subjective states?

Person and Act

To determine the anthropological bases of ethics, Wojtyła analyzes the human act, for the human act must in some way lie at the heart of any ethics. Whether in its structure or effects or the sentiments associated with it, the act is good or bad and thereby relates to the goodness or badness of the agent. With this in mind, Wojtyła intends his principal philosophical work, *Person and Act*, not as an ethical treatise but rather as a kind of prolegomena to ethics. The book's premise is that, as something that originates within the person, the act reveals the person, while at the same time the person forms himself by his freely chosen acts. Thus there is to be expected a connection between the goodness (or badness) of acts and that of the person who performs them. A good person can be expected to perform good acts, but if someone performs evil acts, to that extent he makes himself a bad person. Wojtyła's analysis leads to a concept of the will as that which is the ultimate principle of a person's actions. It is in virtue of his will that the person acquires his moral value as a good or bad person. But before we can advance to the study of the will, we need to see how Wojtyła untangles the relationships among the subjective and objective realms, between the bodily interactions with things in the real world and the inner realm of intentions, thoughts, desires, wishes, and feelings.

Experience and Efficacy

Karol Wojtyła sets out the purpose of his *Person and Act.*

> This study is born from the need to show the objective aspect of that great cognitive process that one can define, at its origin, as the experience of the human being.[2]
>
> This work is not intended to be a kind of commentary, nor yet a "systematic" study, but rather it is a personal attempt to comprehend the subject, an effort at analysis aiming to find a synthetic expression for the conception of the person and act.[3]

---

[2] "Introduzione," in *Persona e atto*, 831.

[3] *Persona e atto*, 857; *Osoba i czyn*, 71.

In a footnote to this second sentence, Wojtyła remarks that he wrote *Person and Act* during the Second Vatican Council and explicitly connects this work with the Council's emphasis (in *Gaudium et Spes*, 76) on the transcendence of the human person. The work, therefore, is an effort to unfold the experience of man objectively, that is, so as to attain objective knowledge and intellectually to grasp what the human person is. In doing so, Karol Wojtyła expects to reveal the person as a being that transcends its physical or material conditions. His strategy for accomplishing this is phenomenologically to analyze the essence of the human act, confident that in doing so he can adequately account for the phenomenological essence of the person who originates (which is to say, performs) the act.

Unlike his phenomenological forebears, Wojtyła does not recognize consciousness as foundational. To regard the person solely in terms of consciousness is effectively to evacuate the concept of the person.[4] This is evident from Wojtyła's analysis of *efficacy*, which he characterizes most clearly in *Person and Act*[5] and which is central to his thought about the will and moral experience. The human act, in order to be an act, must be efficacious or effective. Because by its very essence the act is intended to effect some change in the real order, it cannot reduce simply to an event in consciousness. The act must transcend the order of mental events. Karol Wojtyła is concerned to reject the phenomenalist reduction of human experience, a reduction that can allow the construction of an action only from consciousness. He begins his phenomenological analysis by distinguishing between experiences of acting and of happening, between "what happens in a human being" and "a human being acts."[6] By what experience can we distinguish between acting and happening? It is true that one may falsely "remember" having done something that one did only in an especially vivid dream. Science fiction makes frequent use of imaginative technologies that can create the experience of acting vigorously when in fact the subject's brain is simply responding to artificially fed inputs.[7] One may doubt whether such technology is really possible, but the philosophical

[4] Wojtyła, *Persona e atto*, 872–73; "Person: Subject and Community," in *Person and Community*, 221–23. See also his "Subjectivity and the Irreducible in the Human Being," in *Person and Community*, 209–10.

[5] *Persona e atto*, 917–24.

[6] Ibid., 870, 911–12.

[7] As in the 1999 film *Matrix*, directed by Andy and Larry Wachowski.

issue has troubled phenomenalists and phenomenologists for some time. Descartes famously raised the question whether he was experiencing reality or only dreaming[8] or, indeed, being misled by a powerful "evil genius."[9] If all experiences are "what happens in a human being" (and therefore possibly induced or inducible), then by what criteria may we distinguish actions from passive happenings? Can we save the Aristotelian distinction between *human act* and act *of a human being*? Wojtyła believes that we can and that the experiential key to the distinction is *efficacy*.

Person and Act takes as its starting point the experience "a human being acts." This is a reality that we experience many times each day and that we experience both subjectively ("from within" as one experiences oneself in action) and objectively ("from without" as one experiences the acts of others). If the act is essentially both subjective and objective, than the person himself exists as both subject and object. Just as a reductionist account of the act, whether subjectivist or objectivist, is necessarily inadequate, neither can a reductionist account of the human person suffice, be this account a purely immanentist account or (as is increasingly common in contemporary Anglo-American thought) a scientific materialist one. The person is a being that is at once subject of its own experience and an object in the world. This viewpoint contrasts strongly with Hume's. Wojtyła comments: "Hume develops a purely ephemeral conception of the human being, which for him does not represent an objective being, but rather his Self, which is determined by the sum of its impressions and mental representation."[10] Hume is so intent to avoid admitting causality into his scheme of things that he fails to acknowledge the central role it plays in ordinary human experience. The pie came to be because the baker wanted it and tailored his actions to bring it into being. If we are authentically to grasp the phenomenological essence of this reality "the human being acts," a phenomenalist account is inadequate. The act, precisely as given as a whole in experience, contains within itself the moment of efficacy,[11] for the acting person intends not only to have certain experiences (indeed, he

[8] René Descartes, *Meditations on First Philosophy*, Meditation 1, trans. Donald A. Cress, 3rd ed. (Indianapolis: Hackett Publishing Company, 1993), 19.

[9] Ibid., 22–23.

[10] *Lubliner Vorlesungen*, 305; see also *Persona e atto*, 873.

[11] Wojtyła, *Persona e atto*, 917–21.

may not directly intend the experiences at all) but to set himself in motion to attain some end. This concept of *efficacy* is central and fundamental to all Wojtyła's work on the person and ethics.

Hume argues that even granted this experience, the acting subject does not directly experience the causality by which he acts; he does not perceive the operation of the will upon his body. Arguing that the same necessity governs human behavior as other observed cause-effect interactions, Hume writes:

> If we examine the operations of body and the production of effects from their causes, we shall find that all our faculties can never carry us further in our knowledge of this relation than barely to observe that particular objects are *constantly conjoined* together, and that the mind is carried, by a *customary transition*, from the appearance of one to the belief of the other. . . . When, again, they turn their reflections toward the operations of their own minds and *feel* no such connection of the motive and the action, they are thence apt to suppose that there is a difference between the effects which result from material force and those which arise from thought and intelligence. But being once convinced that we know nothing further of causation of any kind than merely the *constant conjunction* of objects and the consequent *inference* of the mind from one to another . . . we may be more easily led to own the same necessity common to all causes.[12]

Hume's argument is that because we cannot observe the connection between a person's inner experiences of wanting, planning, and deciding, we cannot infer a connection between the person's mental events and the events in the world in which he acts. However, Hume missed the point that Wojtyła notices and develops. What is at stake is not whether one can somehow observe causal mechanisms connecting the will to the body but rather whether one can intend to act at all. Acting is about getting something done. The person who acts does so with an intention. Even if after the fact he can reflect with amazement on the connections among his feelings, intentions, and movements, trying to discern their various relationships, in the execution of the act itself his intention is to effect foreseeable and foreseen changes *by his own agency.* The person in act *intends* to be efficacious. Clearly his experience of acting itself must include the moment of

[12] *Inquiry concerning Human Understanding,* 101–2.

efficacy, the intention and hope that the act will be an intervention in the causal order that will change something in the world or himself.

Consciousness and the Will

We have already remarked on Wojtyła's use of Narziss Ach's work in psychology.[13] Wojtyła writes: "Ach expressed this view by pointing out that in the act of willing, as the representation of his aim emerges, the individual is really conscious that he is the cause of its realization. The 'ego' appears here as the cause of the act, says N. Ach (*Über den Willensakt und das Temperament*, S. 265)."[14] The person experiences himself as author of his act.[15] Wojtyła comments that "the psychology of Ach's school, to the extent that its method of experimentation and field of empirical-inductive science permit, presents the psychological problematic in such a way that it interprets ethical experience in the context of its approach to the lived experience of the will."[16] Unlike Aquinas, whose account of the will is systematic and theoretical, based on the analysis of the powers of the soul,[17] Karol Wojtyła bases his account in experience. Relying on the essential correctness of Thomas's account, buttressed by Ach's findings, he pushes the phenomenological analysis forward in order to develop his own account of the will.

Furthermore, unlike the founders of the phenomenological school, Wojtyła refuses to grant to consciousness the foundational role that phenomenology characteristically assigns it. We may recall Sartre's comment: "Our point of departure is, indeed, the subjectivity of the individual, and that for strictly philosophic reasons. . . . And at the point of departure there cannot be any other truth than this, I think, therefore I am, which is the absolute truth of consciousness as it attains to itself."[18] And Edmund Husserl writes:

---

13 "The Problem of the Will in the Analysis of the Ethical Act," in *Person and Community*, 3, 7; *Lubliner Vorlesungen*, 48–49; *Persona e atto*, 992.

14 *Lubliner Vorlesungen*, 49.

15 Ibid., 70–71, 81–82, 86.

16 "The Problem of the Will in the Analysis of the Ethical Act," in *Person and Community*, 13. The second section of this essay, titled "The Relation of Experimental Psychology of the Will to Ethical Experience," is Wojtyła's fullest discussion of Ach and his school.

17 *ST* I, q. 78, a. 1; q. 82, aa. 1–4.

18 "Existentialism Is a Humanism," 360.

> The phenomenologist, who will only notice phenomena, and know purely his own "life," must practice an *epochē*. He must inhibit every ordinary objective "position," and partake in no judgment concerning the objective world. The experience itself will remain what it was. . . . For one cannot describe any intentional experience, even though it be "illusory," a self-contradictory judgment and the like, without describing what in the experience is, as such, the object of consciousness. Our comprehensive *epochē* puts, as we say, the world between brackets, excludes the world which is simply there! from the subject's field, presenting in its stead the so-and-so-experienced-perceived-remembered-judged-thought-valued-etc., world as such, the "bracketed" world. Not the world or any part of it appears, but the "sense" of the world. To enjoy phenomenological experience we must retreat from the objects posited in the natural attitude to the multiple modes of their "appearance," to the "bracketed" objects.[19]

The problem with this classical phenomenological foundation is that it simply cannot accommodate the common human experience of "a human being acts." The acting person cannot "bracket" the world, because his act is premised upon the expectation that he can effect a change in the world, that his act is efficacious. Therefore, Karol Wojtyła cannot accept consciousness as foundational. Consciousness is not and cannot be an autonomous subject, but rather it is the subjective content of the human being's existence and action.[20] Indeed, the relationship between consciousness and act is exactly reversed from that posited by phenomenology: consciousness emerges "totally in the *voluntarium*, in the dynamism of the human will."[21] And consciousness serves the further function of mirroring the person's acts and experience to him and enabling him to interiorize them. These mirroring and interiorizing functions serve the more fundamental human power of knowledge, and especially the power of self-knowledge.[22] Consciousness is conditioned by the cognitive potentiality to comprehend things. Wojtyła goes on: "To comprehend is nothing other

---

[19] Edmund Husserl, "Phenomenology," *Encyclopaedia Britannica*, 14th ed. (1932), quoted in Forrest E. Baird and Walter Kaufmann, eds., *Philosophic Classics: From Plato to Derrida*, 4th ed. (Upper Saddle River, NJ: Prentice Hall, 2003), 1073.

[20] Wojtyła, *Persona e atto*, 872; "Person: Subject and Community," in *Person and Community*, 226–27, 231.

[21] Wojtyła, *Persona e atto*, 867.

[22] Ibid., 875–76.

than intellectually to grasp the meaning of things or of the relationships among things."[23] Knowledge must transcend consciousness, because these things that consciousness mirrors are the things that the human act engages. When it comes to baking, at issue is not the intentional construction of the egg by consciousness but its suitability for mixing with flour and oil to make the cake. That is to say, the acting person must know the world around him in relation not only to his conscious experience but also in relation to his effective causality as an agent.

Wojtyła's distinction between "a human being acts" and "what happens in a human being" implies that the act cannot be reduced to any prior experience. That is to say, Karol Wojtyła denies that a fully adequate account of an act of a person can be had from what has happened in a human being. Certainly, what happens to a person can motivate or strongly influence an act. The growling stomach insists on being fed. The chemical imbalances associated with bipolar disorder can dramatically affect how a person perceives the world, what he may regard as possible, desirable, or worthwhile. Indeed, Wojtyła warns expressly against the "emotionalization" of consciousness, which occurs when one allows one's consciousness to become "flooded," as it were, by emotions so that they come to overwhelm the person's judgment. Noting that self-knowledge has the capacity to "objectivize even the emotions and sensation," Wojtyła continues:

> For interior integration the control of emotion on the part of consciousness is very important. This control is certainly not exercised outside the will, without its participation, and therefore, only on its basis can moral value be formed. We find ourselves faced with a reciprocal compenetration of consciousness and will; the conscious control of the spontaneous emotive dynamism, which conditions the *voluntarium* which is the proper action of the will, is at the same time conditioned by the will.[24]

We find ourselves here in a nexus of problems ranging from the much-discussed modern issue of freedom versus determinism to the emotivist ethics of Scheler. The key to Wojtyła's analysis of all these issues is the will. From the text just cited in *Person and Act*, it is clear that the will is independent of and in a vital way prior to consciousness. Why? It is by the

[23] Ibid., 875.

[24] Ibid., 899–900.

decision of the will that the emotionalization of consciousness is controlled. Here we may think of Marianne Dashwood (in Jane Austen's novel *Sense and Sensibility*), who is rendered physically ill by the overwhelming heartache of disappointment in love. She takes it as a defining truth about herself that she feels more strongly than her older sister, Elinor (the one with "sense"), and so lets her emotions control and define her. But it is not even necessary to appeal to literature, for it is a common enough experience to encounter those who cannot, because they have long refused to, control outbursts of weeping, anger, melancholy, or the like. The importance of the will in relation to emotion will become more clear in the next chapter, as we consider more deeply Wojtyła's critique of Scheler's ethics. Let us now examine more closely the connection between consciousness and will.

We cited earlier David Hume's critique of the will in his *Inquiry concerning Human Understanding*. In a footnote to that section, Hume continues:

> We feel that our actions are subject to our will on most occasions, and imagine we feel that the will itself is subject to nothing, because, when by a denial of it we are provoked to try, we feel that it moves easily every way, and produces an image of itself (or a "velleity," as it is called in the schools), even on that side on which it did not settle. This image, or faint motion, we persuade ourselves, could at that time have been completed into the thing itself, because, should that be denied, we find upon a second trial that at present it can.[25]

Hume's point is acute. He denies the causality (and hence the freedom) of the will, because the *will cannot be observed in action*. The mechanism (if any) by which the will operates is inaccessible to consciousness. Consistent with his phenomenalism, Hume allows us to note only the correlation between mental events (thoughts, intentions, desires) and events in the world. Others, however, have also noted the same problem. Plato was famously puzzled by evil behavior. One who knows, who truly understands, ought to proceed to do the wise act. And yet, he was himself painfully aware that the most careful philosophical education of the wealthy scion of Dion did not deter the young man from becoming as bad a tyrant as his father. The rational part of the soul should rightfully control

[25] *Inquiry concerning Human Understanding*, 103.

the appetitive, which, left to its own devices, will behave foolishly (at best). But Plato seemed not to have the resources to account for the educated, philosophical soul's deliberate choice of evil. Materialists in our day take a somewhat different approach, denying that the mental has any effect on the physical at all. Therefore the reasons a person might cite for his actions can be nothing more than rationalizations of what his organism did (and was going to do) anyway.[26]

Without doubt, this priority of the will with respect to consciousness is puzzling and has been used to argue that the will itself is a fiction. For instance, arguing against Ryle, Armstrong states, "It follows that not all our acts can spring from acts of the will, but that we must in the end come to acts that spring from mere operations of the will. Operations of the will are mere happenings. They have causes, no doubt, but these causes do not lie in the will."[27] Armstrong distinguishes between acts of the will, which constitute one kind of conscious event, and "mere operations of the will," which are "mere happenings." A thoroughgoing materialist, Armstrong seeks the definitive account of human acts in the chemistry (and ultimately the physics) of the brain. His point here is that the mental acts, the takings of resolve—"I will get up now from bed"—cannot trigger the act of getting up, for even if it could, the taking of resolve would itself require a trigger. Therefore underlying and prior to our conscious acts and decisions must be acts that occur within our organism, acts not subject to conscious control.

If consciousness is the fundamental (or foundational) property of personhood, then this is indeed a serious problem. However, Karol Wojtyła denies consciousness that role, arguing that both knowledge and will are prior to consciousness and form it. Because the human act is both efficacious and conscious, it flows from a power that is both engaged in the world and self-aware. We recall that the act is not merely muscular and physical, but it is directed by knowledge, by the acting person's comprehension of the world, by his understanding of things and how they are. Insofar as it is a human act, the act is not performed in ignorance (so that the comedic character

[26] See Burkert, *Creation of the Sacred*, 26, 66, and Searle, *Minds, Brains and Science*, 95–98.

[27] D. M. Armstrong, *A Materialist Theory of the Mind* (New York: Routledge and Kegan Paul, 1968), 137.

who in his innocent curiosity pushes the alarm button cannot be said to have captured the burglar). The act of the will is therefore a choice for which the agent is responsible. He knows—or is able to know—the consequences of his action, the performance of which is consequently a choice involving those consequences. Most important, however, is that the act of the will is fully realized not in the resolution or in consciousness, but in the act. The act is, of its very nature, *efficacious*, and when one undertakes something efficacious, one's will has thereby undertaken the act. In contrast—but not in opposition—to Aquinas's theoretical account of the will as a faculty of the soul, Karol Wojtyła's account approaches the subject from within human experience. The acting person experiences himself as a willing person, as an efficacious agent. Wojtyła writes, "We call the will in the human being *that which permits the human being to will.*"[28] Concluding his own analysis of Wojtyła's philosophy of the person, Kupczak writes: "The subject of this book, the human person as the efficient cause of his own action, locates the very center of Wojtyła's philosophy."[29]

Freedom and Transcendence

The act of the person is free and cannot be otherwise. The question whether human acts are free or determined is one of the more hotly debated of modern philosophical issues.[30] In a manner prefigured by his analysis in *Love and Responsibility*,[31] Karol Wojtyła addresses the broad issue of determinism and freedom in terms of the relationship between nature and the person. Nature operates in determinate ways, and these activations determine what *happens in* a human being, but not what he does: "Nature manifests itself exclusively in the activations of the subject human being; acts, on the other hand, reveal man as person."[32] Karol Wojtyła does not at all maintain that there is within the human being a

---

28 *Persona e atto*, 961.

29 *Destined for Liberty*, 142.

30 Besides Hume's discussion in the *Inquiry*, see William James, "The Dilemma of Determinism," in *Will to Believe*, 145–83; Felix E. Oppenheim, *Dimensions of Freedom: An Analysis* (New York: St. Martin's Press, 1961); Searle, *Minds, Brains and Science*, chap. 6; and Bernard Berofsky, *Determinism* (Princeton, NJ: Princeton University Press, 1971).

31 As discussed in the previous chapter.

32 *Persona e atto*, 933.

separate power—a will or spiritual mechanism of some sort—that can control the organism. Rather, consistent with his rejection of the "generalized empiricism" that would reduce the order of existence to that of the physical sciences, he holds that the human person is integrated not simply as an organism but as a transphenomenal *suppositum*.[33] This *suppositum* is both an object in the world and an acting subject, two aspects of the person that cannot be separated: "Integration does not eliminate the differences in the manner of self-dynamization of the *suppositum*; it only annuls the possibility of conceiving the person and nature as two distinct subjects of action."[34] Determinism is a problem only if we accept scientific materialism as the last word in metaphysics (which is effectively to deny metaphysics its standing).

In the end, however, it is his phenomenological approach that makes it possible for Karol Wojtyła to avoid the contemporary problematic of freedom and determinism. For Wojtyła, freedom is founded on the experience "I can, but I do not have to,"[35] and, properly understood, this approach escapes Hume's critique. Hume bases his analysis on the recollection of the act,[36] as if the agent says to himself, "I was free, because I could have done otherwise." Here arises the problem of counterfactual conditionals. Consider:

1. Jones did *X*.
2. If he had it to do over again, Jones could have done *Y*.
3. Therefore Jones was free to do either *X* or *Y*.

The problem is with proposition 2. The conditional clause ("he had it to do over again") is a counterfactual, false. Jones will never have it to do over again. Therefore it is as true to deny "Jones could have done *Y*" as to affirm it. The question of freedom can never be settled by such an argument.

However, this is not how Karol Wojtyła addresses the issue. The perspective Wojtyła adopts is that of the acting person as he finds himself in act. For such a one, the proposition "I can, but I do not have to" is an

---

33 *Persona e atto*, 934–35.

34 Ibid., 936.

35 "Mogę—nie muszę." *Osoba i czyn*, 162, 166. The Italian reads, "Posso ma non sono costretto," *Persona e atto*, 978, 984ff.

36 *Inquiry concerning Human Understanding*, 103.

aspect of the reality he faces. In a way, this is the same reality that the existentialists recognized in their analysis of anguish, that the human being is, as it were, condemned to choose. The determinist objection, that one is predetermined to act in a certain way, is bootless. To tell me what I will do (or that my actions are predetermined for me) does not help me decide what I shall do, and even after receiving the predictive intelligence, it falls to me to make up my mind.[37] Wojtyła speaks of the "dynamism of self-determination," which he distinguishes from the dynamism on the natural level.[38] The acting person experiences that it is he who has to put himself into efficacious motion (which is to act) by an act of his own choice and design. That materialist philosophers deny his freedom to do this or dismiss his experience of freedom as an illusion matters not at all. He still has to make up his mind and act (or refrain from acting, but that, of course, is still his own responsibility). Wojtyła's point, therefore, is very simple. The acting person cannot escape his freedom.[39] His action depends not simply on what happens to him, but on his own self, which is the foundation of his freedom.[40]

Horizontal Transcendence

By his act, the person transcends himself. The efficacy of the act reveals and depends upon the twofold transcendence of the person: horizontal transcendence and vertical. By "horizontal" transcendence, Wojtyła means simply that the acting person goes beyond himself to other things: "Crossing the limit of the subject towards the object, that is to say intentionality, can be defined as *horizontal transcendence.*"[41] Underlying this is Karol Wojtyła's insistence that a philosophy of being underlie the phenomenological analysis. He can ignore the phenomenological *epochē*, because to bracket the question of the external world's existence would be to deny

---

[37] See a more complete presentation and discussion of this argument in my *Soul of the Person: A Contemporary Philosophical Psychology* (Washington, DC: Catholic University of America Press, 2006), 187, 228–36.

[38] *Persona e atto*, 979; "Person: Subject and Community," in *Person and Community*, 230.

[39] He can, of course, as the existentialists point out, seek to escape it through inauthentic living. See Jean-Paul Sartre, *Being and Nothingness*, trans. Hazel E. Barnes (New York: Philosophical Library 1956), pt. 1, chap. 2, "Bad Faith."

[40] *Persona e atto*, 980.

[41] Ibid., 982.

this experience, "a human being acts," of its essence as efficacious. This concept of horizontal transcendence has more implications, however, than simply to call classical phenomenology into question.

In virtue of his horizontal transcendence, the acting person is an agent for change in the world. Indeed, he is an intelligent agent, which is to say that he changes the world according to the designs and workings of his mind, his thoughts and imaginations. The person in act envisions the world (or a part of it) in such a possible state and then uses his body to effect those changes. Included in this world, of course, is his own self, as an entity both psychological and somatic. The person can mix eggs and make an omelet. He can also practice the piano and make himself into a musician, or force his body to endure pain in order to become an elite soldier. Therefore this horizontal transcendence involves not only physical, muscular interaction with the things of this world but also intelligence. The motions of the body as it interacts with things realize the rational designs of the intellect (perhaps imperfectly—the putt does not always go into the hole). The act of the body is one expression of the intelligence of the acting person, an intelligence that transcends itself toward the being of things.[42]

Vertical Transcendence

After characterizing horizontal transcendence, Karol Wojtyła proceeds to define *vertical transcendence.*

> However, it is not this [horizontal transcendence] that interests us in the first instance . . . when treating of the transcendence of the person in the act. This is the transcendence that we need for self-determination, transcendence by the very fact of freedom, of being free in the act, and not only by the fact that the volitions are directed intentionally toward their proper object as value-ends. This transcendence . . . can be defined as *vertical.*[43]

---

[42] "Person: Subject and Community," in *Person and Community,* 223.

[43] "Tuttavia non è questa che ci interessa anzitutto . . . , quando si tratta della trascendenza della persona nell'atto. È questa la trascendenza che dobbiamo all'autodeterminazione, trascendenza per il fatto stesso della libertà, di essere liberi nell'azione, e non soltanto per il fatto che i voleri sono intenzionalmente diretti verso l'oggetto loro proprio, in quanto valore-fine. Questa trascendenza, a differenza di quella che abbiamo definito orizzontale, si potrebbe definire verticale." *Persona e atto,* 982.

The very fact of the person's capacity to act freely implies vertical transcendence.[44] Horizontal transcendence is a response to value, as well as an effort to realize a value in a particular situation. Vertical transcendence, on the other hand, questions the value in terms of some standard of good, because the values as presented immediately in consciousness do not, of themselves, validate their own goodness. Karol Wojtyła illustrates this in *Love and Responsibility*, where he analyzes the various aspects of love: attraction, desire, and sympathy.[45] The thrust of his argument is that authentic love needs to be based on truth and not just on the values one finds presented in the experience of an attractive person. Love begins with attraction. "*Attraction is of the essence of love*," Wojtyła writes, "*and in some sense is indeed love, although love is not merely attraction*."[46] Attraction is a matter of feelings, of emotion, as one finds oneself presented with important values. The values at issue in a particular case may vary, as one person is attracted strongly to nobility of character, and another is drawn to sensual or sexual values, and yet another to beauty or wit. Indeed, because most persons are attracted by several values at once, the task is to integrate these values and one's responses to them. Emotion, sentiment, and sensual desire all play a role in love, but neither alone nor in their interaction do they provide adequate direction for love. Sentiment, which has its own inner dynamic, can, as a couple become more emotionally involved with each other, transform into sensual desire, whose finality is sexual contact. Because the experience of values alone does not suffice to guide action, a further, integrating power is needed.

This faculty of integration is the power of the "inner man" to know the truth and thereby to act freely. "*The process of integrating love relies on the primary elements of the human spirit—freedom and truth*."[47] This integration in freedom and truth is precisely the project of vertical transcendence. This transcendence is governed by the orientation to truth, especially truth about the good. From their various perspectives, the psychosomatic and psychological dynamisms of the person—sensation, sensuality, emotion, sentiment, mood, and so on—propose values to consciousness. Reason,

44 Kaczyński, *Verità sul bene nella morale*, 222.

45 *Love and Responsibility*, "Metaphysical Analysis of Love," 73–95.

46 Ibid., 76.

47 Ibid., 116.

however, has the capacity to rise above these perspectives and to ask about the truth. So, for instance, in the case of sexual love between man and woman, emotion and sentiment of themselves may tend to carry the person along, unless braked as it were by the inner self as it chooses to act in truth concerning the two persons and the nature of their relationship. Consequently, Wojtyła can write, "A really free commitment of the will is possible only on the basis of truth. The experience of freedom goes hand in hand with the experience of truth."[48] Vertical transcendence, which depends on the effort to know the truth about the good, is the basis for human freedom. Without this transcendence, it is impossible for the person to be integrated in his acts, for his acts to be his own.

> The person's authentic transcendence in action is realized in conscience, and the *actus humanus* takes shape as the willing and choosing of a "true good" thanks to conscience. Thus the element of conscience reveals both in action and in the efficient subject of action the transcendence of truth and freedom, for freedom is realized precisely through the willing and choosing of a true good.[49]

Buttiglione writes: "The independence of the will from the emotional sphere is explained by its dependence on the truth."[50] What happens in the human being, the appeal of intuited values, cannot determine the will unless the will surrender to them. Because conscience, the application of knowledge about the good to one's behavior, reveals the transcendence of the person toward the absolute good, Karol Wojtyła can here link freedom, conscience, truth, and good into a coherent unity. Transcendence is the key to the human person's spiritual nature;[51] it is another name for the person.[52] Precisely in virtue of this transcendence toward the true good can the person integrate himself in and through his acts.

Integration of the Person in the Act

Unlike animals and machines, the human person does not find his inner dynamisms ordered and integrated for him. Karol Wojtyła writes: "The

[48] Ibid., 117.
[49] Wojtyła, "Person: Subject and Community," in *Person and Community*, 234.
[50] *Karol Wojtyla*, 147.
[51] Wojtyła, "Person: Subject and Community," in *Person and Community*, 233.
[52] Ibid., 230.

promptings of sensuality would give a man all the guidance he needs in his sexual life if, in the first place, his sexual reactions were infallibly guided by instinct, and if in the second place the object of those reactions—a person of the opposite sex—did not demand a different attitude from that which is proper to sensuality."[53] This is a fact insufficiently recognized by contemporary materialists, who maintain that human intelligence and activity are directed toward preestablished ends. Comparing the activities of a sea squirt and an associate professor, Daniel Dennett finds them essentially equivalent, because "[a]ll brains are, in essence, *anticipation machines*."[54] The human brain is able to anticipate more remote and more complex threats and opportunities than that of the sea squirt, but its function is essentially the same. Consistent with empiricist reductionism, Dennett holds that human intelligence is nothing more than a highly successful survival adaptation, the brain being an especially adaptable organ of discernment for the preservation of the individual and the species. However, this account ignores the most distinctive and the truly unique function of the human brain at work, which is to form general concepts. Although the human being does certainly experience drives, desires, and urges similar to other animals, he also experiences the intellectual need to integrate them, to order them according to a principle grasped intellectually. The very fact that a human being can question whether to continue his own life or to satisfy his most basic biological desires indicates that the intellectual integration of his being is no mere epiphenomenological quirk but an essential need.

This integration is a central theme of Wojtyła's *Love and Responsibility*, where at issue is precisely the relationship among the various somatic and emotional factors that enter into human sexual love. In the first chapter, titled "The Person and the Sexual Urge," Karol Wojtyła discusses at length whether the human sexual impulse is an instinct, which he defines as a "*reflex mode of action, which is not dependent on conscious thought*,"[55] or an urge, that is, "*a natural drive born in all human beings, a vector of aspiration* along which their whole existence develops and perfects itself from within."[56] (Let us note here that the instinct as such is studied as a factor in

---

[53] *Love and Responsibility*, 107.
[54] *Consciousness Explained*, 177.
[55] Ibid., 45.
[56] Ibid., 46.

the "biological order" discussed in the previous chapter.) Wojtyła's point in this section of the work is that the sexual drive, strong as it is, can be controlled by the will, that the person can master this behavior, which is instinctive in the lower animals. The problem with the "generalized empiricism" discussed in the previous chapter is that it does not enable us to account for the person's mastery of his sexual drives for their integration. Indeed, the human person is capable not only of managing his sexual impulses but even of denying them for a period or even permanently.[57]

Chapter 2 of *Love and Responsibility*, "The Person and Love," addresses at length the question of integration of the range of impulses within the human being who is sexually and affectively attracted to another. These include attraction; desire; sensuality; goodwill or benevolence; good fellowship; and friendship, any of which can become predominate in a relationship between two persons. The very real issue is how to relate these disparate factors harmoniously and to integrate them into an authentically loving relationship. In a real relationship, if attention is not paid to this matter, then one aspect—most likely sensuality—will dominate, and the relationship itself will disintegrate. Significantly, the first section of that chapter, which analyzes these various factors in detail, is titled "Metaphysical Analysis of Love."[58] This term "metaphysical" indicates that the integration must take place beyond the purely physical plane, as we have already noted, and this returns us to the concept of the *suppositum.*

Will and Suppositum

Although Wojtyła does not present us with a detailed theoretical account of the will, the metaphysical notion of will plays a key role in his ethics. To deny the reality of the will is to render human experience unintelligible. More precisely, without the concept of the will as that power by which the human *suppositum* engages effectively with the world, this experience—"a human being acts"—is unintelligible and effectively denied. Because the person who performs the act cannot be reduced either to a center of consciousness or to a physical entity interacting instinctively with other physical objects, an adequate account of the human person, precisely as given to

---

[57] Ibid., 194–99; see also *Man and Woman He Created Them*, 73.1–77.4, 412–28.

[58] *Love and Responsibility*, 73. "Analiza metafizyczna miłości" in the original Polish, *Miłość i odpowiedzialność*, 69.

experience, requires us to penetrate below the phenomenal level to the transphenomenal *suppositum* that underlies our experience of it.[59] The will is a character or faculty of the *suppositum* as such. That is, the will is neither a physical nor merely a psychological property, nor is it a content (or nexus of contents) of consciousness. Will is that which sets the person into act.

When we claim that it is the will that makes the person act, have we not simply invented a mysterious power unknown to science? No, the will is not mysterious—at least not in the sense proposed by this objection. By saying that the will acts, we assert simply that the person acts *as a person.* If the man strikes his wife in his sleep as a nightmare sends him into a paroxysm of terror, then the man has not acted; certain mechanisms of his brain might have, but not he. *Something happened* in him. When Othello strangled Desdemona, however, *a man acted.* Having considered Iago's allegations and insinuations and the things he had seen (the handkerchief), Othello planned the death of his wife and brought it about. He acted. We say that he made a decision of his will and by his will dynamized himself. But this is to say that Othello himself did the deed and not some part of him or some force outside him. There is a mystery of the will, of course, but it is the mystery we see every day as persons deliberately do things they know to be harmful or bad.

According to Wojtyła's conception, the choice of the will is always the choice of some good, whether as useful, delightful, or fitting. In virtue of the capacity for vertical transcendence, the human person can recognize and choose the good known by reason. Because the will is the ultimate root of the act (when "a human being acts"), that in virtue of which the act transcends "what happens in a human being," there is no going behind the will or explaining it in terms of something else. To be sure, the person in act is influenced, often strongly, by what happens to him, but these happenings do not ultimately determine the act. The decision to act, which is the act of the will, therefore becomes the choice of values and habits. This is to say that when, for example, one looks for an explanation of the criminal act, although the miscreant's upbringing and environment may be helpful for a perspective on his behavior, it cannot provide the ultimate explanation. His options may have been restricted by want of imagination or by limited

---

59 Wojtyła, "Person: Subject and Community," in *Person and Community*, 223–25; *Persona e atto*, 926.

understanding. He may well have experienced his impulses as overwhelming (here the emotionalization of his consciousness). Ultimately, however, the criminal chose his act. Even if the extent to which any given human being is responsible for his acts may be impossible for another to determine,[60] the person himself remains the one responsible for his choice of actions. The choice to perform the act is the decision concerning one's values. Karol Wojtyła writes: "The will is the person's power of self-determination."[61] Therefore, although the choices of the will may reveal much about what has happened to the person, even more do they determine who that person becomes. In virtue of his "vertical transcendence," the person is free and his will has the capacity of free choice. Freedom is the power of self-determination by which the person, who possesses himself, forms himself as a moral agent, as someone good or evil.[62]

Will and the "Freedom of Indifference"

But has this will (and therefore the person) any orientation of its own? Or is it characterized by a complete and indifferent freedom of choice? Addressing the dynamics of the will, Pinckaers writes, "For Ockham, freedom meant essentially the power to choose between contraries, independently of all other causes except freedom, of the will itself—whence the term *freedom of indifference*."[63] The will, so conceived, is radically free, that is, capable of choosing either *A* or not-*A* or *B*, independently of any factor other than its own decision. Kant expresses this conception succinctly in the *Thesis* of the Third Conflict of the Transcendental Ideas in the antinomies of pure reason.

> We must, then, assume a causality through which something takes place, the cause of which is not itself determined, in accordance with necessary laws, by another antecedent to it, that is to say, an *absolute spontaneity* of the cause, whereby a series of appearances, which proceeds in accordance with laws of nature, begins *of itself*. This is transcendental freedom[. . .].[64]

60 See John Paul II, *Evangelium Vitae*, 58–59.

61 "The Personal Structure of Self-Determination," in *Person and Community*, 190.

62 *Persona e atto*, 1023, 1025.

63 Servais Pinckaers, O.P., *The Sources of Christian Ethics*, trans. from the 3rd ed. by Sr. Mary Thomas Noble, O.P. (Washington, DC: Catholic University of America Press, 1995), 242.

64 *Critique of Pure Reason*, B 474.

Kant posits an "absolute spontaneity," a complete independence of the free cause from all extrinsic causality. The free choice is therefore inexplicable, a kind of surd, unrelated to preexisting conditions or factors. Indeed, any force, compulsion, impulsion, or influence that may affect the choice is regarded as a restriction of freedom. Szostek notes that Kant's sharp opposition between determination and freedom has been accepted and adopted by contemporary moral theologians.[65] This freedom must transcend the empirical: "This [Kantian] autonomy is, to put it plainly, *the autonomy of the human being as a rational and not merely 'empirical' subject.*"[66] This conception can lead, however, to new antinomies, as Knauer observes.

> When, on the other hand, as is usually the case, one regards the choice between several goods as the fundamental form of freedom of choice, there then arise irresolvable antinomies. For the decision is either rational but determined, or it is free but irrational. The choice can therefore only be rational when one chooses the greatest good from among the different objects.[67]

It is significant that in this text, not only external forces but *reasons* can be regarded as constraints on freedom. Not only is he unfree who breaks a window while sleepwalking or who, imprisoned for his beliefs, fails to provide financially for his children, but also—to an extent, at least—he who badly wants the car he has just bought or who is intellectually convinced that he best votes by supporting the Green candidate, because like the somnambulant dream and the prison walls, the strong desire and the intellectual conviction condition his choice. It is not hard at all to see Kant's opposition between freedom and the empirical here.

Since freedom and autonomy may not ultimately be conditioned by the empirical, Szostek concludes that according to such theologians the human being is himself "incarnate freedom."[68] Therefore the notion of "freedom of indifference" posits a radically voluntaristic conception of human nature in that the will disposes and determines the human being. Pinckaers writes:

65 *Natur—Vernunft—Freiheit,* 38.

66 Ibid., 39.

67 "Teleologische als deontologische Normenbegründung," 332. Szostek discusses this text in *Natur—Vernunft—Freiheit,* 191, in connection with the problem of rigorism.

68 *Natur—Vernunft—Freiheit,* 155.

"Thus understood, freedom was practically identified with the will, as the origin of willing and acting, as a power of self-determination. In this way it came to constitute, in some way, by itself alone, the very being of the person, as the source of all action."[69] To the extent that a person acts independently of any influence outside himself is the extent to which he is free. Therefore, for many contemporary moral theologians, *freedom* is the principal and fundamental good to be realized by the human person, a freedom whose realization God himself guarantees. Szostek writes for such theologians: "The human being is not only not threatened in his freedom by God, but *God and only God*—especially the God who manifests himself in the light of Christian Revelation—*is* as much *foundation of the human being's autonomy* as also *its transcendental guarantor*."[70] The human person manifests his freedom not by attaining any specific end or by obeying any particular command (or set of commands) but by making his actions entirely his own in the exercise of his freedom.

Will and "Transcendental Freedom"

Closely related to this perspective and its restricted conception of will as merely the power to choose between alternatives is the conception of *transcendental freedom*—"transcendental" precisely because it transcends the empirical order and is therefore prior to any empirical condition or knowledge of the truth. This approach can be traced to Kant's ethical theory, which sharply opposes *nature* and *person* and, coordinated with these, *determinism* and *freedom*.[71] Karl Rahner[72] characterizes this *transcendental freedom* as follows: "the ultimate self-disposability of the person, not only in knowing and therefore not only in self-consciousness, but as self-act."[73] "Freedom is the power of the subject over himself as a unity and a whole."[74] Although this capacity for self-disposal is, to be sure, mediated through the human being's bodiliness, his spatiotemporality, it is not lim-

[69] *Sources of Christian Ethics*, 232.

[70] *Natur—Vernunft—Freiheit*, 135.

[71] See ibid., 38.

[72] See his *Grundkurs des Glaubens: Einführung in den Begriff des Christentums*, 3rd ed. (Freiburg: Herder, 1976), 47–49, 103.

[73] "[L]etzte Sichselbstüberantwortheit der Person, nicht nur im Erkennen, also nicht nur als Selbstbewußtsein, sondern als Selbsttat." Ibid., 47.

[74] "Die Freiheit ist das Vermögen des einen Subjekts über sich als Eines und Ganzes." Ibid., 101.

ited by them. Human freedom, the innermost core of personhood, is not to remain buried in one's reflective interior. Rather, it is that in man which is most creative, by which the person transcends the determination of nature. The key point for the moral life, therefore, lies not so much in the nature of the human being as in precisely the exercise of freedom. Andrzej Szostek writes, "The consequence of such a conception [i.e., Karl Rahner's] of freedom is, among other things, the view that sees the moral value of an act not only in its agreement with the objective norms of morality, . . . but also in that it *manifests freedom*."[75] And further:

> In this conception freedom is regarded precisely in virtue of its essence as not reducible to what is universal . . . but rather receives its norms through its own dynamism: through an interior, individual dynamic that transcends the conclusions of essential norms. Therefore the act of freedom is *morally* of value in that it is an act of freedom.[76]

Although Rahner rejects the notion of the freedom of indifference,[77] the theory of transcendental freedom shares with it this flaw, that it gives decisive priority to the person regarded simply as subject, as center of consciousness and autonomous center of decision. The focus of freedom for Rahner is the person's responsible self-disposition and self-determination. By his categorial act the person objectifies his freedom, in what can be called an "objectivation." Rahner writes:

> Further, this objectivation of the decision of freedom is given in the manner of an open, broader determinability. For this objectivation of a human being's decision of freedom, an objectivation that operates in the objectivity of a common situation of freedom, can become an interior moment of the decision of freedom of another, in which this objectivation can receive a completely different character, without thereby ceasing to be the result of the first act of freedom.[78]

And hence, argues Szostek, Rahner's conception lacks "the orientation of the act of freedom to the truth."[79] Rahner is not arguing that the

[75] *Natur—Vernunft—Freiheit*, 87.
[76] Ibid., 88.
[77] *Grundkurs des Glaubens*, 49, 102.
[78] Ibid., 114.
[79] *Natur—Vernunft—Freiheit*, 237–38.

"objectivation" of one's transcendental freedom can take on any character willy-nilly, regardless of finite states of affairs and the truth of the matter. Rather, in order to protect the transcendental character of the human person and his freedom, Rahner cannot allow a categorial and therefore finite situation to determine that freedom. It follows, then, that the moral life is characterized and its qualifications determined by interior acts and attitudes. This means that the will, to the extent that it is considered, is essentially devoid of its own dynamism or orientation. Will becomes simply the power to effect the creative initiatives of personal freedom.

The importance of these two concepts, the will as "indifferent" and that of creative freedom, will become apparent as we regard Karol Wojtyła's account. If, as Wojtyła maintains, we may speak meaningfully of the truth about the good and, indeed, know this truth, then the intuition of values is governed by the faculty of reason, which is the power to know the truth. The will, conceived as the power to love what is good and to choose values and the acts to realize them according to this truth, must have its own inner dynamism. And it follows further that the creativity of reason cannot extend to the definition of moral norms.

In Aquinas's account, in contrast to the freedom of indifference, the will's power of choice is free only with respect to means to the ultimate end and not to that end itself.[80] This issues in two consequences worth noting here. First, for one who actually experiences the vision of the divine essence, which Aquinas holds to be the ultimate end of the human being,[81] it is impossible not to want that vision or to choose to turn away from it. Second, in the conditions of this life, everything that a human being chooses, he chooses under the aspect of good, as bringing about, contributing to, or realizing what he conceives to be his good. Misconceiving his perfect good, whether through ignorance or an undue attachment to some earthly good, he can indeed direct his will away from the true ultimate good, but it is only in this sense that he is free to reject that good. Aquinas's fundamental point is that the human being is, by his very nature as a rational creature, directed toward God as his ultimate end.

---

80 *ST* I, q. 82, a. 2; I–II, q. 9, aa. 3–4; q. 10, a. 1; q. 91, a. 2; Thomas Aquinas, *Commentary on the* Nicomachean Ethics, trans. C. I. Litzinger, O.P. (Chicago: Henry Regnery Company, 1964), 1.2.21; *De veritate*, q. 22, a. 5.

81 *ST* I–II, q. 3, a. 8.

Wojtyła adapts Aquinas's account, integrating it with his analysis of *values* and *vertical integration.* By the fact that the person experiences the values of things, that he is attracted by values, he is drawn toward goods. The disposition of the human person to go out toward the good is the essence of every "I want something." "To want" means to go out toward a certain good.[82] In this context Karol Wojtyła expressly identifies this *wanting* with the classical notion of *appetitus.* The will, "which forms the action, [and] is the capacity to respond to the values presented," is formed by knowledge. It is the *appetitus rationalis,* because the appetition of the will is inevitably founded on knowledge.[83] Will acts, therefore, on the basis of actively functioning desires, but as these are known by reason. Indeed, we may well understand Wojtyła's account of the relationship between horizontal and vertical transcendence as a rereading of Aquinas's account of the will as rational appetite.

The Soul

In Aquinas's metaphysics, will is one of the powers or faculties of the soul.[84] However, although Wojtyła relies on Aquinas for the foundations of his thought,[85] he devotes remarkably little discussion to the soul as such. We can only speculate on the reasons for this. Certainly in this post-Cartesian intellectual realm, it is hard even to begin discussing the soul without falling or being accused of falling into dualism. We do know, too, that Karol Wojtyła was particularly concerned with the effects of Descartes's turn to a philosophy of consciousness from a philosophy of

---

82 Wojtyła, *Osoba i czyn,* 173–74; *Persona e atto,* 994–95. The Italian renders *wychodzić* ("to go out") as the somewhat weaker *tendere.*

83 *Persona e atto,* 1003–4.

84 *ST* I, q. 82, a. 2. And see Karol Wojtyła, "Thomistic Personalism," in *Person and Community,* 168: "The faculties that express and actualize the soul's spirituality, and thus the human being's spirituality, are reason and free will."

85 The central importance of Aquinas to Karol Wojtyła/John Paul II is manifest and undeniable. See, for example, Wojtyła's *Lubliner Vorlesungen,* 94–101, 386–414; "On the Directive or Subservient Role of Reason in Ethics in the Philosophy of Thomas Aquinas, David Hume, and Immanuel Kant," in *Person and Community,* 57–72; "On the Metaphysical and Phenomenological Basis of the Moral Norm," ibid., 73–94; "Thomistic Personalism," ibid., 167–75; and *Persona e atto,* 861, 926–28, 991–94, 1131–33, 1151–53. See also Buttiglione, *Karol Wojtyla,* 72–82; Kupczak, *Destined for Liberty,* 49–57; and Schmitz, *At the Center of the Human Drama,* 51–54, 60–63.

being.[86] Significantly, in his audiences on the theology of the body, the term "soul" hardly appears at all. In this protracted analysis of human sexuality, love, and marriage, John Paul II does not, as one would expect of a Catholic priest-theologian, focus on the soul in contrast to the body. Rather, he insists that the body reveals the person and is the vehicle for the communion of persons and mutual gift of self that constitutes true love.[87] I suggest that his reluctance to use the term "soul" (at least to any great extent) is strategic. From the start of his adult career, John Paul II's principal concerns were pastoral rather than academic. He wanted to communicate effectively even more than he wanted to make his own contribution to our civilization's body of scholarly writing. He was a teacher and pastor before he was a theorist. Therefore, I suggest, he deliberately avoided this term in order to make clear the truth concerning human beings and their nature without his readers' tripping over dualist interpretations of this term "soul." And so he talked about the same reality but in different terms. Rather than explicating the Thomistic theory, he describes its manifestations in experience. This is especially clear not only in the texts from *Person and Act* cited above but also in chapter 2 of *Love and Responsibility*, where he gives a phenomenological description of the relationship between what Aquinas defines as the intellect and sensitive appetites.

We note, however, that Wojtyła is not reluctant at all to use the terms "spirit" and "spiritual," which, unlike the term "soul," refer to elements of human experience. If "soul" is theoretical, then "spirit" is descriptive. The spiritual is the experience we have of our vocation to transcendence.[88] It is impossible, however, to account ontologically for the will and the unity of the human person without referring to the soul. A nonmaterialist metaphysics of the human person will include an account of the soul, and Wojtyła recognizes this. In *Person and Act* the discussion of the integration of the person in the act is capped and completed by a discussion of the soul as the principle of transcendence and integration.[89] For the human person to be truly master of his act, he must be a spiritual being. That is,

[86] John Paul II, *Crossing the Threshold of Hope*, 37–38, 50–52.

[87] *Man and Woman He Created Them*, 9.4–5, 164–65.

[88] This transcendence need not be *that* transcendent, either. The coach giving the team a pep talk appeals to their team spirit, so that they will transcend their limitations to achieve victory.

[89] *Persona e atto*, 1064–67.

his being and acting cannot consist only in an expression of powers of nature but must be personal. "The manifestations of the spirituality of the human being can neither be understood nor explained without the stability and substantiality of his spiritual element. However, this element's manner of being and acting . . . is not proper to nature, as we have already shown, but to the person."[90] Although this spiritual element or principle, which is the soul, is not accessible to experience (that is, to consciousness), the human being does experience his "self," that he is an "I," and this indicates the direction for a metaphysical analysis of the soul.[91] This analysis, however, is beyond the reach of phenomenology, strictly speaking, but requires the methods of the "philosophy of being."

> We affirmed that the human being does not experience his soul directly. Even the lived experience of the transcendence of the person in the act, in all the elements and aspects of this experience (cf. chapters 3 and 4), do not amount to a direct lived experience of the soul. . . . Both the reality of the soul and the reality of its relationship with the body are in this sense transphenomenal and extraexperiential realities.[92]

The pattern of analysis that we saw Karol Wojtyła apply to the will applies also to the soul. Although the soul is not directly perceived, we recognize its necessity as the principle of integration and transcendence of the person's acts.

Act as Good

Through the human act, we may say that the human soul is revealed, because the act is a rational engagement of the human being with the world, an engagement that reveals the spiritual nature of the human being. The act manifests the person's self-determination and self-possession; indeed, only the being in possession of itself is able to act and thereby to determine itself. As a result, the person is able to—is, indeed, compelled—to decide concerning his transcendence toward the goods he himself has recognized and chosen. In act and only in act is vertical transcendence

---

[90] Ibid., 1062.
[91] Ibid., 1067.
[92] Ibid., 1160.

possible. Even if a person is hindered from significant physical activity, such as through imprisonment or grave illness, he is capable of accepting or rejecting his situation. He can make spiritual use of his plight, communicate with others, and rebel and resist (as political prisoners often do). Here perhaps is one of the most serious weaknesses of Scheler's "value response" theory. The acting person acts not only in response to or appreciation of some value but rather precisely to attain some good. The political prisoner's attempts to communicate with his fellows and to coordinate their resistance do not simply manifest their appreciation of the value of freedom. They attempt to realize freedom for themselves and other members of their cause by confounding the efforts of their captors.

It follows that to do an act is itself a good. Only in act can one realize oneself as virtuous. Only in act can one share in the actions of others to attain the good. Karol Wojtyła identifies this goodness as the personalistic value of the act, which is different from the moral value. "Personalistic value is innate to the realization itself of the act on the part of the person, in that very fact that 'the human being acts' in a manner proper to himself; therefore in the fact that the act possesses a character of authentic self-determination, in it the self-determination of the person, is realized."[93]

Significantly, Wojtyła argues this at the beginning of part 4, chapter 7, of *Person and Act*, "Lineaments of the Theory of Participation," which treats of the acting person in the context of the community and society. Even if that power to act is misused by one's acting immorally, the act retains its value as an expression of the person. Indeed, we experience this in watching the maturing processes of the young, allowing and encouraging them to decide important matters for themselves—and rejoicing when they finally do—while sometimes regretting the choices that they do choose. To deny the person the freedom to act is to violate his personhood, for only in act can he realize himself and transcend his own consciousness.

The Fundamental Question

This perspective brings us back to the fundamental question raised at the beginning of this chapter: What is ethics about? If it is about human acts, then Wojtyła's analysis shows that ethics must go to the core of the human

93 Ibid., 1171.

person, because by his act a person makes himself different, into a different "self" than he was prior to the act. He *becomes* the self he is, realizing his potentialities. The fundamental point is quite simple. The sailor Christopher Columbus set out to find a western route to the Indies. By doing so, he became an explorer. To be sure, the consequences of his act were far greater than even he could have imagined, as his landing in America opened up two unknown continents for European exploration and colonization and decisively changed the course of history. His act had the further consequence that European diseases fatally infected large portions of the indigenous populations. History may judge Columbus's achievements positively or negatively according to these results, but what Columbus himself did, by his own free will and intention, was to explore. He made himself an explorer. Leonardo da Vinci did not. He chose to make himself an artist by painting pictures. The woman who bears a child becomes a mother. In each case, the person by the choice of his acts, which are efficacious, changed the world, opening up unknown trade routes, covering walls with fine images, or bringing a new human being into the world. In acting so, the person is responsible both for what he has effected and for himself as the one who effected it.

The person in act makes himself who he is, because he is the one who has brought this innovation, this beauty, this death and sorrow, this life and joy into the world. By his willed choice of particular values he has done this. In greater part, he forms himself by the choice he has made of himself in the act. The act necessarily involves transcendence toward his higher good, the good that governs the values by which he acts. By the choice of the will, the person chooses what he will value the most. In doing so, he chooses the values in terms of which he seeks to realize his integration of himself. It has been argued that Joseph Stalin was the producer, director, and principal actor of the live "film" called the U.S.S.R.[94] Stalin assigned to each Soviet citizen his role and his lines. He dispensed life and death according to his vision. He tore down and built up. He was, in a meaningful sense, the god of the Soviet Union. His murders and betrayals, his ten-year plans and treaties were ordered according to his own divinity as the transcendent value. He was who he was because of his acts.

---

94 Boris Groys, "Kommunismus wie im Kino: Stalin und die Allmacht des Bildes," *Süddeutsche Zeitung*, March 26–27, 1994, 17.

Had he sat resentfully at his desk, working as a minor bureaucrat, complaining in his own mind about the stupidity of others but never daring to confront them, he would have become a different person—perhaps no more agreeable than the historical Stalin, but different from him. We cannot speak of the individual act as a movement or interaction isolated from the other acts a person performs. Rather, the act falls within a nexus that has meaning, a meaning that the act reinterprets and develops. This meaning is interiorized by the very fact that the person is its author. To decide (as Stalin did) to starve the Ukrainian peasants is not simply an administrative disposition, but it is a claim to absolute sovereignty over their lives. The act is the statement of what is most important, and it serves to determine what the person's transcendent values are. Macbeth was ambitious, to be sure, but his murder of Duncan formed his ambition. After he "murdered sleep,"[95] he advanced his ambitions by additional murders, so that the three witches, themselves icons of evil, could announce his arrival: "Something wicked this way comes."[96]

The deliberate human act originates with the person and not simply with some part or aspect of him. If his urges were true instincts, then we could explain each act by noting that biology will have its way. But this is not the way the human person experiences his act. Even when urges and impulses are very strong, the person can consider the proposed act in relation to the other aspects of his being and to his values. In other words, he experiences the demand to integrate his act into the context of his life, and by doing so, his act is also an occasion of self-integration. This task of integration is itself the act of the person as such, and not of his body and its urges or of his emotional structure alone. Because it is a task of the person as a whole, self-integration may well become a complicated and difficult project. We may think of those afflicted with obsessive-compulsive disorder (OCD). They cannot simply "shut off" the impulse to wash their hands, straighten rugs, or reset the clock. Rather, such a person, availing himself of the help of others, must recognize his compulsions and then negotiate his way through and around them, so that *he* governs his life and not his OCD.[97]

---

[95] Shakespeare, *Macbeth*, act 2, scene 2.

[96] Ibid., act 4, scene 1.

[97] Karol Wojtyła addresses psychological disintegration in general but useful terms in *Persona e atto*, 1075–80.

Although the person may close his eyes to some of its implications, he chooses this act in the context of his being and experience of the world. It is he and not some part of himself that is responsible for the choice that forms this integration. What is it that makes a human person good or bad? Wojtyła argues that, first, it cannot be something that *happens* to a person. No one is good or bad because of the way he was born or even because of how he feels. Nor can a person's goodness (or badness) consist only in some subjective state, as though to be good is a matter of harboring the best or most noble sentiments. The person may feel himself to be good (or evil), but this feeling does not determine his goodness. It is well known that wicked persons can feel very self-satisfied, good about themselves. It is also true that very good persons, who often have tender consciences, can feel themselves to be bad. John Paul II was well aware of the experiences of many Christian mystics who were oppressed by the feelings that they had failed to please God. The person is or becomes good or bad on the basis of acts of which he is the author, because the acts are efficacious. This is what it means for something to be a human act. The good person, therefore, is one who is a substantial principle of good acts, from whom good acts come and can be expected. An evil person is one who is a substantial principle of evil acts. It remains for us next, therefore, to examine our author's account of the goodness or evil of human acts.

CHAPTER 4

The Moral Good

Moral Experience

AT THE HEART of moral experience is the experience of *duty*, of *obligation*, the experience that there is something one is supposed to do. In his encyclical *Veritatis Splendor*, John Paul II wrote: "No one can escape from the fundamental questions: *What must I do? How do I distinguish good from evil?*"[1] Earlier, in the draft of a projected work on moral responsibility, he had written:

> "*What ought I truly to do?*" and "*Why ought I to do* what I ought to do?" In this way are formulated the questions that are innate to the experience of morality as a "fact." . . . At the same time, these questions open to us the path to comprehension. It is a comprehension of duty not only as lived experience but at the same time also as objective *fact*.[2]

In contrast to David Hume, Karol Wojtyła was convinced that there is direct, objective moral experience, experience that is just as real, concrete, and objective as the sensory experience of the physical world. The proof of this is that the acting person confronts the questions cited above: "What ought I truly to do?" and "Why ought I to do it?" These questions arise not from custom or from religious or moral instruction but from the fact of human freedom. Because the acting person, confronted with the possibility of acting, experiences that "I can but I do not have to," he is conscious that

[1] *Veritatis Splendor*, 2.

[2] Wojtyła, *L'uomo nel campo della responsibilità*, 1240.

the direction of his act is his to choose. It lies with him to choose the best act. He can do *A* or *B* or *C*, but not all three. Therefore he must choose, and confronted with the choice, he faces the questions "What should I do?" and "Why should I do the one rather than the other?"

One might well object that these questions do not necessarily imply a moral decision. Should the chess player move his rook to seize the "bishop's" file or his bishop to the long diagonal? Shall we plant tomatoes or flowers in the garden? In neither of these questions is a moral issue at stake. In such cases and in most of life's decisions, one is not confronted with the question of moral evil. Nevertheless, the agent has to decide what to do. He needs criteria or norms for judging what to do. It is, of course, both possible and necessary to distinguish morally decisive choices from other decisions, and we shall reflect later in greater depth upon this. It is worth noting here that we find a certain tension at the foundations of our discussion. Max Scheler and von Hildebrand after him distinguished moral values from other values, so that the choice to tell the truth affirms a moral value and the choice to plant flowers an aesthetic one.[3] On the other hand, Thomas Aquinas affirms that every free human act is morally conditioned, is a moral act.[4] Wojtyła affirms that one experiences morality as a "fact" in the questions "What ought I to do?" and "Why ought I to do it?"—questions that can apply to matters that have no apparent moral import.

The issue before us reveals an ambiguity in our way of thinking about ethics. Moral questions are clearly important; Wojtyła holds that a person makes himself good or bad by his moral acts. On the other hand, a person makes all sorts of vitally important decisions that can dramatically affect his life, without their being a choice between right and wrong. A man may lie to his co-worker about his contribution to the office pool (a morally wrong act), and that evening propose marriage (a morally neutral act) to a young woman. The marriage proposal can more significantly and deeply affect his life and the lives of others than will the lie to the co-worker. About both issues one may ask, "What should I do?" and "Why should I do it?" To one the answer is clear ("Tell the truth"), but to the other we may rightly say there is no right or wrong answer. Wojtyła speaks of a "comprehension of duty" that is experienced as an "objective fact." We

---

3 Scheler, *Der Formalismus,* 124; von Hildebrand, *Ethics,* chap. 19.

4 *ST* I–II, q. 6 prologue.

may ask to what extent and how (if at all) so many of our most important questions can involve a duty or obligation.

Duty

A duty or obligation flows from some norm. The duty to return lost valuables to their owner flows from the norm that a person generally has the exclusive right of access to and disposal of his property. A norm is a principle from which we can derive a universal prescription or proscription, binding every person (at least within a defined population) to perform a particular kind of act or to refrain from some behavior. Different kinds of norms give rise to different kinds of obligations. Karol Wojtyła notes that the concept *norm* is analogous.[5] We may speak of norms of etiquette, legal norms, moral norms, rules of games, and so on.[6] If the answer to the questions "What should I do?" and "Why should I do it?" give rise to norms, then the kind of norms involved will determine the kind of duty involved. The legend is that Ruy Lopez, a Spanish priest and chess player,[7] was once challenged by a fellow priest, who asked him, "Father, if I were to tell you that Christ is returning today and is at the very gates, what would you do?" To which Lopez replied that he would move his rook and play for a quick victory. In this interchange we see two kinds of norms in play. Lopez's critic implicitly appealed to a religious norm, Christ's admonition to be "dressed for action and have your lamps lit" (Lk 12:35), while the chess-playing priest appealed to a principle for winning chess games quickly. However, both norms answer the question "What should I do?" If the player does not control the center, occupy open files with his rooks, and establish mobile pawn chains, he will not win many games. If one is not ready for the Master's Second Coming, he will be judged a useless servant and be cast out into the darkness (Lk 12:41–48).

If norms are analogous, then so are duties. Indeed, we would find it strange to say that the chess player has a *duty* to seize the open file with his rook, even if all the experts agree that he *should* do so. Nevertheless, in the postmortem, the player may well acknowledge that his move was *bad*, that

[5] Compare this with J. J. C. Smart's sharp distinction between moral and nonmoral uses of terms such as "ought," "right," "wrong," "good," and "bad." J. J. C. Smart, *Ethics, Persuasion and Truth* (London: Routledge and Kegan Paul, 1984), 3.

[6] Wojtyła, *L'uomo nel campo della responsibilità*, 1256–59.

[7] For whom the Ruy Lopez Opening, or Spanish Opening, in chess is named.

he *should* have done differently. As we move away from games to more serious matters, of course, the question of duties may take on more recognizable form. For instance, we speak of the social obligation to accept a dinner invitation from one's superiors. Why should we go to dinner at the boss's home? It is expected. If we do not, then I will have been ungracious and my future with the company may suffer. There are legal obligations. Why must I file my taxes by midnight of April 15 and no later? Because the duly empowered legislature has so ordained, and if I fail to file on time I will have failed in a serious responsibility as a citizen. Furthermore, I will be penalized. On the other hand, to whom (other than the reader) is Mr. D'Arcy obliged concerning his choice of a wife?[8] He owes nothing to Elizabeth, to whom he does in fact propose, but his wealthy and disagreeable aunt would make a strong case for his being socially obliged to marry her daughter. At stake are the directions and happiness (or unhappiness) of several lives.

In this context, we might, of course, cite Kant's distinction between hypothetical and categorical imperatives.[9] A hypothetical imperative binds, but only to the extent one wants to attain the end that it is related to. The norms of good chess strategy apply only to one who wants to play well and win. On the other hand, Kant's categorical imperative always applies to every rational being, no matter what he may want or intend. Because a rational being cannot possibly will it to be a universal law that one may lie to evade difficulty, argues Kant, then every rational being in every empirical situation is categorically commanded not to misrepresent the truth. For Kant, moral goodness consists precisely in doing one's duty as reason categorically commands. This approach is indeed tempting if, like Kant, we wish to distinguish the realm of moral values and norms from other realms. Before doing so, however, we must consider more closely the details of the moral life, because categorical duty is not a sufficiently broad category to embrace the whole of the moral life as we actually live it.

The notorious problem with categorical duties is that they are narrowly defined and limited in scope. The most specific moral norms are negative: "You shall not kill," "You shall not commit adultery," and so on. Kant is able to forbid fraudulent promising and suicide, but when he considers charity to the destitute or attending to the development of one's own tal-

[8] In Jane Austen's novel *Pride and Prejudice.*

[9] *Grundlegung zur Metaphysik der Sitten,* 414ff.

ents, he can regard these as only imperfect duties.[10] He lacks the flexibility of an Aristotle, who can find appropriate guidance for positive norms in the mean, that is, in what the reasonable, virtuous person would do.[11] Similarly, because the manualist tradition in Catholic moral theology focused so heavily on moral obligations, expressed in commands (or imperatives), it lacked the capacity to address adequately the richness of the life of love, friendship, and the positive obligations one freely undertakes in life.[12] When pressed by the Pharisees, Christ stated that the first commandment is to love (Mk 12:30–33). The problem is that such commands do not prescribe very many specific behaviors. We identify good parents not by their adherence to rules of parenting but by the devoted care that they give their children. There is no recipe or instruction manual the following of which will make one a good parent. Parents should play with their children but not become their playmates; they must be firm but not harsh. But the limits defining overfamiliarity or firmness may vary in different persons and even in different situations. Similarly, there is no set of activities that adequately encompasses love of God and neighbor, as Christ commanded. If duty (or obligation) is constitutive of morality, in what sense can it be so?

Analogous Norms

When one asks, "What ought I truly to do?" implicit in this question is the premise that some course of action is superior to others, that among the alternatives one can be chosen as best. The question anticipates the possibility of a true answer. That is to say, the question presupposes that one is capable of a rational understanding of the truth, not only of the situation at hand but also of the courses of action available to address it. Because an act is, as it were, intelligence in motion, because the act entails an application of subjectivity to efficacy, the acting person seeks the truth about what he is engaged in. In ordinary human experience this claim is unexceptionable. Every workman, every athlete, every artist, and every

[10] Ibid., 421, 423–24.

[11] *Nicomachean Ethics* 2.6, 1006b36ff.

[12] Pinckaers, *Sources of Christian Ethics*, 14–17, and Servais Pinckaers, O.P., *Morality: The Catholic View*, trans. Michael Sherwin, O.P. (South Bend, IN: St. Augustine's Press, 2003), 37–41. See also Kaczyński, *Verità sul bene nella morale*, 24–25, 28.

parent, when confronted with a challenge to his activity, asks, "But will it work? Will this achieve what we need?" When we consider that every act is directed toward the realization of some good, some end, this question reveals already that to act is to be concerned for the truth about the good.

The second question, "Why ought I to do what I ought to do?" deepens the inquiry into the truth about the good. On one level, of course, the question seeks a deeper understanding of the truth. "You should seize the open file with your rook, because it gives you an avenue of attack." "You should take calcium tablets, because they will forestall the onset of osteoporosis in your old age." Beyond this, however, the question *why* seeks the higher values. This is the perspective Kant has in mind when he distinguishes between acts done in accordance with duty and those done *for the sake of* duty. The shopkeeper who may deal honestly with his customers as a matter of good business practice is not on that account moral.[13] He merely exercises prudent business sense. The question of values comes visibly into play when the question *why* cannot be answered with more information or with a better scientific understanding. It may well be that the action one *ought to* take is contrary to the interests that the acting person has in mind. Ruy Lopez's confrere evidently considered that one's standing before the Judge of the living and the dead was of greater moment than victory in a game. And indeed, this is a challenge not only for the sixteenth-century priest, since each of us experiences the demand to put our acts into the perspective of the goals governing the whole of life. At issue with a particular act is not simply the immediate disposition of things but the unfolding of one's life and the lives of those with whom one lives. When the person acts, he acts for a good. But this good does not stand alone. It is related to other goods. The task of vertical integration is that of integrating one's responses to the various values proposed to one for action. As we shall see, such integration requires some knowledge of the supreme good that governs all lesser or subordinate goods.

Wojtyła's Ethical Interlocutors

To address the question of the foundations of ethics, Karol Wojtyła turned his attention to three principal interlocutors, whom we examine in turn.

---

[13] Kant, *Grundlegung zur Metaphysik der Sitten,* 397.

These were (1) Immanuel Kant and the ethics of duty; (2) Jeremy Bentham and the utilitarian school; and (3) Max Scheler and ethical emotivism. As he considers these, Wojtyła's principal concern, especially with the first two, is not so much to render a thoroughgoing critique as to bring out the underlying principles that define each position and then to compare and contrast them with those that he finds more adequate and appropriate to a Christian moral theory. Therefore, in his critique of Scheler, we may expect also to find the tools to critique G. E. Moore, or in his analysis of the utilitarians the principles for criticizing contemporary consequentialism and proportionalism in moral theology.

Kant

Value of Kant's System

In many respects Kant offers a compelling, albeit thoroughly unrealistic, ethical system. If *duty* is an essential ethical concept, Kant is the philosopher of duty. To be morally good is to do one's duty for the sake of duty. This doing of duty is *disinterested.* Whether the agent benefits from his action or not—indeed, whether or not *anyone* benefits from the action—has no bearing on its morality, provided it was done for the sake of duty. In itself this is admirable. Surely the moral person is the one who does what is right simply because it is right. Furthermore, Kant leaves ethical room for the failure of one whose "heart is in the right place." For an act to be moral, it is not necessary that the effort succeed but only that it be done for the right reason. Indeed, even if one's acts should result in abject failure, making even worse the situation they were meant to address, they can still be morally praiseworthy if done for duty's sake.

We may remark here that one of the central concepts of John Paul II's encyclical *Veritatis Splendor*, the concept that has triggered the most discussion and debate, is that of *intrinsically evil* acts, which may never be licitly performed but are always wrong. This notion of an intrinsically evil act resonates closely with Kant's concept of *duty.* If morality truly imposes obligations to refrain from specific forms of behavior, then one has a duty to avoid performing intrinsically evil acts. Kant's distinction between hypothetical and categorical imperatives clarifies and develops another important aspect of morality. As we have indicated, one can always deny the import of a norm by denying the end to which the norm is directed. If one does not want to play at Wimbledon, then one need not practice one's backhand. If morality is in any meaningful sense to be disinterested, if it is to involve anything resembling a law, then it must surely include exceptionless, universal norms. Kant himself argues that any course of action, however noble or difficult, directed toward and by one's own self-interest can have no moral value.[14] If a person acts on the basis of a hypothetical norm, then he is not so much being morally good as prudent or even shrewd.

Although Karol Wojtyła does not embrace Kant's rationalist ethics based on the categorical imperative, he is clearly indebted to Kant for his "personalistic norm": "This norm, in its negative aspect, states that the person is the kind of good which does not admit of use and cannot be treated as an object of use and as such the means to an end. In its positive form the personalistic norm confirms this: that the person is a good towards which the only proper and adequate attitude is love.[15]

This personalistic norm clearly parallels Kant's "practical imperative," which he derives from his categorical imperative and which reads: "Act in such a way that you treat humanity, whether in your own person or in the person of another, always at the same time as an end and never simply as a means."[16] Now, there are significant differences between these two principles, differences to which we shall attend when we consider the personalistic norm in greater depth. Here we simply observe that the Kantian system gives rise to a demand that the human person be respected in a distinctive way, as a categorical good that must always be respected. Furthermore, from his moral principles, Kant is able to deduce that the human person is endowed with three important characteristics: *dignity*,[17] *freedom*,[18] and *autonomy*,[19] characteristics that Karol Wojtyła will use in and adapt to his own development of ethics.

Finally, though it is little noticed, Kant appreciates the beauty of the moral life. Indeed, it is the aesthetic character of the good will that should motivate one to become moral oneself. A good will is like a jewel that only

---

[14] Immanuel Kant, *Kritik der praktischen Vernunft*, in *Immanuel Kants Werke*, vol. 5 (Berlin: Bruno Cassirer, 1922), Teil 1, Buch 1, Hauptstück 1, §8, Lehrsatz 4.

[15] *Love and Responsibility*, 41.

[16] Kant, *Grounding for the Metaphysics of Morals*, 429.

[17] *Grundlegung zur Metaphysik der Sitten*, 434ff.

[18] Ibid., dritter Abschnitt.

[19] Ibid., 440.

a connoisseur (*Kenner*) of good wills can appreciate fully.[20] It is this fundamentally aesthetic experience of reverence for law that motivates one toward one's duty.

The Obvious Flaws. Kant's ethical system is clearly unworkable. The surest sign of this is that people do not even try to use it to direct their lives. Mothers insist their children not eat too much candy so that they will develop the virtue of temperance. Aristotle would approve. The office worker contributes toward the funeral bouquet of a co-worker's spouse because it will do some good. Mill would approve. But it simply does not happen that anyone not bent on proving a Kantian point will reflect on a proposed action, formulate a maxim, and then test that maxim for rational universality in order to apply the categorical imperative. It is not hard to see why this is so. Kant's ethical system is far too cerebral. For a person to perform a moral act, he must reflect explicitly on the maxim involved and then choose the act for the sake of duty. The good act done simply from habit has no moral worth. "I *will* be true to the wife, I'll concentrate more on my work"[21] are the words not of one established in virtue but of one too prone to infidelity. The point is, of course, that for husbands to be faithful to their wives, patriots loyal to their countries, believers devoted to God, and parents careful of their children, constant reflection on one's duties—accompanied by the reminder to self that these are duties—will tend to hinder the acts and expressions that should flow from virtue or authentically moral disposition. In real life, no one (with the possible exception of an occasional obstinate philosopher) even tries to live a Kantian moral life.

The Critique of Kant

Although Karol Wojtyła finds much that is of value and useful in Kant's thought, he rejects its foundations and much of its structure, and what he does retain, he retains in a significantly different form. The fundamental problem Wojtyła identifies is that Kant effectively cuts off moral obligation from the good. Kant's treatment of *good* in his ethical writings is curious in comparison with Aristotle's. For the Stagirite, good is an object of

---

[20] Ibid., 394.

[21] W. H. Auden, "September 1, 1939," in *The Major Poets: English and American*, ed. Charles M. Coffin (New York: Harcourt, Brace, and World, 1954), 520.

desire and striving.[22] In his *Grundlegung zur Metaphysik der Sitten*, however, Kant states at the outset that we cannot even think of anything good without qualification except a good will.[23] The good will is not an object of desire. It is not useful for attaining any further end; indeed, were one to regard it so, he would show that he did not understand what "good will" even means. Therefore, from the very start it is clear that for Kant, to be good is to be worthy of admiration and imitation, but good is not for possession or attainment. The objective of the Kantian moral person, if we may speak in this manner, is to become good, to have a good will.

At the very start of this study we noted that for John Paul II the highest good, in which all other goods are rooted and find their meaning, is God himself. In this he agrees with Thomas Aquinas, for whom God is the origin and end of all things,[24] the contemplation of whom is perfect human happiness.[25] But it also clearly agrees with Aristotle's view that the First Cause is, as it were, the ultimate object of desire, the love for which moves the Movers of the heavens[26] and whose contemplative activity is the ideal that human contemplation seeks to approximate.[27] Kant sees the goodness of God quite differently. For him, God is neither the principle of all goodness nor an ultimate good to attain. Consistent with the analysis in his *Critique of Pure Reason*, Kant cannot acknowledge that the actual existence of God can be significant to his goodness, at least so far as we human beings are concerned. God's moral significance can lie only in his ideal character. God, the Ideal of pure reason, is also a postulate of practical reason.[28] The challenge to the human being is to be morally good, to have a good will, a will motivated not by sensuality or desire for happiness (which would necessarily yield only hypothetical obligations) but by respect for law itself. Human reason, however, seeks to unite that highest good, morality, with the highest good of human existence in the empirical world, happiness. These two cannot be brought into a real unity, because perfect happiness is

---

22 Aristotle, *Nicomachean Ethics* 1.1.

23 *Grundlegung zur Metaphysik der Sitten*, 393.

24 *ST* I, q. 2 prologue.

25 *ST* I–II, q. 3, a. 8.

26 *Metaphysics* 12.7, 1072b1–4.

27 *Nicomachean Ethics* 10.8, 1178b22.

28 Kant, *Kritik der praktischen Vernunft*, Teil 1, Buch 2, Hauptstück 2, §5, 134.

and can only be an ideal. They can be ideally united in God, Kant acknowledges, but in a God whose real existence cannot be affirmed.

> Therefore the highest good in the world is possible only insofar as one accepts a highest Cause of nature, whose causality has a moral attitude. . . . Therefore the highest good of nature, insofar as it must be presupposed to be the highest good, is a being that through its understanding and will is the cause (consequently the author) of nature, i.e., God. Consequently, the postulate of the highest derived good (the best world) is at the same time the postulate of a *highest* original good, namely, the existence of God.[29]

Within the phenomenal realm, the natural order ruled by the causal laws known to science, there can be no highest good. Nor can pure reason attain to a true knowledge of the Highest Good or Supreme Being. The laws of morality, however, demand an ideal of moral perfection, to which, indeed, every rational being—Kant, his reader, God—is called in virtue of being rational. The human being is challenged, therefore, to act according to a standard of moral perfection that can be described as holiness in an infinite being. It is natural, normal, and inevitable for the human being to desire happiness, and what the moral law obliges, in effect, is that he act so as to be worthy of happiness.[30] How does one reconcile the moral demand with the apparent absence of reward? If we read Kant too analytically, we cannot make sense of this. However, Kant was, in his own way, a visionary. The natural world (the phenomenal realm), properly understood—which is to say, scientifically understood—is a world of perfect order, structured by precise, invariant laws, which admit of no exceptions but which in their simplicity establish a complex, harmonious order. Do not the motions of the moon, planets, and stars fall under the governance of Isaac Newton's elegant formulae? If we imagine the Mind that established this, it is that of a Giver of elegant law. This is the model for the human agent, who is also—like the mind of the First Cause—a lawgiver. The ordinary Prussian shopkeeper who chooses to charge honest prices because duty so requires may not enjoy the profits of his less honest rivals, but he will have the satisfaction of knowing that his good will brings him close to the holiness of the Author of the natural order. Even if he can have no

[29] Ibid., 136.

[30] Kant, *Grundlegung zur Metaphysik der Sitten*, 393.

assurance that such an Author exists or that his acts according to his good will ever accomplished anything worthwhile, he knows that he at least has reflected the divine image of the rational Ideal.

His concern to preserve the concept of duty notwithstanding, Kant completely undermines the truth about the good. According to Kant's premises there can be no truth about the good, because the intelligence that knows truth is not engaged efficaciously with the world through the will. When the coldhearted but dutiful benefactor[31] gives a coin to the little match girl, not only must he ignore his own inclinations, but strictly speaking, he need not even care whether the donation was beneficial. The point is to do the required act according to the good will, not to bring about the good effect. Wojtyła insists, of course, that because the act is efficacious, it is by its very nature related to a value that the agent intends. Within the context of Kant's philosophy, however, the agent is trapped within his own subjectivity. Because the phenomenal realm is completely governed by necessary laws, the realm of freedom must be restricted to the moral. So Kant defends freedom, but in doing so he renders it ineffectual. The human person can indeed act freely, so long as he considers his act from the moral standpoint. Once he views it, however, from the objective standpoint, the freedom disappears. Thus Kant creates a curious kind of moral solipsism by which the agent must be concerned only with the state of his own will and not with the achievement of good results. To put it another way, Kant would have the person develop a good will but renders it impossible for him to be a good human being. Kant saves the notion of obligation but in doing so renders it entirely subjective. One is obliged only to oneself as a rational being.

Utilitarianism

It is fair to say that John Paul II has never had any use for utilitarianism. He betrays sympathy for Kant's project and creatively uses many of Scheler's insights, but throughout his career his attitude toward utilitarianism has been consistently negative. In some respects this can be surprising. Certainly, utilitarianism acknowledges and respects the efficacy of the human act oriented toward the good. Indeed, efficacy is the whole point. Mill wrote: "He who saves a fellow creature from drowning does what is morally right, whether his motive be duty, or the hope of being paid for

[31] See ibid., 398.

his trouble."[32] Even if Kant (at whom this statement was almost certainly aimed) should dismiss the moral value of opportunistic rescuing, the one rescued will be grateful and the rest of us will admire the rescuer's courage and initiative. Indeed, we admire the courage, dedication, and skill of firefighters, surgeons, mountain rescue teams, and soldiers, even if they are paid for what they do. Furthermore, the popular understanding of morality is that one should do good, "make the world a better place." And yet, Karol Wojtyła rejects the philosophy that advocates just this.

In his critique, Wojtyła considers utilitarianism from three perspectives: with regard to its subjectivism, the good it pursues, and its effect on moral norms.

Subjectivism

That subjective feelings lie at the root of utilitarianism is its critical flaw. Despite its appearance of objectivity—the utilitarian seeks what is objectively useful—utilitarianism is founded on feeling. Writes Mill:

> Those who know anything about the matter are aware that every writer, from Epicurus to Bentham, who maintained the theory of utility, meant by it, not something to be distinguished from pleasure, but pleasure itself, together with exemption from pain. . . . The creed which accepts as the foundation of morals Utility or the Greatest Happiness Principle holds that actions are right in proportion as they tend to promote happiness, wrong as they tend to produce the reverse of happiness. By happiness is intended pleasure, and the absence of pain; by unhappiness, pain, and the privation of pleasure.[33]

Mill takes care, of course, to define "pleasure" broadly so as not to restrict it to sense pleasures only. Further, he insists that the happiness at stake cannot be that of the individual agent alone but must be that of all concerned.[34] Nevertheless, the ultimate sanction of utilitarianism is a *feeling*, "the conscientious feelings of mankind."[35] And for Mill the proof of the principle of utility is that happiness, as he understands it, is what everyone finds desirable and that everything else is desired for the sake of happiness.[36]

---

32 Mill, *Utilitarianism*, chap. 2, 18.

33 Ibid., 6.

34 Ibid., 17.

35 Ibid., 29.

36 Ibid., chap. 4, 35–41.

It is instructive to look at the logical structure of J. S. Mill's argument in *Utilitarianism.* His strategy is to present his principle of utility or greatest happiness and then to defend it from all attacks. Indeed, Mill effectively holds that it is the sort of principle that needs only to be understood to be accepted. It suffices to prove the principle that we all want to feel happiness.[37] The bulk of his work is devoted, then, to showing how its critics misunderstand, misrepresent, or confuse the principle. Unlike Aristotle, he does not try to determine the nature of human happiness from an examination of human nature or to determine how the various senses of happiness may be reconciled. Mill's approach is deliberately nontheoretical. Not only does he wish to avoid Kant's subtleties, but following Bentham's example, he wants to avoid any metaphysical commitments. Mill assumes an understanding of human nature, of course, insofar as he implicitly accepts one manner of life as being superior to others. In particular, utilitarianism appears to be an ideal political approach for the modern liberal industrial society. The greatest happiness principle is a useful guide to the eighteenth- or nineteenth-century parliamentarian. What utilitarianism does not—and indeed cannot—do is to show why this way of life is superior, why its pleasures are superior and most worth pursuing. To be sure, Mill is able to argue that one who has experienced the pleasures of the mind can vouch for their superiority; "better to be Socrates dissatisfied than a fool satisfied."[38] As history has already shown, this response is not, in the final analysis, satisfying. We have achieved Mill's dreams of a prosperous, educated, liberal society, and nonetheless we see widespread signs of dissatisfaction and anomie.

The Good of Utilitarianism

It does not suffice to attend to what we *feel* if we do not attend to what we *are.* With feelings at the foundation, there can be no truth about the good, only best guesses, and these may not prove true for everyone. According to the criterion of utility, there is and can be no sense in which a person can be judged good or bad. That is, there is no sense in which the person can strive to be a good person. To be sure, one can certainly strive to realize one's own happiness; one can also strive to be known or recognized as

---

[37] Ibid., 35–36.

[38] Ibid., 10.

good and to do good things. However, there is no meaningful sense in which one can be said to have morally perfected or improved oneself, except perhaps in the weak sense of having shown oneself to be a useful member of society. To the utilitarian, virtue is certainly a good thing, but not because it perfects oneself or one's character. The goodness of virtue consists in the fact that virtuous people tend to be happy and to make life happier for those around them.[39] "Virtue, according to the utilitarian doctrine, is not naturally and originally part of the end, but it is capable of becoming so; and in those who live it disinterestedly it has become so, and is desired and cherished, not as a means to happiness, but as a part of their happiness."[40] The end to be attained is, in the final analysis, not a condition of one's own character but a state of well-being. Properly speaking—according to Mill—prudence and temperance are worthwhile because they promote happiness. If the very possession of these virtues should of itself make the possessor happier, this is only so much the better.

Utilitarianism is a moral theory for good times in a relatively prosperous, advanced society. It does not serve so well for times of crisis or grave suffering. In his *Gulag Archipelago*, Aleksandr Solzhenitsyn shows that the principle "survive at any price" leads to moral degradation.[41] A person may well ameliorate his own situation and even that of those immediately around him by participating in the lies governing the system. In the days of the Communist government's suppression of the Solidarity union and martial law, many Polish parents faced a serious dilemma. Caring for their hungry children, were they to continue with strikes, risking even imprisonment, or were they to accept the regime's strictures and prosper? Father Józef Tischner describes their dilemma: "In recent months, a huge number of Polish families have faced a situation in which they had to decide what heritage should be passed on to their children. . . . These decisions have not come easy. They have had to be made by young people, often without their own place to live, with small children to provide for—people just trying to get by in life."[42]

---

[39] Ibid., 36–37.

[40] Ibid., 37.

[41] Aleksandr Solzhenitsyn, *The Gulag Archipelago, 1918–1956: An Experiment in Literary Investigation*, trans. Thomas P. Whitney, vol. 2 (New York: Harper and Row, 1975), pt. 4, chaps. 1–2, especially 603–10.

[42] Józef Tischner, *The Spirit of Solidarity*, trans. Marek B. Zaleski and Benjamin Fiore, S.J. (San Francisco: Harper and Row, 1984), 76.

In a recognizably utilitarian sense, one can balance the happiness of one's own family against that of the nation as a whole ("If my children can eat well and be warm, then to a marginal extent the social revolution will be slowed"). Tischner's point, however, goes deeper. The nonstriking worker lessens himself by giving in to the regime. He may gain happiness (in the sense that Bentham and Mill understand the term), but he does so at the cost of his own moral maturity. For John Paul II, this moral perfectibility is of great moment, because his end of the person is not simply a state of relative happiness but sanctity. Therefore, in the final chapter of *Veritatis Splendor*, the encyclical on ethical reasoning and moral theology, John Paul II writes of martyrdom as "an affirmation of the inviolability of the moral order."[43] Here we begin to touch on two difficult and controverted ethical issues of which utilitarianism is hard pressed to make sense.

Martyrdom and Moral Demands. First is the moral status of martyrdom. Granted that martyrdom is an ideal of some sort—we do admire and celebrate martyrs—can martyrdom be normative? John Paul II writes:

> In the Old Testament we already find admirable witnesses of fidelity to the holy law of God even to the point of a voluntary acceptance of death. A prime example is the story of Susanna: in reply to the two unjust judges who threatened to have her condemned to death if she refused to yield to their sinful passion, she says: "I am hemmed in on every side. For if I do this thing, it is death for me; and if I do not, I shall not escape your hands. I choose not to do it and to fall into your hands, rather than to sin in the sight of the Lord!" (Dan 13:22–23). Susanna, preferring to "fall innocent" into the hands of the judges, bears witness not only to her faith and trust in God but also to her obedience to the truth and to the absoluteness of the moral order. By her readiness to die a martyr, she proclaims that it is not right to do what God's law qualifies as evil in order to draw some good from it.[44]

Responding to John Paul II's use of this biblical story, Jean Porter takes strong exception to the moral demand presented:

> My initial reaction to this passage was one of shock and dismay. I could not see any real difference between Susanna's case, and the situation of a woman

[43] *Veritatis Splendor*, 92.

[44] Ibid., 91; the story of Susanna is at Daniel 13.

> who is forced at gunpoint, in her own bedroom, to submit to an act of sexual intercourse. . . . It does seem clear that Susanna was subject to coercion. Had she submitted to an unwanted act of intercourse (as countless women, under various kinds of threats, have submitted), she would have done so to preserve her safety and probably her life. Is it clear that *she* would have been guilty of a sexual sin under those circumstances?[45]

John Paul II calls Susanna a witness "to the truth about the good and to the God of Israel."[46] Had she not refused the two elders, she would not have borne such witness. In her response, Porter raises the issue of coercion and sin. If a person does something ordinarily wrong under the threat of death, can she be blamed? Is she guilty of sin? As Porter points out, women of our own time are subjected to lethal threats to compel them to submit to rape.

As we reflect on this dispute, we find ourselves entering a veritable thicket of examples, analyses, and casuistry. Two important points stand out. The first has to do with the nature of the moral act (an issue to which we shall return in greater depth later in this study). What was demanded of Susanna was a positive cooperation with the act of intercourse. The elders had not overpowered her, although it is likely that they could have. In a more recent case, there is reason to believe that even as he wielded his knife, Alessandro Serenelli expected St. Maria Goretti, who was canonized a martyr precisely because she refused him, to cooperate with his desire for sexual relations with her.[47] Clearly in the case of Susanna and arguably in that of Maria Goretti, we have a rape driven not by violent contempt[48] but by the lustful fantasies of the men involved, motivated by the conceit that once the woman has tasted the pleasure she will also enjoy it, that really she wants him or at least can come to want him. If nothing else, he wants her feigned consent.

This is a different case from that of the woman surprised in her bedroom by an intruder or seized in a darkened parking lot at night and then

45 Jean Porter, "Moral Reasoning, Authority, and Community in *Veritatis Splendor*," *Annual of the Society of Christian Ethics* 15, no. 1 (1995): 210–11.

46 *Veritatis Splendor*, 91.

47 See Kathleen Z. Young, "The Imperishable Virginity of Saint Maria Goretti," in "Violence against Women," special issue, *Gender and Society* 3, no. 4 (December 1989): 476, and the sources on Serenelli's motivations and acts.

48 As is apparently the case with many rapes committed by strangers.

overpowered. In such cases, she will be subjected to forcibly attempted intercourse no matter what she does. She can resist, and in some cases her doing so will in fact cause the assailant to call off his attack. It can also happen, however, that her resistance will only enrage the rapist further and lead to further injury and even death. A woman in this situation has quite a different decision to make than did Susanna. She has quickly to make a prudential decision concerning the best way to defend and protect herself. If she submits to the rape, it is not to cooperate. Rather, she has determined that further physical resistance will lead only to more severe injury or death. What she chooses to do, therefore, is to cease futile resistance, an act that cannot be construed as cooperating with her assailant. One is not obliged to fight to the death to protect every good. Therefore the case of the woman raped at gunpoint is in an important respect different, as, indeed, Porter seems to acknowledge.[49]

This distinction of acts—differentiating reluctant cooperation under threat from ceasing futile resistance—does not, however, address Jean Porter's principal concern, which is expressed in the final sentences of the text quoted above: "Had she [Susanna] submitted to an unwanted act of intercourse (as countless women, under various kinds of threats, have submitted), she would have done so to preserve her safety and probably her life. Is it clear that *she* would have been guilty of a sexual sin under those circumstances?" John Paul II does not directly address the question of her guilt in his analysis of martyrdom, or specifically in the case of Susanna.[50] He does, however, affirm that the act in question—a married woman having sexual relations with two men not her husband—falls under "those moral norms which prohibit without exception actions which are intrinsically evil."[51] Although the circumstances are such that Susanna's only hope (apparently) to save her life is to yield to the elders, the act by which she would accomplish this is an act of adultery. That is, to save her life she must voluntarily have intercourse with the elders according to their demands. Should we raise the question of subjective responsibility and personal guilt, we have grounds to argue that her own sin in this affair is

[49] Porter, "Moral Reasoning," 210.

[50] The Scriptural text, however, does impute sin to the proposed act: "But I prefer to fall innocent into your power than to sin in the eyes of the Lord" (Dan 13:23 *The Jerusalem Bible*).

[51] *Veritatis Splendor*, 90.

diminished or even eliminated. (Susanna had time to reflect, but the woman at gunpoint may have only seconds to respond. Furthermore, the setting in which she finds herself may well heighten her fear well beyond Susanna's.) Nevertheless, John Paul II's argument in *Veritatis Splendor*, nos. 90–94, does affirm that moral norms apply, even where respecting their implications can cost a person his life. John Paul would expect the rape victim not to consent to or cooperate with her assailant's act, even though she is not obliged to continue a futile resistance. To be clear, we can and must distinguish between the act of consent to sexual intercourse and that of deciding to forego futile and dangerous resistance.

Developing a similar point, John O'Keefe objects that *Veritatis Splendor* is unrealistically demanding on ordinary Christians and leaves "only room for heroes."[52] His argument continues: "[W]hat kind of church do we want? Do we want a church of perfect heroes, or do we want a church with a little more room for mediocrity?"[53] Going beyond Porter's objection that John Paul II requires the woman threatened with death not to comply with her assailant, O'Keefe argues that one cannot reasonably expect ordinary people in ordinary circumstances always to rise to the state of moral perfection, to respond in the way that the rich young man (of Mt 19:16–22) could *not* bring himself to respond. In a later section of this work we will look in greater depth at the question of exceptionless moral prohibitions. Here our focus is on the goods at stake in human decisions and actions. In his discussion of Susanna (and immediately thereafter, John the Baptist),[54] John Paul II's focus is not on determining the conditions for committing sin, much less those of mortal sin. (Let us recall his remarks on the variations in subjective guilt that might attach to a woman who procures an abortion.)[55] In particular, we cannot read the story of Susanna or John Paul II's interpretation of it as a key for judging women who have fallen prey to vicious men.[56] What he is saying is that one

52 John J. O'Keefe, "No Place for Failure? Augustinian Reflections on *Veritatis Splendor*," in Allsopp and O'Keefe, Veritatis Splendor: *American Responses*, 22.

53 Ibid., 33.

54 John Paul II, *Veritatis Splendor*, 91.

55 *Evangelium Vitae*, 58–59, 101.

56 Although there is a suggestion of this in the biblical story, as the young Daniel takes a swipe at the lesser virtue of the women of Israel vis-à-vis those of Judah (Dan 13:57).

should form one's acts according to norms based on the authentic highest good and not on lesser good. And important as they are to us, our lives and health are not those highest goods. Even if—*pace* O'Keefe—many or most of us fail to realize that good in our actions, and even if the unexpected and horrifying overtake us, our task remains that of directing our acts to a higher good than life itself.

Duty Toward Others. A second moral issue problematic to utilitarianism concerns that of our responsibility to others. Utilitarian morality requires that one strive to maximize the happiness of all concerned.[57] This need not be a state of perfect happiness; utilitarians pride themselves on being realistic. To attain this state of happiness may require some compromise of principle, and the alternative to the compromise may be significant inconvenience or even suffering. The challenge, therefore, is to justify maintaining one's own purity of conscience at the cost of others' happiness, or as one questioner put it to a physician who had spoken against abortion, "How can you justify denying a woman something she needs just so that you can sleep nights?"[58] Is it not selfish to deny another person or group some genuine good simply in order to measure up to one's own moral standard? One of the strengths of utilitarianism is that its appeal to happiness, understood as reasonable pleasure and the absence of pain, is to goods that are in fact universally accepted. This is precisely Mill's point.[59] To insist on adhering to one's own conception of a higher good that trumps those goods that utilitarians can agree upon can constitute an infringement on their participation in the goods as they see them. From a utilitarian viewpoint, moral perfectionism is unreasonable and sometimes unjustifiably selfish.[60] Indeed, precisely this conflict between the conscience claims of the few and the generally acceptable desires of the many has become an important issue of public policy. Is it appropriate for medical providers, on the grounds of personal conscience,

---

57 Mill, *Utilitarianism*, 17.

58 The event was a panel discussion at the University of Notre Dame shortly after the *Roe v. Wade* decision in 1973. Unfortunately, I do not have the date or the names of those participating.

59 *Utilitarianism*, chap. 4, "Of What Sort of Proof the Principle of Utility Is Susceptible," especially 35–36.

60 See Michael Waldstein's discussion of the "selfishness" of morality in his article "Dietrich von Hildebrand and St. Thomas Aquinas on Goodness and Happiness," *Nova et Vetera*, English ed., 1, no. 2 (2003): 448–49.

to refuse to provide medical services that the society as a whole recognizes as acceptable and important?[61]

At the heart of the issue is precisely the good for which we act. Utilitarianism conceives this to be a subjective good, the sense of happiness defined by the enjoyment of pleasure and the absence of pain. There are two important implications of good in this sense. First of all, although Bentham and Mill were both careful to develop the social implications of the greatest happiness principle, because happiness is ultimately a subjective condition, what this happiness consists in can vary from individual to individual. In many respects the free market is ideally suited for meeting the tastes of different individuals; jazz, pop, and classical music lovers all have their radio stations. However, the theory runs into difficulty when individuals and groups find pleasure in things that the majority finds aberrant. For example, although in American and most Western societies the majority of citizens disapprove of pornography, the utilitarian underpinnings of their social ethics inhibit social or legal sanctions against it, except in the case of child pornography, where the offense consists in the abuse of the children who are used. If others are not harmed and a person finds satisfaction in a particular activity (such as viewing pornography), then utilitarianism is hard-pressed to object to it. Indeed, Mill's own principle of personal autonomy forbids interference with the autonomous free choices of other individuals concerning their own enjoyments.[62]

We have a conflict, if not a contradiction. Under the premises of utilitarianism, each person is to be autonomous, free to pursue his own good as he sees fit, so long as he does not interfere with others. Furthermore, the greatest happiness principle requires each individual to be concerned not only with his own happiness but (to a reasonable extent) with that of his neighbors. If this precludes the moral condemnation of experiences that the minority enjoy, it may also preclude conscientious refusal to contribute to the general happiness according to the majority's standards. Precisely here arises a conflict. If the "sole end for which mankind are warranted, individually or collectively, in interfering with the liberty of action of any of their

---

[61] Hillary Rodham Clinton and Cecile Richards, "Blocking Care for Women," *New York Times*, September 19, 2008.

[62] J. S. Mill, *On Liberty* (Indianapolis: Hackett Publishing Company, 1978), 9, 12, 60–61.

number is self-protection,"[63] then what warrant has the social majority for interfering with an individual's liberty of conscience? The only warrant acceptable to utilitarian principles can be the greatest happiness principle, that so far as his personal happiness is concerned the individual is indeed free, but that this happiness (or pleasure) of a clear conscience cannot interfere with the serious needs of his neighbors. Indeed, this is precisely the principle to which Clinton and Richards appeal in the aforementioned article. Let us take note, however, of the implications of this for conscience. If the conscientious objector is himself a utilitarian, then the objection does indeed carry weight, because his conscientious conviction can itself be no more than a personal preference, a condition that gives him personal satisfaction. (One is reminded here of the bumper sticker "If you're against abortion, don't have one.") If, however, the conscientious objection is not founded on utilitarian grounds, then the objector is not compelled by this argument. His obligation is to some other good, one not recognized by the utilitarian norm. As such, his conscientious objection constitutes a rejection of utilitarianism as inadequate to address the moral good at the foundation of his objection. Utilitarianism can address and consider utilitarian objections to a specific course of action, but it must ultimately reject any other moral basis for decision. This means that the utilitarian cannot recognize the moral autonomy, and hence the liberty, of one who embraces nonutilitarian principles. At stake is the status of the good. The conscientious objector opposes the demands upon him precisely because some nonnegotiable good is at stake. But utilitarianism, precisely because it is founded on subjectivity, can ultimately recognize no nonnegotiable goods.

The Norms of Utilitarianism

Moral norms provide the basis for the response to the questions posed at the beginning of this chapter: "What ought I to do?" and "Why ought I to do it?" The fundamental norm of utilitarianism follows from the greatest happiness principle: "[A]ctions are right in proportion as they tend to promote happiness, wrong as they tend to produce the reverse of happiness."[64] Although at first glance this seems to provide a workable moral norm, problems quickly develop as we attempt to specify it more closely *as a norm.* First,

---

[63] Mill, *Liberty*, 9.

[64] Mill, *Utilitarianism*, 7.

one may ask what it means to "maximize happiness." It is clear enough if we compare the child's experience of simply eating cake with that of a party with cake, decorations, and games. An expressway may promote the happiness of many more people than will a new marina for the few who can afford large boats. Nevertheless, beyond such simple cases happiness is not something readily quantifiable, however much we may speak of being more or less happy, nor is there a calculus by which one can balance happinesses. Is it better to choose one moment of blissful ecstasy, even if it be followed by ten years of tedium? (We may note that it is quite common to get into an unsatisfying marriage simply because of the promised bliss of the honeymoon or the fulfillment of a dream for a perfect wedding.) Or is a comfortable life punctuated by periodic amusements and pleasures to be preferred? (But is the bourgeois middle-class life truly happy with no great challenges to courage and personal heroism?) A further problem with treating the greatest happiness principle as a norm is the difficulty of balancing the disparate expectations of happiness among different persons. Is it acceptable to sacrifice the happiness of very few, if their suffering will make possible the happiness of multitudes for generations to come? Or is the obligation to ensure that *everyone* experiences some minimum level of happiness? What is the extent of the norm's application? Mill applies his principle primarily to one's more or less immediate circle and to the well-governed state. Peter Singer, on the other hand, insists that one's concern for the happiness of others must be global in scope.[65] In any case, it is hard to see how the greatest happiness principle could require that an individual significantly sacrifice his own happiness for that of another. Indeed, in his discussion of disabled infants, Peter Singer proposes that parents should not be required to care for them unless it is their own choice to do so, because to care for a disabled child will decrease their own happiness.[66] Insofar as a norm is a principle of obligation or duty, the greatest happiness principle provides no norms, only suggestions.

The Utilitarian Good

Karol Wojtyła's analysis of utilitarianism turns on Thomas Aquinas's analogical uses of the term "good." Wojtyła writes, "The most important distinction, however, is that among the three senses of good: *bonum*

[65] *Practical Ethics*, 318–22.
[66] Ibid., 181–91.

honestum—utile—delectibile (righteous,[67] useful, and pleasant)."[68] The *bonum honestum* is the fitting, the appropriate, good for a human being, whereas the *bonum utile* is the good that is useful for attaining the *bonum honestum.* Therefore "good" (*bonum*) is an analogical term whose primary analogate is the fitting good (*bonum honestum*). Those goods that serve to realize the fitting good are called useful because they bring about the fitting good, regardless of whether they are pleasant or in any other way desirable. Such goods include bitter medicine and expensive antivirus software. Similarly, the attainment of any good or value whatever is accompanied by relief and satisfaction, which constitutes pleasure or delight, and therefore pleasure is desirable not only in itself (as Mill notes) but also as a manifestation of having attained some good. Therefore delightful and useful goods are good insofar as they are related either antecedently or consequently to the fitting good. Wojtyła's fundamental criticism of utilitarianism is that by basing its ethics on the pleasant and the useful, it neglects precisely that in virtue of which these are themselves goods.[69] Thus, in *Love and Responsibility* he argues that attraction and desires do not suffice to direct one's sexual activity.[70] The acting person must seek the truth about the good, and this is necessarily the fitting good, the *bonum honestum.*

For its part, utilitarianism effectively denies the *bonum honestum* in any meaningful sense. According to Hume, Bentham, and Mill, the good for

---

[67] Or "fitting." In "Osoba: Podmiot i wspólotna," Karol Wojtyła characterizes *bonum honestum* by the phrase "dobrem w znaczeniu bezwzględnym i bezinteresownym." *Osoba i czyn,* 385, which the English translation renders "the good in an unconditional and disinterested sense." ("Person: Subject and Community," in *Person and Community,* 230.) The German text of *Lubliner Vorlesungen* uses *rechtschaffen.*

[68] *Lubliner Vorlsungen,* 186. In *Love and Responsibility,* 86, Wojtyła agrees with Aristotle that authentic friendship must be founded on "a genuine good (an honest good)" [in Polish, "dobro prawdziwe (dobro godziwe)"; *Miłość i odpowiedzialność,* 80] rather than on utility or a utilitarian good. In his encyclical on human work we find a parallel distinction among the *bonum* as *fruendum* (to be enjoyed), *utile* (useful), and *dignum* (worthy); John Paul II, *Laborem Exercens,* 9.

[69] See also Wojtyła, "Person: Subject and Community," in *Person and Community,* 249, and "On the Directive or Subservient Role of Reason in Ethics in the Philosophy of Thomas Aquinas, David Hume, and Immanuel Kant," ibid., 60; also *Lubliner Vorlesungen,* 142–43, 249, 282–83, 407, and *L'uomo nel campo della responsibilità,* 1264–66.

[70] *Love and Responsibility,* 107.

which all plans are made and for which all acts are undertaken must be subjective, the experience pleasure (or the avoidance of pain), however these may be conceived. For Thomas Aquinas, however, the *bonum honestum* is an objective reality that the intellect can know and the will strive for. Indeed, only the intellect is capable of recognizing the good as such. Because for Hume, the "grandfather" of utilitarianism, reason is subservient to the passions, reason can have no directive or governing role.[71] The effects of this confusion of goods and of reason's role are far-reaching. Hume and his utilitarian successors undercut the freedom of the human person, who is left under the sway of his passions, drives, and desires. Without there being a true *fitting good* that transcends sense desires (in Wojtyła's terms, *what happens in a human being*) and without the objective, universal power of reason to direct action, the freedom reduces to the arbitrary interaction of urge and impulse (whose ends are always some sort of satisfaction). Without the reason's governance of urges and impulses, the act ceases to be the free act of the person as self-determining and self-possessing. Utilitarianism, as Hume originally expressed it, denies the self-possession of the person in act, and in Bentham and Mill's form it makes that self-possession irrelevant.

Scheler and Emotion

In his ethics, Max Scheler is the anti-Kant. Where Kant sought a thoroughly rational ethics that issues in well-defined duties, Scheler sought an ethics that flows from the heart, or—to be more precise—from the human capacity to intuit and respond to values. Whereas Kant found the *good* in the rationally governed will and the utilitarians in pleasure, Scheler found it in the person himself.[72] One could say that for Scheler, the ethical challenge is simply to recognize the good, interiorize it, and respond to it appropriately. So, Scheler characterizes virtue:

> Virtue has become so intolerable to us most of all because we no longer understand it as an enduring, living, joyful *consciousness of one's capacity and power* to desire and to act for what is right and good in itself and, simultaneously, to

---

[71] See Wojtyła, "On the Directive or Subservient Role of Reason in Ethics in the Philosophy of Thomas Aquinas, David Hume, and Immanuel Kant," in *Person and Community*, 57–72.

[72] Scheler, *Der Formalismus*, 49.

> desire and to act for one's own individual self, as a consciousness of power that flows *out from one's very being*. We understand it rather as a mere dark unfathomable "disposition" and as a natural ability to act according to some prescribed rules.[73]

Scheler goes on to complain that virtue is too often presented as hard to acquire and hard to exercise, when in fact it is something inherently attractive and desirable, if not downright pleasant. In his characterization, acquiring virtue is a matter not of repeatedly performing good acts (as Aristotle taught)[74] but of discovering a "capacity and power" he already possesses. Furthermore, the virtuous person acts "for [his] own individual self, as a consciousness of power that flows out from [his] very being." The truly virtuous person does not need to be commanded, nor does he require imperatives, but his good acts flow from this inner store of goodness, as it were. The task of moral development, therefore, becomes one of unblocking this innate goodness and receptivity for goodness.

In a negative way, Scheler's theory is dominated by Kant. Scheler rejects the core of Kantian ethics, and he does so for the sake of humanity. Kant makes morality rational, the product of rigorous thought. If the benefactor does not reflect on his duty before giving the coins to the misfortunate, if the shopkeeper does not reflect on his obligation to charge fair prices, if the person in economic distress does not reflect on his duty to promise truthfully, then none of these performs a moral act. Scheler finds that abhorrent. Kant dismisses the motions of the heart as empirical, the product of inclination and not of rational duty. Scheler finds them to be the truest fount of morality. Kant's moral realm is a cold, rational place of maxims and analyses; Scheler's is a world rich in values of all kinds, aesthetic, religious, moral, to which the human person can respond. Kant's moral hero, whom we esteem for his adherence to duty, is very much the lone, autonomous individual. Indeed, to be truly moral, he must be completely autonomous, governed only by duty. Scheler, on the other hand, recognizes that we live socially in a world of values, which constitute an ethos. Scheler recognizes the importance of imitating heroes and role models. Kant's ethics is an ethics of command. Scheler's is one of warmhearted response to values.

[73] Max Scheler, "On the Rehabilitation of Virtue," trans. Eugene Kelly, *American Catholic Philosophical Society Quarterly* 79, no. 1 (Winter 2005): 22.

[74] *Nicomachean Ethics* 2.1, 1103a34–b25.

Scheler's Conception of the Person

Karol Wojtyła finds much to like in Scheler's ethics, and he repeatedly returns to the phenomenologist's inspirations. His analysis of shame in *Love and Responsibility*[75] and later as Pope in his theology of the body audiences[76] is expressly indebted to Scheler. Similarly, his discussion of the ethos of Christian marriage in *Man and Woman He Created Them* relies on Scheler's concept of the ethos as a world of values.[77] Nonetheless, he finds Scheler's system inadequate as a foundation for Christian ethics.[78] Despite Scheler's strong emphasis on the person, Wojtyła finds that it is precisely his account of the person that falls short. Scheler characterizes the person thus: "Person can *never* be regarded as a *thing* or a *substance* that might have faculties or powers of some sort, including even a "faculty" or a "power" of reason, etc. Person is rather the immediately experienced *unity* of experience, not only a thing that is thought of as behind and beyond what is immediately experienced."[79]

According to Karol Wojtyła, Scheler's definition fails to account adequately for the human person because by reducing the person to a nexus of subjective experience he misses the moment of efficacy.

> We see that for Scheler the person is not a substance, not a subject in the metaphysical or even the physical sense of the word. . . . The person is correlated with the acts he performs, not in the sense that he constitutes their departure point, but in the sense that he experiences himself interiorly in every act, and in a certain way is everything in every act.[80]

Denying that the person is a substance, Scheler effectively denies what Karol Wojtyła has so strongly insisted upon, that the person is a *suppositum.*

---

75 *Love and Responsibility,* 174–93.

76 John Paul II, *Man and Woman He Created Them,* 27:3–28:6, 240–46; 29:5, 249–50.

77 Ibid., 100:3, 518; 101; 1–11, 520–25; 117b:1–6, 613–15. See also John Paul II, apostolic letter *Mulieris Dignitatem* (Boston: St. Paul Books and Media, 1988), 24.

78 Indeed, this is the thesis of Wojtyła's habilitation thesis, *Valutazione sulla possibilità di costruire l'etica cristiana sulle base del sistema di Max Scheler.*

79 "Person *niemals* als ein *Ding* oder eine *Substanz* gedacht werden darf, die irgendwelche Vermögen oder Kräfte hätte, darunter auch ein 'Vermögen' oder eine 'Kraft' der Vernunft usw. Person ist vielmehr die unmittelbar miterlebte *Einheit* des Er-lebens—nicht ein nur gedachtes Ding hinter und außer dem unmittelbar Erlebten." *Der Formalismus,* 371.

80 *Valutazione sulla possibilità di costruire l'etica cristiana,* 290–91. See also 440.

This is Wojtyła's consistent criticism of Scheler's conception of the human person and indeed of the classical phenomenological conception.[81] As the nexus of experiences, Scheler's person is capable of interior, affective response to values, but he is not capable of realizing them. Indeed, it is not his task to realize them, not as an intentional activity, at any rate. If the personal act is to have any value of its own—particularly a *moral* value—this value must arise only "on the occasion" (*auf dem Rücken*)[82] of the act. Deliberately to aim at realizing a moral value is, in Scheler's mind, Pharisaism, because the focus of the act is not on the value but on one's own goodness.[83] And contrary to Kant, Scheler rejects the role of commands (imperatives) in ethics. His vision of the human person at his best is of one who is responsive to all values as they are in themselves, according to their kinds and relationships. The good person is good and does what is good not because he tries to do so or is commanded to but because his responsiveness to the highest values is such that it overflows, as it were, into action.

Scheler and the Problem of Norms

According to Scheler's conception, we can make no sense of moral norms, for norms are too much like imperatives. Norms of action arise from the reality, the existence of things about which we can ascertain the truth. And norms depend on the truth about the good.[84] Therefore Scheler does not even focus on the questions that for Wojtyła are key: "What ought I to do?" and "Why ought I to do it?" Scheler's entire problematic is centered not on the goods one should effect or acts one should perform but on the state of one's own consciousness in relation to values.[85] In this context we should also note an important theological point. Because Scheler effec-

---

[81] See, for example, "Person: Subject and Community," in *Person and Community*, 219, and "In Search of the Basis of Perfectionism in Ethics," ibid., 53; *Lubliner Vorlesungen*, 36, 45.

[82] Wojtyła, "The Separation of the Experience from the Act in Ethics," in *Person and Community*, 38.

[83] Scheler, *Der Formalismus*, 48. See Karol Wojtyła, *Valutazione sulla possibilità di costruire l'etica cristiana*, 357.

[84] Wojtyła, *Lubliner Vorlesungen*, 37. See also Wojtyła's "On the Metaphysical and Phenomenological Basis of the Moral Norm in the Philosophy of Thomas Aquinas and Max Scheler," in *Person and Community*, 90, and *L'uomo nel campo della responsibilità*, 1029.

[85] Wojtyła, *Valutazione sulla possibilità di costruire l'etica cristiana*, 289.

tively confines himself within the realm of consciousness, there can be for him nothing supernatural, nor can divine commands have moral import. Furthermore, God himself becomes only secondarily important, as the full realization of the value of "the holy" but not as a being in himself.[86] Consistent with Scheler's conception of values in general, that they are independent of their instantiation (so that we may admire heroism whether in fiction or in real life), the highest values of sanctity and holiness need not be instantiated for us to admire and respond to them.

General Response to these Interlocutors

Karol Wojtyła addresses himself to his three interlocutors: Kant, with his deontology; the utilitarians, represented by Hume, Bentham, and Mill; and Scheler the emotivist. In his analyses, he finds important aspects of both Kant's thought and Scheler's to accept and incorporate into his own. But he also has important criticisms, and the bases of his criticisms of all three are closely related.

Subjectivism

All three strains of modern ethical theory reduce to some form of subjectivism. This clearly applies to Hume's and Scheler's ethics, but it applies to the others as well. The Kantian imperative, which Kant regarded as objective, is promulgated by the subject himself. It is the command of his own reason, to which he responds out of esteem for law. The utilitarian greatest happiness principle, which can recognize general patterns and principles, must nevertheless respect its ultimate foundation, which is pleasure. This has become very clear in our own (largely utilitarian) age, during which it is generally accepted that no one can really know or dictate what is good (that is, pleasant) for another person. Whether utilitarian or emotivist, the post-Enlightenment ethician situates the basis of moral goodness in the consciousness or subjectivity of the individual human agent. Ultimately, no "third party" has any warrant for judging a person's moral stance. The best he can do is to object that he himself does not see matters that way. In response to this subjectivism, John Paul II writes: "In order to fulfill its mission, moral theology must turn to a philosophical ethics which looks to the truth of the good, to an ethics which is neither subjectivist nor utilitarian.

[86] Ibid., 397, 410–11, 445.

Such an ethics implies and presupposes a philosophical anthropology and a metaphysics of the good."[87] Having turned from metaphysics, ethics cannot but fall into some form of subjectivism.

Confusion About the Will

Closely related to the subjectivism problem is the loss of the conception of the will. Kant famously held that there is no unqualified good save the good will, but he does not fully develop his conception of will. The will is that which chooses the maxim for action, surely enough, but it is curiously detached from what it actually accomplishes in the world. For Karol Wojtyła *will* is a central concept, because it is by his will that the person himself, in possession of himself and governing himself, dynamizes himself, that is, sets himself into action in the world. "The will is the person's power of self-determination."[88] Wojtyła repeatedly insists on the importance of *efficacy*,[89] because in virtue of his efficacy the person is more than simply a center of conscious experience. No matter how he may experience the world, himself, or the values with which he is presented, he also acts and in doing so engages the world. The concept *will*, expressing this reality of the person as the self-possessed author of his own efficacious acts, is effectively lost in Kant and Scheler.

On the other hand, for utilitarianism what happens in the world is important, since it can affect the general happiness. Paradoxically, however, the will is of little moment for this school, because subjectivity is lost. That is to say, what matters to utilitarians is that favorable events occur, not that the human person bring them about. Hume holds the useful and the agreeable to be the standards for our morality but effectively denies the freedom and therefore the responsibility of the will. In his *Utilitarianism*, J. S. Mill, taking a swipe at Kant, denies that the state of the will is morally significant. Recall his statement: "He who saves a fellow creature from drowning *does what is morally right*, whether his motive be duty, or

---

87 *Fides et Ratio*, 98.

88 Wojtyła, "The Personal Structure of Self-Determination," in *Person and Community*, 190.

89 Besides the texts cited above from Wojtyła's "The Will in the Analysis of the Ethical Act," in *Person and Community*, 3–22, see also "The Problem of the Theory of Morality," ibid., 137, 143, and *Valutazione sulla possibilità di costruire l'etica cristiana*, 354, as well as throughout *Person and Act*, as already noted above.

the hope of being paid for his trouble."[90] The moral rightness of the act lies entirely in its effect, that the drowning man was saved, regardless of the rescuer's intention. As we shall see in chapter 7, this principle becomes important for the evaluation of some contemporary theories in moral theology. Wojtyła holds, however, that in the concept of will, subjectivity—intellect; knowledge and planning; intention and motivation—is joined with objectivity—putting the body in motion causally to effect these changes using these tools and resources. "Will" expresses that it is not a part of the person but the entire being, the *suppositum*, that performs the act.[91] Wojtyła's insistence of the importance of will is key to his further insistence that ethics requires a metaphysical foundation by which the conscious subject is related to and engaged with the existential realm. The human being cannot be considered as simply a medium or a means through which natural causality operates, bringing about its inevitable and inexorable effects. The will, as that by which the person is efficacious and responsible, is a cause of change, of effects in the world.

Moral Norms

The experience of morality as a fact arises from the two questions "*What ought I truly to do*?" and "*Why ought I to do* what I ought to do?" We may say that the first of these points to the question of the content of moral norms and the second to their justification. Karol Wojtyła defines a moral norm thus:

> Norm, in the most general sense of the term, is the name we give to a principle of moral good and evil.[92]
>
> The ethical norm . . . is nothing other than the objectification (and at the same time the concretization) of the truth about the good, of the good tied to a given action of the person, willed in it and realized in it.[93]

---

90 *Utilitarianism*, 18; emphasis added.

91 Wojtyła, *Persona e atto*, 888, 926; Wojtyła, "The Degrees of Being from the Point of View of the Phenomenology of Action," 127.

92 Wojtyła, "The Problem of the Theory of Morality," in *Person and Community*, 139. See also John Paul II, encyclical *Dominum et Vivificantem*, 43 (*Pope Speaks* 31, no. 3 [1986]), and Wojtyła, *Persona e atto*, 1037–38.

93 *L'uomo nel campo della responsibilità*, 1269.

A norm is a truth about some good as good, and as such it is universal or general. *When that truth pertains to the good of a human being as such and to his acts*, it is a moral or ethical norm. "In the final analysis, we can define the ethical norm as the principle of being a good human being (qua human being) and of acting well."[94] If control of the center of the chess board is a norm for the chess player, then the fact that speech exists to represent the mind's understanding of truth is a norm for every human being regardless of his trade, condition, or interests. The chess norm issues in the imperative "Seize control of the central squares," and the norm of speech issues in the imperative "Don't tell lies." For Wojtyła a norm is a truth and not an imperative, and the recognition of the norm must precede moral judgment.

We may contrast Wojtyła's view with Richard McCormick's conception.

> In practical moral matters, the very last thing one arrives at is a moral norm. A moral norm is a generalization about the significance of our actions. It is a conclusion drafted from understanding that significance. When it is up front as the dominant preoccupation, it hinders teaching and learning by bypassing the struggles that lead to understanding.[95]

McCormick tends to see norms as generalized imperatives derived from actual moral experience. If this is the case, however, then such norms are useless for answering Wojtyła's two central questions: "What ought I to do?" and "Why should I do it?" As a generalization, the norm is always after the fact. To be sure, we may recognize that McCormick is right inasmuch as we may learn from past experience how various kinds of acts will turn out, as when health researchers determine that the intake of salt tablets does not help outdoor workers to endure the summer heat better. Nevertheless, since every decision to act intends some good or the realization of some value, it is perforce subject to some governing norm that the acting person, simply in order to proceed into action, needs to discover.

Paulinus Odozor further illuminates the bases of McCormick's concerns about moral norms. Although experience may lead us to generaliza-

---

[94] Ibid., 1272.

[95] Richard A. McCormick, S.J., *The Critical Calling: Reflections on Moral Dilemmas since Vatican II* (Washington, DC: Georgetown University Press, 1989), 120. Also, "Moral norms are generalizations about the significance or meaning of our conduct." Ibid., 14.

tions about our behavior, this does not in itself suffice for the establishment of moral norms, because any straightforward derivation of norms from truths about the world would amount to a confusion of facts and values. Odozor writes:

> The purpose of formal norms is therefore parenetic, intended to remind people of what they are supposed to know and exhort them what to do to avoid sin. . . . Since they presume genuine agreement about what is right and wrong, parenetic discourse or formal norms can only invite, exhort, judge, strengthen, or implore. Ordinarily, they do not inform or instruct.[96]

The norms so conceived are general expressions of value. As such they differ from concrete norms for specific "material" situations, where one might find ontically "right" or "wrong" decisions but not (morally) "good" or "evil" ones, since these depend not on the material circumstances but on the moral values at stake. And indeed, McCormick cites the confusion of *fact* and *value* terms as a principal source of misunderstanding in moral theology.[97] As we shall repeatedly see, Karol Wojtyła conceives norms as truths that concern values. Because a norm is a truth about some value, Wojtyła effectively rejects the sharp distinction between fact-terms and value-terms. As we have seen in chapter 2, the order of nature cannot be value-free; an order conceived without values is itself an abstraction, a creation of the human mind. Thus, in his theology of the body, John Paul II writes: "The understanding of the fundamental meanings contained in the very mystery of creation, such as the spousal meaning of the body . . . , is important and indispensable for knowing who man is and who he ought to be, and therefore how he ought to shape his activity."[98]

Are Moral Norms Founded?

We noted above that although Wojtyła expressed sympathy with aspects of Kant's and Scheler's theories, he thoroughly repudiated utilitarianism, because it disregards or even denies the *bonum honestum*, the fitting good. Reading the classical utilitarian works, one is drawn in by their presumption

96 Paulinus Ikechukwu Odozor, C.S.Sp., *Richard A. McCormick and the Renewal of Moral Theology* (Notre Dame: University of Notre Dame Press, 1995), 43.

97 *Critical Calling,* 136–37.

98 *Man and Woman He Created Them,* 18.4, 200.

that we all know what is good and desirable. Hume calls it the "agreeable," and Mill identifies it with pleasure. Utilitarianism does not see the need to penetrate deeper than what is evident to the reasonably educated member of a sufficiently advanced society. Indeed, to do so might even be dangerous. Hume famously rejects metaphysics and any emphasis on the spiritual that would lead one to embrace "[c]elibacy, fasting, penance, mortification, self-denial, humility, silence, solitude, and the whole train of monkish virtues."[99] Such virtues are neither useful nor agreeable to oneself and do not make one so to others. Karol Wojtyła notes that Jeremy Bentham regards metaphysical considerations as positively dangerous in ethics. Every other fundamental principle than that of the maximizing of happiness is a foundation for despotism and egoism.[100] Indeed, Bentham delights in ridiculing the philosophers, from Plato and Aristotle to his own contemporaries, who claim to find any desirable good other than or greater than pleasure, the sensible well-being of the body.[101] The experiential foundations of utilitarianism are indeed strong. We all do prefer pleasure to pain and strive to attain the one and avoid the other. Bentham continues:

> The life of *A* is filled up with pleasures, all of them ignoble, all of them in the highest degree intense, none of them alloyed by any thing in the shape of pain. In the life of *B*, what pleasures there are, are all of them of the noble kind, but all of them are alloyed with and outweighed by pains. Whose lot, of *A* or *B*, would a man choose, he being in his senses?[102]

Bentham's answer, of course, is that any man would choose the ignoble, for in the final analysis, "ignoble" is but a word, and the pains suffered by *B* are eminently real.

Karol Wojtyła insists that the useful good serves a more ultimate fitting good. Rhetorically compelling as Bentham's arguments may be and reasonable as the more congenial Mill's are, utilitarianism immediately raises practical difficulties, the most evident of which is the simple fact that different human beings find different kinds of things to be pleasant and

[99] *Enquiry concerning the Principles of Morals*, sec. 9, conclusion, 111.

[100] Wojtyła, *Lubliner Vorlesungen*, 342.

[101] Jeremy Bentham, *Deontology*, in *Deontology, Together with A Table of the Springs of Action and Article on Utilitarianism*, ed. Amnon Goldworth (Oxford: Clarendon Press, 1983), 130–47.

[102] Ibid., 141.

painful. Commenting on section 2.3, "Extra-Regarding Prudence: Negative," of Bentham's *Deontology*, Wojtyła remarks, "In a practical way there lies here the weakness of Jeremy Bentham's entire system. The fundamental principle of the maximization of happiness does not provide for conflicts of agreeable things. It is directed toward an ideal harmonious life and life together with others, and on that account is less useful when it comes to establishing the norms for their activity."[103] It is worth noting that this problem continues to be pertinent in our own (still utilitarian) era, where the inability to appeal to a higher good makes difficult the balancing of the desires of diverse populations.

This difficulty points to a more serious one. Hume's and Bentham's utilitarianism is born of a kind of despair that any rationally adequate account can be given of the human good. Indeed, both expressly repudiate religious and metaphysical explanations of human nature. In virtue of his analysis of the human act—more precisely, in virtue of his analysis of the integration and transcendence of the person in the act—Wojtyła concludes that a metaphysical account of the human person is required, that only in terms of such an account can an adequate account of the human good be given. An animal can, as it were, live successfully as a utilitarian, because its instincts are fitted to its needs, balanced and harmonized so that in its proper environment the animal can survive and reproduce. The animal does not, however, think. It cannot imagine for itself a better life, one directed to ends beyond survival of self and species. The animal does not envision a more beautiful world that it can realize by artistic creation. With the human person it is otherwise. Intelligence is not simply a tool for more ingenious adaptation. Intelligence enables the human being to transcend the goods dictated by his nature. Roald Amundsen and his party exerted themselves, risking discomfort, grave injury, and death simply in order to be the first to have reached the South Pole. His rival Robert F. Scott died striving for the same goal.

Even if a utilitarian could object—as Bentham certainly does[104]—that no one can act except in his own interest, it would still remain that the human person himself must determine what shall be a matter of his interest. Fido the dog needs only to look to his visceral feelings to determine

103 *Lubliner Vorlesungen*, 356n30.

104 *Deontology*, 128–29.

that he needs to eat, but Amundsen's interest in the South Pole started in his own mind. There is no human need to visit that place. The polar environment is especially hostile to innate human needs for nutrition, shelter, and warmth. If a Scott or Amundsen can make it his concern, this interest arises not from his nature but from his intellectual ability to transcend *what happens in* him. Catholic priests and religious forgo marriage and its natural pleasures for the sake of serving God and his Church. Many young people forgo marriage for a limited period of time, but precisely the time of greatest sexual desires, in order to complete their educations. Scholars and artists forgo wealth and comfort for the sake of learning or creating. Healthy and strong persons will enter the military, where they may subsequently be killed. All these (and one could multiply examples endlessly) illustrate how the human person does not simply rely on his feelings or attractions to guide his actions. In order to act, the human person needs some conception of what is good. He needs, to the extent possible, to determine what is the truth about the good. Contrary to the implication of utilitarianism, this good is not immediately given to intuition but has to be an object of reason. Only through his intelligence can the human person grasp the truth about the good. Wojtyła writes: "Similar to the lower animals, the human being strives for different kinds of goods. However, this striving has another character precisely because with his understanding the human being recognizes the truth about the good."[105] The inadequacies of utilitarianism demand the intellectual search for the fitting good.[106]

Have Norms an Object?

Kant bases his ethics on moral imperatives. Indeed, we may say that for Kant the norm is everything. However, Wojtyła writes concerning Kant: "The will is not good for this reason, that a truly objective good has become the object of its choice, but exclusively in this, that it is directed according to the law as the a priori form of practical reason."[107] It matters not whether one wants or intends to attain some good or to be good. All that matters is that one obey the moral imperative. In this respect Scheler's

[105] *Lubliner Vorlesungen*, 199. See also *Love and Responsibility*, 107, where we read, "The promptings of sensuality would give man all the guidance he needs in his sexual life if . . . his sexual reactions were infallibly guided by instinct."

[106] *Lubliner Vorlesungen*, 193.

[107] Ibid., 205.

charge of Pharisaism holds true. If the moral heart of Pharisaism is indeed the strict obedience to the letter of the Law because it is God's Law,[108] then Kant's is an Enlightenment legalism whose God is reason and whose Moses is the categorical imperative. Behind Pharisaism, of course, lay the clear awareness of Israel's covenantal obligations to God and of the historical consequences of her disobedience. For the Pharisee, the Law derived its holiness from the God who freed Israel from slavery in Egypt and then punished their disobedience with the Babylonian Captivity. For Kant, it derives its holiness from reason. Kant, therefore, goes far beyond historical Pharisaism, for he separates moral obligation from every good, except that of the will, for which it is the condition.

Wojtyła finds the Kantian ethics inadequate, because it completely fails to account for the nature of the human act. The human act—every human act, by its very nature—intends some good.[109] The person performs his act in order to accomplish something good, to realize some good. When a person asks the moral questions—"What ought I to do?" and "Why ought I to do it?"—he is not asking about the demands that practical reason is placing upon him in the abstract but about how he ought to respond to these desires he experiences for *those* goods in *this* situation. It is *this* proposed act, whether it be to plant a garden, abort a pregnancy, dismiss an employee, or stay at the bar for yet another drink, that he wants to evaluate. Is *this* act good? To this Kant responds that the good to be attained by the act is irrelevant, that the act must be evaluated for its aptitude as a universal law for every rational creature. To be sure, Kant intends his account to deal with "real world" situations—lying, suicide, benevolence to the poor, and self-improvement. Nevertheless, he does not address the full reality of the act as an engagement in the world.

Karol Wojtyła insists over and over that the concept of efficacy is central to understanding the will and the act.[110] Because efficacy is identical

---

108 And this is the thrust of Pharisaism as Jesus criticized it. See Mt 12:1–13; 15:1–9; 19:3–9; 23:13–36; Lk 5:29–39; 7:36–50; 15:1–23; and so on. Jesus' polemic was against a view that made the Law supreme rather than the love of the God who gave the Law.

109 As Aristotle famously observes in the opening sentence of his *Nicomachean Ethics*.

110 *Persona e atto*, chap. 2, 909–23; *Person and Community*, 4, 8, 12–13, 39, 137, 138, 143, 189, 191, 230, 303–4, 332; *Valutazione sulla possibilità di costruire l'etica cristiana*, 354, 365–67, 413–21, 441; and *Lubliner Vorlesungen*, 45, 94.

with efficient causality, its exercise by an intelligent being requires knowledge of the natures of things and the order of nature. Civil engineers need to know the strengths of steel and concrete. Farmers need to know the effects of fertilizer on crops and the environment. Even if today's knowledge is primitive relative to tomorrow's and even if the agent recognizes its inadequacy, he is responsible for what knowledge can be had relative to his act, because he is acting within that order, whether it be the agricultural or the structural or the military realm. Because the act is efficacious and performed for its efficacy, the acting person is responsible for its effects. This is where norms come in. Because the world is a realm of goods, it is not possible to separate the realm of the scientifically knowable from the moral realm, as Kant effectively proposes. A further consequence of this is that the good that one intends by one's act is related to other goods.

A further defect of the Kantian system is that one finds no sense of a hierarchy of goods or obligations in it. In his discussion of a supposed right to lie,[111] Kant insists that under no circumstance may one deceive another or even contemplate such deception (for such is a liar *in potential*), even if a murderer should be asking for the whereabouts of his intended victim. This is consistent, of course, with his ethical principles. The philosophical difficulty is that one cannot relate this duty (i.e., not to lie) to goods such as the safety of a helpless victim, the rights of the potential liar not to disclose his own mind, and public order, nor to the manifest evil of the murderer's intentions. The objection here is not that we have simply to measure Kant's imperative by its practical consequences but that an ethical imperative cannot stand alone as an unsupported law. Rather, it stands in relation to some good, some value, which for its part stands in relation to other values. Such a good is a norm. The stricture against lying lies within a nexus of norms, all of which relate to various goods of varying importance.

These conclusions lead to yet a further consideration. Although Kant is reasonably successful in articulating and defending negative commands (no lying, no suicide), he is unable to provide much in terms of positive direction for life. But if one is to be a good person, it does not suffice sim-

---

[111] Immanuel Kant, *On a Supposed Right to Lie because of Philanthropic Concerns*, in *Grounding for the Metaphysics of Morals* with *On a Supposed Right to Lie because of Philanthropic Concerns*, 63–67.

ply to avoid doing bad things. One needs to develop oneself in a positive way. The question "What ought I to do?" is positive in its thrust. The moral question inevitably involves the question of what good one should live for, and Kant does not provide for this.

Norms and Values

The forward-looking, positive element missing from Kant's ethics is very much present in Scheler's thought. Indeed, Scheler expressly rejects the negative moment in ethics.[112] Scheler's great insight is that the moral life is a matter of responding to values, not only "moral values" narrowly understood, but sensible, aesthetic, and religious, as well as moral, values. The richness of human life derives from the values one intuits. To be a human person alive in the world is constantly to be presented with values that "spring up" unbidden. Real persons daily, indeed hourly, experience attractions and revulsions at every level. In the theater one is horrified by Iago's treachery and Othello's folly. Outside he is charmed by a child playing with her dog. The odor of rotting trash in an alley is irritating, and the memory of Nathan Hale's last words is inspiring. The young person at work is winsome and attractive, indeed sensual and desirable. Furthermore, it is not even essential that these values be instantiated for us to intuit and appreciate them; even though Rick and Ilsa[113] never existed, we sympathize with them and admire their sacrifice.

The ethical challenge is to respond appropriately to these values, which play an important part in our personal formation. The self—the "who I am"—is largely determined by what a person values, a fact that advertisers make great use of as they try to get us to value their products. What Scheler further recognizes is that the tissue of values shared by many persons or a society constitutes an ethos: how we live and what is important to us. Ethos structures life. In his audiences on the theology of the body, John Paul II focused much of his analysis of the relationship between men and women according to the Christian ethos.[114] One of the realities of our human existence is that our lives and values are formed by those with

112 Wojtyła, *Valutazione sulla possibilità di costruire l'etica cristiana*, 379.

113 In the Michael Curtiz 1942 film *Casablanca.*

114 *Man and Woman He Created Them*, 18:4–6, 24:3, 34, 38:1, 44:3, 47–49, and many others.

whom we associate, by our cultural milieu. Related to this is the concept of the moral example, the one who embodies the value. Most often this is a real person—a saint or a hero—but it need not be. Tempted to put my desires ahead of loyalty and the good of others, I may recall Rick's farewell to Ilsa at the airfield and imitate his fictional heroism.

This focus on values provides us with a much richer and more realistic context for our ethics than do questions about stealing expensive medicines from selfish pharmacists, choosing among seven men to fit into a six-man lifeboat, or dynamiting an overweight spelunker whose body is blocking the exit to a flooding cave (to name just some of the dilemmas discussed in contemporary practical ethics). The question of moral norms remains nevertheless: "What ought I to do?" and "Why ought I to do it?" Karol Wojtyła recognized what Scheler's reaction against Kant made it impossible for him to acknowledge, that the experience of and response to values is not enough. In a sense, Scheler lacked moral seriousness in that he failed to acknowledge that the human person is, in virtue of his capacity to act effectively in the world, a force for good or evil. At stake in the moral conflict is not simply the texture of value responses within the experience of the person. Rather, the person stands morally in a true drama where his acts have import for good or evil, where the person himself becomes an agent and source of good or evil.

The Necessity of Norms

To answer our two fundamental questions, those questions that form the basis of moral experience and give rise to the sense of duty, we need moral norms, which have both a teleological and a deontological character. If there are goods to be attained by human action, these give rise to norms. The norms do not themselves prescribe actions. A man asks, "What ought I to do?" To this one might well reply that since he is a father of minor children, he must care for them, effectively expressing the norm that parents are responsible for the well-being of their children. To be sure, this norm may not apply too directly if the decision is between playing golf and cleaning out the gutters. Indeed, one can seldom apply the norm at any specific point in such a way as to say, "Precisely this is what you must do." Certainly the norm prohibits certain acts by the father. He must not abandon his children, although he may leave them to go to war for their country. He must not torment them cruelly, although he may discipline them. The norm is most important in its positive sense. The man who would never abandon or torture his child may need to be reminded (usually by his wife) that his child needs a few hours of his time on the weekend. A good father devotes time to his children, even if one cannot specify that he must spend four hours in athletics or recreational activities per week with them. In other words, the norm guides behavior, even if it does not directly imply that one must perform certain acts under all conditions. Furthermore, as the example of the father implies, a norm can and generally will exclude certain acts as absolutely incompatible with the good represented by the norm.

The Concern of Ethics

Ethics is concerned with moral norms, that is, with those norms that apply to the person simply in virtue of his being a human being. Under Karol Wojtyła's conception, therefore, moral norms presuppose that there are goods that are good for every human person as such. Indeed, we have already (in the prologue) identified God himself as the highest good for every human being. If this is true, that there is one good or set of goods that are such for every human being in virtue of his being human, then on the basis of these goods we can determine basic moral norms. And from these we can deduce or derive moral laws.

In his *Love and Responsibility*, Wojtyła identifies and defends one such norm, which he calls the personalistic norm. In the next chapter, we shall examine his derivation of that norm as well as his application of it to sexual ethics and his theology of the body.

CHAPTER 5

The Personalistic Norm

The Norm

> This norm, in its negative aspect, states that the person is a kind of good which does not admit of use and cannot be treated as an object of use and as such the means to an end. In its positive form the personalistic norm confirms this: the person is a good toward which the only proper and adequate attitude is love.[1]

THE PERSONALISTIC NORM is fundamental to Karol Wojtyła's ethical thought. The norm is not itself a commandment, although the command "Love persons" can be derived from it. Christ stated this commandment to love one's neighbor when the scribe asked, "Which is the first of all the commandments?" (Mk 12:28–31; see also Mt 22:34–40). The scribe's question is a variant of the first question of ethics at the beginning of the last chapter: "What is it that I ought to do?" Christ's twofold answer was, "Love God. Love your neighbor." This commandment to love one's neighbor creates a duty, an obligation, which Karol Wojtyła holds to be based on the personalistic norm. Our purpose here is to investigate this norm, its bases, and its consequences.

1 Wojtyła, *Love and Responsibility*, 41; see also John Paul II, apostolic exhortation *Christifideles Laici, L'Osservatore Romano* (English Edition) no. 6 (1075), February 6, 1989, 1–21; John Paul II, "Letter to Families," *Pope Speaks* 39, no. 4 (July–August 1994): 221; and John Paul II, *Memory and Identity: Conversations at the Dawn of a Millennium* (New York: Rizzoli International Publications, 2005), 133.

The Basis of the Norm: Personal Subjectivity

Early in his theology of the body audiences, John Paul II considers the situation of the first human being, created and placed alone in the garden. The LORD GOD brought the animals to him to name, but the man was unable to find among them a fitting companion. The LORD GOD then cast the human being into a deep sleep, during which he formed the woman. When the man awoke, he exclaimed, "This at last is bone from my bones and flesh from my flesh" (Gen 2:18–23). John Paul uses this episode to analyze human *solitude*, the person's subjectivity.[2] In this encounter with the animals the first man became aware of his superiority to them. John Paul II writes:

> Thus, *the created man* finds himself from the first moment of his existence *before God* in search of his own being, as it were; one could say, in search of his own definition; today one would say, in search of his own "identity." The observation that man "is alone" in the midst of the visible world and, in particular, among living beings, has a negative meaning in this search, inasmuch as it expresses what man "is not." Nevertheless, the observation that he cannot identify himself essentially with the visible world of other living beings (*animalia*) has, at the same time, a positive aspect for this primary search.[3]
>
> [M]an finds himself alone before God, above all to express, through a first self-definition, his own self-knowledge as the first and fundamental manifestation of humanity. Self-knowledge goes hand in hand with knowledge of the world, of all visible creatures, of all living beings to which man has given their names to affirm his own dissimilarity before them. Thus, consciousness reveals man as the one who *possesses the power of knowledge* with respect to the visible world.[4]

Although John Paul II shows how these considerations lead directly to the Aristotelian definition of the human being as *zoón noetikón*, his principal concern and the thrust of his analysis is to characterize the subjectivity of the human person. The *solitude* of the first man is his capacity to be a self. "In fact, solitude also signifies man's subjectivity, which constitutes itself through

---

[2] *Man and Woman He Created Them*, 5:1–7:2, 146–54.

[3] Ibid., 5:5, 149.

[4] Ibid., 5:6, 150.

self-knowledge."[5] Not only does this subjectivity signify a cognitive power, but it is also the basis of man's powers of choice and self-determination.

> The first account of the creation of man . . . contains hidden within itself a powerful metaphysical content. One should not forget that precisely this text of Genesis has become the source of the deepest inspirations for the thinkers who have sought to understand "being" and "existing" [*bytu i istnienia*]. . . . He [man] is defined in a more metaphysical than physical way.[6]

Futhermore, because the first human beings were commanded not to eat the fruit of the Tree of the Knowledge of Good and Evil, they had moral responsibilities, which they could accept and meet or disregard.[7] It is quite a remarkable analysis, really, for in a discussion of the first three chapters of Genesis, John Paul II connects the capacities for reason and will with the sense of aloneness and separation so frequently noted in modern philosophy, especially existentialism. The human person has a deep inner life, which is rooted in his solitude and which can become a barrier between himself and others.

On the other hand, argues John Paul II, it is only with another person that true companionship and authentic communion can be found. This is why, upon meeting the woman, the man in Genesis exclaims, "This one at last is bone of my bone and flesh of my flesh!"[8] He has found someone like himself, a person and true helpmate. In short, the person is never just an object in the world but is also a subject with intelligence and will, capable of choice, self-determination, and moral responsibility. And he is on the lookout for other persons with whom he can enter into communion.

Phenomenal Analysis of Subjectivity

Turning to Wojtyła's philosophical writings, we may rightly say that the subjectivity of the human person is the theme of *Person and Act*, whose notorious difficulty for interpreters lies principally in that it approaches traditional philosophical topics, the human will and act, from the *inside*, from the point of view of human subjectivity. This is, indeed, the key to

[5] Ibid.

[6] Ibid., 2:5, 136; *Mężczyzną i niewiastą stworzył ich*, 12.

[7] *Man and Woman He Created Them*, 7:3–4, 154–56.

[8] Ibid., 8:1–4, 156–61.

understanding Wojtyła's use of phenomenology.[9] If phenomenology is to be taken as the foundation of philosophy, as the key from which all philosophical understanding flows and as the philosophical tool capable of accounting for the sciences, then Wojtyła does not do phenomenology. Classical phenomenology starts from consciousness to discover how the world of objective fact, the world known by science, is constituted in and by consciousness. Wojtyła will not grant to consciousness this foundational role that Husserl gives it, recognizing a more fundamental cognitive level of the human person by which he is able to attain objective understanding of the truth of things. He insists repeatedly that the philosophy of consciousness (of which phenomenology is paradigmatic) must be supported by a philosophy of being.[10]

In *Person and Act* Wojtyła identifies two functions of consciousness, one of which builds upon the other.[11] Because the world is, as it were, given to the subject in his consciousness, a first function is to mirror the world, the subject's life environment. "Consciousness is therefore the reflection or mirroring of all that which the human being comes into objective contact with through any action whatever."[12] This is probably similar to the kind of consciousness the higher animals enjoy. Although this mirroring function is related to cognition, it is not the foundation of cognition, of knowledge and understanding. Indeed, he argues, we best understand the nature of consciousness through the human act. Because the act is a conscious action,[13] consciousness emerges in the *voluntarium*, that is, in the human will. Human consciousness or awareness of the world is conditioned, indeed formed, by the manner in which the human being forms and chooses his act. Therefore, insists Wojtyła, we cannot absolutize consciousness as a kind of independent subject.[14] Human consciousness presupposes and depends upon the human capacities for

---

[9] Buttiglione, *Karol Wojtyla*, 120, 125–29, and Peter Simpson, *On Karol Wojtyla* (Belmont, CA: Wadsworth, 2001), "2. Philosophical 'Prise de Position,'" 7–22.

[10] Wojtyła, *Person and Community*, 46, 49, 219; *Lubliner Vorlesungen*, 401; *Valutazione sulla possibilità di costruire l'etica cristiana*, 308–12; and John Paul II, *Fides et Ratio*, 76, 97. See also Buttiglione, *Karol Wojtyla*, 275ff., and Schmitz, *At the Center of the Human Drama*, 65.

[11] *Persona e atto*, 883ff.

[12] Ibid., 870.

[13] "Czyn jest działaniem świadomym." Wojtyła, *Osoba i czyn*, 76; *Persona e atto*, 864.

[14] *Persona e atto*, 868, 872.

knowledge (or cognition) and will. The first function of consciousness, then, is mirror for the person the environment in which he acts.

Second and more specifically human is the reflexive function of consciousness, which arises from the fact that, knowing and acting consciously in the world, the person is correlatively aware of himself as a subject of experience. Reflexivity means simply the human subject's turning toward himself as a self or an "I,"[15] whose experiences are his own. Through his reflexive consciousness the person can interiorly live (or experience) his own acts, and constitute himself as an "I," or self. In this, Wojtyła is careful to insist that the person *exists* as a *suppositum*, that he is not constituted as a person by his consciousness. The point is only that in virtue of reflexivity does the person become conscious of his personhood and indeed of the personal self who he is and is becoming. Therefore, he can make his acts and experiences as his own.

Consciousness is a consequence, and hence not a condition, of the acting person's capacity to know and to will. Therefore consciousness can (and ought) to be formed by knowledge and will. Furthermore, that consciousness reflects the world of the person, who is thereby conscious of himself as a self or subject, means that the person is, in a way, the center of a world. Although this centrality can well be a source of difficulty and even constitute a moral challenge, it is also the root of the richness of human life. It is the foundation of the truth that the human being is also a cocreator of the world.[16] If the challenge is to form one's own consciousness according to the truth, it remains nonetheless true that each person experiences the world as his own, from his own perspective. The world is formed by what one experiences both as fact and as value, which experience cannot sharply separate.

Person as **sui juris**

As the center of consciousness of his world and its cocreator, the person enjoys a freedom and autonomy that transcend the conditions of the world. This does not mean, of course, that one can successfully disregard how the world objectively is. Rather, it means that the person has at his

15 Ibid., 883–86.

16 Wojtyła, "Thomistic Personalism," in *Person and Community*, 171; John Paul II, encyclical *Centesimus Annus*, 37.

own disposal his own mind to interpret and act in the world. He is self-governing and self-transcending.[17] As a result, the human person can envision a world quite different than the one he is living in and on the basis of that vision become a political revolutionary, a cultural leader, or the like. Or he can deny reality and live as the "star of his own show" in a fantasy world. Persons are moved not by objects and facts but by values, to which a person responds almost spontaneously as appropriate to himself. Furthermore, the human person experiences a desire to transcend himself, to achieve something beyond his own experience, whether this be to see his own grandchildren, to have "made his mark" in the military, to have written or invented something new, or simply to have been part of a significant event. Human persons measure themselves by what they give themselves to. These are the factors that human subjectivity manifests.

The person is therefore governed by laws different from those that govern purely material beings.[18] To set an inanimate object in motion, appropriate physical force, chemical influence, or the like must be applied to it. Plants and animals respond to environmental stimuli in more or less sophisticated ways according to their natures, from the sunflower's turn toward the sun to the jaguar's careful stalking. A physical entity, insofar as it is physical, is governed by the law of the conservation of mass-energy, such that whatever it gives or transmits to another is lost to itself. The person *as person* is not so moved, and this is essential to understanding the personalistic norm.

The person as person is *sui juris*, master of himself. To be sure, one can act upon the body of the person, availing himself of the body's physical properties. So the criminals may bind the bank manager to a chair and then place him before the door as a kind of doorstop. Having deprived him of governance of his own body, the robbers treat the manager as a simple *thing*. However, without that person's cooperation one cannot make full use another's body such that his actions come from within. By this I mean nothing more special or sophisticated than this, that to move a human being's muscles purposefully, his own cooperation is required, and because of the subjectivity of the person, that cooperation is never

[17] Karol Wojtyła, "Trascendenza della persona nell'agire e autoteleologia dell'uomo," in *Metafisica della persona*, 1405–20; also *Persona e atto*, pt. 2, 909–62.

[18] Wojtyła, *Love and Responsibility*, 97.

guaranteed. The patient of another's acts can resist any inducement or threat. The rape victim may scream or fight back. The honest businessman can resist the lure of big money gotten dishonorably. The martyr refuses to betray the truth before the threat of death. The person *as person* does not act without his own personal involvement, without his own consent or at least acquiescence. This does not, of course, mean that the person moves in complete freedom abstracted from all physical conditions. The bank manager may sit blocking the door, unbound but terrorized into submission. The rape victim may submit for fear of being killed. Not only might another person physically constrain the body, but he might enter, as it were, into the subjective world of another. The seducer plays on the maiden's susceptibility to tender affection, and the flirt on the boy's awakening sensuality.[19] Ambition alone did not suffice to move Macbeth to murder Duncan, but also his lady's taunts against his masculinity: "When you durst do it then you were a man;/And to be more than what you were, you would/Be so much more the man."[20]

Indeed, the techniques of mental manipulation are well known and widely practiced in our day by propagandists and advertisers, as well as by seducers, flirts, and conniving spouses. We may say that the art of getting inside another's mental world has become highly developed and valued. The powers of propaganda and persuasion notwithstanding, the individual person can nevertheless consider what is proposed to him and, transcending the images, emotions, sentiments, and reactions that another may present, inquire intelligently about the truth of the matter.

The Inner Structure of Subjectivity

These truths about the nature of the person mean that one cannot, strictly speaking, *use* a person except rarely and exceptionally. One can use a dog by availing himself of its natural instincts to submit to the leader of its pack, to respond to food and positive attention, to learn to obey commands, and so on. Because it has no power to reason and therefore to seek any good other than that toward which its own instincts direct it, the dog lacks subjectivity, spirituality. This disobedient dog is simply obeying an instinct that has not been overcome by the master's training. The civil disobedient, on the other

---

[19] See ibid., 205.

[20] Shakespeare, *Macbeth*, act 1, scene 7.

hand, expressly rejects the conditioning and training that the regime would impose, because he rejects its values. The dog's heroism in rescuing its master results from the pack instinct. The leader must be saved for the pack to survive and thrive. The human hero can and does weigh the dangers. Human subjectivity is always present, in principle at least, to call into question the impositions of another's will. Therefore, it is not possible to use the person *as* person, not without that person's cooperation.

Of course, it is quite possible to subvert the person's subjectivity in order to manipulate him. If the person cannot be used without his own cooperation or complicity, then to use him requires that his subjectivity be subverted or compromised. Subjectivity is founded, as we have already said, on the powers to know the truth and to seek the good. By means of rewards attractively presented and punishments vividly threatened, one may induce a person to change his values. Here the importance of Karol Wojtyła's adoption of phenomenological method comes to the fore. A person ordinarily forms his acts and habits neither on the basis of sheer instinct nor on the basis of cool rational decision. Instead, he lives for the values he has adopted in a world of his experience. The person lives according to an ethos that is formed by his environment (both physical and social) and his own responses to it. Because this world is one of values, a person's responses are tinged with emotion. David Hume and his successors may distinguish neatly between facts and values, but the worlds in which real persons live present facts as values and values as facts. Human experience is never of brute, neutral facts.

This fundamental truth makes it possible to influence or even control a person "from within," as it were. Under the Communist Party rule in Poland (of which Karol Wojtyła had extensive experience), every Pole's world was formed largely by the regime and its expectations. One knew from the constant repetition of the Party's teaching and from the unfavorable consequences of disapproved actions what one was expected to value and to do. The individual person found himself strongly impelled to conform his own mind to the regime's expectations, to yield his own judgment to those expectations. Andrzej Szostek gives a pathetic, if also amusing, example: "I remember a news program on Polish TV several years ago when the announcer, visibly disconcerted, sought to announce the forecasted weather for May 1st in such a way that it did not appear too dreadful and prevent the viewers from participating in the May Day demonstrations."[21] The announcer did not directly fear punishment on the basis of a command that she misrepresent the weather forecast. There was no rule as such. Rather, she had internalized the values of the Party, even though her own professional judgment recognized the absurdity of her position. Citing the writings of the former dissident and eventual president of a free Czechoslovakia, Vaclav Havel, Michael Sherwin comments:

> The rules of this game of make-believe required that every member of society, from the greengrocer to the president, perpetuate the illusion. They were all pushed to participate daily in the many tiny public rituals that validated the ideology of the regime. Havel notes that it was not necessary to believe the lies. Few in fact did. It was only necessary to act as if the lies were true, or at least to remain silent about them. . . . Living within a lie alienates the person from himself, and leads to a "profound crisis of human identity."[22]

Referring to Socrates in Plato's *Crito*,[23] Szostek writes: "In the *betrayal* of the *truth* that he himself knew—and this moment is of decisive significance—he saw a *breach* [*Verstoß*] *with himself*, an offense [*Verstoß*] leading to a far deeper loss of freedom than that of the prison." And he cites Tadeusz Styczeń: "*To save his freedom, to save his fidelity to the known truth and to save himself—that is one and the same.*"[24]

The most blatant way to subvert a person's subjectivity, one used from ancient times, is to torment and harass, to create a world in which the victim's own pain becomes the dominant evil. Solzhenitsyn tells the story of a female prisoner, "M. a former lieutenant and a sniper," in the Kaluga Gates camp of the Soviet Gulag. A woman of "resilient beauty" who had lived a "heroic life,"

---

21 Andrzej Szostek, M.I.C, "Freiheit—Wahrheit—Gewissen" [Freedom—truth—conscience], *Ethos: Vierteljahrsschrift* (Lublin), Sonderausgabe no. 1, 1993, 34.

22 Michael Sherwin, O.P., "John Paul's Theology of Truth and Freedom: A Dissident Phenomenology in a Thomistic Anthropology," *Nova et Vetera*, English ed., 3, no. 3 (2005): 556. The inner citation is of Vaclav Havel, "The Power of the Powerless," in *The Power of the Powerless*, ed. J. Keane (Armonck, NY: M. E. Sharpe, 1985), 30.

23 Under the Communist regime, it was common to speak of Socrates' conflict with the Athenians as a metaphor to address "Kowalski's" (Everyman's) relationship with the regime.

24 Szostek, *Natur—Vernunft—Freiheit*, 244–45. Szostek quotes Tadeusz Styczeń, *Wolność w prawdzie* [Freedom in truth] (Rome, 1988), 13.

M. had been "bought" by a camp trusty, the stock clerk. This man, who had total control of M.'s life, "besieged her so persistently and hard that she could hardly breathe." He had her subjected to the hardest work assignments and to harassment by the jailers. Finally, writes Solzhenitsyn, "I myself saw how, in a twilight pale because of snow and sky, M. went like a shadow from the women's barrack's and knocked with bent head at this greedy Bershader's storeroom. After that she was well taken care of inside the camp compound."[25] A brave, proud, and patriotic woman was humiliated into becoming the mistress of a venal man who controlled the circumstances of her life, who had the power to punish her with the harshest discomfort and ultimately with exile to a Siberian camp. The world of the Gulag was one structured to undermine the *zek*'s[26] earlier values, to replace them with values of its own. Or rather, it so starkly posed the alternative between suffering and even modest comfort and safety that the natural responses of the human organism and psyche took on enormous importance. To have been a military heroine, a skilled sniper and officer in the Red Army during the Great Patriotic War, all fade from the view of one constantly tormented and harassed. Increasingly one's own body and psyche plead that the suffering stop, and the heroine becomes a frayed nervous system. It is worth noting here that prisoners of war and victims of political persecution are often told repeatedly that those back home have forgotten them, that they are without connection to the world without. On their own, they have only their captors for hope.

It is not necessary to torment a person to subvert his subjectivity. Propaganda, advertising techniques, cultish and group enthusiasm practices all tend to subvert the person's subjectivity, replacing the individual's own consciousness of the world or, most often, of some sector of it with that of a dominant group or center of influence. The groupthink of a business concern and the "fog of war" that blinds political or military planners to unusual options reflect the same reality. Groups, powerful persons, social structures, and sophisticated techniques of communication affect us powerfully, transforming the world in our consciousness and thereby potentially subverting our consciousness.

It is tempting and common to consider such phenomena as these in terms of failures of "inner strength." The Polish announcer betrayed her

---

[25] Solzhenitsyn, *Gulag Archipelago*, 2:232.

[26] *Zek* is the Gulag term for "prisoner."

own intelligent mind by her submission to the Party's lies. "M." acquiesced in her own prostitution. And certainly this is true—to an extent. But we misread these situations and, indeed, the structure of our own personhood if, Kantlike, we try to regard the human person as a completely autonomous rational agent. To do so, however, is to ignore the role of values in the person's life and the emotions by which he experiences them.[27] To be a human person is to be continually presented with values of different kinds, of different strengths, and of different origins. These values are related to each other in different ways and together for a world or worlds of values. And a world of values constitutes an *ethos*. This ethos is as much socially determined as individually, if indeed not more so. The United States of America and the People's Republic of China both boast of many intelligent, intellectually curious, reasonable persons, individuals who can and do think critically. And yet one may ask why it is that an American who thinks critically "for himself" will be much less likely to see the importance of social order and harmony than his Chinese counterpart, who will fail to see why the American sets such a premium on individual initiative, independence, and personal freedom. To a great extent Americans think as they do because they are formed by the American ethos, just as Chinese accept a Chinese ethos. Such comparisons show the impact of culture, which grows in response to historical and geographical circumstances. (It is said that the British and the Japanese are such polite peoples because both live on crowded islands.)

Emotionalization of Consciousness

Solzhenitsyn's fellow prisoner "M." formed her life by the ethos of the Red Army, an ethos characterized by pride, discipline, a patriotic sense of dignity. In the Gulag camp, however, the community formed by that ethos no longer supported her. Abstractly considered, the question of using sexual favors to avoid discomfort and to obtain favorable treatment from the authorities is rather simple and straightforward. "M.," however, found herself in a world structured by perverse values, one in which military virtues of courage, diligence, and honor were punished and vice rewarded, in which one's attempts to hold on to personal dignity were constantly undercut. The prisoner's consciousness becomes emotionalized. Karol Wojtyła analyzes the

[27] Wojtyła, *Persona e atto*, 1116–20, 1136–53.

"emotionalization of consciousness"[28] as a condition in which emotion overpowers consciousness such that emotions form experience, that emotions become the principal determinants of one's responses. Although the emotions manifest themselves in bodily sensations, from the person's corporality, they arise as responses to his values. "The human being is conscious of his body and lives it interiorly as well, and moreover he lives his own 'corporeity.'"[29] Emotions *happen* to a person. The consciousness is emotionalized when these "happenings" gain control, as it were, when it is no longer the will that directs the act but the emotion. Ordinarily one's task is to control or manage the emotions, integrating them according to the standards of knowledge, controlling them for the sake of one's interior integration.[30] This is a task for the will guided by self-knowledge. If the task of the person is to govern his own acts on the basis of his personal integration of self, then the emotionalization of consciousness undercuts his self-possession. Rather than truly acting, he is carried away by emotion. "In fact, the emotionalization of consciousness renders difficult or even impossible one's own actualization."[31] Under normal circumstances, the control (or, we might say, management) of emotion is an aspect of maturation. For the person under stress, such as the *zek* in the Gulag, others play on a person's sensations and emotions, compromising the victim's capacity for self-governance, undermining it.

Using the Person

Wojtyła's personalistic norm denies that the person can be an object of use, to be treated as a means to an end. To treat the person as an object of use is effectively to deny his personhood, to undermine his subjectivity. The robbers who bind the bank manager and place him before the door to prevent its being opened clearly do that. It does not matter whether the manager is a human being or a bear, alive or dead. What is important is that he weigh enough and remain where he is put. The task of controlling another's agency is more complex. To use an animal such as a dog or a horse, the human master avails himself of its instincts and natural reactions. The human person shares many characteristics in common with his

[28] Ibid., 896–904.
[29] Ibid., 897.
[30] Ibid., 900.
[31] Ibid., 904.

animal cousins but with this difference: the human person can adopt or reject values presented to him through the senses, feelings, and imagination. He has to integrate them according to some standard (even if it should be to follow what feels good or pleasant). To use a person is to attempt to overwhelm, undermine, or circumvent his capacity for self-integration and self-governance, which is an attempt to negate his personhood, whether it be done by the KGB, the former-suitor-turned-stalker, the manipulative work supervisor, or the temperamental child.

A phenomenological expression that Wojtyła does not use, but that is apt here, is that of *life-world*, which can be defined as the "universally structured realm of beliefs, assumptions, feelings, values, and cultural practices that constitute meaning in everyday life."[32] The structure of values within this life-world constitutes the person's ethos. The life-world is constituted in consciousness by the person's subjectivity. To reform another's life-world is to subvert his subjectivity by pressing beliefs upon him to which his intelligence does not consent and values that do not necessarily reflect his authentic choice of the good. Since subjectivity always belongs to the person, it cannot, properly speaking, be wrested without his consent. Nevertheless, the effort can be made, and this effort constitutes a violation of the person. But to understand wherein lies the violation, we must address the requirement to know the truth about the good.

Truth and Spirit

The human person lives through a life-world constituted by his consciousness and within which he experiences emotionally the facts of the world according to the values that present themselves to him in his life-world. One strength of the phenomenological method is its suitability for analyzing the structures of human experience. Phenomenologists such as (and most notably) Max Scheler can analyze the structure of this life-world with precision and accuracy, showing the way in which values interrelate and stand with respect to each other. The human person, however, is not simply a center of consciousness.[33] Because the person is an efficient cause in the

---

32 Hans-Herbert Kögler, "Life-world," in *The Oxford Companion to Philosophy*, ed. Ted Honderich (Oxford: Oxford University Press, 1995), 488.

33 See Wojtyła, *Persona e atto*, 872–73; *Valutazione sulla possibilità di costruire l'etica cristiana*, 290; and *Person and Community*, 142, 219.

world, because *efficacy* is as essential to his personhood as consciousness, his experience necessarily transcends the phenomena present to his consciousness. For the person to integrate himself in action, it does not suffice to find some ordering principle within consciousness (although that in itself is a difficult challenge), but to order one's life-world and in particular his values such that they are integrated with his acts.

This challenge finds a concrete expression in *Love and Responsibility*, where Wojtyła analyzes the factors that make up *love*.[34] The person in love finds his consciousness filled with the sensations and sentiments of love, whose values give rise to powerful emotions. Wojtyła analyzes love first in terms of *attraction*, of which he writes, "*Attraction is of the essence of love and in some sense is indeed love, although love is not merely attraction*."[35] Attraction arises because the man and the woman regard each other as a good. This attraction is felt, not inferred. In fact, it can be felt strongly as sexual, affective, and emotional factors operate within consciousness. But this makes attraction by itself unreliable. "Where the feelings are functioning naturally they are not concerned with the truth about their object. Truth is for man a function and a task for his reason."[36] He deepens the discussion of attraction by analyzing love as desire, primarily in the sexual sense, and then as goodwill, all of which need to be integrated. And here is the problem. In the case of love between a man and a woman, a variety of powerful factors is at work, from sexual desire to sentiment to camaraderie to emotion. Not only does the person experience these factors, but he must also act upon them. Indeed, where the relationship between man and woman is concerned, the effect of one's actions can be dramatically significant, for the sexual relationship between man and woman can and characteristically does result in the procreation of offspring. Therefore love must be integrated, and neither attraction nor desire nor sentiment nor any other feeling suffices to integrate love. "*The process of integrating love relies on the primary elements of the human spirit—freedom and truth*."[37]

Therefore this life-world and the ethos constituted by its values cannot be a self-contained, solipsistic realm. Because the person is—precisely as

---

[34] *Love and Responsibility*, chap. 2, "The Person and Love."

[35] Ibid., 76.

[36] Ibid., 77.

[37] Ibid., 116.

person—an efficient cause in the world, some aspect of which his actions intend to change, the values intuited and experienced emotionally in consciousness cannot be taken *only* as data of consciousness. That is to say, the person's presence in the world *as person* demands that the world itself be a locus of values or, more precisely, of goods.[38] The response of a man and woman to each other in love may well result in the establishment of a new home, a significant changing of both their lives, and the conception of a baby. In virtue of his power to know the truth about the being of things, the person can critique the world as it appears in his consciousness. The power of reason can know things as they really are. As we noted in chapter 2, this "things as they really are" cannot be reduced to the data of empiricism. The world is in fact full of goods and evils. However, because these goods do not necessarily correspond to the values and order of values as the person experiences them, it falls to the person to determine the truth about the good in his own experience. In other words, a person's life-world is subject to his rational evaluation according to the truth. Indeed, the human person has a primordial obligation to pursue truth. John Paul II pointedly writes: "There is no morality without freedom. . . . Although each individual has a right to be respected in his own journey in search of the truth, there exists a prior moral obligation, and a grave one at that, to seek the truth and to adhere to it once it is known."[39]

The human person, therefore, is not simply a center of experience, a nexus of subjectivity.[40] Rather, he is a being responsible for the truth. As particularly emphasized in the text cited from *Veritatis Splendor*, this responsibility for the truth is fundamental, a "prior moral obligation" to every exercise of freedom. This is not a task that can be accomplished by another on one's own behalf. When Wojtyła writes, "No one else can want for me,"[41] he means more than simply that "only *I* can have *my* experiences." Rather, he means that personhood is something radically incommunicable precisely because the person has an inner life; that is, he is a

38 Here it is worth noting Andrzej Szostek's critique of Karl Rahner's "angelological anthropology," which, argues Szostek, tends to regard the human person as a spirit—or more precisely, a freedom—not integrally engaged with the world. See Szostek, *Natur—Freiheit—Vernunft*, 251–53.

39 *Veritatis Splendor*, 34.

40 Wojtyła, "Person: Subject and Community," in *Person and Community*, 219, 231.

41 *Love and Responsibility*, 24.

spiritual being. "*Inner life means spiritual life. It revolves around truth and goodness.*"[42] "No one else can want for me," because what I want is a good toward which I may direct myself. It is precisely in virtue of that inner life that the human person is able to possess and determine himself by the power of his will, a will that is realized efficaciously. This is a point central to the anthropology of Karol Wojtyła/John Paul II. The human being is not a physical entity with a spirit somehow attached or associated with it. Rather, the human being, as a physical organism in the world, is also a spiritual being. In other words, it is precisely the conscious (and therefore spiritual) subject who is an efficacious agent in the world. It is because man is a spiritual being that John Paul II can define him as "one who seeks the truth."[43] This anthropological conception of the human being as both spiritual and corporeal constitutes the philosophical basis on which John Paul II develops his "theology of the body." If the person as a spiritual being is ordered to truth and goodness as such, then of anything present to consciousness, of any object of experience the person can ask: "Is it true? Is it truly good?" We need, therefore, to examine more closely how John Paul II understands this concept of *truth.*

Truth

In *Fides et Ratio* John Paul II paraphrases Aristotle's definition of truth: to say of what is that it is and of what is not that it is not.[44] Arguing that the desire for truth is a part of human nature, he continues, "It is an innate property of human reason to ask why things are as they are, even though the answers which gradually emerge are set within a horizon which reveals how the different human cultures are complementary."[45] Further on, citing the opening words of Aristotle's *Metaphysics,* he continues: " 'All human beings desire to know,' and truth is the proper object of this desire. Everyday life shows how concerned each of us is to discover for ourselves, beyond mere opinions, how things really are."[46] For John Paul II, then, truth is knowledge of how things really are and why they are as they are.

---

42 Ibid., 23.

43 *Fides et Ratio,* 28.

44 Ibid., 56, 82; Aristotle, *Metaphysics* 4.7, 1011b27. See Wojtyła, *Persona e atto,* 1016.

45 *Fides et Ratio,* 3.

46 Ibid., 25.

What is significant here is his realism, drawn from the Aristotelian-Thomistic tradition. To attain truth, knowledge must transcend the boundaries of personal consciousness to the knowledge of things as they are. Therefore, he speaks in *Fides et Ratio* of the necessity for philosophy to pursue the *truth of being*.[47] The quest for truth requires a metaphysics and not just an epistemology. John Paul II does not himself develop a systematic metaphysics, nor does he provide a fleshed-out theoretical account of truth, choosing rather to develop his phenomenological analyses on the basis of the Aristotelian-Thomistic philosophy of being.[48] His focus in *Fides et Ratio*—and indeed in all his work—is the truth about the human person and his ultimate meaning.

The concern and quest for the truth reveals the spiritual aspect of the human person, since to attain the truth he must rise above the material, sensible order. Through the senses, a human being can indeed become aware of things in the world and their properties, and by his emotions (which are based in the body) the person experiences their value. However, it is only through his power of reason that he can ask and know how things really stand and what is their real value. The reliability of an emotion or sentiment can be competently and accurately judged only by a power higher than the feelings, one that is directed toward the objective truth of things. Based as it is on universal and unchanging ideas and principles, reason is free of determination by physical causes. Furthermore, because this power to know and understand the truth as true is a spiritual (and not material) power within the human being, the person is *responsible for the truth.* His possession of the truth, as well as his ignorance, is his own. Among the truths he is most particularly responsible for is the truth about himself. In John Paul II's thought, self-knowledge is of central importance.[49] The human person is obliged to know himself.[50] This means that the human person cannot accept himself as a given, as though the totality of his experiences and past behavior constitute who he is.

---

[47] Ibid., 5.

[48] Wojtyła, "The Degrees of Being from the Point of View of the Phenomenology of Action," 125–30; "Transcendencja osoby w czynie a autoteleologia człowieka," in *Osoba i czyn,* 480; "The Separation of Experience from the Act in Ethics," in *Person and Community,* 42–43; etc.

[49] *Fides et Ratio,* prologue and 1, 22–23; *Persona e atto,* 877–82.

[50] John Paul II cites the Delphic inscription in *Fides et Ratio,* 1.

Rather, he is capable of knowing the truth about his own nature, his destiny or vocation, and his responsibilities.

Freedom and Will

In virtue of his power to know the truth, the person is able to order himself through his acts to the good independently of what happens in him. He is free. This does not mean that his freedom is a kind of causality separate and, as it were, detached from physical, material causality, as Kant suggests.[51] Rather, knowledge enables the person to direct and govern his physical causality, to determine its practical finality here and now. In virtue of being an animal, the human being is equipped with a variety of organic systems with their respective purposes. The digestive system requires food to process, and the person experiences its needs as hunger. The skin perceives temperature changes, detecting when the ambient air becomes too cold, and the person shivers, experiences "goose bumps," and desires warmth. These are all things that *happen in* a human being, and the human organism's inner dynamics urge a certain kind of response to satisfy the need. Furthermore, on the basis of past experiences, the rational human being recognizes different situations as desirable, exciting, dangerous, challenging, depressing, or otherwise such as may stimulate emotion. A dark forest incites a primordial terror in the heart. The sight of a dear friend causes joy, while a former enemy's appearance rekindles anger and resentment. All these emotions also *happen in* the person, proposing their corresponding responses and urging them. Reason, as Hume argued,[52] cannot simply override these feelings, these bodily desires and emotional reactions. "Willpower" alone (which is simply a kind of inner preaching or motivational speaking to oneself, often coupled with the effort to clear one's consciousness of the unwanted desire) cannot override feelings and their urges. This, however, is not where the will and its freedom lie. Rather, freedom and free choice lie in the capacity to form and govern one's behavior according to the truth, according to an understanding that transcends the desires and urges that happen within. Just as the artisan must work with his materials, overcoming their natural resistance and utilizing their inner

[51] *Critique of Pure Reason*, A 446, B 474, from the *thesis.*

[52] *Treatise of Human Nature*, bk. 2, pt. 2, sec. 3, "Of the Influencing Motives of the Will," 177–82.

structure, so must the free person reform and shape his inclination, emotions, and desires. The alcoholic does not overcome his addiction by perpetually deciding against taking a drink but by restructuring his life, which restructuring may require new social habits, attending Alcoholics Anonymous meetings, and finding different friends, all to support the values that he knows to be authentic goods. The young man who would be chaste learns to avert his eyes from the open blouse of the young woman bending toward him. Competent weight-loss counselors know that a person successfully loses weight and keeps it off not by adopting a particular diet so much as by changing his entire approach to eating and his relationship with food. Freedom is the human person's capacity to govern himself and to direct himself toward ends that he recognizes as and can affirm to be good. In short, Wojtyła's name for freedom is self-determination.[53]

Derivation of the Personalistic Norm

Negative Formulation

> The person is a kind of good which does not admit of use and cannot be treated as an object of use and as such the means to an end.[54]

This is Karol Wojtyła's "negative formulation" of the personalistic norm. Let us first analyze this formulation to find not only its basis but its basis precisely as a moral norm.

"A Kind of Good . . ."

Wojtyła writes that the *person is a kind of good.* Why and in what way is the person a *good*? The theological starting point is the Scriptural testimony that human beings are created in the image of God (Gen 1:26–27). This biblical teaching is central to John Paul II's anthropology: "In [the biblical "beginning"] the revealed truth concerning man as 'the image and likeness' of God constitutes the immutable *basis of all Christian anthropology.*"[55] The

[53] Wojtyła, *Love and Responsibility,* 47, 135; *Persona e atto,* 977–81, 985, 1007, 1026, 1035; "The Personal Structure of Self-Determination," in *Person and Community,* 190; John Paul II, *Man and Woman He Created Them,* 15.2, 186.

[54] *Love and Responsibility,* 41.

[55] John Paul II, *Mulieris Dignitatem,* 6; see also *Redemptor Hominis,* 13, and "Address to a Group of Bishops from the United States on their 'Ad Limina'

creation, according to Genesis, was "good," and after the creation of human beings it was "very good" (Gen 1:10, 12, 18, 25, 31). Even though Karol Wojtyła does not cite this Scriptural teaching in his presentation of the personalistic principle in *Love and Responsibility*, the concept *image of God* is in the background. This is clear from his discussion of the concept in *Mulieris Dignitatem*, where he explores the significance of this image.

> *Man is a person, man and woman equally so* [*Homo persona est, pariter vir et mulier*], since both were created equally in the image and likeness of the personal God. What makes man [*homo*] like God is the fact that—unlike the whole world of other living creatures, including those endowed with senses (*animalia*)—man [*homo*] is also a rational being (*animal rationale*).[56]

That the human being is a rational animal implies far more than the possession of certain powers of the soul (senses, intellect, appetites), for John Paul II proceeds immediately to develop its relational implications. In virtue of her rationality, the first woman is "another I," another subjective self alongside the man. Interpreting Genesis 2 in light of the truth about the image of God, we discover that "man cannot exist 'alone' (cf. Gen 2:18); he can only exist as a 'unity of the two,' and therefore *in relation to another person*."[57] A rational being cannot exist alone but must stand in relation to other rational beings. John Paul presents the naming of the animals in Genesis 2:19–20 as a kind of "test" for the man, in which he discovers that there is none like him, none to be a "suitable helper."[58] To live as a rational being, the human person needs another person. Hence, John Paul II writes, "Man becomes the image of God not so much in solitude as in the moment of communion."[59] To be a person is to stand in relation of mutual gift of self with others.

John Paul develops the specifically intellectual implications of this in his encyclical *Fides et Ratio*, where he stresses the communal character of our reasoning. The isolated intellect contemplating the truth it has acquired on

---

Visit," September 2, 1988, www.vatican.va/holy_father/john_paul_ii/speeches/1988/september/documents/hf_jp-ii_spe_19880902_usa-ad-limina_en.html (accessed September 19, 2006), 4, 8.

56 *Mulieris Dignitatem*, 6.

57 Ibid., 7.

58 *Man and Woman He Created Them*, 5.4–5, 148–49.

59 Ibid., 9.3, 163.

its own is a fiction. Every thinker (which is to say, every human person) needs dialogue with others to attain truth and understanding.

> Their search looks towards an ulterior truth which would explain the meaning of life. And it is therefore a search which can reach its end only in reaching the absolute. Thanks to the inherent capacities of thought, man is able to encounter and recognize a truth of this kind. Such a truth . . . is attained not only by way of reason but also through trusting acquiescence to other persons who can guarantee the authenticity and certainty of the truth itself.[60]

Even one's private thoughts and reflections are conducted in a kind of inner dialogue as one poses problems, questions, objections, and examples to oneself. It is a matter constantly verified in experience that such interior reflections need to be tested against others, that in dialogue one realizes one's rationality. In his encyclical on Christian unity, John Paul II writes: "The capacity for 'dialogue' is rooted in the nature of the person and his dignity. . . . Dialogue is an indispensable step along the path *towards human self-realization*, the self-realization both of *each individual* and *of every human community*."[61] A century earlier, Charles Sanders Peirce had insisted that the very logic of inquiry precludes the individual from being the final judge of truth, that as the work of a community, rational inquiry is of its very nature communal.[62] This community of rationality enables not only an understanding of the world in the various sciences but also the re-creation of the world by human handiwork. This re-creation, of course, must not be understood only in terms of science and technology—the discovery of nuclear power and the building of great bridges—but more importantly in the power to form human societies with their cultures, traditions, and laws. The world human beings live in is itself a creation of the human community.

---

60 *Fides et Ratio*, 33.

61 *Ut Unum Sint*, www.vatican.va/edocs/ENG0221/_INDEX.HTM (accessed January 2, 2003), 28.

62 Charles Sanders Peirce, "Lessons in the History of Science," in *Collected Papers* (Cambridge, MA: Belknap Press, 1965), 1.43ff. See also Adrian J. Reimers, *An Analysis of the Concepts of Self-Fulfillment and Self-Realization in the Thought of Karol Wojtyla, Pope John Paul II*, Problems in Contemporary Philosophy 48 (Lewiston, NY: Edwin Mellen Press, 2001), 136–38.

It follows, then, that the human person is a good. Indeed, by his very subjectivity, every human person experiences himself as a good. This is why a person cares for himself and strives to preserve his own life. But the individual is also a good in relation to others, enriching their humanity by the interchange of rationally ordered goods, manufactured commodities, to be sure, but also through conversation, works of art, literature, law, and the manifold efforts by which persons care for each other. Indeed, it is precisely *as person* that the other is a good. Only a person can appreciate and enrich my personhood. Only persons elicit my rationality, my personal engagement with society and the world. Only a person can bring into my life and that of our society the richness of human creativity, of new ideas. We must note too that in ordinary human experience we encounter the other person as a good when we encounter him *as person.* John Paul II has strongly stressed this centrality of family life for precisely this reason: the family is where the person is formed, learning love and truth. "The first and fundamental structure for 'human ecology' is the family, in which man receives his first formative ideas about truth and goodness, and learns what it means to love and to be loved, and thus what it actually means to be a person."[63] We are encouraged and pleased to see family, friends, and others who show an unfeigned interest in us. The human person is a good.

". . . which does not admit of use and cannot be treated as . . . the means to an end"

Wojtyła's use of the verb "cannot" is significant here, especially when we compare it with Kant's formulation of his practical imperative, "Act in such a way that you treat humanity, whether in your own person or in the person of another, always at the same time as an end and never simply as a means."[64] Wojtyła's norm is in the indicative voice, while Kant's is in the imperative. Kant's formulation allows for the possibility that one may treat another person (or even oneself) as a means; Wojtyła states that the person *does not admit of use* and *cannot* be treated as a means. He can say this because he has examined more closely and specifically what it is to be a person, whereas Kant's concern was to carve out space and conditions for

63 John Paul II, *Centesimus Annus*, 39; see also his apostolic exhortation *Familiaris Consortio* (Boston: St. Paul Editions, 1981), 17–18, and Karol Wojtyła, "The Family as a Community of Persons," in *Person and Community*, 316–20.

64 *Grounding for the Metaphysics of Morals*, 429.

morality in a causally determined world. For Kant there is, strictly speaking, no question of an encounter with another person. In Kant's world the other is encountered as a phenomenon, which is, as such, subject to the laws of nature governing the phenomenal world. His personhood is not, therefore, given in experience. The respect due to him is based on the acknowledgment that he too is a rational being who lives his own life as *noumenon*, which is to say as a moral being. There can be no question of my entering into communion with him in a shared subjectivity such as John Paul II describes. Because the other is and can be for me nothing other than phenomenal, I can, in the first instance, treat him as a means to an end. Indeed, this will be my "default" stance toward him. The import of Kant's practical imperative is that I may not stop at this but must always take care to treat him also as an end in himself.

For Karol Wojtyła, however, the situation is quite different. As we have already noted, the person *as person* simply cannot be an object of use. His overpowered body can be restrained and used, and another can seek to subvert his subjectivity in order to impose his will, in which case the person consents, even if only minimally, to being used or treated as a means. Therefore Wojtyła asserts his personalistic norm in the indicative rather than the imperative mode. But if the norm is indicative, a proposition representing a fact, how can it be normative? How can it entail imperatives?

Imperatives and the Personalistic Norm

In his analysis of *participation*, of "acting together with others,"[65] Wojtyła argues that prior to the moral value is the *personalistic value* of an act, which itself is normative. This personalistic value arises from the fact that the act arises from the person who is its author and simultaneously fulfills him (or leads toward his disintegration as a person, if the act is evil). To perform an act is itself a value.[66] From this emerges the normative content:

> If the personalistic value of the act is a fundamental value that conditions . . . ethical value and the ethical order, then also that norm of acting that results directly from this has fundamental significance as well. It is not an ethical norm in the strict sense of the word . . . , but it is a norm of the completion

[65] Wojtyła, *Persona e atto*, pt. 4, "Participation," 1167–1213.

[66] Ibid., 1173.

> of the act, a *norm* of one's *personal subjectivity*, an "interior" norm, which is about the assurance of the self-determination of the person, hence his efficacy, transcendence, and integration in the act.[67]

Karol Wojtyła intends to justify the moral proposition that it is wrong to use another person, treating him as a means to an end. Indeed, in *Love and Responsibility* he uses this norm to establish that certain forms of interpersonal behavior are morally wrong and that others are to be fostered.[68] Plainly, Wojtyła is not intimidated by Hume's stricture against inferring an "ought" from an "is." Indeed, as we saw in chapter 2 above, the "order of nature," which is also the order of creation, is an order not only of ontic structures but also of goods. To Karol Wojtyła's mind a fact can and generally does have a value. Norms are truths about the world and not simply subjective evaluations. This point is central to his later arguments in *Veritatis Splendor.* A moral norm is stated in the indicative mode because facts are not, after all, neutral. The *neutral fact* is found only in the abstractions of that "generalized empiricism which seems to weigh so heavily on the mind of modern man."[69] Therefore it is not that we impose or invent values that we "find" in the world but that the realm of neutral facts is itself an abstraction. The person is a *good*, which means that there are appropriate and inappropriate ways to respond to the value that the person is and represents.

The moral task confronting any person as a rational being is to tailor his actions to the authentic good. As we have already stressed, the person lives in a world of values. Even if it be possible to consider the world abstractly as a realm of neutral facts, as soon as one participates in it, as soon as his engagement with the world becomes a matter not simply of abstract scientific consideration but of *praxis*, then the facts become structured with and formed by values. The task of intellectually sorting out true from false goods is in some cases fairly simple. Amusing as it may seem to tease the neighbor's Rottweiler, the dog's mien, fangs, and strength promote prudential reflections. The reasonable person reflects on the finitude of his funds and develops at least a modicum of prudence. Although

67 Ibid., 1182.

68 See *Love and Responsibility*, 121–23, 218–19, 228–30. As this pertains to the economic sphere, see John Paul II, *Laborem Exercens*, 7.

69 *Love and Responsibility*, 57; see also 226 for Wojtyła's concrete application of this.

Friday's paycheck can purchase abundant Saturday pleasure, a reflection on the needs of the coming fortnight tempers the gratification of sense and fosters the virtue of thrift. Indeed, there is scarcely an adult who has not developed some virtue on the basis of reflections about the goodness of certain values presented to his consciousness. Of course, the goods one must respond to do not exist only on the horizontal level, as though one's only judgments have to do with managing money and avoiding danger. There are higher goods that govern our lives, goods that no person can long avoid responding to. That courage is a virtue precisely about facing dangers that are worth risking one's life for[70] implies that there are goods greater than life.

One good to which a person must respond is the person—one's own self, of course—but also the other person, his neighbor. Wojtyła's personalistic principle is that the person is a good that cannot be used as an end. That which one uses as an end is a tool or instrument, an extension of one's own corporality and therefore efficacy. The instrument is an aid to the efficacious realization of one's own will, as the acting person works to effect a change in the world. And herein lies the problem with using a person. That person, precisely insofar as he is a person, has his own will. He acts on the basis of his own understanding and valuation of the world about him to attain the good he has chosen for himself. The person being used as a tool really has a mind of his own. It is worth noting here that those who are being so used and who have no way effectively to make their activity their own (such as slaves or those forced by necessity into degrading servile work) resent their overseers and often, whether deliberately or not, undermine the work forced upon them. The disconnection between one's own subjectivity and the work one is forced to do gives rise to the experience of *alienation.*[71] It follows that to use a person or to *attempt to use* a person is a violation of that good which he is. The attempt to use another is unrealistic and can succeed only to the extent that the personhood of the other is denied. In this respect we may note that those intent on dominating and controlling others grievously resent the other's insistence that he too has a mind and a will. Because to use another person

---

[70] Aristotle, *Nicomachean Ethics* 3.6, 1115b2ff.

[71] Wojtyła, "Person: Subject and Community," in *Person and Community*, 257; John Paul II, *Centesimus Annus*, 43.

is to deny and nullify a genuine good (the personhood of another human being), to try to use another person is morally wrong.

Positive Formulation

> In its positive form the personalistic norm confirms this: the person is a good toward which the only proper and adequate attitude is love.[72]

The positive formulation of the personalistic norm is a surprising innovation in philosophy. From the perspective of Christian Revelation, of course, the requirement to love one's neighbor is fundamental, as Wojtyła himself notes in his discussion of the norm.[73] However, the thrust of his argument in *Love and Responsibility* is philosophical. He writes:

> Strictly speaking the commandment says: "Love persons", and the personalistic norm says: "A person is an entity of a sort to which the only proper and adequate way to relate is love." The personalistic norm does, as we have seen, provide a justification for the New Testament commandment.[74]

Before proceeding, however, to examine the philosophical basis of this positive formulation, we must consider a second theological point, drawn from one of John Paul II's favorite texts of the Second Vatican Council:[75]

> Indeed, the Lord Jesus, when He prayed to the Father "that all may be one . . . as we are one" (John 17:21–22) opened up vistas closed to human reason, for he implied a certain likeness between the union of the divine Persons, and the unity of God's sons in truth and charity. This likeness reveals that man, who is the only creature on earth that God has willed for itself, cannot fully find himself except in sincere gift of self.[76]

In context this quote compares the human person with the Persons of the Trinity, whose personhood consists in relation,[77] implying that human

---

72 Wojtyła, *Love and Responsibility*, 41.

73 Ibid., 40.

74 Ibid., 41.

75 See Pascal Ide, "Une théologie du don: Les occurrences de *Gaudium et spes*, no. 24, 3 chez Jean-Paul II," *Anthropotes* 17 (2001): 149–78, 313–44.

76 *Gaudium et Spes*, 24.

77 Thomas Aquinas, *ST* I, q. 40, aa. 1–2.

personhood is likewise relational and that just as God is himself a communion of Persons, so too must the human person live in communion. In this text, the Council identifies the human being as "the only creature on earth that God has willed for itself." From his very origin, the human person does not exist for the purposes of some greater entity, but for himself. As the context and development of *Gaudium et Spes* makes clear, the Council is not affirming the radical autonomy or total independence of the human being in relation either to God or his fellows. Rather, as the first chapter of the pastoral constitution makes clear, the human being is endowed with his own dignity precisely because of his intellect and conscience, in virtue of which he enjoys authentic freedom.[78] "For its part, authentic freedom is an exceptional sign of the divine image within man. . . . [H]ence man's dignity demands that he act according to a knowing and free choice."[79] The human being, according to the Council, is not simply a tool or a part of a larger scheme of things.[80] Nevertheless, the human being realizes and fulfills himself only by freely giving of himself to others, in love. To put it in the terms we have been using, the person realizes his value as a person in serving the good of others.

Here we glimpse the inherent complexity of interpersonal relationships. If the person is not to be an object of use, because as person he directs himself according to his own understanding and will, then how might one relate appropriately to him? It does not suffice simply to learn from him what he desires and provide that for him, for the efficacy of his own personhood requires that he himself strive to realize the good. One does not love, therefore, simply by *doing for* or by meeting material needs.[81] Furthermore, if one needs the assistance or aid of another person, how can one appropriately avail oneself of that aid without *using* the other? In general, how can society, which by its very nature requires interdependence, function without persons using each other? This problem becomes especially acute when we consider that one person in question may be under another's authority. The general sends the foot soldier into a dangerous battle. The overseer instructs the worker to exert himself in tedious labor.

---

78 *Gaudium et Spes*, 15–17.

79 Ibid., 17.

80 On this see ibid., 12, 14.

81 On this see, John Paul II's discussion of the "primacy of things over persons" in his encyclical letter *Dives in Misericordia*, 11.

Although neither the soldier nor the worker enjoys nor wants to undertake the task assigned, the superior insists. The young husband, having forgone sexual intimacy for the weeks following his wife's delivery of a child, wants to have relations with his wife (whose hormonal responses to the child may leave her with little desire for such intimacy). Is this a case of using another, if her desires do not correspond to his ardent impulses? Furthermore, even if one person should willingly consent to be a sort of slave for the pleasure or convenience of the other, thereby making of himself a free gift, does not this very fact constitute the beloved's response as a kind of using?

Let us pause momentarily to situate this issue more broadly. At stake here is not simply the solution to a difficulty in Wojtyła's text but in fact a fundamental anthropological conception. Whether we consider the problem of *using* another in the various interactions of domestic, civil, commercial, military, and even religious life, or the conception of *love* insofar as it entails doing good for another, we necessarily confront a tension between the objective, factual reality of the other as a physical entity in the world and the subjective reality of the other in his freedom and interiority. St. James famously rebukes those who give their poor neighbor nothing while wishing him: "Keep yourself warm and eat plenty!" (Jas 2:16). But one may also remark that love cannot amount simply to *doing for* or *giving to* another. If, as Rahner and his intellectual heirs suggest, the person is to be identified with his freedom,[82] then it becomes extremely difficult to express the difference or even to find the boundary between loving and using. The interaction between persons, considered insofar as they are objects in the world, reduces to an exchange of ontic goods. Truly to love another as person requires above all that his freedom be affirmed.[83] Such a position comes very close to Kant's, with his sharp distinction between the objective realm of the *phenomena* and the freedom of the *noumena*. The acting person may do good for the other's *body*, but in doing so, does he serve the other *person*? How can he take advantage of another's resources and capabilities without using him? Although we commonly recognize that love must express what is within another ("It's the thought that counts"), we realize that the measure of true love cannot be simply the level of freedom

82 Rahner, *Grundkurs des Glaubens*, 49; Szostek, *Natur—Vernunft—Freiheit*, 38, 88–89, 155.

83 Szostek, *Natur—Vernunft—Freiheit*, 217.

and creativity of its acts. True love must address the beloved's needs for the good. We shall return to these questions in chapter 8.

Karol Wojtyła resolves the problem of use in relationships in terms of the good. The union or communion of two persons cannot, strictly speaking, be a substantial union. Even in the sexual union (by which the man and woman become "one flesh"), the two remain distinct human persons;[84] John Paul II speaks in his theology of the body of "bi-subjectivity."[85] Though their bodies may be joined in a common act and expression of devotion, each has his or her own experience of the act. Each is a center of his own subjectivity, acting on the basis of his own understanding of the truth and desire for the good. The union of two persons can only come to be in terms of the good, specifically in terms of a shared good, a common good.[86] This common good "is not simply the sum total of particular interests; rather it involves an assessment and integration of those interests on the basis of a balanced hierarchy of values; ultimately, it demands a correct understanding of the dignity and the rights of the person."[87] Wojtyła writes:

> I may want another person to desire the same good which I myself desire. Obviously, the other must know this end of mine, recognize it as a good, and adopt it. If this happens, a special bond is established between me and the other person: the bond of a *common good* and of a common aim. This special bond . . . constitutes the essential core around which any love must grow. In any case, love between two people is quite unthinkable without some common good to bind them together. This good is the end which both these persons choose.[88]

We can contrast this with any system of compulsion or totalitarian imposition, realities with which Wojtyła had direct personal experience. In *Centesimus Annus*, he writes:

---

84 The identification of man and woman as "one person" is a particularly serious error of Stephen Clark's analysis of the marriage relationship. See Stephen B. Clark, *Man and Woman in Christ* (Ann Arbor: Servant Books, 1980), 85.

85 *Man and Woman He Created Them*, 91.6, 481; 92.4, 484.

86 Wojtyła, "Person: Subject and Community," in *Person and Community*, 254; *Love and Responsibility*, 29–30.

87 John Paul II, *Centesimus Annus*, 47.

88 *Love and Responsibility*, 28.

> In the totalitarian and authoritarian regimes, the principle that force predominates over reason was carried to the extreme. Man was compelled to submit to a conception of reality imposed on him by coercion, and not reached by virtue of his own reason and the exercise of his own freedom. This principle must be overturned and total recognition must be given to the rights of the human conscience, which is bound only to the truth, both natural and revealed.[89]

Similarly, in a more immediate community and in the communion of two persons, the appeal to a principle other than truth as the source of agreement quickly becomes an appeal to force or superior power of some kind.

The common good does not bind persons together only inasmuch as each desires it as a good, similar to a theater audience's common desire to see the performance. None in the anonymity of the audience cares for the others. (Indeed, one may prefer that fewer people be in attendance, to leave room to spread out one's coat.) The common good binds persons together insofar as each desires the good for the other, that the other attain the good as his own. To love means not simply to provide the beloved with what is good, therefore, but to desire that the beloved realize his own good. This is manifest in the rearing of children, as the wise parent does not simply provide goods and services but enables the child increasingly to provide for himself. This is the reason why true friendship involves a willingness to share in common work. If, as Aristotle says, a friend is "another self," then friendship is about sharing virtuous activities in a common life, marked by conversation and thought.[90] In communion each desires not only the common good, but that good precisely because the other so desires it as a good. "I may want another person to desire the same good which I myself desire," writes Wojtyła. "Obviously, the other must know this end of mine, recognize it as a good, and adopt it."[91] And if the love is to be real, then I will desire the goods the beloved desires.

Such a conception precludes use, because the good is desired precisely as the good that the beloved desires. To be sure, the relationship is different where a personal communion is not in question, such as the relationship between a military officer and a conscripted soldier. There the officer

---

[89] John Paul II, *Centesimus Annus*, 29; see also 44.

[90] *Nicomachean Ethics* 9.9, 1170b.

[91] *Love and Responsibility*, 28.

may well be unaware of the conscript's state of mind, whether he wishes to serve as a soldier or to fight in this war. The understanding of common good in the social and political sphere must include a normative moment according to which the individual is understood to share in the obligations for mutual protection, funding of infrastructure, and so on. At stake is what Thomas Aquinas calls "civic fellowship."[92] Even in such cases, the conscript cannot be treated as simply a tool for use, another weapon in the war, but he must be regarded as fellow citizen with whom one is in solidarity. If the conscript fails to recognize this, then to a certain extent he fails in his virtue as a citizen obliged to his fellow countrymen. And members of a society rightfully expect their fellows to be virtuous.

A deeper concern is the nature of this common good. According to *Gaudium et Spes*, 24, a human being finds himself only in sincere gift of self. If this is to be understood as Wojtyła proposes, then this gift of self must be in service of the good that the recipient is himself ordered to. One does not love the absent homeowner by entering his home and repainting the interior, even artistically with the highest-quality paints. Nor does one love the bank robber by providing him with superior weapons and a getaway car. Indeed, such a gift is, as it were, the negative image of the situation with the conscript. The officer makes it possible for the conscript nobly to love his country by defending it. The donor to the bank robber enables further and worse ignobility. If, however, the text from *Gaudium et Spes* is true, this gift of self must be in reference to a good that is both authentically and universally good. It must be a genuine good for every human being. This is the topic we will examine more closely in the next chapter. The intelligibility of the personalistic norm in its positive formulation depends on the existence or reality of such a good. If there is a good that is an authentic, fitting, and overarching good for every human being, such that one person can help another to the personal attainment or achievement of that good, then we may truly say that "the person is a good toward which the only proper and adequate attitude is love." If such a good be lacking, then what is best for one person may well differ from the good of his fellows, and the common good of two can depend only on their mutual agreement. It would be impossible to affirm that each owes another anything but justice, understanding by this a kind of truthfulness

[92] *ST* II–II, q. 26, a. 8.

and mutual equity in their dealings. If, on the other hand, the person is a good that does not admit of use, and if the person exists and lives for a good that is transcendent and universal, then the only way in which one can relate at all to him, without falling into a violation of the norm as negatively formulated, is in love, that is, by serving him to attain his own authentic good.

In arguing this, of course, we cannot pretend that all questions concerning human relationships, and in particular social ones, are immediately answered. As Karol Wojtyła notes in the final chapter of *Person and Act*, the attitude of opposition or resistance may well be the most appropriate expression of solidarity with one's fellows in society.

The Imperative

The imperative "Love persons" is derived from the personalistic norm, and the derivation is evidently straightforward, granted the foregoing. If the personalistic norm be true, then one who fails to love in effect does two things. First, he attempts the impossible, which is to use a person. In saying "he attempts the impossible," of course, we cannot imply that in a practical sense he fails to attain his objective. Quite often he does attain his objective. However, his effort to use the other becomes a seduction or even an attempted compulsion of the other's will. As such he reduces the other to an object, a nonsubject, and hence a nonperson. To put it another way, his intentional image of the other is as a tool or means for the satisfaction of desire and not as a good to be valued for itself. Second, in failing to love and in using the other, he neglects the transcendent good that is both his own and the other's good and in its place substitutes a good of his own choosing, toward which he directs not only himself but the one he is using. To use another, to fail to love is therefore to turn oneself away from the transcendent good.

An imperative is, of course, a command. Whence comes this command? And what is its force? By its very essence, command or imperative comes from one with authority to enforce it by rewards and punishments. When Kant, who rejected the notion of a God who intervenes directly and historically into the affairs of human beings, sought to account for the authority of his imperatives, he acknowledged God as practical Ideal in terms of which the attendant moral disintegration of the immoral person could be understood as punishment or condemnation and the beauty of the morally good will could be seen as reward. Karol Wojtyła, as we have noted at the opening of this work, finds in God the origin and meaning of all good. Therefore, as we reflect philosophically on the imperative, we need not resort to any kind of Kantian philosophical mythology. Therefore, without disregarding that the authentic good lies in a personal God, we can examine the consequences of both compliance with and disobedience to the imperative to love in terms of the relationship with the good. Wherein are the rewards and sanctions that attach to the command resulting from the personalistic norm?

Since for Karol Wojtyła love consists precisely in disinterested gift of self,[93] only by loving others can the human being find himself, realize himself. Referring to *Gaudium et Spes*, 24, John Paul II writes, "This *finding of oneself in one's own gift becomes the source of a new gift of self* that grows by the power of the inner disposition to the exchange of the gift and in the measure in which it encounters the same and even deeper acceptance and welcome as the fruit of an ever more intense consciousness of the gift itself."[94] That is to say, this gift of self, rather than evacuating the self, enriches it in such a way that the person comes actually to possess himself more fully and creatively precisely in the gift. If to act is, as Wojtyła argues, the way by which one realizes himself as a person, then for the act actually to attain this self-realization it must be an act of love. An evil or wicked act is, precisely as such, a disintegrating act,[95] one that cannot fulfill the person because it is not directed toward the authentic good as known but rather to some value whose goodness is only apparent. Good acts are precisely those that direct the person in transcendence toward the good, and not simply his own personal good or subjective experience of the good but the realization of this good in the lives of others. One "sanction" against failure to love is, therefore, a loss of meaning to one's life. This is not merely a psychological event. Rather, this loss is of the fullness of good itself. Indeed, John Paul II expressed this unequivocally:

> Man cannot live without love. He remains a being that is incomprehensible for himself, his life is senseless, if love is not revealed to him, if he does not

93 *Love and Responsibility*, 95–96.

94 *Man and Woman He Created Them*, 17.5, 197; see also 78.4, 431.

95 Wojtyła, *Persona e atto*, 1075–79; *Lubliner Vorlesungen*, 407.

encounter love, if he does not experience it and make it his own, if he does not participate intimately in it.[96]

Clearly this understanding of self-fulfillment and self-realization is different from and, indeed, opposed to that proposed in the thought of those, especially in contemporary popular publications, who propose fairly well-defined and articulated conceptions of self-fulfillment as a nexus of enriching experiences and the means to attain them. The principal of these conceptions is that proposed by utilitarianism, according to which the good is, in the final analysis, that which pleases, that which the human being finds subjectively satisfying.[97] Closely akin to utilitarianism is the modern conception of the self as autonomous and that precisely in its etymological sense as self-legislating. It is ultimately only the autonomous individual who can determine or define what is good for himself, so that any externally imposed or proposed overarching good under which his personal good is to be subsumed is ipso facto an infringement on his autonomy. This understanding was perhaps most clearly and dramatically stated by the Supreme Court of the United States: "At the heart of liberty is the right to define one's own concept of existence, of meaning, of the universe, and of the mystery of human life."[98]

Thus does the question of norms come down to the question of the good, in particular to the relationships among useful goods, pleasurable (or delightful) goods, and fitting goods. And to this question we turn in the following chapter.

---

96 *Redemptor Hominis,* 10.

97 Mill, *Utilitarianism,* 7, 13–14, and see Karol Wojtyła, "Jeremy Bentham: 'Deontologie oder die Wissenschaft von der Moral,'" *Lubliner Vorlesungen,* 339–56.

98 Majority opinion of the United States Supreme Court in *Planned Parenthood of Southeastern Pennsylvania v. Casey,* 505 U.S. 833 (1992).

CHAPTER 6

The Fitting Good

God and the Good

POPE JOHN PAUL II, philosopher, theologian, and pastor of the Church, does not treat the existence of God as a purely religious matter distinct and separate from the realms of science, art, and everyday activity. We have already seen this in his arguments that the biological order is an abstraction from the order of existence, which is the natural order considered precisely as created by God. We must note this simply because the Enlightenment heritage separates sharply the realm of science, the objectively knowable, from that of religion and values.[1] That God—a Being almighty, omniscient, and eternal, Creator of all other beings, Author of their meanings, and Exemplar of every good—exists is, to John Paul II's

[1] The paradigmatic expression of this might well be Kant's *Religion within the Limits of Reason Alone*, especially in bk. 3, 98–100, where he argues, "There is only *one* (true) *religion*; but there can be *faiths* of several kinds," by "faiths" meaning formal religions with dogma and worship. William James, "The Varieties of Religious Experience," in *Essays in Pragmatism* (New York: Hafner Publishing Co., 1948), "Conclusions," 128, in which he characterizes specific beliefs in an almighty God as "over-belief," sketches what has become our contemporary expression of this. In his analysis of the intellectual climate within which *Veritatis Splendor* appeared, Kaczyński argues that "the theology of creation becomes fundamental to moral theology," precisely because one's moral theology, as well as philosophical ethics, rests on one's account of human nature, on philosophical anthropology. See Kaczyński, *Verità sul bene nella morale*, 29.

mind, a suitable object of human knowledge.[2] Furthermore, this God is the Good, the ultimate and perfect good from which all other goods somehow derive.[3] John Paul II teaches: "Only God is good, and of goodness he possesses infinite perfection. God is the fullness of every good. Thus, just as he 'is' all the fullness of being, in the same manner he 'is good' with all the fullness of good."[4]

And because God is good, his creation is good. "The biblical description of the creation has a character at once ontological—that is, it speaks of beings—and axiological—that is, rendering testimony to values. Having created the world as a manifestation of his infinite goodness, God created it to be good. This is the essential teaching that we draw from the biblical cosmology."[5]

The good creation is a work of the Creator's love for the human being, and therefore a gift.[6] That creation has the nature of the gift is important, because a gift is by its very essence given in freedom. The world is not some necessary emanation from the power of an impersonal being or system. Rather, it serves the Giver's purpose to provide for the good of those to whom he gave the world and its goods. Therefore this gift-character, both ontological and axiological, is rooted in the being of things.

Being and Good in Aristotle and Aquinas

Comparing the conceptions of *good* in the thought of Aristotle and Aquinas, Karol Wojtyła explores their respective accounts of the relation-

---

[2] John Paul II, "Con la ragione l'uomo può giungere alla conoscenza di Dio" [By reason man can arrive at knowledge of God], general audience, March 20, 1985, and "Gli uomini di scienza e Dio" [Scientists and God], general audience, July 17, 1985, in *Catechesi sul Credo*, pt. 1, "Dio Padre e Creatore."

[3] On this compare Joseph Ratzinger, who writes: "Plato was right when he identified the highest divinity with the idea of the good. . . . [T]he three questions, concerning truth and good and God, are but one single question." Joseph Cardinal Ratzinger, *Truth and Tolerance: Christian Belief and World Religions*, trans. Henry Taylor (San Francisco: Ignatius Press, 2004), 230.

[4] General audience, September 11, 1985, in *Catechesi sul Credo*, pt. 1, "Dio Padre e Creatore."

[5] General audience, January 29, 1986, ibid.

[6] John Paul II, *Man and Woman He Created Them*, 13:3–4, 179–80; 14:3, 182; *Dominum et Vivificantem*, 37; *Laborem Exercens*, 12; *Redemptor Hominis*, 8; and general audiences of October 2, 1985; January 8, 1986; and January 29, 1986, in *Catechesi sul Credo*, pt. 1, "Dio Padre e Creatore"; also Wojtyła, *Sources of Renewal*, 46.

ship between *being* and *good*.[7] For Aristotle the good is the object of an aspiration, a desire. Wojtyła writes: "The fact of the aspiration and the end striven for connected with this fact form the experiential basis of the philosophy of the good and thereby of ethics."[8] The good for Aristotle is not constituted as such simply in virtue of its being the object of desire, however, but rather by its being adequate to human nature. The good corresponds to the nature of the human being. It follows, therefore, that the Aristotelian ethics is genuine, founded as it is on happiness, which is the genuine good for the human being.[9] Consequently, the question of happiness, of what this genuine good consists in, becomes central for the understanding of the truth about the good, and indeed to determine the essence of happiness is a central problem of *Nicomachean Ethics*. What is important for Wojtyła is Aristotle's insight that there is a good adequate to the human being, a good that can be known and striven for. Aristotle identifies it as a good that forms the active life but that, as philosophical contemplation, must ultimately participate in the contemplative activity of the gods.[10] How one attains this good is notoriously unclear and has given rise to a great deal of analysis of the Stagirite's ethics.

According to Karol Wojtyła's reading, Aquinas carries Aristotle's analysis a metaphysical step further: If Aristotle's conception of the good for the human being is essentialist, then Thomas's is existential. The essence of the human being as a rational and social being implies that certain goods are appropriate to him, that there is an excellence that characteristically belongs to the rational animal. "Human good turns out to be activity of soul exhibiting excellence, and if there are more than one excellence, in accordance with the best and most complete."[11] However, writes Wojtyła: "Aristotle's conception of good, in which teleology comes to the fore, was thoroughly transformed in the doctrine of St. Thomas. In his philosophy he brings the aspect of existence into the foreground, for which reason his conception can rightly be designated existential."[12] God the Creator is the

[7] "Auf der Grundlage des sittlichen Guten," in *Lubliner Vorlesungen*, 260–303.
[8] Ibid., 263.
[9] Ibid., 271.
[10] *Nicomachean Ethics* 10.8, 1178b21ff.
[11] Ibid., 1.7, 1098a16.
[12] *Lubliner Vorlesungen*, 273.

fullness and perfection of being itself and as such is the fullness of good. Other things are good insofar as their perfection approaches the divine.

> The Creator sees in himself the highest exemplar of all created natures. He knows these natures through their likeness to the exemplar, that is, insofar as they reflect his nature. Herein lies the core of his normative system. Striving toward the end does not alone create the system, nor is it even determined by a being's similarity to the Creator. . . . Only his exemplarity expresses anything about the system of norms, for the Exemplar is the transcendent measure for everything that is directed toward him.[13]

Aquinas's metaphysical step is to link the good with being. To the extent a thing shares in the fullness of being (which is God himself, for God is *ipsum esse subsistens*) is the extent to which it is good.

To an extent, this conception of God as the fullness and perfection of good is reminiscent of Plato's idealist notion of the form of Good.[14] Plato's Good, however, was above all an object of knowledge and not of aspiration or action.[15] Thus, we find in Plato an otherworldly intellectualism that is hard to connect with moral norms. On the other hand, Karol Wojtyła finds something in Aquinas we cannot find in Aristotle and which must needs go beyond the Stagirite's essentialism. For Aristotle the measure is the good *for man*, and this is why in his discussion of happiness he says that human beings can be happy, but only "as *human beings.*"[16] For the human being, however, there is a transcendent order of perfection beyond the immanent goods of human nature, one that reaches to being itself. The divine goodness is the goodness of being itself, a perfection that lacks nothing, suffers nothing, desires nothing, but is all in all.[17] How this good can be the good for a human being is problematic. Being omnipotent and without flaws, God never suffers the frustration of his will. The human person lacks this perfection of power. Perfect in intellect, God is never mistaken. Human beings are constantly uncertain and in error. God wills only what is good, but human beings find themselves desiring and

[13] Ibid., 276–77.

[14] *Republic*, 6–7.

[15] *Lubliner Vorlesungen*, 110, 125, 280.

[16] *Nicomachean Ethics* 1.10, 1101a20.

[17] See Thomas Aquinas, *ST* I, qq. 4–11. See Wojtyła, *Lubliner Vorlesungen*, 290.

yearning for all sorts of inappropriate things. To say that a human being can somehow attain to the pure goodness of Subsistent Being itself is, at the very least, to demand a stretching of philosophical conceptions. Let us trace Wojtyła's argument.

The Roots of Goodness in Being

Karol Wojtyła bases his analysis of God as the fitting good for human beings on Aquinas's argument that good consists in *modus, species, et ordo,* that is, in measure, species, and order. In his *Disputed Questions on Truth,* Aquinas writes:

> The relation implied in the word *good* is the status of that which perfects. This follows from the fact that a thing is capable of perfecting not only according to its own specific character but also according to the act of being which it has in reality. In this way the end perfects the means to the end. But since creatures are not their own act of existing, they must have a received existence.[18]

Wojtyła then proceeds to cite the next paragraph of Aquinas's text as especially significant.

> Thus every good, being perfective in accordance with both its specific character and its act of being, has measure, species, and order: species in its specific character [*ipsam rationem*], measure in its act of being, and order in its status as perfective.[19]

The good is therefore identical with the being of the thing, with its essence and its existence. The good is rooted in its form (*species*), which, as it were, sets the standard of the thing's perfection, which perfection must be realized in being. The order is the thing's orientation toward its own proper good or perfection. That is, the perfection or good of a thing presupposes

---

[18] *De veritate,* q. 21, a. 6; *ST* I, q. 5, a. 5. See Wojtyła, "Die Frage nach dem Maßstab des Seins," in *Lubliner Vorlesungen,* 273–77.

[19] *De veritate,* q. 21, a. 6. In *Lubliner Vorlesungen,* 275, Wojtyła cites the text in Latin: "Unumquoque bonum, inquantum est perfectivum secondum rationem speciei et esse simul, habet modum, speciem, et ordinem. Speciem quidam quantum ad ipsam rationem; modum quantum ad esse, ordinem quantum ad ipsam habitudinem perfectivi."

not only its form but also everything that is presupposed by and is consequent on the form.[20]

The goodness of a creature is measured on the one hand according to its own form (a tall, sturdy oak with full foliage is a *good* oak) and on the other hand according to the participation of that creature in the divine goodness. Every created good is a reflection or manifestation of the divine good,[21] and some creatures can reflect this divine good more perfectly than others. For example, living things more nearly reflect the goodness of the living God than do the nonliving. Most notably, however, the rational being, the human person created in the image and likeness of God, still more perfectly reflects God's perfection and therefore his goodness. Wojtyła writes: "*The higher stages of participation in that absolute fullness of existence, which God represents, come to expression in the more perfect nature of the created being.*"[22] The fact that the human being, as a creature, is formed means necessarily that he is limited. In virtue of its form, any thing is a *this* rather than a *that.* Underlying this analysis is Karol Wojtyła's insistence that the "order of existence" (or "of nature")[23] is the totality of relationships among existing entities. This is an order not only of mechanical relationships, such as the mechanisms by which an RNA molecule replicates itself or by which the process of natural selection preserves advantageous modifications in a species, but also of goods, as we showed in chapter 2.

If the human being is a limited being, finite in the face of the divine infinity, in what way can the human person be *capax Dei*? Karol Wojtyła responds that the measure of a thing's perfection is realized in its striving toward God, and the human person is capable of expressly, consciously, and deliberately yearning for God. In this way the teleology of Aristotle is united with Plato's philosophy and the thought of St. Augustine.[24] God, the Exemplar (the "Form of the Good") is also the fullness of being. As Exemplar, he is the model and origin of all created being. Every created thing reflects something of the Exemplar who has brought it into being. Among creatures in this world, the human person, however, is uniquely

---

[20] *ST* I, q. 5, a. 5.

[21] *ST* I, q. 6, a. 4.

[22] *Lubliner Vorlesungen*, 276.

[23] The reference is again to the important paragraph at *Love and Responsibility*, 57.

[24] *Lubliner Vorlesungen*, 299.

capable of the imitation of God. In virtue of his knowledge and love for the good, he transcends himself and the world about him toward the perfect good.

Imitation and Moral Norms

Aquinas's existential innovation transforms the Aristotelian ethics, because God the Exemplar becomes the transcendent measure for everything directed to him. "Therefore every being possesses an immanent and a transcendent measure. The immanent measure is derived from the inner relationships that govern a given being, which are derived, for instance, from the relationship between form and matter. The transcendent measure arises from the yearning for the divine being, its highest perfection."[25]

The human person is able to direct himself toward his freely chosen ends, and therefore his direction of himself toward the Creator and Exemplar lies in his own power. This fact gives rise to moral norms. Karol Wojtyła continues:

> This turning toward the end is a result of the perfection of the being. . . . This turning toward the end remains in connection with the being and its actions. However, this exemplarity is tied up with the understanding, with knowledge formed by understanding. If a being not only acts according to understanding but also knows it by its understanding, then in its action it cannot free itself from the consequence of this exemplarity which permeates the world of beings. This consequence is the norm.[26]

Let us note two important aspects of this text. First, one of the criticisms of Pope Paul VI's *Humanae Vitae*, a criticism that John Paul II was particularly concerned to address,[27] was that Paul VI had fallen into "physicalism" or "biologism," reducing moral laws to laws of nature, as though Paul were

25 *Lubliner Vorlesungen*, 277.

26 *Lubliner Vorlesungen*, 277. The German translation reads: "Die Hinwendung zum Ziel ist ein Ergebnis der Vollkommenheit des Seins. . . . Diese Hinwendung zum Ziel verbleibt in einem Zusammenhang mit dem Sein und dem Handeln. Die Vorbildhaftigkeit aber ist mit dem Verstand verbunden, mit dem verstandesmäßigen Erkennen. Handelt ein Wesen nicht nur nach dem Verstand, sondern erkennt es auch mit dem Verstand, so kann es sich in seinem Handeln nicht von der Konsequenz der Vorbildhaftigkeit lösen, die die Welt der Wesen durchdringt. Diese Konsequenz ist die Norm."

27 See *Veritatis Splendor*, 47–48; *Man and Woman He Created Them*, 125:2, 637.

saying that where sex is concerned, it is impermissible to contravene or interfere with natural processes. Although this was not what Paul VI was saying, the relationship between moral norms and the patterns and laws of nature most certainly needs to be explicated. We recall the revisionist objection that moral theologians err by confusing fact-description (*Tatsachenbegriff*) and value-description (*Wertbegriff*).[28] From his early philosophical writings to his papal works, John Paul II implicitly rejects this distinction but consistently maintains that truths themselves are value-laden, that there are no bare physical facts, no value-free beings in the real order. Of course, this does not mean that we can simply "read off" moral imperatives from nature's processes, but it does mean that those processes are embedded within an order of goods and themselves participate in those goods. The text from *Lubliner Vorlesungen* cited above intends to provide a kind of primordial or fundamental norm in terms of which other norms can be formulated. This norm is that in virtue of his power to understand the structure of reality and to know the real world around him (this knowledge being based on that understanding), the human person is responsible for his acts. This is not simply a matter of his being able to predict outcomes, although it certainly includes this. The person who engages in sexual intercourse can know that such activity can well result in conception and pregnancy. More important is the fact that this responsibility is founded on an *understanding* of the world in relation to its Exemplar. By "understanding" we mean, of course, not only the general facts but the order underlying them.

The second aspect is that a being is perfected in its turning toward its proper end. In his *Lubliner Vorlesungen*, Wojtyła stresses repeatedly that the goodness of a thing consists in its perfection.[29] Later on, in his encyclical *Veritatis Splendor*, he addresses the question of morality in terms of Christ's challenge to the rich young man, "If you would be *perfect* . . ." and then proceeds to analyze this perfection in terms of the imitation of Christ.[30] The encyclical shows us, of course, the direction in which we are to find this perfection, this imitation of the Perfect Good. As early as the *Lubliner Vorlesungen*, however, Wojtyła is clear that this ultimate end for

---

28 McCormick, *Critical Calling*, 58, 136–37.

29 *Lubliner Vorlesungen*, 173, 177, 179, 196, 243, and notably 244: "Der Akt bedeutet immer Vollkommenheit, er ist beim hl. Thomas also ein zentraler Begriff der ganzen metaphysischen Philosophie des Guten."

30 John Paul II, *Veritatis Splendor*, 16–21.

the human being is God. Karol Wojtyła writes that in Aquinas's conception, "Aristotelian perfectionism and teleologism is joined to the revealed truth about God as Creator and End."[31] If a thing is perfected only by turning toward its proper end, then the human being is perfected only in its turning toward and, indeed, striving for, God as his final end.

The Vision of God and the Human Good

Karol Wojtyła accepts Aquinas's account of human happiness as the vision of the divine essence: "Because the Essence of God is the fullness of good, the immediate knowledge of this essence yields the fullness of happiness."[32] Although this vision cannot be attained under the conditions of this life, any participation in genuine good is a participation in God's perfect happiness. Like Aquinas, Wojtyła is faced with the difficulty of reconciling this transcendent end with the limited goals accessible to the human person and the necessarily finite powers he can exercise. This end, we must note, is not simply very hard to attain but is absolutely beyond the capability of human beings in this life. Aquinas addresses this question with his long analysis of human acts, virtues, and vices in the *Summa theologiae* II, followed by the discussion of Christ and his work in the *tertia pars.* Although he relies upon the account of the human act and its object in *Veritatis Splendor*, John Paul II does not retrace Aquinas's account of the moral life in detail. Rather, he turns his attention to the *experience* of the moral life.

Considered experientially, the vision of the divine essence poses immense problems. Although one may use terms such as "bliss," "perfect fulfillment," and "all-consuming joy" and point to experiences such as the encounter with earthly beauty and the joys of earthly love, it is impossible to say what this vision of God is like.[33] Furthermore, the absolute inequality of the encounter with God raises the question of the retention of human personality and identity. If God is to be "all in all,"[34] then how can the finite human being avoid being completely absorbed and annihilated?

---

31 *Lubliner Vorlesungen*, 176; see also 173–74.

32 Ibid., 175, and *Love and Responsibility*, 137–38. John Paul II, *Crossing the Threshold of Hope*, 73, and *Centesimus Annus*, 41. See also Thomas Aquinas, *ST* I–II, q. 3, a. 8.

33 On this compare Benedict XVI, encyclical *Spe Salvi*, November 30, 2007, 12, where he speaks of being immersed in an ocean of unending love.

34 Eph 1:23.

To understand any thing, the human intellect must "become that thing" by abstracting its form and becoming informed by it, so that the understanding soul is, in a way, that thing. The chemist knows not only the chemicals and their compounds; he thinks "chemically." Those who know something have internalized it by having let their minds become informed by it. So, to know God directly and immediately, the soul, specifically its intellectual power,[35] has to be conformed to God. In order for the vision of God to be such as Aquinas holds, the human intellect must therefore become "deiform."[36] The divine form, by which God is what he is, must inform the human intellect. But since God's essence, what he is, is his very being (*ipsum esse*),[37] the vision of God must consist in the human intellect's somehow becoming (*ipsum esse*) being-itself.

Aquinas's account gives rise to a host of conceptual problems, which admit of only the most formal treatment. We simply do not know directly and cannot reliably imagine what such deiformity can be *like*. It also raises serious problems concerning the identity and personality of the human subject having the vision of God. The human person is a finite being, and in significant ways defined by his finitude, indeed, by his limitations. If "I" am Ludwig van Beethoven, then I speak German, not English, and certainly not Chinese. Beethoven's "I" expresses himself with stunning originality, discipline, and creativity through music but tends to write maudlin prose when overwrought (consider his "Heiligenstadt Testament"). Beethoven had extraordinary musical gifts as both a performer and composer, but he also suffered from increasing deafness during his most productive years. His artistic output, which transcended the limitations of classical form, became the model and inspiration for the subsequent Romanticism in music, which for its part so transcended Beethoven's innovations that for a composer in our day to return to Beethoven's forms would be anachronistic and unacceptable. While we may speculate what Beethoven might have done with the electric guitar, he was in fact limited to the acoustic instruments of the early nineteenth century. Although we rightly marvel at the creative genius of a Beethoven—or a Mozart or a Shakespeare or a Michelangelo—genius that in some ways transcends the

---

[35] *ST* I–II, q. 3, a. 5.
[36] *ST* I, q. 12, a. 5.
[37] *ST* I, q. 3, a. 4.

creator's limitations, it remains true that every human creator is a finite creature whose self is limited by space, time, culture, and even physical conditions. And what we are considering now is that this creator of beautiful music is to be conformed to the perfectly beautiful Creator of all things in all their beauty. Must we say that all that is distinctive and personal to Beethoven (or anyone else) is absorbed and lost in the overwhelming perfection of the divine essence? Does the Divine Perfection obliterate human personality? We must reconcile the apparently limited nature of the human person with his destiny somehow to appropriate the infinite good that is God. To begin our analysis, we turn first to consider the human being's direct and perforce limited engagement with the world in his work.

Human Creativity, Work, and Engagement with the World

Karol Wojtyła's account of the transcendence of the person makes it clear that the human being is inextricably metaphysical, that a purely naturalistic, immanent, or "horizontal" account of the human person and his good is not adequate to its subject. As a philosopher working under a Communist regime in dialogue with Marxists and later as Pope, he devoted significant attention to human work: "And work means any activity by man, whether manual or intellectual, whatever its nature or circumstances."[38] It is clear from this definition that *Person and Act* itself constitutes an analysis of human work. This definition of work is deliberately broad, encompassing not only the strenuous labor of the quarry worker but also the scholar's research, the musician's practice and performance, the mother's nursing, and even the child's play. What John Paul II most certainly did not want was to restrict the notion of *work* only to economic activity. Money or economic value cannot constitute an adequate measure for human work, even if much work is and ought to be remunerated.[39] Our predilection for considering work in economic terms deserves a preliminary examination in terms of materialist naturalism, Marxism, and economic liberalism.

Work and Materialist Naturalism

Human work has survival value. We can attribute the survival and hegemony of our species to the distinctively human capacity to work intelligently.

---

[38] John Paul II, *Laborem Exercens*, prologue.

[39] Ibid., 6, 15.

Human ingenuity and creativity make it possible to manage water resources with dams and canals, heat our homes in cold climates, defend ourselves from stronger predators, hunt prey more efficiently, grow edible plants in abundance, and so on. In terms of natural selection, human intelligence is advantageous and therefore is naturally selected. And indeed, we read in the writings of cultural evolutionists that all manifestations of human work and activity derive from the survival advantage conferred by the capacity for intelligent work, that all human work traces back to this survival advantage. To such evolutionary reductionism one can object that human work is not only functional, but it is also cultural. Even if the lever, inclined plane, and gyrocompass should serve human survival, it is not clear how Mozart's *Jupiter* Symphony does. Let us consider the implications of this.

Mozart's forty-first symphony did not spring full-blown into the world, abruptly bursting into a silent Vienna. It is a manifestation of a musical form that itself evolved historically from song, dance, and worship. From ancient times, human beings have used music to help structure their lives. And, to be sure, the function of music has often been quite practical. The lullaby does help baby to sleep, and the sailors' chantey keeps them pulling the ropes in unison. The important stories of ancestors and past adventures are more easily remembered with rhythm, rhyme, and melody. And yet, if human culture were rooted only in survival advantage, we have gotten no closer to explaining Mozart's work. The Volga boatmen need not *sing* "Heave ho!"[40] It suffices for the foreman to call it out. Mama can simply mutter soft tones to baby, if all that is needed is an effect. The cultural setting exceeds the requirements of effectiveness, and the reason is quite clear. The cultural artifact serves a different purpose than the purely functional. Culture relates work to some good beyond the product of the work.

Any cultural manifestation, any artwork brings unity to diversity and multiplicity. A rhythmic "heave, ho" or "one, two" suffices to keep the barge haulers pulling together, but the Volga boatmen had their own song, one they had inherited from their fathers and grandfathers, one that was much different from those sung along the Erie Canal. And even today, as mechanized barges sail the Volga, Russian choruses sing the "Boat Song" to express an aspect of the Russian soul. The unity at issue here is not simply

[40] In Russian, "Ey ukhnyem, ey ukhnyem": the opening words of the "Volga Boat Song."

that of a work crew but of a people extended in space and time. Similarly, the point of the legends and stories passed on in tales, ballads, and epic poems is not simply to provide examples of how problems can be solved but to pass on the common life of a people. Furthermore, the shape of a people's artifacts is culturally determined. Pioneers and nomads may well use available materials to erect their shelters, but once the bare necessities are met, then even tents take on cultural significance and become symbols of those who dwell in them. This is, of course, why anthropologists can identify the origins of ancient tools and artifacts. Each people has a "way we do things" that is reflected in its work and the products of its work. John Paul II addresses the cultural inheritance of the worker, who enters into the labor and working traditions of those who have gone before.

> Working at any workbench, whether a relatively primitive or an ultramodern one, a man can easily see that *through his work he enters into two inheritances*: the inheritance of what is given to the whole of humanity in the resources of nature, and the inheritance of what others have already developed on the basis of those resources, primarily by developing technology, that is to say, by producing a whole collection of increasingly perfect instruments for work. In working, man also "enters into the labour of others."[41]

That which brings unity to a people or a community is ipso facto good, for the good of any being is lost through the loss of its unity. The unity of a community is not simply physical, as though it were constituted simply by residence in a particular region or by common biological ancestry and physical resemblance. At the basis of the community's unity must lie a common life, a *doing things together*, which arises from common activity toward shared goods. Although among these values survival and a modicum of prosperity will be essential, the community is not constituted solely by its need for survival as its absolute good. To the extent that a people or community has a *way of life* is the extent to which it is identifiable as a people, to which the community is a good *of this sort*. It is not simply that the members of the human community support each other in a common concern for survival and material well-being but that they also strive to maintain the community as such as a bearer of certain traditional values. A people clings to its heritage because the people itself and not only

[41] *Laborem Exercens*, 13.

its members must survive. "Inseparable as they are from people and their history," writes John Paul II, "cultures share the dynamics which the human experience of life reveals. They change and advance because people meet in new ways and share with each other their ways of life."[42]

Work is therefore a cultural reality and cannot be reduced only to its survival effectiveness. The worker transforming the world about him by his labor does so in the cultural context, which is to say as part of a community extended in space and time. His work, even if performed alone, is shared in that it is a part of a tradition of work. Japanese saws cut on the pull stroke, and Western saws on the push. Furthermore, the laborer's work is a participation with others in a social and economic context. In virtue of these contexts and connections, work cannot be considered in isolation, as simply the realization of some material change in the world (a ditch dug or a field planted), but must be considered as part of the development of the culture. Work manifests and sustains the community as a community. The community, be it so small as the family or so large as the nation, is an overarching good that is realized and sustained in the individual's work. In other words, authentic human work participates in the common good of the community and realizes the community as a good.

Marx and Work

The Catholic scholar in postwar Poland was perforce engaged with Marxism. The underlying philosophical ideology of the regnant regime still claimed the allegiance of its intellectuals and was opposed to that of the scholars in the Catholic universities. For Marx, the drama of history lies in the conflict between classes: "The history of all hitherto existing society is the history of class struggles."[43] The worker—*this* worker—is determined in his significance by his membership in the working class. His work is proletarian, which means that it is exploited by the bourgeoisie or capitalist class. Because of the inherent condition of exploitation that results from the very structure of capitalism, he is alienated from his work. This alienation is imposed on him and his fellows by the capitalistic forces of production. It is important to note that this condition of alienation is

[42] *Fides et Ratio*, 71.

[43] Karl Marx, "Manifesto of the Communist Party," in *The Portable Karl Marx*, ed. Eugene Kamenka (New York: Penguin Books, 1983), 203.

objective, not a subjective feeling or condition that the worker can address on his own (for instance, by taking a greater interest in his work or by suggesting ways to improve the product). The alienation arises from the fact that he has sold his work to the capitalist, who then exploits it for profit to increase his capital. Just as one who sells his farm has alienated it, so too is the worker's labor alienated. Even such remedies as a higher wage or improved working conditions fail to address the root problem of alienation, for the worker's work is not his own. He works to increase the capitalist's profit. Or, rather, his work is exploited by the capitalist for the increase of profit. The only solution to the problem of exploitation, therefore, is the abolition of capital and the communization of the means of production. The working class will cease to be exploited only when, *as a class*, the proletariat owns the factories and farms.

Writing about the dialogues with Marxists on the subject of atheism, John Paul II notes:

> But oddly enough, this kind of controversy with Marxism was brief. It soon came about that man himself—and his moral life—was the *central problem under discussion*. . . . When I wrote the book *The Acting Person*, the first to take notice of it, obviously in order to attack it, were the Marxists. In fact, my book represented an unsettling element in their polemic against religion and the Church.[44]

John Paul goes on to observe that although he had not written the book as a direct attack on Marxism, its emphasis on the person and his morality constituted a real challenge to the bases of Marxist thought. In *Person and Act* and later in his papal encyclicals, Wojtyła argues that alienation does not arise simply from the external conditions of labor. If the act originates from within the subjectivity of the worker, then external conditions alone cannot constitute his alienation from his work. Marxism regards the worker only insofar as he is an object in the production cycle, as a unit in the process. If, however, this worker is a person with an *inner life*, then his alienation cannot consist only in an object relationship between his work and its physical conditions. In his poetry, Karol Wojtyła reflects on the worker.[45]

44 *Crossing the Threshold of Hope*, 199.

45 During World War II, young Karol Wojtyła worked in a stone quarry. See Weigel, *Witness to Hope*, 55–56, and Szulc, *Pope John Paul II*, 115–16.

> No, not just hands drooping with the hammer's weight,
> nor the taut torso, muscles shaping their own style,
> but thought informing his work,
> deep, knotted in wrinkles on his brow,
> and over his head, joined in a sharp arc, shoulders and veins vaulted.[46]

The work flows from the will of the worker. He has chosen to perform this work and to do so in concert with others, as an employee of this company or in this sector of the economy. To be sure, his choice may well be restricted and less than completely free. He may be working in a field for which he is overqualified or unsuited, simply because more appropriate work is not available. He may be treated unjustly, underpaid and abused by his supervisors. His work may be hard and harmful.

> They laid him down, his back on a sheet of gravel.
> His wife came, worn out with worry; his son returned from school.
>
> Should his anger now flow into the anger of others?
> It was maturing in him through its own truth and love.
> Should he be used by those who come after,
> deprived of substance, unique and deeply his own?[47]

Although his qualifications are his strong back and arms, rather than his intelligence, the quarry worker is author of his own work. He knows how the work can be done well, and if management or his fellow workers hinder his doing the work well, he is angry. The workers give each other a hand and help the "new guy" learn the tricks to being both safe and productive. In his act the worker realizes himself, because his act is his own. "Proletarian" does not define his self. It is he alone who determines whether he works well and intelligently and in harmony with his fellows. Within the Marxist conception, however, his works have meaning only insofar as they participate in the inevitable collapse of capitalism and the coming revolution of the proletariat. In Marxism, the person disappears, subsumed into the class. The Marxist worker produces wealth to be turned

[46] Karol Wojtyła, "Material," from the cycle *The Quarry*, in *Easter Vigil, and Other Poems*, trans. Jerzy Peterkiewicz (New York: Random House, 1979), 29.

[47] Karol Wojtyła, "In Memory of a Fellow Worker," from the cycle *The Quarry*, ibid., 33.

into capital. His ultimate goal, the establishment of the dictatorship of the proletariat, is not actually related directly to his work. Indeed, it need not even be something that the individual worker desires or strives for. His ultimate good is not his own and lies beyond his control. Karol Wojtyła's analysis, in effect, denies this, allowing instead the worker—including the quarry worker—to be author of his own acts, engaged in the worth of his own productions.

Work and Economic Liberalism

Similar to Marxism, indeed almost like a photographic negative, is the individualism of economic liberalism. For classical liberalism, the individual is sovereign, master of himself.[48] What liberalism shares in common with Marxism is the premise that work is measured by economics alone, that its only value is objectively determined. Whatever work one does is undertaken after a kind of cost-benefit analysis. The worker expends effort, whether muscular or intellectual, to produce a product or service that can be exchanged for wealth or consideration of some sort. The individual is inherently selfish, necessarily so. To be sure, one may work in concert with others and for the benefit of others (such as one's family, company, or town), but this shared work manifests only an enlightened self-interest. The good to be attained is the material benefit that interaction with the environment can realize.

The ethics of economic liberalism is utilitarianism, which takes as the highest good—indeed, as the *sole* good—the maximization of pleasure broadly understood. One can endure five days of drudgery for the sake of a pleasant weekend. An individual may devote years of hard and often unpleasant work to the project of amassing sufficient wealth to be able to spend his middle age enjoying personal comfort and relative superiority over others. As we noted earlier, success is the only real norm of utilitarianism. If an act "worked," produced the desired result, then the act was good and right. What is most significant, however, to Karol Wojtyła is that the criteria of good and evil are entirely subjective. Pleasure is the subjective experience of good as a good. "Pleasure is, of its nature, a good for the moment and only for a particular subject, it is not a super-subjective or trans-subjective good. And so, as long as that good is recognized as the

---

[48] Mill, *On Liberty*, chap. 1, 9.

entire basis of the moral norm, there can be no possibility of my transcending the bounds of that which is good for me alone."[49] One may well sacrifice one's own immediate pleasure for the sake of social harmony, so that more persons than I will enjoy pleasure. Indeed, Mill insists that his utilitarian principle demands precisely this: "[The happiness which forms the utilitarian standard of what is right in conduct is not the agent's own happiness, but that of all concerned. As between his own happiness and that of others, utilitarianism requires him to be as strictly impartial as a disinterested and benevolent spectator."[50] Taken as a principle for public administration, this is reasonable and workable. And, indeed, one often gets the sense in Mill that he is not always speaking so much to the question of individual morals as to public administration, that he envisions a rational, benevolent way to order the increasingly prosperous, but socially unequal, society of Victorian England.

As an ethical principle, however, Mill's principle of utility fails. However one qualifies his presentation of it, the "greatest happiness principle," founded as it is on pleasure as its ultimate basis, cannot escape Wojtyła's critique. Pleasure is purely subjective, an aspect of the inner life,[51] and as such it founds no objective norm. In *Love and Responsibility* Wojtyła considers the popular position that two mutually consenting adults can agree to share their bodies sexually for the sake of mutual pleasure. He comments: "[T]here can be no genuine reciprocity based only on desire or on a 'consumer' attitude. For such an attitude does not really seek a response to love in the form of reciprocity, but only the appeasement, the full satisfaction of desire. It is at bottom the merest egoism."[52] His point here is simply that there can be no sharing of a pleasure. Two persons can share sexual activity, of course, just as they can share a meal, participation in sports, or a conversation. The pleasure, however, is the subjective experience of the event. To be sure, two persons may well have similar experiences of the same thing, and it can be gratifying to discover that someone close to you feels much the same way as you do. It is also often the case, however, that two persons experiencing the same thing may experience

[49] *Love and Responsibility*, 37–38.
[50] *Utilitarianism*, 11.
[51] Wojtyła, *Love and Responsibility*, 32.
[52] Ibid., 88; see also 126–27.

very different feelings in regard to it. This is often the case, in fact, with sexual encounters. If, then, two persons engage in sexual activity for the sole purpose of mutual pleasure with no reference to any further good, then in fact they share nothing together except the physical encounter. The encounter can be a total failure for one partner but thoroughly enjoyable for the other. What pertains to the pair pertains *mutatis mutandis* to the society as a whole. If Mill's greatest happiness principle is the measure of the good, then all that can be had is a multiplicity of members experiencing varying degrees of satisfaction—or dissatisfaction. It is famously impossible to make everybody happy.

Liberal Happiness. There are two complementary solutions to this problem of attaining the "happiness" required by the greatest happiness principle. The first is to recognize that regardless of subjective dispositions and desires, certain objective conditions apply to all human beings: they need food, clean water, lodging, education when young and employment when mature, and so on. Happily, these are all things that public authorities can either provide or foster, and the liberal political and economic regime is, in fact, generally competent to provide such conditions. The prosperous liberal society is not necessarily the home of crowds of the subjectively pleased, but its people are decently fed, clothed, employed, and generally provided for. Utilitarian public administration can and does work fairly well.

The second aspect of the "happiness" required by the greatest happiness principle lies beyond public administration and indeed beyond any universal description or provision. If happiness is pleasure, then it is the subjective state of being pleased. Although Mill rightly insists that *pleasure* need not be construed as merely the satisfaction of the senses, even the highest satisfactions—the joys of friendship, the theater, music, intellectual discovery—regarded only inasmuch as they are pleasures, are inherently and irredeemably subjective. Even if many persons of good breeding and education would derive great personal satisfaction from a performance at La Scala, there is no universal law or principle to determine that every such person will. In fact, such pleasures are arguably more subjective than those of sense, for almost every human being will find pleasure in the satisfactions of the most basic biological needs. However, the satisfaction of the higher faculties can vary from person to person, as each finds pleasure in a different configuration of goods. The structuring of one's life to derive maximum satisfaction or pleasure is entirely a personal matter. Although there may well be general principles that one is wise to follow (become as educated as possible, refrain from abusing alcohol and addictive drugs, cultivate friendships with good people), it remains that to each person there is his own preference. There is no *right* way to live, no *right* form of satisfaction. The ultimate good is radically privatized, so that there can, in principle, be no objectively known *common good* for all. An immediate implication of this is that the role of public authority is to mediate and balance the private goods of its citizens in such a way that as many of them as possible can attain the good they desire.

What, Then, of Work? As so conceived by liberalism, work becomes problematic. If the end and measure of human activity is pleasure, then it becomes difficult to ascertain the value of work as such. Certainly, there are some for whom work is pleasurable, those who enjoy their work and find it fulfilling. But for most, work inevitably involves drudgery. Indeed, almost every form of work has unpleasant aspects. It follows then, that the value of work can be only instrumental, that it provides goods and services by which the worker and his neighbors can realize their own happiness. Work is not integral to one's good or one's happiness but ancillary. The worker effectively negotiates a trade-off, devoting himself to toil in order to enjoy its fruits at another time. We note that this trade-off becomes a fairly complex matter, fraught with unpleasant surprises and difficult choices. One can, like Dickens's Scrooge, devote long years to work alone in the hopes of enjoying great wealth at some distant day, or he can minimize his work and "live for the moment," with the expectation that he may never prosper materially. A perfect job may turn out to be unexpectedly unpleasant, perhaps because of an overbearing supervisor or disagreeable co-workers. Most significant, it is only those privileged by wealth and social standing or by their life in modern Western societies who can choose the form of their work and consider it in terms of satisfaction. For most human beings throughout human history, work has been imposed, not chosen for personal satisfaction. We could go on with examples, but the central point is this, that the activity of work has no necessary connection with the pleasurable good it realizes. And so in the liberal economy work is increasingly oriented toward the creation and satisfaction of subjective desires, toward the creation and marketing of new products, the fostering of new and more technologically sophisticated needs, and the transformation of art and entertainment into an industry for constant amusement.

Transcendence and Work

In Karol Wojtyła's analysis of work and creativity, we find a perspective quite different from the modern variants just described. Not only does work create products, but "[i]n creating we also fill the external material world around us with our own thought and being."[53] Wojtyła compares this with God's own creative activity, which brought the world into existence, and "God saw that it was good" (Gen 1:25). Human work thus develops, as it were, its own order of goods. By intelligence, imagination, and initiative the human race has brought about an order of goods more exactly adapted to human needs than that provided by nature.[54] By clearing land and planting grains in orderly rows, by domesticating certain animals, and by harnessing animal and eventually chemical energy, human beings made the land more productive and human life less precarious. Furthermore, in providing for their needs, human beings have done so decoratively, with an eye to the beautiful and the tasteful. Human intelligence developed dyes for clothing and paints for walls (even the walls of caves!). Pillars holding up roofs became stylized and even ornate. Peoples established libraries and schools to preserve and pass on their knowledge. The result of all this human activity is an interrelated network of human creations that constitute the world we have inherited. The purpose and the effect of work are to fill the world with goods—not just products but interrelated goods.

The implication of this is that human work is not only the effecting of changes. Because the worker shares in the creativity of the Creator, his labor is always transcendent. The human worker imposes a human order within the context of the cosmic order established by the Creator. This expresses exactly the truth that all human work is culturally conditioned. To be sure, work settings and conditions may often well be subhuman and anticultural. No doubt the conditions in English and European mills blinded Marx to the cultural aspect of work. Indeed, in his critique of the bourgeoisie, he decried precisely the loss of work's cultural aspects:

---

53 "Thomistic Personalism," in *Person and Community*, 171–72.

54 John Paul II, *Laborem Exercens*, 5; see Vatican Council II, *Gaudium et Spes*, 53.

> The bourgeoisie, wherever it has got the upper hand, has put an end to all feudal, patriarchal, idyllic relations, it has pitilessly torn asunder the motley feudal ties that bound man to his "natural superiors," and has left no other nexus between man and man than naked self-interest, than callous "cash payment." . . . The bourgeoisie has stripped of its halo every occupation hitherto honored and looked up to with reverent awe. It has converted the physician, the lawyer, the priest, the poet, the man of science, into its paid wage laborers.[55]

Even direr have been the conditions of slaves, who have no control over their work. Nonetheless, the human person seeks to impress the seal of his own personhood on his work. Dave the Slave, an African American slave in South Carolina during the first half of the nineteenth century, produced pottery that is still in demand.[56] More common in the modern era has been the formation of labor unions, which not only served as organizations to protect workers' rights but also constituted a reality that belonged to the workers. If laborers were alienated from management and therefore from the companies they worked for, they nevertheless had the union. And the unions had their own structures, songs, celebrations, and traditions—their culture. Many contemporary management theorists have come to recognize that workers are more productive and happier when they realize that their own intellectual contributions are valued and used, when they are partners and not simply tools in the manufacturing process.[57]

From this creative interaction with the work of the Creator there derives an enhanced dignity of work. The human being is not simply, in virtue of his superior intelligence, a more effective worker in the sense that a cat is a more effective hunter than the less intelligent dog, but with his fellows and with God the Creator he is a coartisan of the human world. The worker creates not just an artifact but the physical and aesthetic characteristics of the world for future generations. Work is more than "just work."

The Creator's Work

Discussing the work of God as Creator, John Paul II emphasizes the Trinitarian implications of the creation.

---

[55] "Manifesto of the Communist Party," 206.

[56] See "Dave the Slave," www.davetheslave.org.

[57] See William Ouchi, *Theory Z: How American Business Can Meet the Japanese Challenge* (Reading, MA: Addison-Wesley Publishing Company, 1981).

> In the light of these apostolic texts [referring to the writings of Sts. Paul and John] we can affirm that the creation of the world finds its model in the eternal generation of the Word, the Son, of the same substance of the Father, and its source in the Love that is the Holy Spirit. This Person-Love, consubstantial with the Father and the Son, together with the Father and the Son, is source of the creation of the world from nothing, that is, of the gift of existence to every being.[58]

The creation of the world is not simply, therefore, an exercise in divine power and planning but rather a work of wisdom and love. The model, the archetype as it were, of the creation is the Eternal Word of God: "Through him all things came to be" (Jn 1:3). The creation reflects the divine mind, as the artwork reflects and reveals the artist's mind. More significant for our current discussion is the role of the Holy Spirit, whom John Paul calls the "source" of God's gift of existence to every being. Following Thomas Aquinas,[59] John Paul II gives the third Person of the Trinity the name "Love."[60] The creation is, therefore, a work of love, a gift. John Paul II further develops this theme of love in creation in his theology of the body audiences.

> The creator is he who "calls to existence from nothing" and who establishes the world in existence and man in the world, *because he "is love"* (1 John 4:8). . . . [T]hat account often repeats, "God saw everything that he had made and indeed, it was very good" (Gen 1:31). Through these words we are led to glimpse in love the divine motive for creation, the source, as it were, from which it springs: *only love, in fact, gives rise to the good and is well pleased with the good* (see 1 Cor 13). As an action of God, creation thus means not only calling from nothing to existence and establishing the world's existence as well as man's existence in the world, but . . . it also signifies *gift*; a fundamental and radical gift, that is, an act of giving in which the gift comes into being precisely from nothing. . . . [*C*]*reation is a gift,*

---

58 General audience, March 12, 1986, in *Catechesi sul Credo*, pt. 1, "Dio Padre e Creatore."

59 *ST* I, q. 37, a. 1.

60 John Paul II, *Dominum et Vivificantem*, 10; also his general audience of April 18, 1990, in *Catechesi sul Credo*, pt. 3, "Lo Spirito Santo datore di vita" (1989–1991), www.vatican.va/holy_father/john_paul_ii/audiences/alpha/index_it.html (accessed January 31, 2010).

> *because man appears in it, who, as an "image of God," is able to understand the very meaning of the gift* in the call from nothing to existence.[61]

If the incarnate Word is the model or archetype of the creation, reflecting the wisdom and intentions of the Creator, and if the purpose of the creation is love, a realization of the Love between the Creator and the Word, then creation itself falls within the Trinitarian dynamic of wisdom and love. The text from the theology of the body audiences adds this, that this love is directed beyond God himself. Because the human being is an "image of God," that is, a being capable of its own acts of knowing and loving—with its own subjectivity—he is capable of receiving the gift, appreciating it, and responding to it. It is as though the gift cannot be a gift until there is a recipient capable of recognizing it as such. The primary gift to the human being, according to these texts, is existence itself. Not only does God the Creator provide the human being with good things, such as the Garden of Eden with all its riches, but he gives him his own existence as a person, that is, as one who possesses his own life, who shapes and determines himself as a person, choosing what kind of person he shall be.

Let us note too the phrase "*only love, in fact, gives rise to the good.*" Only what is gift, brought into being and given in love, is good. What does not flow from or originate in love is not good.[62] The creation is good because it originates within and comes from the inner richness of the perfectly and supremely good God himself. His love, expressed in the gift of creation to the human person, is a gift of himself in that it is a gift of his wisdom, power, and bounty for the benefit of human beings. Most important is the gift of being "in God's image" (Gen 1:27), for it means that the human being is a person, author of his own acts based on his understanding of the truth and his choices in love. Human acting reflects, in a way, the creative action of God. We might say that love is God's characteristic mode of acting, and he has given it to human beings to share in that mode. And for the human act to give rise to the good, the authentic good, it must be an act of love.

---

61 *Man and Woman He Created Them,* 13.3–4, 180.

62 It is important not to take this simplistically, as if to say, for instance, that the child conceived of rape is an evil because he does not originate in love. The rapist—or any other maker of evil—is not the sole, exclusive, and completely adequate cause of that which is brought into being.

These considerations put us in a position to return to the question of the "fitting good" for human beings, that participation in God which constitutes the transcendent end of finite human life and activity.

Participation in the Infinite Good

The human agent has neither God's ineffable wisdom nor his omnipotence. Indeed, no matter what he does, the human worker depends on the materials in his environment, as well as on the contributions of his fellows, both known and unknown, directly and indirectly connected to him. And as we have noted already, the effects of his acts are always finite. The human being is clearly incapable of attaining to God under his own power. How does the finite attain to and relate to the Infinite? In the thought of Karol Wojtyła/John Paul II we can identify three key principles.

Cocreation

Because the human being has the power to know of God that he exists and that he is one, and to conceive of the universe as a whole, and because his will (despite his limited powers) can extend to all good,[63] he is the image of God. In virtue of his rational and free personhood, the human being is a kind of cocreator, a creative being. The first way in which the human agent participates in the Infinite Good is by way of imitation and cocreation. Working in the world God created, the human being is quite really working with God. Sharing in God's work, one works with God. Karol Wojtyła writes:

> We are creators because we think. . . . Creating as derived from thinking is so characteristic of a person that it is always an infallible sign of a person, a proof of a person's existence or presence. In creating we also fill the external material world around us with our own thought and being. There is a certain similarity here between ourselves and God, for the whole of creation is an expression of God's own thought and being.[64]

Later, in *Centesimus Annus,* John Paul II develops this conception further:

> The original source of all that is good is the very act of God, who created both the earth and man, and who gave the earth to man so that he might

[63] See Thomas Aquinas, *ST* I–II, q. 2, a. 8.

[64] "Thomistic Personalism," in *Person and Community,* 171–72.

> have dominion over it by his work and enjoy its fruits (Gen 1:28). . . . The earth, by reason of its fruitfulness and its capacity to satisfy human needs, is God's first gift for the sustenance of human life. But the earth does not yield its fruits without a particular human response to God's gift, that is to say, without work. It is through work that man, using his intelligence and exercising his freedom, succeeds in dominating the earth and making it a fitting home. In this way, he makes part of the earth his own, precisely the part which he has acquired through work.[65]

As a "cocreator," the human person can therefore be considered a partner with the Creator in the development and management of the creation. As such, he approaches the creation not as something of his own to exploit but as the handiwork of another, entrusted to his care.[66] This is not simply a matter of doing chores or meeting immediate survival and comfort needs. Because the human being is a person, he can know the truth about the world about him and internalize it. As a spiritual being, the human person can embrace the whole of creation in his understanding, however imperfect that understanding might be, and situate himself and his work in the context of that whole.[67] The human person is inherently a metaphysician. The creature who is a person grasps, albeit imperfectly and in part, what the Creator in the perfection and comprehensiveness of his creative wisdom makes. Even this distant participation in the wisdom of the Creator gives rise to wonder, admiration, and an inclination to worship.

Conformity with God's Love

Imitating the Creator's work in his own labor, the human person participates in God's gift of love. Indeed, his calling is to do so. Recalling the teaching from *Gaudium et Spes* (24.3) that "man, who is the only creature on earth which God willed for itself, cannot fully find himself except through a sincere gift of himself," we discover the concept of *union* among persons joined with that of *gift of self.* Just as the Persons of the Trinity live eternally the gift of self, each to the others, in perfect union, human persons can

---

[65] *Centesimus Annus,* 31; see also John Paul II, "Letter to Artists," www.vatican.va/holy_father/john_paul_ii/letters/1999/documents/hf_jp-ii_let_23041999_artists_en.html (accessed December 14, 2007), 1.

[66] John Paul II, *Sollicitudo Rei Socialis,* 28.

[67] See John Paul II, *Fides et Ratio,* 83.

attain unity "in truth and charity," a state that can be attained only through sincere gift of self. Characterized here is love, which as eros desires and seeks to attain union with the beloved and as agape gives of itself generously.

John Paul II develops this conception of love at great length and in detail in his catechesis on the theology of the body. In his analysis of the initial encounter of the man and woman in Genesis 2, he remarks on their twofold discovery of each other as persons and as sexually determined, factors in virtue of which they could enter into communion.[68] Furthermore, this nature of this communion is signified by their bodies, by the "spousal meaning of the body."[69] Existing as male and female, their bodies signified that each was created to be given as a gift to the other, a gift that is uniquely and fully signified and realized by sexual union. Because they are *persons,* this gift could be realized only by the man and woman themselves.[70] That is, it is not that God gives the woman to the man but that she gives herself and he reciprocates by the gift of himself. For the man and woman in marriage this gift of self is total, such that each becomes, as it were, the possession of the other. Because no love, no union is possible without a shared good,[71] the complete gift of self means that the two share all the goods of their life together. This goes beyond the formula "What's mine is yours and what's yours is mine" to a commitment on the part of each to seek to realize the highest good for the beloved, "that I may serve for the realization of the best for you."

Spousal love, which is complete, lifelong, and exclusive, offers a paradigm for other loves, for other relationships of communion, be these familial, social, civic, or of any other sort. Love is always a gift of self that seeks the good of the other. Two persons create a communion of persons as they give of themselves each to the other for the sake of a shared good.

In his first encyclical, John Paul II wrote: "In reality, freedom is a great gift only when we know how to use it consciously for everything that is our true good. Christ teaches us that the best use of freedom is charity, which takes

---

68 *Man and Woman He Created Them,* 9.1–10.5, 161–69.

69 Ibid., 14.4, 185; Wojtyła, *Mężczyzną i niewiastą stworzył ich,* 49. See Wojtyła, *Miłość i odpowiedzialność*, 87–92; in *Love and Responsibility,* 95–96, the English translator renders "miłość oblubieńcza" as "betrothed love," and the Italian translation, *Metafisica della persona* (Milan: Bompiani, 2003) renders it as "amore sponsale."

70 *Man and Woman He Created Them,* 13.2ff., 179–85.

71 *Love and Responsibility,* 28–29.

concrete form in self-giving and in service. . . . The full truth about human freedom is indelibly inscribed on the mystery of the Redemption."[72]

It is in this capacity to love that the human person most fully imitates God.[73] Although the human being is finite and imperfect, he can strive to love fully, that is, to give fully of himself. Because the "full truth about human freedom is indelibly inscribed on the mystery of the Redemption," Christ's salvific death becomes the model for human perfection in love. This is why the final chapter of John Paul II's encyclical on moral theology turns to the consideration of martyrdom.[74] That the person can imitate God for God's sake means that he shares something with God, that he has become "like God," not in power or wisdom, to be sure, but in that which is most characteristic of him, the generosity of his love.

The characteristic of love is to seek union with the beloved. Man and woman come together sexually in love to realize and express their union. Although this love is realized as love in the total gift of self, there is in this a "having" of the other, which is one of the great paradoxes of love.[75] And just as man and woman give themselves to each other in marriage, so has God given himself to the Church in Christ (Eph 5:32). Indeed, this is the Scriptural pattern of God's relationship with his People from the time of the prophets.[76] The dynamic of divine love, like that of love between two humans, is that of the gift; God gives himself to his beloved in the hope that his love will be received and reciprocated with the beloved's gift of self. This reciprocity in love establishes a certain equality of footing between the two, for love can be given only in freedom. The implication of this is that the human person can love God. Lest this sound trite from repetition, we must recall that for Aristotle such a concept would be nonsense. Although the human intellect can reflect on the First Cause and gain some knowledge of it,[77] there was for Aristotle no possibility of a human being's entering into a relationship of love with this entity. What we can do is to admire and wonder at it.[78] The dynamic of divine love,

72 *Redemptor Hominis,* 21.

73 John Paul II, *Man and Woman He Created Them,* 16.3, 191.

74 *Veritatis Splendor,* 90–94.

75 Wojtyła, *Love and Responsibility,* 86–87.

76 John Paul II, *Man and Woman He Created Them,* 93.1–3, 487–88; 94.6–95.7, 493–99.

77 Aristotle, *Nicomachean Ethics* 10.8. See also *Metaphysics* 12.7–10.

78 *Metaphysics* 12.7, 1072b24ff.

however, is such that it necessarily divinizes the human lover, raising him, as it were, to the level of God.[79] It is because of this that John Paul II can hold that the image of God is realized not only in the rationality of the individual human soul but especially in the communion of persons.[80]

Procreation

Distinctive among the works of human beings for its meaning, its expression, and its effects is the sexual union between man and woman. This act is intended to and is able to express the fullest love possible between two human beings, the complete gift of self, one to the other. The act is, indeed, often referred to as *lovemaking*. Sexual intercourse is also distinctive because it is the only human act in which the Creator can be directly and creatively involved. When the couple unite sexually and a child is conceived, then the Creator himself gives that child its soul.

> A relationship between spirits which begets a new embodied spirit is something unknown to the natural order. Nor yet can the love of man and woman, however powerful and profound in itself, do this. . . . The essence of the human person is therefore—in the Church's teaching—the work of God himself. It is He who creates the spiritual and immortal soul of that being, the organism of which begins to exist as a consequence of physical relations between man and woman.[81]

The effect of the act, when it has a productive effect, is a being whose existence is caused not only by the act but by God himself. The human couple are therefore directly involved with a new creation on the part of God. The implications of this fact are astounding and philosophically disconcerting. It is only when a man and a woman unite sexually[82] that God

---

79 This is a constant refrain in Christian thought. See Thomas Aquinas, *ST* I, q. 12, a. 9; *De veritate*, q. 10, a. 11. From a different angle, consider Søren Kierkegaard's *Philosophical Fragments*, in *Philosophical Fragments [and] Johannes Climacus*, ed. and trans. Howard V. Hong and Edna H. Hong (Princeton, NJ: Princeton University Press, 1985), chap. 2, 26–34.

80 *Man and Woman He Created Them*, 9.3, 163; *Mulieris Dignitatem*, 7.

81 Wojtyła, *Love and Responsibility*, 55; see also John Paul II, *Familiaris Consortio*, 11.

82 Excepting, of course, the singular case of God the Son's Incarnation in the Virgin's womb and those cases where the union of man and woman is mimicked technologically by in vitro fertilization. In this latter case, the natural process of intercourse is replaced by medical procedures by which sperm and egg are brought together.

brings into being a human soul. Furthermore, whenever a man and a woman do succeed in conceiving a child, the Creator is compelled, as it were, to create a rational and therefore spiritual human soul. Although the act of sexual union is intended to be an act of love, as we shall discuss in the next section, it retains its creative efficacy in any case—whether the man forces himself upon an unwilling woman, or a woman conceives to compel a man's fidelity, or, indeed, if egg and sperm are united in a petri dish. That is to say, therefore, that this natural process, which can be analyzed and even replicated in a laboratory, always and necessarily implicates the direct intervention of the Creator God.

Nor can one easily reject these implications—although there certainly are many who do[83]—in order to reduce human conception to a purely natural, biological process. When Wojtyła writes: "A relationship between spirits which begets a new embodied spirit is something unknown to the natural order," the issue is not simply how a physical process can cause a metaphysical entity (the soul) whose existence cannot be detected by physical means, although this is an important question, but how any process governed only by physical laws can give rise to a spiritual being, one that has an inner life, by which it governs its own life in accord with its own understanding of the truth about the good. That mother and father are such beings cannot be attributed to their physical structure alone,[84] but neither is there a way by which they can directly transmit this spiritual nature to another being. If God is not involved, then another account for this remarkable innovation of spirituality must be given. Plato's proposal that the soul must preexist the man[85] attempts to address precisely this problem. This problem is not simply the contemporary problem of how a physical entity can be conscious[86] but the deeper and more decisive question of how a physical being can orient itself toward a good that transcends its physical nature, and this according to the crite-

[83] So Charles Darwin notes that his account of the origin of the human species ought to pose no particular problem concerning the soul, since we already know the individual human being arises from a natural process. See his *Descent of Man* (Princeton, NJ: Princeton University Press, 1981), chap. 21.

[84] See Reimers, *Soul of the Person*, chap. 6, "Reality and Nature of the Soul."

[85] *Phaedo* 72e–77c.

[86] See, for example, Dennett, *Consciousness Explained*, and John R. Searle, "Consciousness, Its Irreducibility," in Honderich, *Oxford Companion to Philosophy*, 153.

rion of truth known according to the canons of reason. This is what Wojtyła means when he insists that the sexual urge has "an existential and not merely biological character."[87] Rather, it is "bound up with the very existence of the human person—that first and most basic good."[88]

This capacity for procreation, remarkable as it is in itself, entails the further project of rearing and educating the offspring. John Paul II writes: "The task of giving education is rooted in the primary vocation of married couples to participate in God's creative activity: by begetting in love and for love a new person who has within himself or herself the vocation to growth and development, parents by that very fact take on the task of helping that person effectively to live a fully human life."[89]

Whether believers in God or not, parents take on the quasi-divine role of creating and governing a world for their small children to live in, as they educate them to take up their places in the broader world later on. While the higher mammals may train their offspring (as both domestic cats and cheetahs teach their young to hunt prey), human beings can and generally do educate their young in spiritual matters, teaching them virtues and introducing them to the life of the mind and the possibilities of artistic expression. At stake here is not only religion as such but also the development of the mind and a sense for the world and the child's place in it. The parent, educating his child, is taking on a divine role, that of the teacher of the fundamental realities. The parent creates a "world" for his children to live in, a world structured with domestic order, rhythms, customs, beauty, and moral standards; then, as the child matures, the parent introduces him increasingly to the broader world outside the home, interpreting it to him. This is not simply an ideal; it is what every parent does. Parenthood is a role like that of God in the child's life.

The Fitting Good

We now turn our attention to the ultimate realization of the *fitting good.* Whether in work or in love or in procreation and education, the human person remains within his earthly finitude. He is subject to suffering and death and, more perilously, to moral evil. So long as he lives he may pervert

87 *Love and Responsibility,* 52.
88 Ibid.
89 *Familiaris Consortio,* 36.

his labor, be faithless in love, and betray the needs of his children. In the foregoing we have described how he images God, but this account does not address how he may see him or experience him. Nevertheless, the entire moral life is directed toward this encounter with God.

Immortality and the Life of the Resurrection

In his philosophical works Karol Wojtyła does not provide much account of the condition of the soul postmortem and its experience of God. And in his pastoral writings he turns his attention immediately to the life of the resurrection, to that state in which, after Christ's Second Coming, the dead will be raised. In his theology of the body audiences in particular, John Paul II addressed the vision of God in his discussion of the resurrection of the body.[90] For John Paul II the immortality of the soul is not a primary concern or significant theme. This does not mean, however, that he ignores the philosophical question of the postmortem condition of the soul. In his essay "Thomistic Personalism," Wojtyła affirms the soul's immortality, and he intends to do so in continuity and harmony with Thomas Aquinas's account. In doing so, however, Wojtyła focuses on the "eternity of the person." "The truth of the immortality of the soul is simultaneously the truth of the indestructibility of the person."[91] He is not being careless here. Karol Wojtyła wants to assert that although the soul may be immortal, the person is eternal. Granting that true eternity belongs only to God, who is by his nature above and beyond time, the human person is eternal because he is spiritual. That the person is a spiritual being is not in the first instance a theoretical conclusion of metaphysics but a consequence of the reality of a person's experience of himself and his inner life. In *Love and Responsibility*, Wojtyła writes, "*Inner life means spiritual life. It revolves around truth and goodness.*"[92] That the person can transcend himself and the material plane toward truth and good and beauty proves that he is a spiritual being. Indeed, this is what "spiritual" means; "[i]nner life means spiritual life." The person is, therefore, eternal because he is spiritual.

---

90 *Man and Woman He Created Them*, chap. 3, "Christ Appeals to the Resurrection," 64.1–72.7, 379–412.

91 "Thomistic Personalism," in *Person and Community*, 175.

92 *Love and Responsibility*, 23. See also *Persona e atto*, 989, 1027–28, 1060–61.

> Eternity belongs to the person, however, in the sense that whatever is spiritual is indestructible, that is, by nature capable of lasting without end.
>
> This is one aspect of the eternity of the person, and it is connected with another aspect. The values by which the person as such lives are by nature transtemporal, and even atemporal. Such values include truth, goodness, and beauty, as well as justice and love, and, in general all the values by which the person as such continually lives. One can say, therefore, that the very content of the person's life points to the eternity of the person.[93]

Although it is consonant with such an argument, it would be a mistake to read this passage as a proof for the immortality of the soul. The eternity of the person consists in his transcendence which is oriented toward truth and good. The brute animals act so as to survive and continue the existence of their respective species. In this respect, they are bound to the earth. The human person, however, can live for values transcending temporal and material ones. Those, such as tyrants and camp commandants, who would degrade the dignity of others characteristically strive to reduce them to caring only for their basic material needs and for relief from pain. If a person's sole concern is to assuage his own hunger and to escape torment, then his humanity is degraded. Conversely, even those who do not believe in an afterlife usually find their meaning in something transcendent, whether in creation of beauty, discovery of truth, or some significant impact on the future of the human race.

It is particularly important to recognize that this *eternity of the person* is manifest and can be realized in this life. Of course, one can live entirely materialistically, which is to say, for his own comfort and physical satisfaction. However, even in such lives there is betrayed a yearning for the infinite, whether in the hopes one has for one's children, in the enjoyment of music, even in one's own sense of wounded pride upon being insulted. When Terry Malloy[94] complains to Father Barry, the unofficial chaplain to the dock workers, "If I spill [testify to the authorities], my life ain't worth a nickel," and the priest replies, "And how much is your soul worth if you don't?" what is directly at stake is not the afterlife but Malloy's character in this life. The small-time thug who "coulda been a contender" faces the

93 Wojtyła, "Thomistic Personalism," in *Person and Community*, 175.

94 Portrayed by Marlon Brando in the film *On the Waterfront*, directed by Elia Kazan (1954).

seriousness of the question of his character. In the boxing ring he could have fought for the championship, but what Father Barry challenges him to do is to direct his life to the truth, to practice justice. The priest calls him to his inner life, to reflect on the demands of truth and the good, specifically to tell the truth about evils being perpetrated against his fellow workers. Even in this life, the person is spirit and capable of living as such.

However, the person who yearns for the infinite is also constrained by the material conditions of this life and his body. In the film *On the Waterfront*, Terry Malloy is almost killed by the mobsters. Mozart died before finishing his *Requiem*, and Aquinas before completing the *Summa theologiae*. Beethoven's orchestration of his later symphonies was flawed by his inability to hear. This does not mean that the spirit can be entirely contained by this world. If we may speak of the "eternity of the person," it remains true that only God is eternal. If the person is spiritual in virtue of his orientation to the truth, beauty, and good, his bodiness and materiality render his attainment of these inevitably partial and imperfect. However, much as he may transcend himself toward pure and perfect Being (*ipsum esse subsistens*), the human being remains a being in a qualified sense.

For a variety of theoretical reasons, it is necessary to give an account of the condition of the separated soul after death. Following a tradition of philosophical reflection going back to Plato, Aquinas reasons that, because of its rationality, the soul must be immortal.[95] There is a further theological concern too. If the human being is to be resurrected, then there is needed a principle of continuity between the man who has lived a mortal life and the same man subsequently resurrected. If the human being perishes completely at death, then there can be no resurrection but only a creation of a new being. In view of these factors there is a clear theoretical necessity for an account of the soul and its postmortem condition. However, when we turn to the Scriptures, what we find is the hope of a future resurrection, a new life for the whole human being.[96] The Scriptures do not much speak of eternal life for the soul alone. It is in this context that

---

95 Thomas Aquinas, *Aristotle's* De anima *in the Version of William of Moerbeke and the Commentary of St. Thomas Aquinas*, trans. Kenelm Foster, O.P., and Silvester Humphries, O.P. (New Haven: Yale University Press, 1951), 3.10, 743.

96 So Mk 12:25; Mt 22:28–32; 25:31–46; Lk 20:36; Jn 6:40; 11:21–26; 1 Cor 15:12–57; and so on.

John Paul II addresses the fitting good for the person as such, and this good is the contemplation of God in the life of the resurrection.

John Paul II and Resurrected Life

In his theology of the body audiences, John Paul II had defended the importance of the body in its sexual differentiation as male and female for the Creator's plan, arguing that the relationship between husband and wife is a kind of primordial sacrament of the creation. But if the love of husband and wife is by its nature bodily, that is, sexual and oriented toward marriage and procreation, then what can be made of Christ's interchange with the Sadducees, and especially of Christ's words, "For at the resurrection men and women do not marry; no, they are like the angels in heaven" (Mt 22:30)? These words—the reference to angels, in particular—suggest sexlessness and even immateriality in the life of the resurrection. And yet such a state seems to be incompatible with our nature as bodily, sexually differentiated beings.

Citing Luke's words, "[T]hose who are judged worthy of a place in the other world and in the resurrection from the dead . . . can no longer die, for they are the same as the angels[97] and, being children of the resurrection, they are sons of God" (Lk 20:35–36), John Paul II writes:

> This statement allows us above all to deduce *a spiritualization of man according to a dimension that is different from that of earthly life* (and even different from that of the very "beginning").[98] It is obvious that we are not dealing here with a transformation of man's nature into an angelic, that is, purely spiritual nature. . . . Resurrection means restoration to the true life of human bodiliness, which was subjected to death in its temporal phase.[99]

What does this mean, that man will be "spiritualiz[ed] according to a dimension that is different from that of earthly life"? To answer this we must first recognize that even in this mortal life, the human being is a spiritual being, because he can orient himself toward and center his life

---

[97] ισάγγελοι, "like or the same as angels."

[98] By the "beginning" John Paul II means the conditions of human nature as originally created and intended by the Creator, as reflected in the first three chapters of Genesis.

[99] *Man and Woman He Created Them*, 66.5, 389.

around the true and the good. As John Paul notes, the Psalmist writes that even in this life, "You have made him little less than the angels" (Ps 8:6, RSV). He then continues: "One must suppose that in the resurrection this likeness [to God] will be greater: not through a disincarnation of man, but by another kind (one could also say, another degree) of spiritualization of his somatic nature, that is, by another "system of powers" within man. The resurrection signifies a new submission of the body to the spirit."[100]

Under the conditions of this present life, the human spirit is indeed hindered by Original Sin, that is, by the workings of concupiscence, but it is also limited by its very nature. Knowledge of the truth is always tinged with uncertainty and the possibility of error, because all knowledge originates in sense knowledge. Even the most profound human thoughts must be developed in phantasms, in symbols created by the body. Here we need only consider the extent of scholarly debate that expressions of human wisdom, such as the writings of Aristotle, have given rise to. To this day, learned scholars write journal articles and deliver papers, debating what the Stagirite really meant. And if to interpret Aristotle's writings is difficult, so too is even the task of clearly formulating one's own expression. Such limitations as these are a result not of sin but rather of the natural limitations of the human intellect in this life. Human knowledge of spiritual realities is not direct but mediated through material media, through sense representations.

John Paul II's notion of "another kind of spiritualization" would seem, therefore, to amount first of all to a more immediate access and response to the truth and the good. Those who share the glory of the resurrection will enjoy a direct knowledge of God (which, of course, necessarily exceeds the powers of the senses), who is the Author of all truth and the Exemplar of all good. Furthermore, the resistance that our native sinfulness poses to the spirit will be decisively overcome. That is, the whole person will respond naturally and promptly according to the authentic order of goods in relation to the One who is the perfect good, without having to overcome the resistance of concupiscence, those desires that aim at the satisfaction of the senses and human pride. The spiritualized body will respond promptly in love, without the natural hindrance of weariness and the dread of insuperable obstacles. While it may be silly to wonder if those resurrected in glory may be able to fly or walk through walls, it seems perti-

[100] Ibid.

nent to speculate that the resurrected person will have no difficulty doing whatever good work of love may be appropriate for him.

Encounter with God

In this condition of the resurrection to glory, the human person will enjoy the perpetual vision of God himself.

> The eschatological communion (*communio*) of man with God which is constituted thanks to the love of a perfect union, will be nourished by the vision "face to face," by the *contemplation* of the most perfect communion—because it is purely divine—which is, namely, the *Trinitarian communion of the divine Persons* in the unity of the same divinity.[101]

Certainly this agrees with St. Thomas Aquinas's argument that our perfect happiness and fulfillment is the eternal contemplation of the divine essence,[102] and with the much more recent pronouncement of the Second Vatican Council: "The root reason for human dignity lies in man's call to communion with God. From the very circumstance of his origin man is already invited to converse with God."[103] Such a communion is plainly beyond our this-worldly capacity to describe. There is no saying accurately "what it's like." This does not mean, however, that we are completely incapable of rendering an account of it.

The text from *Gaudium et Spes* speaks of this communion with God in terms of conversation, an interaction between persons, an intelligent exchange between intellectual beings. And this is, indeed, precisely how John Paul II represents this state of contemplation: "As a consequence of the vision of God 'face to face,' *a love of such depth and power of concentration on God himself* will be born in the person that it *completely absorbs the person's whole psychosomatic subjectivity*."[104] The human person in glory will respond to the divine Gift of Self with his entire being, body and soul, with his "psychosomatic subjectivity." John Paul II continues:

> This concentration of knowledge ("vision") and love on God himself—a concentration that cannot be anything but a full participation in God's

[101] Ibid., 68.1, 394.
[102] *ST* I–II, q. 3, a. 8.
[103] *Gaudium et Spes*, 19.
[104] *Man and Woman He Created Them*, 68.3, 395.

> inner life, that is, in trinitarian Reality itself—will at the same time be the discovery in God of the whole "world" of relations that are constitutive of the world's perennial order ("cosmos"). This concentration will above all be man's rediscovery of himself, not only in the depth of his own person, but also in that union that is proper to the world of persons in their psychosomatic constitution.[105]

In three points John Paul II characterizes the dynamic character of the contemplation of God in glory. In the simplicity of that eternal gaze is *first* the participation in the reality of the Trinity, Father, Son, and Holy Spirit. As participation this is necessarily more than simply observation (if mere observation of such a reality could even make any sense), but a being involved. In his theology of the body, of which this text is a development, John Paul II has already developed the notion of the *unity of the two*, the marriage of the man and the woman, as a participation in the Trinitarian love. Indeed, so strong is this participation that he identifies marriage as a sacrament of creation.[106] The earthly life of love in the communion of persons (of which marriage is paradigmatic) foreshadows the participation in the life of the Trinity. *Second*, the simple gaze upon God is also the discovery in him of the whole world of relations that constitutes the cosmos. We may here recall Wojtyła's earlier discussion of the distinction between the "natural order of existence" and the "biological order."[107] This gaze is a kind of sharing in the "mind of the Maker." That which we grasp only partially and via abstraction in the sciences of this life appears in its full order and harmony when seen in the Creator's light. And as a consequence there is, *third*, the rediscovery of oneself. This rediscovery is of marvelous import.

The great problem that arises when we try to consider what the contemplation of the Author of all things, who is Infinite, Eternal Perfection, indeed Being itself, is that the puny human self will be swallowed up. It is not at all unreasonable that the Gautama envisioned Nirvana as a state without desire or craving, without pleasure or pain, without Self.[108] Says the Buddha: "He for whom things future or past or present are nothing,

105 Ibid., 68.4, 396.

106 Ibid., 19.3–4, 202; 96.1–7, 503–6.

107 *Love and Responsibility*, 57.

108 Arindam Chakrabarti, "Buddhist Philosophy," in Honderich, *Oxford Companion to Philosophy*, 107–9, and Arindam Chakrabarti, "Nirvana," ibid., 623.

who has nothing and desires nothing—him I call a Brahmin."[109] What John Paul II proposes, however, is that this encounter with the Infinite is the occasion for a rediscovery of self. This rediscovery becomes intelligible when we attend to two factors. First, the inner life of the Godhead is itself a community of Persons in love. Second, the human person in this life discovers himself "only through sincere gift of self."[110] And indeed, this is a common enough human experience, that in the love for another (or for others) one best and most truly finds himself. The Beatific Vision will therefore be the fulfillment of what the human person lives imperfectly in this life. It is the fulfillment of human subjectivity, of the spiritual being oriented to truth and the good in love, precisely by his union with the One who is Truth and Goodness itself.

---

109 Gautama Buddha, *The Dhammapada*, chap. 26, "The Brahmin," in *Introduction to Philosophy of Religion: Readings*, ed. James Kellenberger (Upper Saddle River, NJ: Prentice Hall, 2007), 19.

110 Vatican Council II, *Gaudium et Spes*, 24.

CHAPTER 7

A "Truth About Evil"?

IN *VERITATIS SPLENDOR* John Paul II maintains that there are acts that are of themselves *intrinsically evil.*

> One must therefore reject the thesis, characteristic of teleological and proportionalist theories, which holds that it is impossible to qualify as morally evil according to its species—its "object"—the deliberate choice of certain kinds of behavior or specific acts, apart from a consideration of the intention for which the choice is made or the totality of the foreseeable consequences of that act for all persons concerned.[1]

This comment, which introduces the section of *Veritatis Splendor* on "intrinsic evil,"[2] affirms on the one hand that certain kinds of behavior or specific acts are "according to [their] species" morally evil and further that "teleological and proportionalist" theories of morality deny that such characterization is possible. The question of intrinsically evil acts and universally binding moral proscriptions became the flash point of the early responses to and analyses of *Veritatis Splendor.* With this doctrine concerning intrinsically evil acts, we may speak of a "truth about evil."[3] John Paul II affirms that there are acts which *by their very nature* are evil, that we can identify certain forms of behavior that cannot be made good by extenuating circumstances or higher motives. He goes on to list some examples of

[1] *Veritatis Splendor,* 79.
[2] Ibid., 79–82.
[3] John Paul II, *Dominum et Vivificantem,* 48.

intrinsically evil acts: "[w]hatever is hostile to life itself, such as any kind of homicide, genocide, abortion, euthanasia and voluntary suicide," as condemned by Vatican II;[4] contraceptive practices, as proscribed by Pope Paul VI in *Humanae Vitae*;[5] and idolatry, immorality, adultery, sexual perversion, theft, greed, drunkenness, reviling, and robbery, as warned against by St. Paul (1 Cor 6:9–10).[6] John Paul II's position poses two distinct problems for us. The first is that of the locus of the evil in the act itself, its foundation. What is it that can make an act intrinsically evil such that no circumstance or intention can redeem it? The second problem is that although John Paul II ascribes the rejection of the Church's teaching (which includes his own authoritative papal pronouncements) to teleological theories, his own account is clearly teleological.

If John Paul II's position were strictly deontological,[7] the first problem would be readily solved (although further problems would then be raised). If the criterion by which any act is evil is that it contravenes divine command, then it would be fairly easy to determine the morality of an act. This criterion would, however, be extrinsic to the act in the sense that it is not by understanding the act itself that one understands its evil but, in the final analysis, by the manifest command of God. Such a position results from a purely juridical conception of the moral law. If the moral law depends ultimately upon divine command, then knowing and interpreting divine commands becomes the central task of moral theology, which for its part ceases to be related meaningfully to philosophical ethics.[8] In fact, some of John Paul II's critics seem to read him in precisely this way, interpreting his insistence on the authority of the Magisterium to mean that he, the Pope, claimed to be the ultimate definitive interpreter of moral right and wrong, God's Supreme Court, as it were. Under such a

4 *Gaudium et Spes*, 27.

5 *Humanae Vitae*, 14.

6 These lists are cited in *Veritatis Splendor*, 80–81. See also *Dominum et Vivificantem*, 55.

7 As, for instance, Charles Curran and William Spohn maintain; see William C. Spohn, "Morality on the Way of Discipleship: The Use of Scripture in *Veritatis Splendor*," in Allsopp and O'Keefe, Veritatis Splendor: *American Responses*, 99, and in that same volume Charles Curran, "*Veritatis Splendor*: A Revisionist Perspective," 230.

8 Here we may fall into the dilemma in which Socrates trapped the priest Euthyphro 2,400 years ago. See Plato, *Euthyphro* 10a to the end.

conception, moral theology and, indeed, reasoning in general play but a minor role in comparison with the power of the Magisterium authoritatively to pronounce on the contents of the law.[9]

In fact, John Paul II rejects a legalist, "divine command" approach to moral reasoning. In his principal philosophical work on sexual ethics, he wrote (as Karol Wojtyła) that although one may well draw up sets of rules for Catholic moral theology, the true task is to found moral norms on incontrovertible truths about fundamental values, most especially on the value of the person.[10] As we have seen already, the moral theology and philosophical ethics of our author have a strongly teleological note. This is especially evident in the first chapter of *Veritatis Splendor*, which is a kind of commentary and reflection of Christ's encounter with the rich young man,[11] who is searching for the ultimate good. He has obeyed the Ten Commandments and asks, "What more do I lack?" John Paul II comments:

> *To ask about the good*, in fact, *ultimately means to turn towards God*, the fullness of goodness. Jesus shows that the young man's question is really a *religious question*, and that the goodness that attracts and at the same time obliges man has its source in God, and indeed is God himself. God alone is worthy of being loved "with all one's heart, and with all one's soul, and with all one's mind" (Mt 22:37). He is the source of man's happiness.[12]

---

[9] See Bernard Häring, "A Distrust That Wounds," in Curran and McCormick, *John Paul II and Moral Theology*, 42, and also McCormick, "Some Early Reactions to *Veritatis Splendor*," 29. Also Maura Anne Ryan, " 'Then Who Can Be Saved': Ethics and Ecclesiology in *Veritatis Splendor*," in Allsopp and O'Keefe, Veritatis Splendor: *American Responses*, 11; Ronald R. Burke, "*Veritatis Splendor*: Papal Authority and the Sovereignty of Reason," ibid., 123, 130. See also McCormick, "Some Early Reactions to *Veritatis Splendor*," 28–29; Burke, "*Veritatis Splendor*: Papal Authority and the Sovereignty of Reason," 119 and especially 124: "The Pope is involved here in serious business. He wants to leave no room for doubt regarding the authority of the Magisterium or the subservient role of moral theologians." Also, Éric Fuchs, *La morale selon Jean-Paul II: Réponse protestante à une encyclique* (Geneva: Labor et fides, 1994), 52; Robert Somerville, "Les encycliques du pape et l'évangile," in *Paroles de pape, paroles protestantes*, ed. André Birmelé et al. (Paris: Les bergers et les mages, 1995), 62, 64; and Schneider, "*Wer Gott dient, wird nicht krumm*," 97.

[10] *Miłość i odpowiedzialność*, 14; "Author's Introduction to the First Edition," in *Love and Responsibility*, 16.

[11] Mt 19:16–23.

[12] *Veritatis Splendor*, 9.

In this text we find a fundamental norm of John Paul II's moral theology: God is the highest good and most worthy of love. Thus can he go on to say, "*The moral life presents itself as the response* due to the many gratuitous initiatives taken by God out of love for man. It is a response of love."[13] The command that flows immediately and directly from this norm is "Love God," and so John Paul II cites the fundamental commandment of Deuteronomy 6:4–5: "Hear, O Israel: The Lord our God is the one Lord. You shall love the Lord your God with all your heart, and with all your soul, and with all your might."[14] This is a positive commandment that itself designates no particular evil, except that of refusing to love God. Whence come the negative commandments and intrinsically evil acts? John Paul II begins to answer this question in the very next section of the encyclical, where he points to the Law, to the Decalogue, the first tablet of which directs us to love God. Beyond this, the commandments of the second tablet direct us to the love of neighbor. "The commandments," says John Paul II, "of which Jesus reminds the young man are meant to safeguard *the good* of the person, the image of God, by protecting his *goods*."[15] These represent the basic conditions for love of one's neighbor, of which they are the first step, expressing the dignity of the human person. Although mere obedience to the commandments does not suffice for love of neighbor, the commandments do constitute a necessary condition for that love. In this way John Paul II begins to find the deontology implicit in the teleology of the human person living for love of God.

Intrinsece malum and the Object of the Will

A human act is evil if it contravenes a moral norm. This is clear from the fact that a moral norm expresses the truth about the good. Karol Wojtyła writes, "The ethical norm . . . is nothing other than the objectification (and at the same time the concretization) of the truth about the good, of the good tied to a given action of the person, willed in it and realized in it."[16] Since

[13] Ibid., 10.

[14] Ibid.

[15] Ibid., 13.

[16] *L'uomo nel campo della responsibilità*, 1269. Elsewhere he writes, "Norm, in the most general sense of the term, is the name we give to a principle of moral good and evil." "The Problem of the Theory of Morality," in *Person and Community*, 139. See also *Persona e atto*, 1037–38.

the will is to be ordered to the good—by his will the person is to love what is good and choose according to the truth about the good (as he understands this)—one behaves badly by choosing against the good, just as the chess player whose move leaves the king exposed has made a bad move. To choose against a moral norm is to choose a value contrary to the true good, in effect, denying the good as known to reason and hence the truth in favor of some other value that is presented to sense or emotion. Such as choice is founded on concupiscence rather than on the love for the true good.

In his theology of the body audiences, John Paul II characterizes the human being after the Fall as the "man of concupiscence,"[17] and he does so in terms of the Johannine "threefold concupiscence": "the concupiscence of the flesh, the concupiscence of the eyes, and the pride of life."[18] Concupiscence so understood is broader than the sensual concupiscence that craves the pleasures of the flesh. *Concupiscence of the eyes* encompasses the desire for possessions, for material things, and the *pride of life* is that form of concupiscence that would assert the self in pride and domination. It is clear, therefore, that not all concupiscence results from the stirrings of the flesh. For the sake of gain a man might well deny himself pleasure; consider Dickens's Scrooge. Dominated by vainglory—the pride of life—a person may risk comfort, goods, and even life itself. The feelings that arise from the latter two forms of concupiscence have more the character of emotion than of sense craving. These feelings, be they urges of sensual desire or emotions stimulated by pride or the desire to possess and use, can become powerful to the point of dominating a person's psyche. As such they may seem—and for the moment *be*—irresistible.[19] They represent values that supplant the good known objectively by reason. What all three forms of concupiscence have in common is that the values to which they are directed are not those known by reason, which is the only power by which the person can know things as they really are. Governed by the values presented by the threefold concupiscence, the person's acts cannot be referred to the fitting good, the true good.

[17] *Man and Woman He Created Them,* 26.1–3, 234–36; in Polish, "człowiek pożadliwości," *Mężczyzną i niewiastą stworzył ich,* 86.

[18] 1 Jn 2:16. The citation is drawn from Waldstein's translation in *Man and Woman He Created Them,* 26.1, 234.

[19] See the discussion of "emotionalization of consciousness" in Wojtyła, *Persona e atto,* chap. 1, sec. 5, 896–904, and the analysis of emotion, 1119–21, 1136–40.

It is not the commandment as such that makes a human act intrinsically evil. Rather, an act is specified as morally good or evil according to its *object,* which is intrinsically related to the moral norm. Here it is worth citing at length from John Paul II's text:

> Reason attests that there are objects of the human act which are so by their nature "incapable of being ordered" to God, because they radically contradict the good of the person made in his image. These are acts which, in the Church's moral tradition, have been termed "intrinsically evil" (*intrinsece malum*): they are such *always and per se,* in other words, on account of their very object, and quite apart from the ulterior intentions of the one acting and the circumstances.[20]

Some "objects of the human act" simply cannot be ordered to God. They are absolutely incapable of being so ordered, that is, of expressing love for God or neighbor. To explain the expression "object of the human act," John Paul II refers to Thomas Aquinas's analysis.

> Now, in a voluntary act, there is a twofold act, namely, the interior act of the will and the external act, and each of these acts has its object. The end is properly the object of the interior act of the will, while the object of the external action is that on which the action is brought to bear. Therefore just as the external act takes its species from the object on which it bears, so the interior act of the will takes its species from the end, as from its proper object.
>
> Now that which is on the part of the will is formal in relation to that which is on the part of the external action, because the will uses the limbs to act, as instruments . . . . Consequently the species of a human act is considered formally with regard to the end, but materially with regard to the external act. Hence the Philosopher says[21] that "he who steals that he may commit adultery is, strictly speaking, more adulterer than thief."[22]

The point that Aquinas is making is that just as the external act has an object on which the body's actions are brought to bear, so too does the internal act, which is to perform *this particular external act for this end.* The man is aiming his pistol at his rival and pulling the trigger, and these

---

[20] *Veritatis Splendor,* 80.

[21] Citing Aristotle, *Nicomachean Ethics* 5.2, 1130a24.

[22] *ST* I–II, q. 18, a. 6.

are not random motions. They are what he has chosen to do, and the choice to do these actions is the internal act. John Paul II summarizes thus: "The object of the act of willing is in fact a freely chosen kind of behavior."[23] This object is not, he adds, "a process or an event of the merely physical order. . . . Rather, that object is the proximate end of a deliberate decision which determines the act of willing on the part of the acting person."[24] The object of the act of willing, therefore, is simply what the acting person intends to do. Rhonheimer summarizes the concept: "The object of the human act is by no means a simple 'physical good' or 'nonmoral good,' as would be, for example, a human life or property. Rather, the object of a human act is always a willing and with this, as the encyclical affirms, 'a freely chosen behavior': it is a kind of action, as, for example, 'to kill an innocent man,' or 'to steal.' "[25]

Consistent with his position stated elsewhere that moral evil arises only within the will,[26] John Paul II locates the *moral object* in the will. This means that the object is not some pattern of motion and therefore that it cannot be the sequence of events considered as such that is immoral. The ingesting of a particular pharmaceutical is not of itself evil,[27] nor is the firing of a rifle horizontal to the ground in the direction 36 degrees from due north. However, if the ingesting or the firing is the act of a human person (a human act), it has been commanded according to the will of the person

23 *Veritatis Splendor*, 78.

24 Ibid.

25 Martin Rhonheimer, "La prospettiva della persona agente e la natura della ragione practica," in Melina and Noriega, *Camminare nella Luce*, 170.

26 John Paul II, *Centesimus Annus*, 4; *Memory and Identity*, 37. See also Karol Wojtyła, "The Transcendence of the Person in Action and Man's Self-Teleology," in Tymieniecka, *Analecta Husserliana*, 9:207; "The Problem of the Theory of Morality," in *Person and Community*, 129–61.

27 The obvious allusion is to contraception, and concerning this see Paul VI, *Humanae Vitae*, 15. But consider also the recent controversy of the United States Food and Drug Administration's approval of thalidomide as a treatment for multiple myeloma, a form of cancer. The drug had been outlawed in 1962 after its use to remedy morning sickness during pregnancy resulted in serious deformities of infants. When the FDA and its counterparts in other countries recently approved the drug for myeloma, many of those affected by its earlier use protested that a drug that had caused such harm to unborn children ought never to be allowed on the market. In their opinion, the drug itself is to be regarded as an evil. See Thalidomide Victims Association of Canada, www.thalidomide.ca/home/.

who decides, "I will take this pharmaceutical now" or "I will fire this rifle in that direction now." Furthermore, the acting person acts on the basis of an understanding of the consequences of the act. The drug will have known effects. The path of the rifle bullet will endanger this living being. This means that the intention is written into the act.[28] The gunman chooses to shoot at the beer can on the log, at the deer, or at his rival. What he intends to do determines the motions that he enacts. (Of course, the act of murder is quite independent of the means used, whether one fires a rifle, stabs with a knife, or deliberately misleads his victim into mortal danger.) Therefore, when John Paul II writes that "there are objects of the human act which are so by their nature 'incapable of being ordered' to God," he is referring to the acting person's choice of a kind of behavior whose end cannot be ordered to God. To fire a rifle can be ordered to a fitting good, but to murder Jones cannot.

The Revisionist Objections

Many contemporary moral theologians have objected strongly to this account. R. Preston writes, "The examples it [*Veritatis Splendor*] gives of intrinsically evil acts from *Gaudium et Spes* are unconvincing; mostly they do not define acts in the abstract, but with the circumstances or conditions which make them evil."[29] Perhaps more clearly to the point, Richard McCormick argues:

> Within the past twenty-five years, many Catholic moral theologians have adopted a form of teleology in their understanding of moral norms. . . . However, common to all their analyses is the insistence that causing certain disvalues (ontic, nonmoral, premoral evils) in our conduct does not ipso facto make the action morally wrong. The action becomes morally wrong when, all things considered, there is no proportionate reason justifying it.[30]

McCormick proceeds on this basis to identify some confusions that arise in moral theology from the failure to observe this distinction between

[28] See also Rhonheimer, "La prospettiva della persona agente," 170: "Per questo, all'interno del discorso morale non esiste nessuna contrapposizione fra le nozioni di 'oggetto' e di 'fine'. L'oggetto è, per l'appunto, *un tipo* particolare di fine."

[29] R. Preston, "*Veritatis Splendor*: A Comment," *Studies in Christian Ethics* 7 (1994): 40.

[30] McCormick, *Critical Calling*, 134.

moral and *nonmoral* or *premoral* values. Among these are the confusion of fact-words and value-words and of the pairs "right-wrong" and "good-bad."[31] So, when the Second Vatican Council condemns "any kind of homicide, genocide, abortion, euthanasia,"[32] it has already, by its very choice of words, "loaded" the discussion with moral values.[33] The terms themselves entail moral evaluation. On the other hand, should one use such terms as "causing the death of another human being, a particular population, a fetus, a person in pain," then one has expressed the premoral situation. By the very meaning of the word, *murder* is morally wrong, but the question for moral theology is whether *this* particular taking of a human life is murder and hence morally wrong. From the revisionist (or proportionalist) perspective, the acting person is confronted with a choice of realizing an array of premoral goods and evils—or better, values and disvalues—by his act. To choose to pursue an admittedly dubious legal prosecution, for example, may result not only in the death of a man innocent of any crime (one premoral evil) but also in the preservation of one's nation from invasion (invasion being a much graver premoral evil).[34]

Reflections on "Double Effect"

The concept of "proportionate reason," as cited above by McCormick, and this distinction between premoral and moral goods (or evils) arises from Peter Knauer's reflections on the implications of traditional "double effect" casuistry,[35] in which he argued that all moral judgments involve the weighing of

31 Ibid., 136–37.

32 *Gaudium et Spes*, 27.

33 Several moral theologians have criticized the use of this conciliar text on the basis that the Second Vatican Council itself never referred to these acts as *intrinsece mala*, and its intention in presenting this list appears to be quite different from the use John Paul II makes of it. See Paolo Carlotti, Veritatis Splendor: *Aspetti della recezione teologica* (Rome: Libraria Ateneo Salesiano, 2001), 153.

34 The allusion, of course, is to Caiaphas's advice at John 11:49–50. Although the use of this example may strike some readers as unfair, Caiaphas was most certainly weighing the disvalue of the death of one man (and that man arguably a blasphemer) against the catastrophic disvalue of the loss of a nation. Clearly, he did not recognize the distinctive ontological and salvific status of the one whom he was prepared to sacrifice. We shall return to this specific example later in the analysis.

35 Peter Knauer's work on the principle of double effect can be said to mark the beginning of the proportionalist tradition in moral theology. See Christopher Kaczor, introduction to *Proportionalism: For and Against*, ed. Christopher Kaczor (Milwaukee: Marquette University Press, 2000), 11.

premoral goods. Although for the Scholastics the application of this principle was rare, "marginal," and infrequent, Knauer maintains: "In reality, virtually all acts have a double effect; in almost every act, a gain is tied to a loss (injury)."[36] Their reason for this is that any action can be described independently of the reasons for undertaking it. Knauer instances the word-couples "killing and murder," "termination of pregnancy and abortion," and "amputation and mutilation" as cases where the second, morally laden term receives its moral value from the reasons for its being undertaken.[37] Similar is J. Fuchs's analysis, cited by Andrzej Szostek, of the morality of removing the diseased uterus from a pregnant woman: "The theory [of double effect] overlooked that the evil at stake is such not in the moral sense but in the premoral . . . and that therefore its realization occurs . . . not as a separate human action with its own morality but as an element of an action that is specified through the establishment of an end."[38] McCormick similarly gives the fairly common example of the removal of a fetus from a pregnant woman who will die otherwise. According to the principle of double effect, he argues, one may remove the fetus to save the mother's life. The death of the woman and the death of a fetus are both premoral evils. What is at stake, therefore, is not the morality of this or that act but rather the weighing of the corresponding basis for the choice of one premoral good over another.[39] In Fuchs' similar case, he takes a slightly different, albeit related, approach, considering the relationship between the ontically good end and the premoral evils that must be accepted to realize it. In short, whereas the Scholastics proposed that in rare cases one might choose to perform an act one of whose unintended consequences was an evil, the revisionist theologian argues that every act is the choice to attain some good at the cost of some evil. It is good to walk

---

[36] Peter Knauer, "Zu Grundbegriffen der Enzyklika '*Veritatis Splendor*,'" *Stimmen der Zeit* 212, no. 1 (January 1994): 22. See also Knauer, "Teleologische als deontologische Normenbegründung," 323, and "The Hermeneutic Function of the Principle of Double Effect," in Kaczor, *Proportionalism*, 25–26.

[37] Knauer, "Zu Grundbegriffen der Enzyklika '*Veritatis Splendor*,'" 25.

[38] J. Fuchs, "Der Absolutheitscharakter sittlichen Handlungsnormen," in *Für eine menschliche Moral: Grundfragen der theologischen Ethik*, vol. 1 (Fribourg, Switzerland [Freiburg, Schweiz]: Universitätsverlag, 1988), 245f., cited in Szostek, *Natur—Vernunft—Freiheit*, 178.

[39] Richard A. McCormick, S.J., "Ambiguity in Moral Choice," in Kaczor, *Proportionalism*, 209.

to the store, even at the cost of shoe leather and the risk of getting a blister on the foot, if one derives a sufficient benefit to offset the harm.

However, if the choice is among premoral goods, whence do we derive the *moral goodness* or *moral evil* of the act? Knauer appeals to the concept of *entsprechende Grund* ("proportionate reason"): "An act can be 'evil in itself' [*in sich schlecht*] only if one has no 'proportionate reason' for allowing or causing some harm but rather in the final analysis contradicts the reason for the action."[40] Knauer characterizes "proportionate reason" as follows:

> The reason for an action is "proportionate" only when the action is justified *in the long run and as a whole* for the premoral value or value-complex it strives for, this value-complex being formulated as *universal*. . . . Conversely, the reason for an act is not "proportionate" *if the action is not justified for the value or value-complex that it strives for but is instead counterproductive to it*, or if it sacrifices other values.[41]

The physical description of the act itself does not avail for judging its morality,[42] but only the reasons for its performance. It follows therefore that one cannot judge Jones's deliberate killing of Smith to be immoral on the basis of the act as described. If Jones had a proportionate reason—such as to protect his own life—then the act is warranted. In response to the objection that in legitimate self-defense one does not directly intend the death of his attacker, that the decisive distinction is that between direct intention and an indirect permission, Knauer responds that these distinctions between "direct" and "indirect" or "causing" and "allowing" can be founded only on the legitimacy of the *proportionate reasons* at stake: "As long as the allowing or causing of harm is not justified through a 'proportionate reason' it is 'direct' in the moral sense and itself determines the 'end of the act.' "[43] In the case of self-defense, therefore, at issue is not whether Jones intended to see Smith dead but whether his action of using lethal force "in general and in the long run" affirms the value of life. In such a case—as indeed with virtually every act that any person might perform—

40 "Zu Grundbegriffen der Enzyklika '*Veritatis Splendor*,' " 22; "Hermeneutic Function of the Principle of Double Effect," 26.

41 "Zu Grundbegriffen der Enzyklika '*Veritatis Splendor*,' " 23.

42 Knauer, "Teleologische als deontologische Normenbegründung," 348. See also Curran, "*Veritatis Splendor*: A Revisionist Perspective," 238.

43 "Zu Grundbegriffen der Enzyklika '*Veritatis Splendor*,' " 24.

what is at stake is a balancing of premoral goods and evils. By his inaction, Jones would allow his own death at the hands of Smith. Knauer's criterion is intended to provide a criterion for determining which evil to allow or cause. The project of proportionalism must therefore entail the establishment of the criteria for determining how the respective harms or premoral evils consequent upon an action (or inaction) are to be balanced.[44]

An especially illuminating perspective on the implications and the bases of this conception is the application by both Knauer and Louis Janssens to the promulgation of traffic laws. Janssens argues that the "dynamic character of morality" flows from the principle that "wherever ontic evil can be lessened it must be lessened."[45] This "dynamic character" arises because the conditions under which human beings live constantly change. For example, public officials must frequently reevaluate their policies concerning vehicular traffic, since the development of faster and more powerful vehicles creates new, hitherto unknown risks of harm. For the responsible officials not to adapt laws and driving regulations to changing conditions could be to put more of the populace at risk or harm, and such failure would therefore be immoral on their part.[46] The choices to change speed limits, to replace intersections with roundabouts, or to widen highways all become moral choices between good and evil. Knauer makes a similar observation.[47]

This attention to the prudential decisions of public officials is not a side issue but indicates a fundamental change in the understanding of morality. At issue is not simply whether public officials are obliged to adapt public safety policies to changing conditions but whether officials act wickedly in choosing speed (which motorists generally value) over maximal safety; after all, it is likely that highway deaths would drop dramatically if motorists were to travel at forty miles per hour on superhighways

[44] See Joseph Ratzinger, "Christian Faith as 'the Way': An Introduction to *Veritatis Splendor*," *Communio: International Catholic Review* 21, no. 2 (Summer 1994): 201, and Ratzinger, "Il rinnovamento della teologia morale: Prospettive del Vatican II e di *Veritatis Splendor*," in Melina and Noriega, *Camminare nella Luce*, 41; also Michael D. Place, "*Familiaris Consortio*: A Review of Its Theology," in Curran and McCormick, *John Paul II and Moral Theology*, 188. For a nice summary of some of the more important approaches to this question, see McCormick, "Ambiguity in Moral Choice," in Kaczor, *Proportionalism*, 166–214.

[45] Louis Janssens, "Ontic Evil and Moral Evil," in Kaczor, *Proportionalism*, 138.

[46] Ibid., 136–37.

[47] "Hermeneutic Function of the Principle of Double Effect," 34–35.

and correspondingly slower on lesser roads. The proportionalist thesis is that moral choice is ultimately about balancing goods and evils in the situations one encounters such that to prefer ontic evils over goods always constitutes moral evil. We see this perspective perhaps most explicitly in Janssens' utopianism:

> This insight into a better world originates in the dynamic qualities of our human nature which is essentially tending toward the future. In other words, the utopian speculation is inherent in the history of man. . . . The utopia is also an expression of the faith that history has a future; and it is an expression of the idea that we must feel responsible for the ideal of the betterment of the world when we act. The *concrete material norms* of morality hold the ideal of the utopia before us and continually suggest a future which is more suitable for man.[48]

Our moral responsibility reduces to the general requirement to make the world a better place. Plausible as this may seem at first glance, such a requirement quickly breaks down. What does this utopian ideal mean? Should automobiles, vehicles that enable us to do business, visit friends, and expand our experience—and that consume fossil fuels, filling the air with hydrocarbons, and cause immense human suffering from accidents, as well as more than fifty thousand deaths annually—have been invented? Did the Wright brothers behave immorally by inventing the vehicle from which the bomber would descend? Surely one of the lessons of the history of technology is that the military mind is quick to adapt new inventions for more efficient and effective wartime killing. Janssens has given us a standard that is very hard to apply.

Summarizing from his own analysis of proportionalist moral theology, Szostek holds that such theologians must find the basis of moral right and wrong not in the acts but in the "subject's *fundamental stance* concerning that which he regards as good and right."[49] The physician who removes the diseased uterus may reasonably be said to have taken the life of the unborn infant, even if he wishes that this outcome were not necessary and his intention is to save the mother. If this act is not to qualify as a culpable killing, as murder, the moral goodness of his act must derive from his intent. These

[48] "Ontic Evil and Moral Evil," in Kaczor, *Proportionalism*, 142–43.

[49] *Natur—Vernunft—Freiheit*, 180.

considerations relate directly to the linguistic or terminological objection that to use value-words (such as "murder") is already to have determined the moral value of the act. Granted that murder is always wrong, because "murder" means "unjust killing,"[50] the question still remains whether *this* act of bringing about the death of a human being is unjust in such a way as to qualify as "murder." In the background here, we may clearly perceive David Hume's phenomenalism: the act is an event in the world falling under a given factual description, expected to bring about certain other events and states of affairs, which may be good or evil (in a premoral sense). The choice of an act is therefore the choice among premoral goods and evils. According to such a conception of the human act, little sense can be made of the notion of an act that is *intrinsically evil* in itself.

Let us note in passing that such a perspective makes it hard to grasp the moral distinction between artificial contraception and natural methods of family planning. Both Paul VI[51] and John Paul II[52] have argued that although artificial contraceptives and sterilization are morally unacceptable, a couple may delay or forestall conception of a new life by recourse to the infertile periods within the woman's menstrual cycle. Many object to this that the pontiffs are splitting hairs, that recourse to basal temperature readings and the testing of mucus are every bit as artificial as pills, patches, and IUDs.[53] The critical point, however, is that both approaches to the exercise of sexuality allow for acts of sexual intercourse that do not result in conception. If the behavior is the same and the results are the same, are not the acts the same? The revisionist moral theologian can respond that, yes, the acts (sexual intercourse or copulation) are the same, that the only difference lies in the circumstances in which the acts are performed.[54] (Similarly, the

---

50 McCormick, *Critical Calling*, 136. See also James Gaffney, "The Pope on Proportionalism," in Allsopp and O'Keefe, Veritatis Splendor: *American Responses*, 63, and in that same volume, Curran, "*Veritatis Splendor*: A Revisionist Perspective," 232. We will note shortly that, these authorities notwithstanding, the definition of murder is not "illicit or unlawful killing."

51 *Humanae Vitae*, 16.

52 *Man and Woman He Created Them*, 122.1–125.7, 628–39, and *Familiaris Consortio*, 32. See also Wojtyła, *Love and Responsibility*, 237–44.

53 I could cite numerous conversations, but see also Luke Timothy Johnson, "A Disembodied Theology of the Body: John Paul II on Love, Sex, and Pleasure," *Commonweal*, January 26, 2001.

54 Odozor, *Richard A. McCormick and the Renewal of Moral Theology*, 97.

revisionist theologian will maintain that in the cases of loving marital intercourse, adulterous relations, and rape, the acts are the same but the circumstances different.) For his part, however, John Paul II effectively maintains that the acts are different, that the couple using natural methods relies on virtue (specifically chastity) to govern their sexual behavior and its results, while those using contraceptives have given the lie to the intrinsic meaning of the act, thereby changing it fundamentally.[55]

The Structure of Acts

Precisely here do we find the key to a kind of systemic misunderstanding surrounding *Veritatis Splendor.* When this encyclical appeared, many contemporary moral theologians complained that they could not recognize themselves or any thinkers they knew as holding the positions criticized in chapter 2 of the encyclical, while many of their critics thought John Paul II's critique was precisely on the mark.[56] Indeed, some proportionalist theologians took positive offense at the charge that, for example, they affirm that a good end can justify an evil act. One could say that one side (or both) is being obtuse or disingenuous, but the reality seems to be less pernicious. Between these two sides we find a significant difference in their respective understandings of the human act. Consistent with the post-Enlightenment perspective on the ontological neutrality of events and things in the world, revisionists see the act as an in-principle neutral event whose moral character must derive from a balance, proportion, or relationship among premoral goods and evils. John Paul II, however, argues that this is not an adequate account of the human act, that such objections inevitably prescind from the "*perspective of the acting person.*" It is precisely this perspective from which we must consider the object of the moral act.[57] That is to say, the acting person is not merely an observer confronted with choosing between two or more arrays of premoral values and disvalues, but he is himself the cause of his own acts. The fire chief may well have to choose between rescuing the trapped children or devoting all his

55 *Man and Woman He Created Them,* 127.4–5, 643–44; 128.4, 646; 131.1–2, 652–53.

56 See Gaffney, "Pope on Proportionalism," 61, 67; Curran, "*Veritatis Splendor*: A Revisionist Perspective," 237; McCormick, "Some Early Reactions to *Veritatis Splendor,*" 11–12, 14, 20; Fuchs, *La morale selon Jean-Paul II,* 41; and Carlotti, Veritatis Splendor: *Aspetti della recezione teologica,* 129–30.

57 *Veritatis Splendor,* 78. See Rhonheimer, "La prospettiva della persona agente e la natura della ragione practica," 169–224.

resources to keep the blaze from igniting a gas storage facility. No matter what, something bad will happen, and it is up to him to minimize the damage. Such a scenario does not, however, accurately represent the moral choices and acts represented by the commission of murder, genocide, abortion, and so on. The moral agent is not simply choosing among possible configurations of premoral good and evil in the world.

Let us consider the case example of the foreign traveler who emerges from the jungle into a Latin American village where a tyrannical captain threatens to kill all the villagers but will spare them if the traveler will kill the village headman. Might a person not be excused for killing or even be obliged to kill the one in order to save the life of many?[58] Implicit in this example is that the traveler's challenge is to select between two alternative concatenations of good and bad, of values and disvalues. He may choose a state of affairs in which all the people of the village lie dead or one in which only one person is dead. The situation apparently poses a moral dilemma because both states of affairs lie within the traveler's power to realize. He can preserve the lives of the villagers but at the cost of performing an act that is ordinarily regarded as morally abhorrent, an act that he would ordinarily describe as murder and therefore as wrong. As we consider such dilemmas, it is not hard to see Hume's parricide tree lurking in the background. The facts themselves are devoid of moral value.

Such analyses as presented in the South American village dilemma overlook the "perspective of the acting person" in the sense that they ignore the moral agency of the acting person. The fire chief who abandons the endangered children to direct his resources to preventing the catastrophic explosion can be said to have chosen between two scenarios. His capacity to act (by allocating personnel and equipment) is limited, and whatever he does, his acts can be good. Whether he has performed well or ill is simply a prudential matter. The traveler's choice is different, however. His own option for action is to murder, which the *Catechism of the Catholic Church* characterizes as the "*direct and intentional killing*" of a human being.[59]

---

[58] Charles Curran discusses this hypothetical case in his *Directions in Fundamental Moral Theology*, 177–78, 183, arguing that for the traveler to kill the headman could be morally defensible.

[59] *Catechism of the Catholic Church* (Ligouri, MO: Ligouri Publications, 1994), 2268. It is important to note that this definition does not contain value-terms such as "unjust" or "unlawful."

The traveler is required to take direct lethal action against the village headman for the sake of ensuring that he dies. If his aim is bad and he only wounds the headman, then under the tyrannical captain's terms he must administer a second killing shot. The headman must die by the traveler's agency and intent.[60] And this is the point. Although the further intention, the more ultimate goal—that the lives of the villagers be saved—is undeniably good, the act he has chosen is the killing of an innocent man, which is murder.[61] We cannot say that his proximate end is the saving of the village, for the act he chooses is to kill the headman.

At stake here is the structure of the human act, of the manner in which the human act is to be conceived. Karol Wojtyła characterizes an act as a dynamization or setting into motion of oneself to attain some end. The act, so he argues, is to be efficacious,[62] which is to say that an act is intended to effect some change in the world or in the acting person. This is directly consonant with Aquinas's argument that the human being always acts for an end.[63] As we consider this in detail, it becomes apparent that "act" is an analogous term. That is to say, because an act is an efficacious bodily motion in space and time, it can both be linked with other acts and subdivided into constituent acts.

We can illustrate this with athletic acts. Why was the man not in his office on Saturday afternoon? He played tennis instead. His boss may judge this playing to have been a *bad act* (since there was much work to be done), but his physician may have considered it a *good act* (since he had advised vigorous exercise). So, playing tennis is *an act.* But as part of the act, the man served the ball to his opponent. If the ball landed in his opponent's service court, then *the serve was good* and contributed to victory, one of the ends for which the man plays. However, the apparently

60 We may contrast this with the case of the police officer who shoots a dangerous suspect. Even though he "shoots to kill," aiming for the chest, once he has brought down the suspect and rendered him harmless, the officer will summon medical help to treat the suspect's injuries.

61 Thus the case is different also from that of a driver who has lost his brakes and must choose between running into one man or a crowd of schoolchildren. He intends to kill no one, only to minimize the damage with the resources available to him.

62 Here I am following, in summary fashion, Karol Wojtyła's analysis in pt. 1 of *Person and Act,* especially chap. 2.

63 *ST* I–II, q. 1, a. 1.

successful service may have been bad, if the player stepped on the baseline, thus committing a foot fault. Regardless of the physical and psychological benefits of the act of playing tennis and of the coordination of toss, backswing, and follow-through, the service was bad, because the footwork was bad. Indeed, when we consider just this one aspect of the game, we discover a nexus of acts that are called into play: the toss, the backswing, the footwork, and the follow-through. And indeed, advanced players devote effort simply to practice the toss alone. The point of this example is that in every case where we speak of "an act," the event in question may well be a constituent part of some other act and may well admit of being analyzed into subacts. (If the tennis example seems unconvincing, consider the act of driving a car and the detailed instruction that is involved in teaching a teenager how to perform this act.) This becomes important as we attempt to determine what is the *object* of the will in choosing an act.

To clarify the application of this to morality and the moral object of the act, let us consider an argument Peter Knauer presents.[64] In order to support his position that the object of the act is determined by its "proportionate reason" (*entesprechende Grund*), he recalls an article he had read many years before, in which the author argued that organ donations by living donors were not morally permissible, because an evil—self-mutilation by allowing the removal of one's organ (Knauer suggests the kidney)—is performed to attain some good. But since it is a fundamental moral principle that one may not do evil to achieve a good, the transplant must be evil. In arguing against this position, Knauer writes: "Here it is not at all a matter of two different acts, the first of which is evil and which then cannot be justified through the second. Instead, what is at stake is from the start a single act, whose "object" or "end of the act" is the saving of another human being's life."[65] It follows therefore that the morally qualified act is the total act of surgical transplantation to save a life. Richard McCormick writes: "Finally, Knauer argues, correctly I believe, that we must be careful to analyze an act accurately. Organ donation from a living donor is not two acts, one a means to the other. It is a single act whose very object is saving the life of the recipient."[66]

---

64 "Zu Grundbegriffen der Enzyklika '*Veritatis Splendor*,'" 14–26.

65 Ibid., 25.

66 McCormick, "Some Early Reactions to *Veritatis Splendor*," 21.

Although Knauer is right to defend the moral goodness of organ transplantation, his own argument is mistaken. The reduction of the nexus of acts in question to one act of saving a life is not convincing. Should the surgeon removing the kidney nick it with his scalpel, his transplantation colleague would complain that the first surgeon had botched his work, had performed *his act* poorly. Furthermore, were the organ removal performed on an unwilling donor, for example, or without anesthetic, we would rightly object that such a procedure is immoral; the immorality would arise precisely from the act of performing invasive surgery on an unwilling patient or in subjecting him to avoidable excruciating pain. Knauer's intellectual opponent erred not in regarding the act of removing an organ from a donor as a morally qualifiable act but in wrongly qualifying its morality.

This kind of argument could stand, if it were possible to maintain a kind of *practical atomism*, according to which an act could be characterized in itself according to its object without consideration of component subacts. If the act of *saving a life by surgical transplantation* were atomic, then we could accept Knauer's reasoning. However, like the act of playing tennis, this act of surgical transplantation is itself a synthesis of component acts, each of which is susceptible of analysis in terms of *its* object. Should one of the component acts of an act be immoral, then its immorality cannot be redeemed by the broader, overarching act of which it is a component. As a stage in transplanting a kidney, the physician has to remove the organ from a live donor. If that act were indeed immoral, as Knauer's unnamed opponent proposed, then the act of transplantation would indeed be immoral.

The Status of Ontic Evil

The real difficulty here is Knauer's underlying principle, accepted by his adversary, and indeed by most proportionalist theologians, that moral evil is constituted by the unwarranted permission or causing of premoral (or ontic) evil. But is this in fact true? Or might the very notion of premoral (ontic) evil need to be questioned? Janssens defines "ontic evil" as "any lack of a perfection at which we aim, which can keep our acts from being human acts in the real sense (*ST*, I–II, 6, 8). We call ontic evil any lack of a perfection at which we aim, any lack of fulfillment which frustrates our natural urges and makes us suffer. It is essentially the natural consequence of our limitation."[67]

Janssens continues:

> Wherever ontic evil can be lessened it must be lessened. This obligation reveals the dynamic character of morality. There are two reasons for this obligation. The first one follows from the definition of morality: moral activity fundamentally concerns the truly human development of man and society and the struggle against ontic evil which impedes this development. The second reason follows from the meaning of our activity in the world: by our activity we must turn the world of nature into a world of culture.[68]

Although ontic evil is often identified with Aquinas's notion of physical evil,[69] Aquinas himself does not characterize morality in terms of the causation and avoidance of physical evils. Janssens speaks accurately enough of evil as any lack of perfection, but in applying this to human beings he does not raise the question of the perfection of the human being as such. We may speak of ontic evils in relation to many kinds of standards of perfection. We kill trees in order to carve their wood into beautiful statues. Parents cause pain and frustration to their children as punishments in order to perfect their offspring morally. "Daddy" insists that his child take a fearful jump into the swimming pool despite the child's manifest fear. The young athlete finds it a grave misfortune that his small stature disqualifies him from sports competition at the next higher level.[70] As Janssens observes, there is a kind of evil that results simply from our creaturely limitations. Existence in the world is characterized by the occupation of space and time, which of itself limits one's movements and the movements of neighboring things. As physical things interact, they change

---

67 Janssens, "Ontic Evil and Moral Evil," 119. See also 127, where he characterizes ontic evil as "a lack of perfection, a deficiency which frustrates our inclinations. We label it *evil* when it affects a human subject insofar as it appears to the consciousness as a lack and a want, and to the extent that it is detrimental and harmful to the development of individuals and communities."

68 Ibid., 138.

69 See, e.g., Knauer, "Hermeneutic Function of the Principle of Double Effect," 26, 31, as well as "Teleologische als deontologische Normenbegründung," 325.

70 This example is not absurd, because hereditary shortness can be treated—and in places is being treated—with growth hormones so that talented, but comparatively small, boys can attain their athletic dreams.

each other; things wear out. To survive, animals must eat other living things. All these can be regarded as evils of a sort.

If the permission or causation of ontic evils constitutes a moral evil, then not only moral theology but natural theology too becomes enmeshed in paradox and antinomy, because the Creator himself has caused a world in which evil (especially the evil of animal and human suffering) is inevitable. If God is conceived as good, then how can he have created a world in which sentient beings suffer? If God is morally perfect, as well as omniscient and omnipotent—and our conception of God requires this to be so—then he never does anything morally wrong.[71] Van Inwagen proposes, in effect, that God is powerless to do otherwise than to allow evil in the world he creates precisely because in any world governed by orderly laws, some bad things will result; some sentient beings will suffer. To prevent this would require God's constant and massive interference in the order he had created.[72] Although Van Inwagen argues that such an argument need not subvert traditional beliefs in God, it is hard to avoid the inference that God is either limited in his power or is morally obtuse.

At issue is the status of natural or physical evils. In this context we cannot fully address (much less solve) the "problem of evil" as understood by contemporary natural theology, except to say this: natural or physical evils do not constitute evil. If God has created limited beings, then these beings are necessarily limited in their goodness, and these limitations cannot constitute evil. The goodness of a thing correlates with the degree of being it enjoys, with its participation in the perfect being that is God. A thing and its behavior is good or evil to the extent that it is ordered to the Creator and shares in his goodness. To be sure, this principle does not suggest a ready solution to the question of animal suffering,[73] but it does indicate the answer to the question of the relationship of human morality to physical or natural evils. Of all creatures in the visible world, only the human being is capable of ordering himself by his own acts toward or away from his Creator. Morality is constituted by what is good or bad not for some inanimate or living thing or even for the human body under some aspect

---

[71] Peter Van Inwagen, *The Problem of Evil: The Gifford Lectures Delivered in the University of St. Andrews in 2003* (Oxford: Clarendon Press, 2006), 62–63.

[72] Ibid., 123.

[73] An issue to be addressed in a future work.

but rather for the human person as a whole in the perspective of his ultimate end, his highest good.

Evil and the Will

In examining the writings of proportionalist, consequentialist, and other revisionist moral theologians, we seldom find significant discussion of the moral characters of persons. The discussion is invariably in terms of acts, habit, choices, and ends, but little is said of the will and of the manner in which moral good or evil pertains to the person himself. Here we must recall John Paul II's account of the human will, discussed in chapter 3. Because that by which the human being is dynamized is the will, the person's act is ultimately explained by the decision of the will. In the jungle example, therefore, the reason that this man, the village headman, has died here and now, is that the traveler has decided that, insofar as it lies with him, the headman will die. But what about the greater evil, the deaths of the entire village? Anguished though he may be, no matter what he does, the traveler is not responsible for their deaths. But could he not have prevented them? The invariable precondition attaching to such dilemmas is the requirement of absolute certainty on the part of the moral agent. In this case, the stipulation is that the traveler is absolutely certain that if he kills the headman, then the captain will keep his part of the bargain, and that if he does not, then the villagers will all die. In real life, however, there can be no such certainty, only probabilities. The tyrannical captain seems not to be one whose promises most intelligent people would accept. (Perhaps he wants to implicate an imperialist Yankee in the headman's murder.) Perhaps a battalion of government troops are in hiding, waiting for the opportune moment to attack the revolutionaries. Perhaps a volcano will erupt or lightening strike. The implication of these uncertainties is not simply that the circumstances surrounding the situation are hard to determine. Rather, they show that this traveler—and, indeed, any moral agent—has not at his disposal a comprehensive knowledge of reality. Nor does he enjoy the power to determine the future of the entire situation. What he governs directly by the power of his will is *himself.* Regardless of possibly hidden government troops, volcanoes, the captain's possible treachery, the traveler determines that this man must die. He is not the lord of all creation but only—if he chooses—of the headman's continued life.

According to John Paul II's analysis, the traveler's killing is an act incompatible with the love of God. In order to preserve the rest of the villagers, the traveler chooses to hate the headman. He is clearly *using* him, taking from him his life so that the others may be saved. This is *prima facie* a violation of the personalistic norm, that a person is a good that does not admit of use. What makes the action wrong, therefore, is not the ontic disvalue of death but the moral disvalue of deliberately bringing about an innocent man's death. This is why we may indeed legitimately use value-words in describing human acts. Every human act expresses the intent of the agent's will. (To be sure, it may often be that only the agent himself, and not some outside observer, knows the true intent of his act.) As such it is morally determined. It may be that "ontically considered," the line between medicating a suffering person for pain and overmedicating in order to bring about death is blurry (how much opiate is too much?), but the line between intents is not. One can intend either to alleviate pain or to kill, and it may be that no one other than the agent himself knows the intent. It is in this sense that a physical description of the act, such as an independent observer might give, is inadequate to determine its morality. Nonetheless, there is an intent, and it determines the action morally.

If the *object of the act* of willing is "a freely chosen behavior,"[74] then the choice of that behavior as chosen has its intended end. By his act, the rifleman intends to bring about the death of his rival, to stop the aggressor, to test the trigger mechanism, or to demonstrate his own accuracy as a marksman. To be sure, the act will be surrounded by circumstances that may render a good act evil (as to fire recklessly at a target when others might enter the line of fire). John Paul II's point is that there can be no circumstances that will render a morally evil act good. The saving of the village does not redeem the deliberate killing of the headman. The acquisition of vital intelligence does not make the spy's adultery morally good.

The intrinsically evil act is one that cannot be directed toward the final end of the human being. The fitting end for the human person is eternal communion with God. Although this communion can be realized only in the next life, we can nevertheless participate in it in this life as well. If, as Aquinas holds, the soul of one who sees the Divine Essence must become

---

[74] John Paul II, *Veritatis Splendor*, 78.

"Deiform,"[75] then this deiformity must somehow characterize the earthly human being as he heads toward that ultimate goal. And indeed, he does so precisely insofar as he imitates Christ.[76] The intrinsically evil act, therefore, is one that Christ himself could not have chosen, for it is inconsistent with his own love. Furthermore, Jesus did not realize all the ontic goods that he could have.[77] He rebuffed the man whose brother cheated him out of part of his inheritance (Lk 12:13).[78] He walked through a crowd of crippled people at the Pool of Bethesda before choosing just one crippled man to heal (Jn 5:1–9), and after miraculously feeding five thousand, he hid himself to avoid their making him king (Jn 6:15). Clearly, Jesus *could* have ended poverty and famine for his followers, and he *could* have restored the Kingdom of Israel. He allowed the authorities to commit the consummate injustice of deicide, when he had the power to summon legions of angels to his defense (Mt 26:53).

Here we arrive at the core of John Paul II's analysis of moral evil. Arguing that through this deicide, the Holy Spirit demonstrates the relationship between moral evil and the cross of Christ, John Paul goes on to say,

> The "convincing" [concerning sin in Jn 16:7ff.] is the demonstration of the evil of sin, of every sin, in relation to the Cross of Christ. Sin, shown in this relationship, is recognized in the entire dimension of evil proper to it, through the "mysterium iniquitatis" (2 Thes 2:7) which is hidden within it. Man does not know this dimension—he is absolutely ignorant of it apart from the Cross of Christ.[79]

If we reflect on the decisions and behavior of the principals in the crucifixion of Christ—Peter, Judas, Caiaphas, Pilate, the soldiers, and the rest—it is not hard, using principles from proportionalist moral reasoning,

75 *ST* I, q. 12, a. 5.

76 John Paul II, *Veritatis Splendor*, 16.

77 Knauer addresses this dilemma in "Teleologische als deontologische Normenbegründung," 327. If morality is simply a matter of bringing about the best result in every situation, we wind up with a kind of moral rigorism, one that Peter Singer arguably falls into with his arguments concerning the responsibilities of Americans to redistribute their wealth. See his *Practical Ethics*, chap. 8.

78 It seems to me that the man was probably morally in the right but with a dubious legal claim. Why else would he betake himself to the well-known prophet and righteous man rather than to the legal authorities, who could enforce a valid will?

79 *Dominum et Vivificantem*, 32.

to justify or at least subjectively excuse all their behavior. Peter was under extreme emotional stress, overtired and confused when he denied Christ. In recent years, some have speculated on Judas's motives. By forcing the issue, he could help Jesus by causing the crisis that Jesus would use his power to overcome. If so, then perhaps Judas had simply misunderstood his own role. Caiaphas and Pilate were both in very difficult political, social, and military straits, concerned with the fates of entire peoples and not simply with the fair treatment of one man. Although not all the arguments on behalf of these principals may be equally convincing, they can all be plausible. And this is the point. No one involved with the crucifixion directly set out to kill God. No one said, "Good be damned! I choose to bring about great evil." And yet, with the cooperation of all these, the ultimate moral evil was performed.

Precisely in this context, John Paul II refers to the "mystery of evil" (*mysterium iniquitatis*), which can be fully recognized only with the aid of the Holy Spirit. This mystery of evil goes far beyond the claim that human agents can err or selfishly misjudge their true priorities. Rather, the high priest of God's People, a man who prayed and read the Scriptures daily, and Peter, the Rock on whom the Church was to be founded and who shared Jesus' daily life, could choose grievously against God. Such a choice is not simply a mistake or a misjudgment of the balance of premoral goods. It is a choice contrary to the fundamental moral norms that God deserves to be loved above all and that the person is not to be used but rather to be loved. Such a choice is possible for a human being, and in so choosing he sets himself against the order of love that his Creator has authored out of his love. In choosing against the fundamental moral norms, the human person effectively usurps the prerogatives of his Creator and chooses love of self to the contempt of God.[80] Therefore, the intrinsically evil act is one that cannot be chosen in union with Christ and that, in fact, separates one from Christ precisely in that it sets one's will against God, who, as Supreme Good, is the Author of all good.

The human being is capable of recognizing God and his will, of knowing the truth about God. This capacity for God is written into the constitution of the human being as the image of God. John Paul II writes:

---

80 See Karol Wojtyła, *Sign of Contradiction* (New York: Seabury Press, 1979), 82–83.

> And if the visible world is created for man, therefore the world is given to man. (Gen 1:26, 28, 29) And at the same time that same man in his own humanity receives as a gift a special "*image and likeness*" to God. This means not only rationality and freedom as constitutive properties of human nature, but also, from the very beginning, the capacity of having a *personal relationship* with God, as "I" and "you," and therefore the *capacity of having a covenant*, which will take place in God's salvific communication with man.[81]

The human person is responsible for the truth, the truth about himself and about God, who has given him his life as a creature within a good creation. This responsibility makes possible the radical evil of sin: "At the root of human sin is the lie which is a radical *rejection of the truth* contained in the Word of the Father, through whom is expressed the loving omnipotence of the Creator."[82] The mystery of iniquity is this: that the human person can reject this truth about the good and choose the lie instead. The ultimate cause of this turning to untruth can ultimately be found only within the core of the person himself, in his will.

A consequence of the relationship between moral evil and the will is that the evildoer incurs *guilt*, of which he must repent and for which he must make reparation.[83] Guilt arises not from misjudgment, nor does it arise from the erroneous choice of a badly balanced concatenation of premoral goods and evils. To be sure, the scrupulous may experience feelings of guilt for goods left undone, and the innocent may blame himself for a tragic accident. Feelings are not always an accurate guide to true guilt.[84] The professional "hit man" may feel nothing amiss in his emotional life. Nevertheless, if John Paul II is right that the evil act arises from the core of the person, making the person himself evil, then it follows that this evil will have repercussions in the life of the evildoer.[85] The reality and nature of

---

81 *Dominum et Vivificantem*, 34.

82 Ibid., 33.

83 John Paul II, apostolic exhortation *Reconciliatio et Paenetentia*, www.vatican.va/holy_father/john_paul_ii/apost_exhortations/documents/hf_jp-ii_exh_02121984_reconciliatio-et-paenitentia_en.html (accessed October 7, 2005), 13.

84 Charles E. Curran's position (in "Conscience in the Light of the Catholic Moral Tradition," in *Conscience*, 18) that the "most adequate" criterion of a good conscience is "peace and joy" thus will prove inadequate, unless Curran can provide an objective measure of "peace and joy."

85 *Reconciliatio et Paenetentia*, 17.

guilt are clearly portrayed scripturally in Cain's defensive response to God, "Am I my brother's keeper?" (Gen 4:9) and his subsequent recognition that his murder has made him an outcast (Gen 4:12–14), as well as in Psalm 51: "For I know my transgressions, and my sin is ever before me" (Ps 51:3). After killing Richard III's brother, the Duke of Clarence, the Second Murderer's conscience reappears: "A bloody deed, and desperately dispatch'd! How fain, like Pilate, would I wash my hands of this most grievous murder."[86] And of course, the theme of Dostoevsky's *Crime and Punishment* is that the criminal has so harmed himself that he *needs* his punishment to redeem his guilt.

The evil of the act arises from the will. The moral evil is not that a man dies but that a person has willed the death of this man. In some respects it may be good that a man die. A person suffering severe pain may wish for death as an escape. Because all must inevitably die, relatively healthy old persons eventually begin to experience a desire to "get on with it" and pass from this life. Such a desire is not suicidal but rather a sense that it is now time for this life to be over. Certainly it is only through death that one may come to eternal life, that one can attain his ultimate end. Nevertheless, even though death may, from such perspectives, be a kind of good for some person, to decide to kill a human being is an evil.[87] Let us explore more exactly why this is so.

Because norms are the basis for his answering the fundamental moral question, "What ought I to do?" the human choice to act must be guided by moral norms, by the truth about the goods that are at stake in his actions. John Paul II has identified two fundamental norms. The first is this: "*To ask about the good*, in fact, *ultimately means to turn towards God*, the fullness of goodness. . . . God alone is worthy of being loved 'with all one's heart, and with all one's soul, and with all one's mind' (Mt 22:37)."[88] That is, God is the highest Good and most worthy of love. From this we derive the command "Love God." The second is the personalistic norm: "[T]he person is the kind of good which does not admit of use and cannot be treated as an object of use and as such the means to an end, [but rather] a good towards which the only proper and adequate attitude is

[86] William Shakespeare, *The Tragedy of King Richard III*, act 1, scene 4.

[87] See John Paul II, *Evangelium Vitae*, 47.

[88] *Veritatis Splendor*, 9.

love."[89] And this norm issues in the command "Love persons." In claiming that there are certain acts that are intrinsically evil, John Paul II is saying that in choosing these forms of behavior, the person sets his will against the good as known in truth. For example, to murder (deliberately and directly to kill) an innocent person is to treat that person as an object and to cut him off from the foundational good of life itself, foundational because all other earthly goods are had only when one is alive.[90] The truth about this person (who is a good) is that he possesses his own life, over which he alone exercises an appropriate mastery.[91] The murderer not only violates that person (who ordinarily wants to cling to his own life) but denies the good that his personhood is. He overrides that good by his choice to eliminate it.

Sin: Usurping the Divine Order

The person who chooses to perform an intrinsically evil act effectively chooses to create a new reality, one in which that good represented by the norm is denied. The person in act, as a knowing being, is a creative being within the Creator's order.[92] This is to say that each of us lives and acts within a life-world, the ordered world of our own understanding and values. This world is, to be sure, incomplete and imperfect. Nevertheless, it is a world in the sense that the cougar's environment is not (at least not for the cougar). The world of the human person is a coherent whole, structured according to knowable principles, at least some of which are known, and governed by knowable laws, some of which are also known. Furthermore, this world is also the work of the Creator, whose perfect wisdom and power have made it to be exactly according to his intention.[93] The creation is "very good" (Gen 1:31). Although the human person grasps that the world is an ordered whole, only the Creator grasps the order in its entirety. Despite the immense range and infinite concern of his intellectual powers, the human person can conceive only imperfectly the structure and order, and thereby

---

89 Wojtyła, *Love and Responsibility*, 41.

90 John Paul II, *Evangelium Vitae*, 18, 57.

91 See Thomas Aquinas, *ST* I–II, prologue, and Vatican Council II, *Gaudium et Spes*, 24: "man, who is the only creature on earth God has created *for its own sake*" (emphasis added).

92 John Paul II, *Laborem Exercens*, 4.

93 See the important discussion of the human being's relationship with the natural and human environments in John Paul II, *Centesimus Annus*, 37–38.

the goodness, of the creation. Thus, the human sciences develop. What human beings can readily know, however, are fundamental moral norms.

Within the creation, the Creator has made many persons, each of whom is a rational subject and an efficacious agent in the world, each of whom he has destined to communion with him.[94] The personalistic norm states that the person is not an object of use but rather is appropriately and adequately related to only in love. To violate this norm is a violation of the Creator's intended order of things. It is, as it were, to substitute an order of one's own for the Creator's. The murderer (or rapist or torturer or abortionist, or anyone who performs an act in violation of the moral norm) by his action contradicts the Creator's order, replacing it with an order based on the moral agent's own determination of what the good is to be. Because the person in act must always refer to truth,[95] having applied his intelligence to the needs, values, and state of affairs he is acting upon, his act represents a kind of living judgment on the truth of the matter.[96] By violating the personalistic norm, he violates the truth concerning the person concerned, effectively denying that personhood, and therefore denies the finality for which that person is created. This is so, because the person is destined to union with God through action governed by his own subjectivity. The Creator does not simply grant him that union but awaits his love in response to Him. The person who contravenes a moral norm re-creates the world, as it were, or perhaps we might say, acts in a world of his own re-creation, in such a way that would subvert the Creator's intention. In this way, the sinner establishes his own standard of the good, has authored his own truth about the good. And this is the root of human malice and the *mysterium iniquitatis.*

A particularly clear and important example of this appears in John Paul II's theology of the body, in the discussion of Christ's words: "Whoever looks at a woman to desire her has already committed adultery with her in his heart."[97] If Christ's words are not to be interpreted as simply a kind of restatement of the ninth commandment, "You shall not covet your neighbor's wife," then a deeper understanding of what constitutes "adultery in

---

94 John Paul II, *Veritatis Splendor*, 9; *Mulieris Dignitatem*, 5. See also Vatican Council II, *Gaudium et Spes*, 19.

95 Wojtyła, *Persona e atto*, 1010–13.

96 See Reimers, *Soul of the Person*, chap. 5, especially 164ff.

97 Mt 5:28. John Paul II's analysis is at *Man and Woman He Created Them*, 24.4–25.5, 229–33; 35.1–41.1, 267–90.

the heart" is needed. John Paul II begins his analysis by observing that the ancient translations of the text render it "has already made her an adulteress in his heart"; the Greek word *meucheuō* is transitive, not intransitive as the modern translations render it.[98] This is an important clue to Christ's underlying thesis. Since adultery is a sin—in the Old Testament a crime—that by definition requires two persons, at least one of whom is married, we may ask how one person can commit adultery "in the heart." John Paul II responds by directing our attention away from the ancient Jewish legal tradition, for which adultery was primarily a juridical matter, to the prophets, for whom adultery was a matter of personal betrayal, the betrayal of a covenant relationship of love. Adultery was the preferred prophetic metaphor (especially in Isaiah, Hosea, and Ezekiel) for Israel's infidelity to its covenant with the Lord. And in this, according to John Paul II, can we discern how adultery in the heart can be constituted.

"Adultery in the heart" is the matter not of a physical act but rather of an interior breach of the covenant with one's spouse, a covenant of mutual and entire gift of self, whether or not an adulterous act is performed. Like adultery, concupiscence "is an inner detachment from the spousal meaning of the body."[99] Furthermore, Christ's words were "whoever looks at *a woman*," not "at *another woman*," allowing in principle that one can commit adultery in one's heart even with one's own wife.[100] The man who so regards any woman, even his own wife, has "made her an adulteress" in his own heart. John Paul II explains:

> He shows in this way who the woman "is" at whom he "looks to desire," or rather who she "becomes" for the man. Thus the intentionality of knowledge determines and defines the intentionality of existence itself. . . . [The woman] is deprived of the meaning of her attraction as a person so that this attraction, while belonging to the "eternally feminine," has become a mere object for the man: *that is, she begins to exist intentionally as an object for the possible satisfaction of the man's sexual urge.*[101]

---

[98] John Paul II, *Man and Woman He Created Them*, 24.4, 229, text and footnote. In the footnote, John Paul lists several translations in modern Western languages.

[99] Ibid., 39.5, 286.

[100] Ibid., 42.6, 295.

[101] *Man and Woman He Created Them*, 41.1, 290.

From this it is clear that the adulterer (or adulteress) has chosen to live and act according to an order other than that established by the Creator. The woman, a person created with her own dignity and subjectivity, has become for the man, that is, according to his interior vision of reality, a mere object for the satisfaction of his sexual and emotional desires. The lustful man (or woman), who regards the other as an object for his sensual satisfaction, lives in a world of his own, not in that which the Creator fashioned as a gift to him.

"Ontic" Evils: Suffering

In the light of the earlier analysis of proportionalism and consequentialism, we may well ask about the status of "ontic" evils. Are we not morally obliged to prevent or alleviate suffering? That disaster threatens is not an event without moral consequences. The person, an intelligent and efficacious agent, can intervene when things go badly and work to correct them. The imminent flood can create a responsibility to help fill sandbags.

John Paul II describes suffering as the experience of any kind of evil,[102] and this characterization is worth noting, for it inverts the way in which we frequently understand suffering.[103] Ordinarily we regard the suffering itself as the evil, so that the task is to get rid of this undesirable experience or sensation. The physician, however, will frequently find real value in his patient's pain, which can reveal the nature of the underlying ailment. Medical wisdom dictates that one never seek simply to eliminate pain lest in doing so a serious disease be masked. This is John Paul II's point concerning suffering in general, and it therefore changes the focus of much of our analysis: we ordinarily think of evils, at least the most important evils, in terms of the pain they cause to persons. However, if suffering is the experience of an evil, if suffering is therefore consequent upon some underlying evil, then the important thing is to determine what that evil is and address it.

"Thus," writes John Paul II, "the reality of suffering prompts the question about the essence of evil."

> Christianity proclaims the essential *good of existence* and the good of that which exists, acknowledges the goodness of the Creator and proclaims the

---

102 Apostolic letter *Salvifici Doloris* (Boston: St. Paul Editions, 1984), 7.

103 See Adrian J. Reimers, "Human Suffering and John Paul II's *Theology of the Body*," *Nova et Vetera*, English ed., 2, no. 2 (Fall 2004): 445–59.

> good of creatures. Man suffers on account of evil, which is a certain lack, limitation or distortion of good. We could say that man suffers *because of a good* in which he does not share, from which in a certain sense he is cut off, or of which he has deprived himself. He particularly suffers when he "ought"—in the normal order of things—to have a share in this good, and does not have it. Thus, in the Christian view, the reality of suffering is explained through evil, which always, in some way, refers to a good.[104]

Clearly any kind of damage to the body is an evil, for it interferes with the proper functioning of the human organism and thereby directly affects the efficacy of the human person in his actions in the world. Similarly, a mental illness such as depression or paranoia is an evil, for it hinders the person's knowledge of himself and the world, and it distorts his emotional response to reality. Poverty, political oppression, enslavement, discrimination, and other such social realities are evil insofar as they prevent or hinder persons from freely pursuing their own good. And if existence is essentially good, then annihilation, the deprivation of existence itself, is a grievous evil. We all experience this in the natural fear of death.

There is also, of course, a suffering that accompanies evildoing. The thief suffers anxieties from his fear of capture, and the addict experiences genuine physical pain as his body craves the drugs to which he has subjected himself. On one level, such suffering is easily accounted for in terms of the frustration of one's aims or the habitual (or habituated) functioning of the physical organism. There is a deeper level of suffering, however, than this, one that pertains directly to the moral evil one has embraced, which one normally experiences as *guilt.*[105] This is intended to lead to *remorse*, which John Paul II identifies as a sharing in God's own "repentance at having made man": "Is it not an echo of that 'reprobation' which is interiorized in the 'heart' of the Trinity and by virtue of the eternal love is translated into the suffering of the Cross, into Christ's obedience unto death?"[106] There is a suffering that attaches to the evil of wrongdoing, but, unlike pain, it is a suffering that does not *impose itself* upon the unwilling. One can ignore the pangs of guilt. If God is the Supreme Good and communion with him the goal of human life, then the worst evil is to be

---

104 *Salvifici Doloris*, 7.

105 Reimers, "Human Suffering and John Paul II's *Theology of the Body*," 449–50.

106 *Dominum et Vivificantem*, 45.

deprived of this communion. The pain of this deprivation will be immense and eternal.

The effect of this analysis of suffering is to relativize all "ontic" evils, the "heartache and the thousand natural shocks that flesh is heir to."[107] Evils are truly evil to the extent that they undermine the person in his being as a person, his integration, and not simply in his psychosomatic integrity. Wojtyła has characterized the person as a self-determining and self-transcending being, whose integration as a self is achieved through his own acts. It may well be the case, therefore, that an "ontic" evil can become a good for a person who deals with it courageously or creatively. The loss of great inherited wealth may be the impetus that inspires a young person to develop his own talents and take greater responsibility for his life. John Paul II's own life can illustrate the benefits of adversity, if we consider his trials under the Nazis and then the Communists as a kind of preparation for the leadership he came to exercise as Pope. The common human experience of adversity sheds light on Aquinas's response to the objection that because there is manifest evil in the world, God cannot exist. Aquinas responds, "This is part of the infinite goodness of God, that he should allow evil to exist and out of it to produce good."[108] As does the Exemplar, the image (that is, the human person) can draw good out of evil.

If "ontic" evils are thus relativized, then have we not relativized moral good and evil? If we recall John Paul II's qualification that the goodness or evil of the object of the act must be regarded from the "perspective of the acting person," then it is clear we have not. To inflict an evil on another person is to hinder or deny that person's good. Should one do this knowingly and deliberately, even in the awareness that the other person can "rise to the occasion" and cope well with the evil, is to fail in love. However much Adam's fault may have been rendered "happy" by Christ's redemptive sacrifice, it remained a sin for Adam,[109] who saw not a stage in the unfolding of God's redemptive plan but an opportunity to satisfy his desire for a forbidden but tasty fruit that was also, so said the serpent, the key to rivaling God's knowledge. To hold a strategically vital position, the colonel may

---

[107] William Shakespeare, *Hamlet*, act 3, scene 1, the soliloquy "To be or not to be."

[108] *ST* I, q. 2, a. 3 ad 1.

[109] Easter Proclamation (*Exultet*), Easter Vigil, *Daily Roman Missal* (Chicago: Midwest Theological Forum, 2003), 442.

so dispose his troops that the Third Platoon will suffer severe casualties, but his act is not murderous. He and his troops are engaged, even at the risk of their lives, in the common effort to defend their nation. By contrast, when King David ordered Uriah to be exposed to death, his intent was to see his soldier killed (2 Sam 11:14–25). If a tactical advantage accrued from the Hittite's death, it was purely accidental. More to the point, that the proverbially wise King Solomon should be born of Uriah's widow, Bathsheba, cannot after the fact justify David's depriving Uriah of his fundamental good of life. This man, who had chosen to serve his king as a soldier like the members of the Third Platoon, was prepared to give his life in battle to achieve victory. But his life was taken for another purpose, by the king who used him to conceal his own adultery with the widow. In short, what governs each situation is not simply the "ontic" evil of a man's having died but the *act* of a person choosing in one case to arrange that death and in the other to accept the other's willingness to sacrifice himself (or themselves) courageously for the sake of a common good.

Norms and the Common Good

It is clear, then, that the moral evil does not depend on a weighing or evaluation of goods and evils considered generally but is determined in terms of the fundamental norm governing one's relationship with his fellows, the personalistic norm that a person is not to be used as a means but rather is to be loved. Indeed, the positive formulation of the personalistic norm is decisive for understanding how one can morally be involved in the evils of this world. To hold almost any kind of responsibility or authority is to find oneself having to hurt people. The employer must lay off employees or dismiss those who are unproductive. The commander must send his soldiers into harm's way. Parents must discipline their children, and teachers must give low or failing grades. In all such cases, those affected feel themselves harmed and even badly used. Any of these evils can result in a person's feeling injured and becoming embittered.

Although to love another person means, in part, to desire that person's good, it does not suffice to desire all that the person desires. Love must be reciprocal, communal. That is to say, two persons love each other by desiring for each other some higher good to be realized as good for each and for both. Husband and wife desire not only the pleasures of each other for each other but also the goods of progeny and family life.[110] By a kind of extension, members of a community, be it a nation or a corporation or a university or any other group, share a common good and therefore can love each other according to the common good that unites their community. Thus an American motivated by patriotic love will strive to realize justice for and with his fellows, the attainment of a more perfect union, domestic tranquility, common defense, and general welfare, and to secure the blessings of liberty.[111]

Since the common good for which all human beings are destined is God himself, then to love one's fellow human being ultimately means to help him to God. To be sure, not all believe that this communion is their true good, and this means that one cannot always love another on one's own terms.[112] Love does not mean sharing in the evil, foolish, or simply erroneous choices of the beloved. This point becomes particularly acute in the social and civic sphere, where choices are made by consensus and where democratic processes presumably settle all disputes concerning action. Indeed, it is argued that a moral prohibition (against procured abortion, for example) can legitimately be enacted into law only if it is based on a consensus.[113] John Paul II's response to this is particularly forceful, as he rejects the relativism implicit in contemporary civil understandings of the common good. He writes:

> Democracy cannot be idolized to the point of making it a substitute for morality or a panacea for immorality. Fundamentally, democracy is a "system" and as such is a means and not an end. Its "moral" value is not automatic, but depends on conformity to the moral law to which it, like every other form of human behavior, must be subject. . . . But the value of democracy stands or falls with the values which it embodies and promotes.[114]

He continues:

> Laws which authorize and promote abortion and euthanasia are therefore radically opposed not only to the good of the individual but also to the

[110] Wojtyła, *Love and Responsibility*, 28–30, 84–88.

[111] Constitution of the United States of America, Preamble.

[112] See the discussion of "solidarity" and "opposition" in Wojtyła, *Persona e atto*, 1195–99.

[113] McBrien, *Catholicism*, 1009.

[114] *Evangelium Vitae*, 70.

common good; as such they are completely lacking in authentic juridical validity. Disregard for the right to life, precisely because it leads to the killing of the person whom society exists to serve, is what most directly conflicts with the possibility of achieving the common good.[115]

Of course, John Paul II insists that this common good is higher than any earthly good, warning in that same encyclical that an exclusively this-worldly perspective will necessarily lead to the tyranny of a "culture of death."[116] In other words, the "truth about evil" is that evil is the turning away from transcendent good, which is God himself.

Intrinsic Evil and "Hard" Cases

As noted earlier, much of the critique of the notion of intrinsically evil acts has arisen from reflection on the notion of "double effect." If an act can be justified whose effect is the same as an intrinsically evil act, then are we not merely splitting hairs in order to justify what common sense tells us is the right thing to do? Similar problems arise with stealing (may the poor man steal bread from the rich to feed his starving children?) and lying (the SS is at the door and Jews are hiding in the attic), as well as with many other prohibitions. And so, to take the example of stealing, one argues that since the earth's goods are intended for all of humanity and since the institution of private property exists to provide for orderly and secure access to these goods, the truly destitute person in dire need may justly access necessary goods in the possession of his neighbor without violating the moral norm concerning private property. Appeal is made to the higher norm by which the norms about private property are founded. The discussion can admittedly become complex and open to dispute. (Granted that one may lie to the SS about the Jews in the attic, may one then lie to American immigration authorities about undocumented Mexicans hiding in the basement?) We ask why it is so important that we even try to split such hairs. There are two kinds of answer.

The first answer is that norms are necessary to avoid sliding into relativism. Without them we have no assurance that we are acting according to the truth, which is precisely what constitutes moral goodness. This was

---

[115] Ibid., 72.
[116] Ibid., 64.

very much John Paul II's point in the texts cited above from *Evangelium Vitae*. The second answer touches the profundity of the relationship between the person and his acts. The intrinsically evil act is such precisely because it cannot be reconciled with the love the human person is called to have for God and neighbor.[117] If eternal communion with God is the fitting good for every human person, a good to be realized in part even in this earthly life, then the one who chooses against the moral norm has *by his very act* chosen against such communion. As argued in the preceding chapter, this communion is attained through participation in and imitation of the divine love. We stand before a kind of paradox. Our morality depends on our imitation of God but is undermined by our usurping the divine prerogatives. The liar, who seeks deliberately to mislead another who is entitled to the truth, "plays God" by, as it were, restructuring the order of reality according to his own design rather than to that which really obtains. The judge who condemns the innocent man in order to prevent serious and imminent civil unrest (or the jungle traveler who kills the village headman) has assumed the power of life and death over another. Our destiny, and therefore our dignity, lies in our participating in God's creative wisdom by our coming to know the truth and especially by our participating in his love by giving of ourselves for him and for our neighbor. The choice of a serious immoral act, one that violates the norm that God is to be honored as highest good or that violates the personalistic norm, is in itself a choice against God's created order, which is the order of love. As such it makes the one who chooses such an act to be a rival to God. Such a person's will is set in opposition to the highest good, and this in a direct and existential way.

It follows, therefore, that although casuistic reasoning may well be called for when the application of moral norms is complex or doubtful,[118] the doctrine of intrinsically evil acts transcends legalistic concerns. The intent of casuistry, legitimate as such reasoning may often be, can never legitimately be to determine how one can perform desired acts by finding a "loophole" in the moral norm.

---

[117] John Paul II, *Veritatis Splendor*, 12–13, 52, 72.

[118] John Paul II, *Veritatis Splendor*, 76.

CHAPTER 8
The Truth About the Good

IF COMMUNION with God is the *fitting good* for human beings, then this should profoundly affect how we should live our lives. Indeed, this is the premise underlying John Paul II's encyclical *Veritatis Splendor*, which argues precisely that it is on the basis of the truth about that ultimate, fitting good that Catholic moral teaching rests. In this concluding chapter we will examine some ramifications of John Paul II's conception of the moral life and the truth about the good.

Transcending Legalism

One of the themes we find most consistently stressed among "revisionist" or progressive moral theologians is the rejection of legalism, a mistrust of any deductive approach to morality based on the essences of things.[1] Richard P. McBrien writes, "According to the deontological model (employed in the pre-Vatican II manuals of moral theology), conscience keeps before us the demands of God's law. According to the teleological model (employed by Thomas Aquinas), conscience keeps before us our ultimate end."[2] Because the traditional moral theology of the manuals was deductive and legal, the focus of moral thinking was on obligations and

1 See Carlotti, Veritatis Splendor: *Aspetti della recezione teologica*, 19; Odozor, *Richard A. McCormick and the Renewal of Moral Theology*, 61; Schneider, "*Wer Gott dient wird nicht krumm*," 97; and Curran, *Moral Theology of Pope John Paul II*, 60.

2 *Catholicism*, 968; see also Curran, "Conscience in the Light of the Catholic Moral Tradition," in *Conscience*, 19.

prohibitions rather than on themes such as happiness, friendship, suffering, and love.[3] Such moral theology had little room for discussion of such realities as the Beatitudes or the gifts of the Holy Spirit, since these could not be objects of obligation.[4]

The Moral (Ir)relevance of Revelation

As a result of the focus on moral obligation, a "double morality" arose in moral theology, according to which a general secular morality applies to all human beings and then a set of specifically Christian duties oblige the followers of Christ.[5] If human reason is capable of arriving philosophically at a natural law that applies to all, then it would appear that Christian Revelation can add nothing decisive to morality without risking the condemnation of all pagans of good will. That is to say, if faith is decisive to the moral life, then those who do not have the gift of faith must be condemned to living wrongly. Conversely, if reason can know the moral law without reference to Revelation, then faith would appear unnecessary to morality. To be sure, one does not need to be a Christian to know that stealing, murder, and betraying trust are wicked things to do. It is commonplace to observe that many nonbelievers are better behaved than many Christians. But if this is the case, then what difference does Revelation make? And what can be the value of faith, unless perhaps to provide an extra supernatural assistance to follow through with obedience to moral law? One can point, perhaps, to specifically religious laws, the commandments of the first tablet of the Decalogue. The natural law does not dictate that God shall be worshipped on the Sabbath or that his name shall not be taken in vain (although even pagans were cautious about misusing the names of divinities). One might also note that in the ethical thought of ancient Greece and Rome, humility was not regarded as a virtue. However, it is strange (at least) to reduce the Christian ethos to that of Aristotle with the additional provisions that one worship appropriately and be humble too.

This particular issue gains additional importance in the context of contemporary moral discussion in the public forum as Christians attempt to

---

3 Pinckaers, *Sources of Christian Ethics*, 17–30.

4 Ibid., 263; see also Ratzinger, "Il rinnovamento della teologia morale," 35–36.

5 Servais Pinckaers, O.P., *Pour une lecture de* Veritatis Splendor (Paris: Éditions Mame, 1995), 26; see also Curran, *Directions in Fundamental Moral Theology*, 11, 34.

influence legislation and public mores. As Christians object to such issues as legalized abortion or the rights of homosexual couples to attempt marriage, their opponents frequently object that Christians are seeking to force religious beliefs and morality on a populace that does not accept the authority of the Church or the Scriptures. To this the apologists for the Christian positions will ordinarily respond that no such imposition is at stake, that these positions are proposed on the basis of rational arguments accessible to all, believers and not. In other words, the Christians argue that there is nothing distinctively Christian about the moral laws that they follow. But if this is the case, then we may rightly ask what is distinctive. If on the basis of its distinctive lifestyle early Christianity was known simply as the Way (see Acts 22:4; 24:14, 22),[6] then we might expect it to be governed by a morality in some way distinct from that of the surrounding culture. These objections are serious, perhaps indeed insuperable, if morality is nothing more than obedience to revealed divine law.

"Perfect" and Ordinary Christians

A further consequence of legalism was that among Christians one could distinguish the morality of those who sought to be perfect and those who merely wanted to meet the requirements for salvation.[7] According to such a schema, everyone is obliged to obey the commandments and meet a minimum level of religious observation in order not to be damned. In this respect the laws of the Church were especially helpful, requiring attendance at Sunday Mass, confession and communion once each year, and observance of specific rules concerning marriages, the introduction of children to the sacramental life of the Church, and so on. Then for those who wanted (as a kind of option) to do more—to be really holy—there are not only such options as conformity to the Beatitudes (Mt 5:3–12), attendance at weekday Masses, and various avenues of meditative and contemplative prayer but also the evangelical counsels of poverty, chastity, and obedience. To be sure, Christ listed love of God and love of neighbor as the two great commandments (Mt 22:36–39), but their application

[6] Precisely in this context Joseph Ratzinger points out: "Non va infatti dimenticato che il cristianismo, nei suoi inizi, si definì *odos*, una strada, un cammino: non una teoria, ma la risposta alla domanda 'come vivere?' e 'che cosa fare?'." "Il rinnovamento della teologia morale," 40.

[7] Pinckaers, *Pour une lecture de* Veritatis Splendor, 27.

proved hard to codify, except insofar as Jesus himself stated, namely, that on these "depend all the law and the prophets" (Mt 22:39). The problem for legalism, of course, is that it is very difficult, if not impossible, to reduce love to a prescribed series of actions. And so, writes Pinckaers, "We have, on one hand, a morality limited to a minimum of observances and to the concern to avoid mortal sin, and on the other hand, a pursuit of perfection that is accomplished above all by ascetic practices and supplementary observances."[8]

Further Difficulties with Legalism

Legalism requires knowledge of the law. For this reason, professional and business people hire attorneys to advise them through the thickets of contract, tort, and tax law. To do otherwise, to rely on "common sense," is to risk legal and financial disaster. Necessary as this may be in certain spheres of activity, it does not present an adequate model for the moral life. The spontaneity of the daily moral life seldom leaves room for the cautiously calculating legal analysis characteristic of contract making and complex finance. One simply does not have the leisure or expertise to consult handbooks of moral theology before taking decisions to act. Maria Goretti had no chance to consult her catechism or her parish priest about the moral correctness of submitting to Alessandro Serenelli's sexual advances. He had a knife and demanded an immediate response. In fact, we commonly think of the good person as the one who does not have to think long, if at all, about the right thing to do.

Here we do well to recall Richard McBrien's contrast: "According to the deontological model . . . , conscience keeps before us the demands of God's law. According to the teleological model . . . , conscience keeps before us our ultimate end."[9] As we have seen, John Paul II, especially in *Veritatis Splendor*, appears to ground his moral account teleologically and not directly on law. But is this accurate? Certainly the person confronted with a moral choice may well have the moral law before his mind. Any small child having heard, "Absolutely no candy before dinner" is keenly

[8] "On a, d'une part, une morale limitée à un minimum d'observances et au souci d'éviter le péché mortel, et de l'autre, une recherche de la perfection qui se fait surtout par l'ascèse et par un supplément d'observances." Ibid.

[9] *Catholicism*, 968.

aware of Mother's command. More pertinently, the paradigmatic example of the past four decades would be the Catholic married couple deciding about the use of artificial contraception. What is very clear to them (assuming that they have, in fact, been informed concerning Church teaching) is the moral stricture, the teaching of the "official Church" against the use of contraceptives. In short, we do often have the moral law clearly in mind as we confront moral issues. In other instances, however, we have our end in view. The Marine strives to live up to the ideals of the Corps. For love of his wife the business traveler does not even consider accepting the allurements of an attractive colleague. In some circumstances teleological considerations predominate. "Yes, I could cheat, but then how could I live with myself? I would have betrayed my highest values." What all this shows is not an ambivalence or lack of clarity about moral strictures but rather a need for a deeper analysis than McBrien's dichotomy suggests.

Formation in Love

We return here to the question of the *fitting good*, which, according to John Paul II, must govern the moral life. In general, a final cause dictates the form of a thing for which it is the end or good. The tool is designed to fulfill its function. More to the point, the human person tailors his acts and, to a significant extent, even his body to become what he intends to be. To become that which he is not yet, the athlete or musician devotes himself to hours of training that will both form his body and habituate his responses, depriving himself of pleasures that others enjoy. Similarly, the dieter may put a note or cartoon on the door of the refrigerator to remind him of his weight-loss goal. The desire for some attainable good of itself creates a kind of deontology, a set of laws, obedience to which will foster achievement of the goal and disobedience to which will frustrate the good. The violinist's life is different from the tennis player's. More to the point, the life of the Christian, directed to the attainment of union with God, must be decisively and decidedly different from that of a nonbeliever simply because the Christian forms his life so as to attain his destiny of communion with God, a destiny that he has already begun to live out. The significance of this becomes clearer as we apply this principle to our two problem cases: (1) the problem of a "double morality," one for unbelievers and one for Christians, and (2) the distinction between "elite" and "ordinary" Christians.

"Double Morality"

The problem is this. On the one hand, there is held to be a natural law, which applies equally to all human beings, whether Jewish, Christian, or nonbeliever or even atheist. On the other hand, as we learn from St. Thomas Aquinas[10] and John Paul II,[11] the Christian lives for union with God himself. Have we returned in a new way to Richard McBrien's dichotomy, teleology for the Christians and the deontology of natural law for the rest? If so, then those without Revelation can (and must) reason philosophically to the prescriptions of the natural law, while believers respond to Revelation's promises of eternal life. This is not, however, how John Paul II saw the moral life, and therefore it is not how he saw the moral law. Indeed, as we investigate this, we will also glimpse his conception of the relationship between philosophy and theology, between reason and faith.

At issue are the questions (1) what is the supreme good, and (2) how does one relate to it morally? Like Thomas Aquinas before him, John Paul II does not hold that there is a separate supreme good or that there are distinctive moral norms for Christian believers in comparison to nonbelievers. Rather, he makes his own the judgment of the Second Vatican Council that the dignity of every human being is rooted in his destiny to divine communion: "The dignity of every human being and the vocation corresponding to that dignity find their definitive measure in *union with God*."[12] If the foundations of Christian morality are teleological, then so are those of morality *simpliciter*. Every human being is to live in such a way as to direct himself toward the perfect goodness of his Creator and to conform his acts to the standard of good established by the Creator.

This question of "double morality" is therefore precisely the question of the supreme good. The Christian morality arises from the response human beings must make to God as Supreme Good. The problem posed to us is that not everyone accepts that God is as Christians understand him, or

---

[10] *ST* I–II, q. 3, a. 8.

[11] *Veritatis Splendor*, 11–12.

[12] John Paul II, *Mulieris Dignitatem*, 5; see Vatican Council II, *Gaudium et Spes*, 19.

indeed that he even exists. It may seem inappropriate to impose the requirements derived from Christian belief in a supreme creating and redeeming God on those who do not accept Christian Revelation. However, if God does in fact exist, if he is personal and has chosen to engage with us human beings, and if we are personally responsible to him, then these facts do pertain to all human beings. If some do not believe in God, either that he exists or that he is concerned about our relationship with him, then those who do so believe would seem to be responsible to communicate these truths to them. If God is real, personal, and concerned for humans, then ethics must be theocentric because God is the highest good. Those who do not share these beliefs about God[13] live for some other good as highest. For most people in our contemporary civilization, this good is some variant of that described by John Stuart Mill in his *Utilitarianism.* What this means is that the so-called double morality comes down to a difference of understanding concerning the highest good. This, however, is not how the question generally appears.

The problem of a "double morality" arises not from considerations of an ultimate end but from a deontological conception of morality. To put it simplistically, but fairly accurately, we think that Christians have their rules, Muslims have theirs, and secular humanists have theirs. Nobody has any right to impose his own rules on members of another group. The prohibition of artificial contraception is (presumably) a Roman Catholic rule, which does not bind (and therefore ought not be applied to) those who are not Catholic. If this is how we conceive ethics, and if we conceive of the natural law as the universal set of moral rules, those principles, prescriptions, and proscriptions upon which all can agree as applying to all, then we do indeed wind up with a double morality. If by "natural law" we mean a system of moral rules deducible entirely and exclusively from human experience and knowledge without reference to God—*etiamsi daremus non esse Deum* (as though there were no God)—then divine Revelation would be ethically superfluous, valid only insofar as it provides additional witness to the human race's accumulated wisdom. Neither the

[13] It should be noted that in all this, we pass over the differences among those who believe in one self-revealing God. Christians, Jews, and Muslims—not to mention to various subgroups among each of these religions—will account differently for the expectations God has of his human creatures.

Scriptures nor the Church could, in virtue of their divine character, provide authoritative moral guidance. But this dilemma arises only if we consider morality, as well as the natural law itself, as a system of rules unrelated to any overarching good.

John Paul II's account, especially as presented in *Veritatis Splendor*, avoids this problem of "double morality," precisely because he founds his account on the existence of a supreme good for which all are destined. To be sure, problems do arise from the facts that different men disagree about the nature and existence of this highest Good and, among those who agree to his existence, on his revealed intentions and will. Yet even those who do not know God and those able to receive his Revelation are by their nature inclined and obliged to seek the highest good and conform themselves to it as best they can.[14] Concerning this we may note the historical witness of Aristotle, who reasoned to the existence of a first mover, a supreme divine being.[15] So distant is this being from the human mind that we have difficulty conceiving of it, much less knowing it directly. Nonetheless, in Aristotle's *Nicomachean Ethics* the Stagirite concludes that the best life is one spent contemplating the truth about the highest beings and, so far as possible, imitating them. That is to say, for Aristotle, the truth about the highest being leads to a response of admiration and awe that structures human life. Even more striking is the personal example of Socrates, a pagan who saw his vocation to pursue wisdom as one divinely ordained.[16] According to John Paul II's standards, Socrates' death for the truth merits for him recognition as a martyr.[17] This ancient philosopher, who criticized the stories of the Olympian gods without denying the existence of higher beings,[18] pursued wisdom and sought to inspire his fellow Athenians to care for their souls. Socrates seems to have accepted the underlying truth of Athenian religious belief—hence he instructed that a cock be sacrificed

---

[14] See John Paul II, *Fides et Ratio*, prologue and 1–5, and *Veritatis Splendor*, prologue and 1–2.

[15] *Physics* 8.6; *Metaphysics* 12.6–9.

[16] Plato, *Apology* 21a–23b; 28e–30b.

[17] John Paul II, *Salvifici Doloris*, 22: "This glory must be acknowledged not only in the martyrs for the faith but in many others also who, at times, even without belief in Christ, suffer and give their lives for the truth and for a just cause. In the sufferings of all of these people the great dignity of man is strikingly confirmed."

[18] Plato, *Euthyphro* 6b–d; *Republic* 377e–380b.

to Asclepius after his death[19]—and it is Apollo, the god of Delphi, whom he obeys and to whom he writes a poem in his last days.[20] Although Socrates does not present a clear conception of what God must be, he clearly accepts that the popular religion of ancient Greece manifests something true about the divine, even if the popular and mythical conceptions have to be purified by philosophical reflection.[21] This belief, inchoate and unsatisfactory as we may find it, was sufficient for this ancient pagan to structure his life upon, forming his ideals and virtues.

Therefore, the difference between the Christian believer's grasp of natural law and its requirements will differ from that of the nonbeliever according to the differences in their conception of God, that is, of the highest principle of meaning and value in the universe. For Aristotle the First Cause, because of its surpassing beauty, is deserving of human admiration and imitation, while the Christian, believing that the Triune God creates, redeems, and sanctifies him, responds with complete self-sacrificial love. Based on the Scriptural conception of the human being as the "image and likeness" of God (Gen 1:26), the Jewish and Christian ethos regards all human beings as entitled to a fundamental respect, which the Greeks could not discover.[22] At the root, then, of the "double morality" is not a conflict of moral codes but rather a difference between conceptions of reality and understandings of what is the truth. This appears to be a problem of contemporary secularism, which has settled on "generalized empiricism"[23] as the standard of truth and utilitarianism as the standard of good. These provide us with "neutral languages" for us to discourse about true and false, good and evil, but their very structure precludes all reference to the transcendent. As a result, the good person is the one whose behavior conforms to currently accepted and agreed-upon standards of behavior and comportment. And, to be sure, one does not need a religious

---

19 Plato, *Phaedo* 118a.

20 Ibid., 60d.

21 As Plato does in *Republic.*

22 See Aristotle's discussion of slavery and "natural slaves" in *Politics*, trans. C. D. C. Reeve (Indianapolis: Hackett Publishing Company, 1998), 1.2, or Plato's remarkable eugenics proposal, which rather casually includes the infanticide of the unfit, in *Republic* 5, especially at 460b–461d.

23 See Wojtyła, *Love and Responsibility*, 57.

faith to refrain from cold-blooded murder, to pay one's bills, to be kind to children at Christmas, and to treat colleagues respectfully.

"Elite" and "Ordinary" Christians

Just as a proper teleological understanding clears away the problem of the "double morality," so too does it render impossible any distinction between "elite" and "ordinary" Christians because all Christians—indeed, all human beings—are called to live for the same ultimate end. The very origin of such a distinction is a flawed conception of divine law, which arises from an inadequate understanding of God's revelation of himself. The legalist model of Christian morality tends to foster an understanding of God's law based on the functioning of positive civil law. The good, law-abiding citizen is obliged to conform his behavior to the requirements of the law as stated in the pertinent legislation. To be sure, a citizen may go beyond the requirements of the law, say, by volunteering for hazardous military service, but such service is entirely voluntary and not required for good citizenship. (And even under military conscription, no citizen is obliged to enter the more dangerous elite units.) The sanctions of the law are normally clear, so that one knows what sanctions will obtain should he fail to obey the law. Although the courts cannot command one's heart to love the country or to be enthusiastically patriotic, one does well to obey the legislator lest the sheriff exercise his authority and deprive one of money or freedom. We obey because, failing to obey, we fall subject to the sanctions of a superior power. If we so regard the divine law and its Legislator by comparison with the civil law model—God has given his law, and all power lies ultimately in his hand—we can easily conceive of two basic levels of Christian commitment: the one consisting in strict obedience to the law, and the other in a "going beyond" to achieve exceptional sanctity.

Not only does such a conception regard God merely as a strict legislator and judge, but what is more serious, it fails to recognize him as the Supreme Good. Rather, God is conceived as the *giver* of good or evil, according to one's deserts, and one obeys his laws in the expectation of thereby avoiding punishments and receiving his rewards, dreading (according to the words of the traditional act of contrition) the "loss of heaven and the pains of hell." Under this conception, one's true good, that for which one chooses one's acts, is one's own state of well-being. If happiness is simply a very good reward that God gives to those who obey him, then a teleological ethics does indeed collapse into utilitarianism, because the standard of the good is the same. The good is "what pleases me." All that is added is a kind of supernatural giver of unimaginable pleasure to those who please him and intense pain to those who offend him. The concern about such a conception seems to underlie Father Tadeusz Styczeń's objection to Aquinas's account of happiness, as we shall see shortly. This conception, however, is far from what Aquinas intended, and, more to the point, it is antithetical to John Paul II's thought.

If God is the fitting good (*bonum honestum*) for a human being, then he is so for every human being. In his letter preparing for the new millennium, John Paul II writes: "The whole of the Christian life is like a great *pilgrimage to the house of the Father*, whose unconditional love for every human creature, and in particular for the 'prodigal son' (cf. Lk 15:11–32), we discover anew each day. This pilgrimage takes place in the heart of each person, extends to the believing community and then reaches to the whole of humanity."[24] From this it follows that "the degree of personal sanctity does not depend on the position one occupies in society, much less in the Church, but only on the degree of charity experienced (cf. 1 Cor 13). A lay person who generously receives the divine charity in his heart and life is holier than a priest or bishop who receives it in a mediocre fashion."[25] If the measure of sanctity is charity, or disinterested self-gift to God, then clearly every Christian (and indeed every human being) is called, precisely in virtue of being human, to sanctity, because it is only in terms of a relationship of eternal personal intimacy with God that the human person can be fulfilled. To propose a two-tiered vision of the Christian life would therefore constitute an effective denial of this destiny to the lower tier, as though those who had fulfilled their moral obligations (obeyed the commandments, said their prayers, and so on) would receive a pleasant place

[24] Apostolic letter *Tertio Millennio Adveniente*, www.vatican.va/holy_father/john_paul_ii/apost_letters/documents/hf_jp-ii_apl_10111994_tertio-millennio-adveniente_en.html (accessed June 20, 2007), 49; see also his general audience, August 11, 1999, "La vita cristiana come cammino verso la piena communione con Dio," www.vatican.va/holy_father/john_paul_ii/audiences/1999/documents/hf_jp-ii_aud_11081999_en.html (accessed February 3, 2010).

[25] John Paul II, "La vocazione dei laici alla santità," general audience, November 24, 1993, www.vatican.va/holy_father/john_paul_ii/audiences/1993/documents/hf_jp-ii_aud_19931124_it.html (accessed July 24, 2006), in *La chiesa nel Credo.*

in heaven, while those who lived for holiness would enjoy eternal friendship and intimate fellowship with God.

Pure Deontology and Phenomenologists' Objections

Several contemporary Catholic phenomenologists, including some important interpreters of the thought of John Paul II, have objected to the teleological interpretation of human destiny in relation to morality and, indeed, to the Thomistic conception of will and good. These thinkers draw their inspiration principally from Max Scheler's friend and philosophical admirer Dietrich von Hildebrand. It is worth our while briefly to pause here and sketch the outlines of von Hildebrand's conception, which differs not only from Aquinas's but also, as we shall see, from Karol Wojtyła's.[26]

The central conception of von Hildebrand's moral philosophy is *value response*.[27] On this concept the whole of his Christian ethics turns, so that what is concupiscent and prideful in man (these being the two centers of human wickedness) are opposed to the "value-responding center."[28] One becomes good, according to von Hildebrand, precisely by responding to authentic values, and one becomes evil by responding out of pride and concupiscence. In von Hildebrand's thought, *value* holds priority over *good*. Values are the fundamental givens to which we are called to respond, because they and only they are important in themselves.[29] Values are irreducible ultimate realities.

> Many attempts have been made to reduce value to something other than itself. But these attempts are futile and vain because the notion of value refers to an ultimate datum, not only in the sense that it is grasped solely in an original intuition and is undeducible (this would also apply to the color red), but also in the sense that it is a fundamental datum which we necessarily always presuppose.[30]

---

[26] Others see a strong connection between von Hildebrand's thought and that of Karol Wojtyła. See, for example, Harvanek, "Philosophical Foundations of the Thought of John Paul II," 6. Later in this work I will defend the position that Wojtyła's conception is decisively different from that of von Hildebrand.

[27] Von Hildebrand, *Ethics*, chap. 17.

[28] Ibid., 412ff.

[29] Ibid., 73.

[30] Ibid., 95.

If this is so, then we may ask what becomes of those ends we have traditionally called "goods." Von Hildebrand responds by distinguishing among three levels of importance: (1) the "subjectively satisfying," (2) the "objective good for the person," and (3) the "important in itself."[31] Of these, only the third has moral value, although one may seek the others without moral blame, depending on the circumstances and, in the case of the subjectively satisfying, what the satisfaction consists in. Von Hildebrand fairly thoroughly rejects the Aristotelian conception of the moral life,[32] and his thought is certainly difficult to reconcile with that of Thomas Aquinas. Behind von Hildebrand's ethics lie three important philosophical positions: (1) the value-neutrality of factual being, (2) a conception of the will as simply the power to command acts, and (3) concern to protect the purity of the person's moral response from the taint of self-interest. These are positions that derive from Scheler's ethical and personalist views, even though they cannot be deduced *in toto* from those. It will be useful for our future investigations to look at each of these factors here.

The Value-Neutrality of Factual Being

This is a point on which von Hildebrand is particularly clear.[33] Values are not constituted by the qualities of a being or the relationships it may have with other beings. Rather, factual being, in and of itself, is neutral as to value. This principle applies directly to human morality, because human acts receive their moral character only in relation to the values at stake.[34] The acts of a person to attain goods that are merely subjectively satisfying or that are objective goods for the person are, as such, without moral value. A person can perform appropriate acts that are morally acceptable without having behaved well morally, if his acts are not performed in response to a moral value that is expressly recognized.[35] Indeed, the fundamental moral value is that of moral value as such. Von Hildebrand distinguishes between the "morally conscious" man, who acts expressly for the sake of moral goodness, and the "morally unconscious" man, who may well act rightly but does so without awareness of or intention to realize moral values. Thus,

[31] Ibid., chap. 3, "The Categories of Importance," 34–63.

[32] See ibid., 104, 133–34, 258, 306, 376–77.

[33] Ibid., 102, 229, 231, 251, 400.

[34] Ibid., 342, 405.

[35] See ibid., 342, for the criteria by which an act is morally good.

von Hildebrand allows for a kind of value-neutrality of human actions in their ontological constitution.[36] Just as one can encounter and know objects in the world and yet remain blind to the values associated with them, so too can one perform acts that realize ends and goods—even acts that may perfect oneself—and yet act without moral significance.[37]

Will as the Power to Command Acts Indifferently

In von Hildebrand's ethical system, the will plays a decidedly subordinate role to what he calls the "spiritual center," which is the locus of value response. Distinguishing two senses of "will," he writes:

> When used in a larger sense the term "will" seems to embrace all responses whether volitional or affective. In this sense, love, veneration, esteem, are called acts of will. When used in the narrower sense it is restricted to the specific act which is at the basis of all actions. . . . We shall thus use in our context the term "will" or "willing" only in the strict sense in which it is synonymous with the volitional response.[38]

Will, so conceived, has no orientation of its own toward the good but is the faculty of what Crosby calls "arbitrary freedom"[39] and what Pinckaers identifies with the "freedom of indifference."[40] The moral value of the act performed depends not on the will, therefore, but rather on the person's response to the moral values perceived in the situation. Although von Hildebrand allows the person to become morally good through his responses (unlike Scheler, who eschews every concern by the subject for his own moral goodness), moral goodness is not attained by the decisions of the will, by one's acts. In principle, a person may will the choice of the highest good and still remain morally indifferent (although, to be fair to von Hildebrand, such a choice would be highly unlikely and unrealistic). Nowhere in his *Ethics* does von Hildebrand directly connect moral goodness with the will and its acts.

---

36 By contrast, Thomas Aquinas holds that every human act is ipso facto a moral act. See *ST* I–II, q. 6 prologue.

37 Von Hildebrand, *Ethics*, 257.

38 Ibid., 199–200.

39 John F. Crosby, *The Selfhood of the Human Person* (Washington, DC: Catholic University of America Press, 1996), 37.

40 *Sources of Christian Ethics*, 331–32.

Self-interest and the Purity of Moral Response

A tone of admiration for moral heroes (such as Socrates) and saints pervades von Hildebrand's works. Repeatedly, persistently he points to the examples of goodness and holiness of great saints and invites us to admire them. One could say that his *Ethics* itself springs from his own value response to the lives of those he truly admires, and one thing he is particularly keen to defend is the genuineness of their virtue. The great strength of his value-response theory is its stress on selflessness. The value response is not the desire for some good for oneself, nor is the value something the response to which directly benefits the person responding.

> [N]either the moral nor the intellectual value of the adequate response is the basis for the principle which declares that an adequate response is due to every object endowed with a value. Not for the sake of the responding person, but for the sake of the value of the object to which the response is addressed, should the adequate response be given. The relation between a value and the oughtness of the adequate response to it is one of those ultimate principles belonging to the very basis of the universe. It is one of those principles which have often escaped a philosophical *prise de conscience* despite the fact that they are self-evident and always presupposed by us. But as soon as we focus on them in a really philosophical *prise de conscience*, we realize their ultimate character and this excludes any further "why."[41]

Von Hildebrand is careful to distinguish the value response from everything that contributes to the *objective good for the person*, which includes not only food and water but also education, skills, and even Aristotelian virtues.[42] Although von Hildebrand affirms that the truly good person, the saint, attains the great benefit of the vision of God, his acts can have no taint of self-interested seeking of this benefit.[43] Clearly, von Hildebrand shares Scheler's concern to avoid "Pharisaism," the perversion of performing acts purportedly for some good but with the further intention of benefiting oneself either by the self-congratulatory attainment of some level of moral perfection or by simply getting into heaven. Both philosophers, and

---

[41] Von Hildebrand, *Ethics*, 248.
[42] Ibid., 393–94.
[43] Ibid., 221–23.

their philosophical heirs, are anxious to preserve morality from the taint of self-interest. The moral act, in order to be fully praiseworthy, must be performed or chosen simply for its own sake and not for the benefits that accrue from it. By rooting morality entirely in the value response and reducing the role of the will to the choice of options in a value-neutral physical order, von Hildebrand has protected it from this taint.

This ideal of phenomenological deontology has found expression among some of Wojtyła's contemporary interpreters, most notably Father Tadeusz Styczeń and Josef Seifert.[44] Styczeń argues: "The moral obligation, of which we have experience, of taking a specific decision or of completing a determinate act does not, in fact, appear to us as depending on the consciousness of an ultimate end and of the desire to attain it. . . . Moral obligation, therefore, does not result as a function of the ultimate end of the human being."[45]

And further on: "In short: the experience of moral obligation pronounces itself in favor of the rejection of the model of ethics which takes the ultimate end as its starting point."[46]

Given Styczeń's prestige as a close friend and immediate disciple of Karol Wojtyła,[47] we need to take seriously his objection and account. First of all, Tadeusz Styczeń does not deny that happiness and morality are intrinsically related. His concern is that an ethical theory that connects moral character to happiness would reduce all ethical decisions to choosing that which fosters one's own happiness, and by doing so will evacuate the central moral notion of duty.[48] Thus, in an earlier essay he raises the objection that the eudaemonist ethics of both Aristotle and Aquinas may well reduce to simply a theory of attaining happiness.[49] In response, he argues that the moral obli-

---

44 For a good summary of their common position and a defense of its relationship with Wojtyła's thought, see Seifert, "Karol Cardinal Wojtyła (Pope John Paul II) as Philosopher and the Cracow/Lublin School of Philosophy," 182–90.

45 Tadeusz Styczeń, "Premessa: Karol Wojtyła: Un filosofo della morale agli occhi del suo discipolo," in Wojtyła, *Metafisica della persona,* cviii.

46 Ibid.

47 Indeed, Father Styczeń was among those present at Pope John Paul II's bedside when he died April 2, 2005. See George Weigel, *God's Choice: Benedict XVI and the Future of the Catholic Church* (New York: HarperCollins, 2005), 77.

48 See Kaczyński, *Verità sul bene nella morale,* 163.

49 "Zur Frage einer unabhängigen Ethik," 121–22.

gation to perform a given act cannot depend on one's desire to attain happiness, even if in the end this attainment of happiness does indeed depend on the moral act.[50] The root of these objections is a contrast or tension between the subjective, my personal satisfaction, and the objective, disinterested moral good. In many respects, Styczeń's ethical stance appears as a variant of the Kantian, emphasizing the centrality of duty in contrast to any kind of self-interest. Also like Kant, Styczeń relies heavily on the importance of the autonomy of the human person, an autonomy that is drawn from the demands of reason's relationship with truth.[51]

Styczeń is concerned to protect the rightful autonomy of ethics, to preserve the moral "ought" from reduction to something else, as clearly obtains in utilitarianism.[52] In particular, he wants to show (among other things) that this "ought" cannot rightly be reduced to the orientation toward happiness, that to say that one "ought" to do that which will make him happy is to say that one "ought" not do anything, at least not in a strict sense. Unfortunately, Styczeń's interpretation rests on a misunderstanding of Aquinas's account of the role of the ultimate end with respect to ethics. Styczeń writes, "In the concern to determine the moral 'ought' the Aristotelian viewpoint dominates [in Aquinas's ethics]. The moral 'ought' (but also the moral good and evil of human acts) is determined according to its relation to the last end of man." Here Styczeń cites *Summa theologiae* I–II, qq. 18–21, and he adds, "Thomas, however, does not doubt that the form of the moral act can only be teleological . . . Eudemonia is the norm of the moral."[53] Father Styczeń's argument, briefly stated, is that because the human act receives its moral species from its end and since the end of man is happiness, the act is to be judged (in St. Thomas's scheme) according as it promotes happiness. The act is but a means to happiness. Several representatives of the phenomenological tradition, including Scheler, Dietrich von Hildebrand, and Josef Seifert, have sharply criticized such an instrumentalization of the moral

50 "Premessa," cix.

51 See Tadeusz Styczeń, "Verità, libertà e amore nell'enciclica *Veritatis Splendor*," in Melina and Noriega, *Camminare nella Luce*, 472, 475.

52 This is a concern that Karol Wojtyła clearly shared. See his "Transcendencja osoby w czynie a autoteleologia człowieka," 481, and "Transcendence of the Person in Action and Man's Self-Teleology," 203.

53 "Zur Frage einer unabhängigen Ethik," 119, 121.

act.[54] The question, however, is whether Aquinas's account of happiness falls to this critique.

The solution to this problem depends on the nature of happiness as the ultimate good and its relation to individual acts. Although Thomas follows Aristotle formally, his different conception of man's ultimate happiness takes on a decisive character (although one can argue that Aristotle too saves the notion of ethical obligation).[55] For Aquinas, happiness does not and cannot function as an operative moral norm. As John Langan comments, "Thomas does not present the first principles of practical reason as conditional imperatives of the following form: If you wish to attain perfect beatitude, then do *X* and avoid *Y*."[56] For one thing, human acts of themselves are, of their own causal properties, insufficient to bring about the ultimate end. If human happiness, man's ultimate end, consists in God himself,[57] there is and can be no human act adequate to attaining this end. Happiness as Aquinas conceives it cannot be a state of subjective satisfaction,[58] but this is precisely how von Hildebrand[59] explicitly and Styczeń implicitly conceives it.

Furthermore, the foundational principles of natural law and morality in Aquinas are *per se nota* principles and not prudential judgments.[60] Aquinas himself says that an act is good or evil according as it has its proper fullness of being, including its species, which is determined by the end.[61] The end by which the act is specified is the good, as known by rea-

---

[54] See Scheler, *Der Formalismus*, 10–11; von Hildebrand, *Ethics*, chap. 23; and Josef Seifert, *Essere e persona: Verso una fondazione fenomenologica di una metafisica classica e personalistica* (Milan: Vita e pensiero, 1989), chap. 1.

[55] As indeed Karol Wojtyła himself holds. See his *Lubliner Vorlesungen*, 264: "Entgegen einer solchen Annahme [i.e., that Aristotle's ethics is simply a kind of catalogue or summary of good behaviors] behaupte ich, daß die Ethik des Aristoteles trotz allem eine richtige Ethik darstellt, das heißt eine Lehre vom menschlichen Tun, gestützt auf den normativen Grundsatz, also daß sie von der Norm durchgedrungen ist."

[56] John Langan, S.J., "Beatitude and the Moral Law in St. Thomas," *Journal of Religious Ethics* 5, no. 2 (1977): 187.

[57] Thomas Aquinas, *ST* I–II, q. 3, a. 8; cf. John Paul II, *Veritatis Splendor*, 9, and *Centesimus Annus*, 43.

[58] *ST* I–II, q. 2, a. 6; q. 3, a. 2; q. 4, aa. 1, 2.

[59] Von Hildebrand, *Ethics*, 306.

[60] Langan, "Beatitude and the Moral Law in St. Thomas," 187.

[61] *ST* I–II, q. 18, a. 1.

son; the standard for moral matters is reason, and it is from the rational end that the act is called good or evil.[62] Styczeń's argument hinges on the end-directedness of human acts, as stated in *Summa theologiae* I–II, qq. 18–23, and on the ultimate order of the will to happiness.[63] However, in the passages concerned, St. Thomas himself does not connect the end of the individual act directly to the ultimate end of man. The step between the two is not so immediate as Styczeń seems to suggest.

Here an important distinction comes into play. The first principle of the will is the last end, which is happiness. This is a principle, not of cognition, but of appetition. When we ask about moral principles, we are inquiring after the principles of practical reason. The first principles of practical reason are intellectual principles, by which the good is known. "Therefore [the rational creature] has a share of the Eternal Reason, by which it has a natural inclination to its due act and end; and this participation of the eternal law in the creature is called the natural law."[64]

The phenomenological intuitionist school, represented by Styczeń, von Hildebrand, Seifert, and Crosby, works with a different conception of will than do Aquinas and Wojtyła. The intuitionist conception of the will is as the power to choose between alternatives and command actions. For these philosophers, the moral task is to find and embrace those values that transcend their own desires and the fulfillment of their human nature, because considered in relation to such innate desire and self-fulfillment the good can amount only to an "objective good for the person" but not the good as such.[65] Therefore, in von Hildebrand's ethical theory, the will plays a relatively minor role in the moral life, which is governed instead by the *value-responding center.* He writes: "The act of willing which arises freely, inasmuch as it cannot be considered a link in a chain of causality, has its sufficient reason in the nature of the person; this nature is endowed with the

62 Thomas Aquinas, *Summa contra Gentiles* III, 9.1; *ST* I–II, q. 18, a. 5.

63 "Zur Frage einer unabhängigen Ethik," 121. Thus he writes, "Thomas does not doubt that the form of the moral act can only be teleological. The moral qualification of an act is expressed for him—similarly to Aristotle—without reserve in this, whether it is a fitting or unfitting means for attaining the last end, i.e., happiness." The second sentence here does not follow immediately from the first; in fact, Aquinas does not draw this conclusion in this way.

64 *ST* I–II, q. 91, a. 2.

65 Von Hildebrand, *Ethics*, chap. 29, 393–404, especially 396. See also Crosby, *Selfhood of the Human Person*, 199.

mysterious capacity of engendering an act of will and of starting a new chain of causality."[66] The basis of freedom and hence the moral value is rooted not in the will but "in the nature of the person." Is this not simply saying the same thing as, say, Aquinas but in different terms? No, it is not, because for von Hildebrand the nobility of the person and his moral center consists in his deep inner responsiveness to values.[67] Further, to protect the disinterestedness of the value response, these philosophers deny that the human person has an innate teleology toward the good itself. Therefore, the choice of the will for the good cannot be rooted in the human being's natural desire or inclination toward good. It must be, as far as the person's inclinations are concerned, absolutely disinterested and unaffected. This position, of course, is not far from Kant's requirement that the moral agent act not only according to duty but from duty.[68] The will, so conceived, has no object of its own and as such is subject to no governing norms other than the dictate of law.

A closer examination of their respective works will, of course, reveal significant differences among these writers, especially between Styczeń and von Hildebrand. What they all share in common is the insistence on the primacy of intuition. By this they intend something different from and more fundamental than a kind of mental impression (intuition in the popular sense). Rather, they understand intuition as the grasp in consciousness of a *given*, an essence that is irreducible to anything more fundamental. For von Hildebrand, the objects of these intuitions are values. For Styczeń, they are moral duties or obligations.[69] These values or duties, respectively, are not rooted in the being of things, such that by knowing things according to their ontological natures one can deduce or reason to the values they represent or embody or the moral obligations that pertain to them. To be sure, Styczeń recognizes the intrinsic dignity of the human person as one deserving of love, a dignity founded on the autonomy of the person as a subject—indeed, he insists on it. In this he draws very close to Wojtyła's personalistic norm.[70] However,

---

66 *Ethics*, 291; see also 258, 268.

67 Ibid., 319.

68 *Grounding for the Metaphysics of Morals*, 397–99.

69 Styczeń, "Verità, libertà e amore nell'enciclica *Veritatis Splendor*," 475; see also Kaczyński, *Verità sul bene nella morale*, 164.

70 As he is indeed well aware. See "Verità, libertà e amore nell'enciclica *Veritatis Splendor*," 475, where he refers expressly to the German translation of the essay "Person: Subject and Community."

Styczeń's account of the person, to the extent that he offers one, is much closer to Kant's in the *Grundlegung* than to Aquinas's or Aristotle's. Whether the irreducible intuition is of values or moral duties, this phenomenological intuitionism tends to regard the objectively knowable realm of facts as in itself devoid of value. At the least, this school fails to (and is perhaps unable adequately to) provide an account of the ontological grounding of values or obligations in existing things.

According to Aquinas, the human person can know the goodness of things as they are, both according to the notion of good itself and in relation to the universal good. For its part, the will is naturally inclined toward the good as such (*bonum universale*), which can be known not through the senses but only by the power of reason. Thus the person can present to his will not only the self-satisfying goods that senses perceive and sensitive appetites incline to, but he can have also present to his will the good as such.[71] It is precisely here that we find the roots of moral obligation. A free being enjoying free choice of the will, man can choose among the goods presented by his cognitive powers. To choose according to the goods known by sense or according to some other limited criterion of good is to turn away from the good in general, and St. Thomas calls this "malice."[72] Because the human being can recognize God as his last end—his ultimate happiness—he must therefore direct himself to God. Aquinas writes: "[God] is man's last end; and it is our duty to refer all our actions to the last end. Consequently whoever does an evil deed not referable to God does not give God the honor due to him as our last end."[73]

Moral obligation stems from the fact that man is ordered to the good through the power of reason. If he fails to use that power or puts it to the service of some relative good rather than the universal good, then he has done evil and turned away from good. We may conclude that although Thomas Aquinas clearly holds to eudaemonism, he escapes the charge of destroying moral obligation. His teleological ethics does indeed preserve the essentials of morality, including the possibility of selfless action.

---

71 Thomas Aquinas, *In Aristotle's* De anima, 3.12, 771; see also *Commentary on the* Nicomachean Ethics, 1.10, 129.

72 *ST* I–II, q. 78, a. 1.

73 *ST* I–II, q. 21, a. 4; see also I–II, q. 19, a. 10.

This discussion of eudaemonism and the phenomenological intuitionists is particularly pertinent for the analysis of Wojtyła's thought, not only because he speaks in terms of "self-realization" and "self-fulfillment,"[74] but because especially in his writings on sexual morality he has been concerned to give an adequate account of human desires and longings as a good. This is clearly thematic in *Love and Responsibility*, where from a phenomenological analysis of the "elements" of love as attraction, desire, goodwill, sympathy, and friendship, he moves directly to a discussion of "duty," of love as entailing obligations for which one is responsible.[75] The immediate problem is that if human sexual love not only inevitably involves strong desires but is in fact structured upon them, then how is it possible for sexual love not to reduce to utilitarianism, to the use of the beloved for one's own satisfaction? This theme is further developed theologically in John Paul II's theology of the body. The subtitle of the original Polish manuscript is "Odkupienie ciała a sacramentalność małżeństwa" ("Redemption of the body and the sacramentality of marriage"), and early in his discussion he says that the direction of the analysis is given by Romans 8:23, "[W]e ourselves . . . groan inwardly as we wait for adoption as sons, the redemption of our bodies."[76] John Paul II's concern is not simply that human beings need to be redeemed from sin but that the *body*, with its concupiscence, inevitable in this life, needs to be redeemed. If the body in its original nakedness was to have been—and therefore is intended yet to be—a sign of disinterested, sincere love, how can it be redeemed from its concupiscence?

The important text from *Gaudium et Spes*, 24.3, "[M]an . . . cannot fully find himself except through a sincere gift of self," a favorite text of John Paul II, poses this paradox sharply. Generally speaking, it seems impossible to perform a truly selfless, disinterested[77] act if one has in mind his own attainment of moral goodness. Can a person be said to be in

---

[74] Indeed, I have personally observed and participated in conversations with other scholars in which precisely these objections were at issue.

[75] *Love and Responsibility*, 73–95, 119. The English "duty" renders the Polish *powinność* ("duty, obligation"), *Miłość i odpowiedzialność*, 107.

[76] *Man and Woman He Created Them*, 4.5, 145.

[77] It should be noted that in the Polish translation of the Latin, *sincera* (English "sincere") is *bezinteresowny*, "disinterested." We may recall that the *bonum honestum* is the "disinterested good," according to Wojtyła.

pursuit of the good if in the back of his mind—but foremost as ultimate criterion—he intends to preserve his own standing as a morally good person? How can one save his life only when ready to lose it?[78]

To a great extent the problem is illusory, arising from an equivocation, a certain slipperiness of meanings. Every good that a particular person wants or strives to achieve is such precisely because *he* wants it, because *he* is striving for it. One can, of course, embrace some good, even a lofty good, for one's own satisfaction. To serve dinner at the homeless shelter because it "gives me such a good feeling to help" or to throw oneself into a cause in order to have some strong commitment to structure one's life may well be self-serving. However, if one selflessly gives his efforts, his treasure, and himself for some good, then he is necessarily committed to that. His personal engagement with that good cannot but have a reciprocal effect on his own life. He invests himself in it as the good he has chosen. The question, then, that lies before each human person is: What good shall I live for? This good, even if disinterestedly pursued, becomes "my" good, because it is the goal or end that "I" seek.

Community and the Common Good

Reading *Person and Act*, with its focus on the consciousness and efficacy, the self-governance, self-realization, and self-fulfillment of the person, one might well infer that, like most modern thinkers, Karol Wojtyła has so focused on the individual as center of consciousness and knowledge that he fails to account for the social or communal character of the human being. Certainly, his intellectual predecessors—we may think of the Enlightenment figures, such as Descartes, Hume, and Kant, as well as of Husserl and his neo-Cartesian philosophy of consciousness—emphasized the autonomy of the individual as a knower and moral agent. It is clear, however, from his entire corpus that John Paul II was acutely concerned with the human being as an inherently social being. Not only did he precede *Person and Act*[79] with *Love and Responsibility*,[80] an investigation of the necessity of and conditions for interpersonal communion, but he appended a seventh chapter on intersubjectivity by participation to *Person*

[78] See Styczeń, "Premessa," cix.

[79] *Osoba i czyn* was published in 1969.

[80] Published in 1960 as *Miłość i odpowiedzialność*.

and Act,[81] precisely to address the fact that when the human person acts he does so "with others." In 1976 he then further addressed the question of intersubjectivity in his important essay "Person: Subject and Community,"[82] developing his argument in continuity with the framework already developed in *Person and Act*. During his papacy the social nature of the human being and his need for communion with others constituted a major theme.

As background to John Paul II's conception of interpersonal communion, we may consider two texts from the Second Vatican Council's Constitution on the Church in the Modern World (*Gaudium et Spes*), a document strongly influenced by the personalism of then Cardinal Wojtyła.[83] The first of these texts appears in the opening chapter, on human dignity, immediately after an introduction of the Scriptural notion of man as "created 'to the image of God.' " "But God did not create man as a solitary, for from the beginning "male and female he created them" (Gen. 1:27). Their companionship produces the primary form of interpersonal communion. For by his innermost nature man is a social being, and unless he relates himself to others he can neither live nor develop his potential."[84]

We note the Council's inference that man is social because, from the beginning, male and female were made for each other, for "companionship." Indeed, the human being is social in his "innermost nature." This text is particularly pertinent to our present discussion, because precisely these concepts and this line of thinking reappear in John Paul II's catechesis on marriage, his "theology of the body." The second text is one that we have already noted in this study from *Gaudium et Spes*:

> Indeed, the Lord Jesus, when He prayed to the Father, "that all may be one . . . as we are one" (John 17:21–22) opened up vistas closed to human reason, for He implied a certain likeness between the union of the divine Persons, and the unity of God's sons in truth and charity. This likeness reveals

---

81 *Persona e atto*, 1167n73.

82 Karol Wojtyła, "Osoba: Podmiot i wspólnota," *Roczniki Filozoficzne* 24 (1976): 5–39; English translation in *Person and Community*, 219–61.

83 Weigel, *Witness to Hope*, 159–60, 166–69. For example, see Cardinal Wojtyła's interventions in Vatican Council II, *Acta synodalia Sacrosancti Concilii Oecumenici Vaticani II*, vol. 4 (Vatican City: Typis Polyglottis Vaticanis, 1977), pt. 2, 661–62; pt. 3, 242.

84 *Gaudium et Spes*, 12.

> that man, who is the only creature on earth which God willed for itself, cannot fully find himself except through a sincere gift of himself.[85]

As we have seen, this is a text that John Paul II makes his own throughout his teaching, and, indeed, precisely in relation to human communion.

Goods for Sharing

It is tempting to regard the person's relationship with the good, including the "fitting good" (*bonum honestum*), as a dyadic relationship. The person *receives* the good and then *has* it. He *incorporates* it into himself somehow or *experiences* it. Perhaps the good *transforms* him. The model suggested by our very way of speaking is of one entity (the human person) that is autonomously related to some other entity (his good). So regarded it is hard to see how communion in the good is possible, and especially how the good can be realized through "gift of self." But such a model relies implicitly on a materialist conception of the good, that the good is some thing or sensible experience. The key for Karol Wojtyła/John Paul II is that true goods are spiritual goods. This is so, because man is a spiritual being, a being with an inner life. "*Inner life means spiritual life. It revolves around truth and goodness.*"[86] We may consider this inner life by turns in relation to truth and goodness.

The search for and possession of truth, although it touches the human person most intimately (indeed, it forms him), is not an autonomous, solitary event. The solitary knower is a fiction, made plausible by Descartes's meditations[87] and Hume's theory of impressions and ideas, but a fiction nevertheless. In his encyclical on faith and reason, John Paul II addresses this directly. After defining the human being as "*the one who seeks the truth*,"[88] he goes on to argue that the search for truth is a communal affair. "From birth, therefore, they are immersed in traditions which give them not only a language and a cultural formation but also a range of truths in which they believe almost instinctively."[89] After acknowledging that through the process of growth into maturity the person will doubt much

---

85 Ibid., 24.
86 Wojtyła, *Love and Responsibility*, 23.
87 As narrated in his *Meditations*.
88 *Fides et Ratio*, 28.
89 Ibid., 31.

of what has been proposed to him as true and subject it to critical inquiry, John Paul II remarks that there nevertheless remain many more truths that are simply believed on the authority of others. This body of truths is, however, far more than simply a collection of neutral data. The truths a person believes structure the world he lives in. We—all of us—live in a world formed by the thoughts and beliefs of other persons. The very languages we use are received from others, from a linguistic tradition.

"In believing, we entrust ourselves to the knowledge acquired by other people."[90] This injects a certain inevitable dependence into our intellectual and moral lives. What a person possesses most intimately, the thoughts of his mind and the values embraced by his heart, are largely received from others in faith. This is not to be confused with the temporary situation of the pupil who learns what the teacher requires until he is old enough to verify it on his own, as one can in fact do with many mathematical truths. The human person is a knower within a knowing community, and that community plays a critical role in the formation of his own knowledge and values. (This is not to say, of course, that an individual cannot question and reject what his community has given him. Copernicus rejected the Ptolemaic astronomy, and Martin Luther broke with many teachings of the Catholic Church.) Furthermore, a person's critique of the truths he has received takes place in the context of his community. He responds to them, argues against them, justifies himself in relation to them. From this John Paul II goes on to a deeper point about our human community:

> It should be stressed that the truths sought in this interpersonal relationship are not primarily empirical or philosophical. Rather, what is sought is the truth of the person—what the person is and what the person reveals from deep within. Human perfection, then, consists not simply in acquiring an abstract knowledge of the truth, but in a dynamic relationship of faithful self-giving with others. It is in this faithful self-giving that a person finds a fullness of certainty and security. At the same time, however, knowledge through belief, grounded as it is on trust between persons, is linked to truth: in the act of believing, men and women entrust themselves to the truth which the other declares to them.[91]

---

[90] Ibid., 32.
[91] Ibid., 32.

This papal text is a direct development of the argument presented in his earlier philosophical essay, "Person: Subject and Community," where he characterized the interpersonal dimension of community in terms of the *I–thou* relationship. In that relationship, "there *ought* to be a mutual self-revelation of persons: the partners *ought* to disclose themselves to each other in their personal subjectivity and in all that makes up this subjectivity."[92] In virtue of the mutual unveiling, members of a community entrust themselves to each other.

John Paul II's point here is quite clear, provided we put aside the blinders that philosophers too often wear and consider what communication normally is. It is tempting, especially for the philosopher, to reduce communication to the exchange of meaningful utterances, analyzing the conditions of meaningfulness and truth, the roots of miscommunication, and so on. In fact, however, interpersonal communication is indeed an entrusting of oneself as one seeks to learn from the other—or as two persons try to sort out together—the configuration of the world about them, a world of value-laden facts. This is especially clear if we consider the communication between parent and child or between mentor and pupil. Nevertheless, this entrusting takes place in many other situations, such as learning one's way in a new town, mastering a new skill, determining what to do about a diseased tree on the property, and so on. In that most objective of spheres, the empirical sciences, the communal character of knowledge is of central importance. The results of an experiment are not accepted until others have reproduced and analyzed it. A theory is not established until the relevant community of scientists accepts it. Charles S. Peirce, arguing that the inquiring community is intrinsic to logic, writes, "He who would not sacrifice his own soul to save the whole world, is, as it seems to me, illogical in all his inferences, collectively. Logic is rooted in the social principle."[93]

Aristotle comments that the purpose of legislation is to make men good, for it requires them to conform their actions to the ends and ideals of the community.[94] And indeed, as members of a community communicate among themselves about the goods around which that community is structured, they form themselves and each other according to those ideals

92 Wojtyła, "Person: Subject and Community," in *Person and Community*, 245.
93 Charles Sanders Peirce, "The Doctrine of Chances," in *Collected Papers*, 2.654.
94 Aristotle, *Nicomachean Ethics* 2.1, 1103b4.

or norms. They communicate and develop patterns of behavior, ways of seeing things, and values, and as they do so the social norms are formed and integrated more or less completely into the lives of the members. Analyzing Aristotle's dictum, Aquinas argues that the goodness that men attain under the legislation (and customs) of the community is relative to the goodness of the legislator's will.

> Since virtue is "that which makes its subject good," it follows that the proper effect of law is to make those to whom it is given, good, either simply or in some particular respect. For if the intention of the lawgiver is fixed on true good, which is the common good regulated according to Divine justice, it follows that the effect of the law is to make men good simply. If, however, the intention of the lawgiver is fixed on that which is not simply good, but useful or pleasurable to himself, or in opposition to Divine justice; then the law does not make men good simply, but in respect to that particular government. In this way good is found even in things that are bad of themselves: thus a man is called a good robber, because he works in a way that is adapted to his end.[95]

The Larger Community

Shared life, therefore, is sharing in goodness. Persons in community serve, whether wittingly or not, to make each other better according to some standard of good. In *Person and Act*, Karol Wojtyła devotes an extended discussion to the concept of *participation*,[96] by which he means the "acting together" with others for the sake of a common good. After rejecting both radical individualism, which makes the community superfluous, and collectivism, which effectively denies the subjectivity of the person, Wojtyła considers two fundamental attitudes that characterize participation: *solidarity* and *opposition*.[97] Both these attitudes are unthinkable without the foundation of a commitment to the *common good*.[98] Solidarity is the standing with one's fellows for the sake of their fitting good, for the attainment of the good that one shares with them. Equally important, however, is the attitude of opposition with respect to those whose actions hinder or

[95] *ST* I–II q. 92, a. 1.

[96] *Persona e atto*, chap. 7.

[97] *Persona e atto*, 1195–1200.

[98] See also Wojtyła, "Person: Subject and Community," in *Person and Community*, 246–54.

counter the attainment of the common good. The importance and implementation of these attitudes becomes clear if we keep in mind the situation in which Professor Wojtyła lived and worked, the situation of a patriot in a nation dominated by an alien power. The Pole had to be true to Poland, its language, culture, religious faith, and customs,[99] but to do so he had to oppose the Communist regime imposed by Soviet Russia.

In his social encyclicals, Pope John Paul II carries this conception of the person's participation in the common good further. For example, his encyclical on human work insists that human work is inherently personal, if also communal: "Man has to subdue the earth and dominate it, because as the "image of God" he is a person, that is to say, a subjective being capable of acting in a planned and rational way, capable of deciding about himself, and with a tendency to self-realization. *As a person, man is therefore the subject of work.*"[100]

It is in virtue of this personalist character of work that labor must hold priority over capital; the worker is never only a tool for capital.[101] However, this personalist character does not mean that work is individualistic. Indeed, work is virtually always social in character. It has economic and social ramifications, and ordinarily it is performed together with others.

Most significant is that the worker shares in the activity of the Creator, and, says John Paul II, "within the limits of his own human capabilities, man in a sense continues to develop that activity, and perfects it as he advances further and further in the discovery of the resources and values contained in the whole of creation."[102] The paradigm of work is the farmer or artisan who produces something, a good. Agriculture, the various trades, and manufacturing, which constitute the major portion of the world of work, are directed to the production of useful products. Paradoxically, however, these are not the chief human goods, however useful or necessary they may be. John Paul II repeatedly emphasizes the principle that the human person is more important than any thing, that the proper

---

[99] John Paul II, homily, Victory Square, Warsaw, June 2, 1979, www.vatican.va/holy_father/john_paul_ii/homilies/1979/documents/hf_jp-ii_hom_19790602_polonia-varsavia_ge.html (accessed January 3, 2008).

[100] *Laborem Exercens*, 6; see also *Centesimus Annus*, 13.

[101] *Laborem Exercens*, 12, 15. This is effectively an application of the personalistic norm to the economic realm.

[102] Ibid., 25.

measure of the human being is who he is and not what he has.[103] Work is a fruit of and expresses a culture, and those who labor both participate in and develop their culture, their society's way of "doing things." The worker incorporates his culture into his own work, transmitting it through his work and stamping his own personality on it. The good of work, then, is not simply that one is contributing economically to his own survival and that of his fellows but also that he is a part of the whole, one who is working together with his neighbors and making a contribution. Through his work he belongs more fully to his community.

Furthermore, the very activity of working is a participation in the work of the Creator, whether the working person is aware of this or not. Adapting his understanding to the materials of his work, his mind adapts to that of the Creator, and imitating the patterns of nature's interactions, he imitates the work of the Creator. The worker is doing something Godlike, applying creative intelligence to the creation of something good. Furthermore, working together with others is a sharing in the good, not simply in causing something new to exist that may be useful but in the process of melding the efforts and intelligence of several persons in a common project.[104] Irrespective of the objective existence of the object of work, the work itself represents a sharing of goods.

The Married Couple

Particularly important in the thought of John Paul II is that communion formed by the love of husband and wife, a communion that gives rise to the fundamental community of the family. Characteristically, two persons marry in the hope of finding happiness. Although at certain times and places marriages have been arranged or entered into for political, economic, or dynastic purposes, it remains true that most enter into marriage with at least the hope of happiness. One may willingly accept employment or undertake schooling that promises to be unpleasant if these things will pay off in the future, but

[103] John Paul II, *Centesimus Annus* 20, 29, and especially 36; *Redemptor Hominis*, 15–16; encyclical *Redemptoris Missio*, 59, *L'Osservatore Romano*, January 28, 1991, weekly English ed.; *Man and Woman He Created Them*, 133.3, p. 662; "Letter to Families," 222–23.

[104] To be sure, other factors can well enter into the work situation, factors such as hidden agendas, selfishness, or laziness, among others, that will darken or obscure this element of shared creativity. Nevertheless, the work itself will contain these positive elements.

we enter marriage in the hopes that the married life itself will be happy. The married couple hopes for love, a home and family of their own, and stability of life together. People marry not so much to *obtain a good* as to *live the good.* Marriage and family life constitute the good that is entered into.

This point is significant, because, although love and marriage involve moral issues, the decision to marry is not generally a moral issue inasmuch as one does not ordinarily fulfill a moral obligation by marrying (or refraining from marriage).[105] On the other hand, marriage is a decision and act that thoroughly transforms one's life, creating new obligations and opportunities. Marriage entails a significant sacrifice of freedom. We might take note of some of the dark humor surrounding weddings: the tradition of the bachelor party as the last night of "freedom," a man's use of the expression "ball and chain" to refer to his wife,[106] and the very real dependence that the bride often enters into, reflected in the folk song complaint "When I Was a Single Girl." If the most important moral aspects of our lives, those most characteristically involving good and evil, are governed only by moral obligations that admit of codification, then, remarkably, this very important decision falls outside the scope of morality. This is a curious result when we consider that marriage involves particularly intimate relationships of love, which one is advised to enter into only with care and mature reflection. The choice of the goods of marriage introduces the new spouses into a dramatically different form of life than they had lived previously.

John Paul II calls the love of husband and wife "spousal love," by which he means a love of total gift of self.[107] In his earlier work, *Love and Responsibility*, he had characterized this love so: "Betrothed [spousal] love differs from all the aspects or forms of love analyzed hitherto. Its decisive character is the giving of one's own person (to another). The essence of betrothed love is self-giving, the surrender of one's 'I'."[108] To marry, according to John Paul II, is to give oneself entirely and exclusively to one's spouse, to

---

105 It may be worth commenting here that even in cases where there appears to be an obligation, such as when a premarital pregnancy is involved, the requirement that marriage be entered into freely implies that there can be no unqualified moral obligation to enter into a marriage.

106 The Spanish word for "handcuffs" is *esposas*, which literally means "wives."

107 *Man and Woman He Created Them*, 15.3–5, 188–89; 78.4, 431.

108 Wojtyła, *Love and Responsibility*, 95–100. The Polish *oblubieńcza* is rendered "betrothed"; see *Miłość i odpowiedzialność*, 87–92, and *Mężczyzną i niewiastą*

be entirely his or hers alone. Of course, this is not the place to explore all the ramifications of this love. Here we focus simply on the goods that are exchanged in this love. Love is possible only on the basis of some common good, and so it is with spousal love, where the goods at stake are the ends of marriage: *procreatio*, *mutuum adiutorium*, and *remedium concupiscentiae*.[109] And indeed, when couples marry they ordinarily have these in mind, at least in some sense. They want to conceive, bear, and raise children (*procreatio*) and to share a life together (*mutuum adiutorium*). Furthermore, they want to enjoy sexual intimacy with each other in a way that is appropriate, implicitly rejecting inclinations to promiscuity or self-indulgence. On the other hand, it can be said that before all these ends, they want each other and to give to each other. The ends of marriage serve to flesh out the existential realization of the gift of self.

What is it that makes another's gift of self so wonderful, so surpassing a good for which one forsakes the single man or woman's comfortable life, financial independence, and greater freedom to pursue rewarding opportunities? The first is the attractiveness, the beauty, of the beloved.[110] Characteristically, a person comes to love another after having been strongly attracted, and the basis of that attraction is ordinarily characterized as "beauty." The lover desires the beauty of the beloved, if not to possess it, then at least to admire it and to bask in its presence.[111] This experience of beauty, the desire to admire it and incorporate it into one's life, is one of the vital elements of falling in love. What we dismiss as infatuation is most frequently fascination with beauty. In his *War and Peace*, Tolstoy gives us a perceptive insight into the power of the gift of beauty. When the beautiful Elena Kuragina accepts Pierre Bezukhov's proposal of marriage, Bezukhov is awestruck that someone so beautiful should agree to marry him, and indeed, even though he knows that he does not truly love Elena, he carries the engagement forward, simply because of the honor of being accepted by one so beautiful. To be offered the gift of another's beauty is ordinarily

---

stworzył ich, 44–45, 49. In *Man and Woman He Created Them* the original Italian adjective *sponsale* is rendered "spousal." Other translations render that adjective as "nuptial."

[109] Wojtyła, *Love and Responsibility*, 66–69.

[110] See John Paul II, "Letter to Families," 20; *Man and Woman He Created Them*, 108.6, 554.

[111] See the further analysis in Reimers, *Soul of the Person*, 79ff.

experienced as a signal honor. To be sure, there always remains the task (which Bezukhov did not carry through) of discerning the true goodness beneath apparent beauty, and one mark of maturity is the ability to recognize beauty more substantial than the merely physical. Nonetheless, it is ordinarily gratifying when someone beautiful makes a gift of that beauty. Incorporating the beauty of the other person into one's life holds the promise of making one's own life beautiful.

Besides the aspect of beauty (whether physical or spiritual), there is in marriage the gift of each others' bodies in sexual relations. Despite the protestations of contemporary cynics and empiricists, sexual relations between human beings are not ordinarily experienced as simply a biological interaction, a release of physical tension and nothing more. (Of course, by living a sufficiently promiscuous life, one can come to the state at which sexual encounters acquire this purely physical kind of character, but this is an aberration and is recognized as such, even by those who act in this way.) The human being normally experiences feelings of shame at having his sexual values exposed to the view, the perception, of others, and therefore the person tends to conceal those parts of the body that are most characteristically masculine or feminine, the characteristics that definitively distinguish one as male or female.[112] The initial thrill of the sexual encounter, therefore, lies in the powerful emotional realization that this person intends, whether now or at some future time, to give to me the gift of her femininity or his masculinity in this complete way.[113] Subsequently, as a couple live out their married life, the freshness of married sex is maintained primarily and most effectively by the couple's ongoing recognition that their every sexual encounter has the nature of the gift.

Finally, until very recently, the procreation of children has been recognized as one of the great goods of married life.[114] And even in contemporary society, most parents take pride in their children, finding in them a reflection or continuation of themselves. As a couple raises its children,

---

112 Wojtyła, *Love and Responsibility*, 174–193; John Paul II, *Man and Woman He Created Them*, 26.4–28.6, 236–46.

113 John Paul II, *Man and Woman He Created Them*, 110.5–9, 568–72.

114 This appears to be no longer the case in Western culture, according to a 2007 study by the Pew Research Center, *As Marriage and Parenthood Drift Apart, Public Is Concerned about Social Impact*, July 1, 2007, pewresearch.org/assets/social/pdf/Marriage.pdf.

they invest time and effort into far more than maintaining their offspring's existence. Parents of every culture, class, and station strive to inculcate their values into their children, teaching them how to live and indeed to live rightly—how to work, what kind of work is worth doing, how to treat other persons, how to relate to the broader society, what behavior is moral and what immoral, how to seek and know God. Engaged in this project, father and mother need to become of one mind (more or less) as they teach and form their children, and as they do this, they can enrich each other, developing their own perspectives and understanding of their life and their values.[115]

These goods of marriage clearly transcend purely material things. In their mutual gifts of self the spouses can find their lives and themselves enriched. Receiving a spouse's gift of self, a person knows himself to be valuable, an important part of the universe, at least for this one person. The husband and wife affirm each others' beauty and value. Furthermore, they expand each other's understanding, intellectually and artistically interpreting the world they live in and build up together. This is true not only of those who are most culturally aware, those with sufficient wealth and education to avail themselves of the resources of high culture, but it applies equally to working-class and rural families, as well as to the peasantry of ages past and the poor of today's third world. Parents decorate the home and teach their children how to act and to think about the world around them. Further, by the sheer exigencies of living together, the couple can grow in virtue, correcting their faults for the sake of their love. If a couple are happily married, that is, living together their initial gift of love, then the acquisition and exchange of material things becomes of relatively minor importance to them. The best gift is the gift of the person, the sharing in the wisdom and love of a human being who gives himself to you.

The Common Good

The common good is the basis for unity in love among human beings.[116] Important as it is, *common good* is a concept that is little understood in the modern, post-Enlightenment world. It is fair to say that for a modern democratic state, the common good is that collection of goods that all or

---

[115] John Paul II, "Letter to Families," 7–9, 11, 16; *Familiaris Consortio*, 36ff., 43.

[116] See Wojtyła, *Love and Responsibility*, 28–29.

at least most members of the society recognize as such and as worth striving together for. According to the Enlightenment conception, the common good is established by consent rather than by any preexisting human nature or ontological reality.[117] The people chooses its own common good. So conceived, the common good can consist only in material goods and in the conditions and systems for acquiring and distributing material goods. Practically speaking, this means that the common good of the American society, and indeed, of most European societies and Australia, Korea, and Japan, consists in the rule of law under reasonably democratic legislators, appropriately regulated free markets, and access to natural sources of wealth. By contrast, John Paul II characterizes the common good as "the good of all and of each individual,"[118] and it is in terms of this good that the structures and procedures of a society and its government are to be judged.[119] Indeed, in his encyclical on the Gospel of Life, John Paul II writes:

> To be actively pro-life is to contribute to the renewal of society through the promotion of the common good. It is impossible to further the common good without acknowledging and defending the right to life, upon which all the other inalienable rights of individuals are founded and from which they develop. A society lacks solid foundations when, on the one hand, it asserts values such as the dignity of the person, justice and peace, but then, on the other hand, radically acts to the contrary by allowing or tolerating a variety of ways in which human life is devalued and violated, especially where it is weak or marginalized. Only respect for life can be the foundation and guarantee of the most precious and essential goods of society, such as democracy and peace.[120]

---

[117] I simplify here somewhat, ignoring the Romantic conception of the common good as the true will of the people, as proposed by Jean-Jacques Rousseau and realized in the French and Russian Revolutions. See Piotr Nowakowski, "The Natural Law in Jean-Jacques Rousseau's Philosophy and Its Social and Pedagogical Consequences" (paper presented at the International Symposium on Natural Law, Catholic University of Eastern Africa [CUEA], Nairobi, Kenya, February 6–8, 2007).

[118] *Sollicitudo Rei Socialis*, 38.

[119] John Paul II, *Centesimus Annus*, 58; see also *Laborem Exercens*, 20, and especially *Evangelium Vitae*, 70.

[120] *Evangelium Vitae*, 101.

In John Paul II's conception, *common good* therefore precedes that of any publicly agreed-upon common value. That is to say, the common good is the good for each member of the society even prior to his own valuing it as such. Central among the goods that make up the common good is the good of life itself, a good that radically pertains to the individual as a person. In *Centesimus Annus,* he remarks, "[U]ltimately, [the common good] demands a correct understanding of the dignity and the rights of the person,"[121] directly relating this in the footnote to the discussion of the common good at *Gaudium et Spes,* 26, where the Second Vatican Council discusses the common good in relation to "the exalted dignity proper to the human person" and his "universal and inviolable" rights.

The World Community

John Paul II makes his own the characterization of "common good" used by the Second Vatican Council: "the sum of those conditions of social life which allow social groups and their individual members relatively thorough and ready access to their own fulfillment."[122] The key to the Council's definition of "common good" is the concept of *fulfillment* of the human person. On this depend the rights of the human being and his duties. The fulfillment of the person, according to John Paul II, is his realization as a subject capable of knowledge and love, a realization that can occur only in relation to the truth. In his catechesis on the theology of the body, John Paul II develops this notion at great length, examining how the communion of man and woman in marriage enables them to realize themselves and their personhood in love. The principles at work there, however, are not restricted only to that relationship but rather apply to other communions, to communities, and to society itself.[123] Marriage is a kind of paradigm of the self-gift that should characterize all human relationships.[124] The individual person approaches the good in communion and in community with others. Culture forms him according to its understanding of the good, and in turn the individual forms his culture and influences his fellows. This good necessarily has a spiritual character,

121 *Centesimus Annus,* 58.

122 Vatican Council II, *Gaudium et Spes,* 26. This definition is also taken up in the *Catechism of the Catholic Church,* 1906–7.

123 See John Paul II, *Man and Woman He Created Them,* 133.1, 660.

124 *Gaudium et Spes,* 24.

because the higher goods by which human beings are formed and direct their lives must be transcendent. The fact that values must be judged in relation to truth demands a vertical transcendence.[125] The good turns out inevitably to have a spiritual and therefore a personal character.

Conclusion

The phrase "truth about the good" recurs significantly in John Paul II's writings from his early scholarly works and into his papal works, most notably in *Veritatis Splendor.*[126] It is a major theme in his writings and a key to his understanding of anthropology, both philosophical and theological, and ethics. By understanding how John Paul II conceives the truth about the good and why he insists on its importance, we can grasp the roots of his personalism and its relationship with the thought of his intellectual predecessors, especially Aquinas and Scheler. That there is a *truth* about the good demands that the person be understood ultimately in terms of the philosophy of being—metaphysics—and John Paul II straightforwardly embraces the metaphysical thought of Aristotle and Aquinas. However, the question of the *truth about the good* does not normally arise as such in Aristotelian-Thomistic thought, not in the way in which John Paul II addresses it. To be sure, Thomas asks and answers the question of the respective relationships between "good" and "true" with "being,"[127] as well as their relative reciprocal priorities.[128] In his analysis, the Angelic Doctor moves on the theoretical plane, but John Paul II wants to address the issue from the perspective of experience, and particularly the experience of values. Although the good cannot be rooted in the subject's personal experience of values, as Scheler implies, John Paul II does not repudiate Scheler. Rather, John Paul II takes the experience of the conscious and acting subject as his starting point, the subject who finds himself drawn to act in response to the values he experiences and those values that seem good to him to realize. He starts, that is to say, from much the same place as Scheler and in terms remarkably similar to the German phenomenologist's. Scheler

125 Wojtyła, *Persona e atto,* 982–83.

126 *Veritatis Splendor,* 30, 32, 61–64, 75, 82, 91, 104, 110.

127 *De veritate,* q. 1, a. 1; *ST* I, q. 16, aa. 1, 3; *Commentary on the* Metaphysics *of Aristotle,* 6.4.1230–44.

128 *De veritate,* q. 21, a. 3; *ST* I, q. 16, a. 4.

identifies the good as an intentional element in human experience, as a value that structures his moral life. What Scheler misses, the factor that renders the philosophy of being necessary, is the moment of efficacy. The human act changes things; it brings good or evil to the world and into the lives of persons. The agent who effects these changes is himself good or evil according to his acts. Therefore he needs to know the truth about the good.

The *truth about the good* is the source of moral norms. "The ethical norm . . . is nothing other than the objectification (and at the same time the concretization) of the truth about the good, of the good tied to a given action of the person, willed in it and realized in it."[129] Properly understood, this is the central conception of John Paul II's ethics and philosophical anthropology. This *truth about the good* is not a purely moral principle, a kind of deontological primary law, a variant on Kant's categorical imperative. Rather, because there is a truth about it, the good is an inextricable aspect of the real order, of the order of creation. As John Paul II insists in the opening chapter of *Veritatis Splendor*, God is the "One who is good," and as such he is the Source and Author of all good, including—indeed, especially—the good for the human person. Because it is "very good" (Gen 1:31), his creation has the character of a gift to his human creatures. These statements may appear as commonplace devotional meditations, but John Paul II insists that they are literally true, which implies that any conception that prescinds from the order of good is an "abstraction" and therefore not a complete representation of the truth of things.

A particularly important kind of creature is the human being, who is created in the image of God himself. Indeed, this doctrine that the human being is in the image and likeness of God is the essential starting point for any Christian anthropology.[130] As a rational and free creature, the human being is a *person*, the master of his own acts. The meaning of his freedom is that the person is capable of self-governance. By his freely chosen acts, the human person forms himself according to the standards of good that he chooses, according to the values he embraces. The moral task of the human person arises precisely from the fact that he can determine how to act according to his knowledge of the *truth about the good*. The good is to be found in the created order around him and especially in his relation-

---

129 Wojtyła, *L'uomo nel campo della responsibilità*, 1269.

130 John Paul II, *Mulieris Dignitatem*, 6. See also *Dominum et Vivificantem*, 34, 36.

ships with other persons. Karol Wojtyła argues that precisely because the person is a *good*, a fundamental norm applies to him: the personalistic norm. The person is a good that does not admit of use; rather, the only appropriate response to a person is love. This is not simply a moral principle but a truth about what a person is, about what pertains to a free, self-determining being who bears in himself the image of God.

Because the good is an aspect of the created order, we can speak of the *natural law*, which is simply the order of goods according to which the Creator has structured his creation. Key to understanding this order are the two fundamental norms, *truths about the good*, that we have already identified: (1) God is the Supreme Good, the "One who alone is good," and (2) the personalistic norm. From these we can evaluate other goods and so discover the provisions of the *natural law*. This *natural law* is not identical with the laws of nature discovered by the various physical sciences (which are, as we have already noted, abstractions from the real order). Hence to charge John Paul II with the error of "biologism" or "physicalism" is to misunderstand him.[131]

The *truth about the good* is expressed most perfectly in God himself, in his eternal Word, and because the Word has become flesh and dwelt among us (Jn 1:14), Jesus Christ is the way by which human beings can attain to the good. This is why John Paul II makes much of the *sequela Christi* in the opening chapter of *Veritatis Splendor*. Jesus' role cannot be simply that of a moral exemplar or teacher, or even of simply a judge. John Paul II means to flesh out the teaching of Vatican Council II that only in the incarnate Word is the mystery of man, his origin and destiny, made clear.[132] He is saying that every human being needs Christ, that only in Christ can the human person make complete sense of his life, and only in following (or imitating) Christ can one live according to the complete *truth about the good*.

John Paul II's analysis entails a fairly thoroughgoing rejection of the foundations of post-Enlightenment conceptions of truth and good. Recognizing that the person acts on the basis of values and furthermore that the nexus of his values structures his world, giving it its ethos, John Paul II

---

131 John Spinello, *The Genius of John Paul II: The Great Pope's Moral Wisdom* (Lanham: Sheed and Ward, 2007), 89.

132 See Vatican Council II, *Gaudium et Spes*, 22.

first recognizes the existential inadequacy of the Humean sensationalism to account for human experience. David Hume's and indeed every sensationalist account of human experience fails to account for what millions of human persons experience every day. No one in severe pain or swept up in the delights of love can affirm the sharp distinction between fact and value. The utilitarian account does incorporate the ordinary human experiences of pleasure and pain as impetuses to action, but it fails to address the fundamental question of morality, the question that impels the acting person to seek moral norms: What should I do? As such, the utilitarian account must ultimately destroy ethics, simply because it can provide no solid norms, no guidance as to what one *ought* to do. The reason for this is that it cannot transcend the boundaries of this-worldly experience. Utilitarianism fails to identify what the useful must be useful for and what it is that is worthy of taking pleasure in, namely, the transcendent *fitting good*, the *bonum honestum*. It is necessary, therefore, for the rational being, the person, intellectually to investigate the *truth about the good*, and to embrace that Good when it has been found.

Bibliography

Works by Pope John Paul II/Karol Wojtyła

The Acting Person. English translation of *Osoba i czyn.* Translated by Andrzej Potocki. Vol. 10 of *Analecta Husserliana: The Yearbook of Phenomenological Research*, edited by Anna-Teresa Tymieniecka. Dordrecht: D. Riedel Publishing Company, 1979.

"Address to a Group of Bishops from the United States on their 'Ad Limina' Visit." September 2, 1988. www.vatican.va/holy_father/john_paul_ii/speeches/1988/september/documents/hf_jp-ii_spe_19880902_usa-ad-limina_en.html (accessed September 19, 2006).

Catechesi sul Credo. Pt. 1, "Dio Padre e Creatore." General audiences, 1985–1986. www.vatican.va/holy_father/john_paul_ii/audiences/alpha/index_it.html (accessed September 3, 2003).

Catechesi sul Credo. Pt. 2, "Gesù Figlio e Salvatore." General audiences, 1986–1989. www.vatican.va/holy_father/john_paul_ii/audiences/alpha/index_it.html (accessed July 27, 2004).

Catechesi sul Credo. Pt. 3, "Lo Spirito Santo datore di vita." General audiences, 1989–1991. www.vatican.va/holy_father/john_paul_ii/audiences/alpha/index_it.html (accessed January 31, 2010).

Centesimus Annus. Encyclical. *L'Osservatore Romano*, May 6, 1991, weekly English ed., 5–16.

La chiesa nel Credo. General audiences, July 10, 1991–January 3, 1996. www.vatican.va/holy_father/john_paul_ii/audiences/index.htm (accessed July 24, 2006).

Christifideles Laici. Apostolic exhortation. *L'Osservatore Romano* (weekly English edition), no. 6 (1075), February 6, 1989, 1–21.

Crossing the Threshold of Hope. New York: Alfred A. Knopf, 1994.

"The Degrees of Being from the Point of View of the Phenomenology of Action." In Tymieniecka, *Analecta Husserliana*, 11:125–30.

Dives in Misericordia. Encyclical. Boston: St. Paul Editions, 1980.

Dominum et Vivificantem. Encyclical. *Pope Speaks* 31, no. 3 (1986): 199–263.

Easter Vigil, and Other Poems. Translated by Jerzy Peterkiewicz. New York: Random House, 1979.

Evangelium Vitae. Encyclical. New York: Random House, 1995.

Familiaris Consortio. Apostolic exhortation. Boston: St. Paul Editions, 1981.

Fides et Ratio. Encyclical. Boston: Pauline Books and Media, 1998.

Homily. Victory Square, Warsaw, June 2, 1979. www.vatican.va/holy_father/john_paul_ii/homilies/1979/documents/hf_jp-ii_hom_19790602_polonia-varsavia_ge.html (accessed January 3, 2008).

I fondamenti dell'ordine etico. Bologna: CSEO, 1980.

Laborem Exercens. Encyclical. Boston: St. Paul Editions, 1981.

"Letter to Artists." www.vatican.va/holy_father/john_paul_ii/letters/1999/documents/hf_jp-ii_let_23041999_artists_en.html (accessed December 14, 2007).

"Letter to Families." *Pope Speaks* 39, no. 4 (July–August 1994): 208–45.

Love and Responsibility. English translation of *Miłość i odpowiedzialność*. Translated by H. T. Willetts. San Francisco: Ignatius Press, 1993.

Lubliner Vorlesungen. Translated by Annaliese Danka Spranger and Edda Wiener. Stuttgart-Degerloch: Seewald Verlag, 1981.

Man and Woman He Created Them: A Theology of the Body. Translated with an introduction and index by Michael Waldstein. Boston: Pauline Books and Media, 2006. Original Italian, *Uomo e donna lo creo*, general audiences, 1979–1984, text available at www.vatican.va/holy_father/john_paul_ii/audiences/alpha/index_it.html (accessed September 3, 2003).

Memory and Identity: Conversations at the Dawn of a Millennium. New York: Rizzoli International Publications, 2005.

Metafisica della persona: Tutti le opera filosofiche e saggi integrative. Milan: Bompiani, 2003.

Mężczyzną i niewiastą stworzył ich: Odkupienie ciała a sakramentalność małżeństwa [Man and woman he created them: Redemption of the body and the sacramentality of marriage]. Lublin: Wydawnictwo KUL, 2008.

Miłość i odpowiedzialność. Lublin: Towarrzystwo Naukowe KUL, 2001. Translated into English as *Love and Responsibility*.

Mulieris Dignitatem. Apostolic letter. Boston: St. Paul Books and Media, 1988.

"Osoba: Podmiot i wspólnota." *Roczniki Filozoficzne* 24 (1976): 5–39. Translated into English as "Person: Subject and Community," in *Osoba i czyn*, 371–414.

Osoba i czyn: Oraz inne studia antropologiczne. Lublin: Towarzystwo Naukowe KUL, 2000. Translated into English as *The Acting Person.*

Persona e atto. Italian translation of *Osoba i czyn.* Translated by Giuseppe Girgenti and Patrycja Mikulska. In *Metafisica della persona.*

Person and Community: Selected Essays. Translated by Teresa Sandok, O.S.M. New York: Peter Lang, 1993.

Person und Tat. German translation of *Osoba i czyn.* Freiburg im Breisgau: Herder, 1981.

Reconciliatio et Paenetentia. Apostolic exhortation, 1984. www.vatican.va/holy_father/john_paul_ii/apost_exhortations/documents/hf_jp-ii_exh_02121984_reconciliatio-et-paenitentia_en.html (accessed October 7, 2005).

Redemptor Hominis. Encyclical. Boston: St. Paul Editions, 1979.

Redemptoris Missio. Encyclical. *L'Osservatore Romano,* January 28, 1991, weekly English ed.

Salvifici Doloris. Apostolic letter. Boston: St. Paul Editions, 1984.

Sign of Contradiction. New York: Seabury Press, 1979.

Sollicitudo Rei Socialis. Encyclical, 1987. www.vatican.va/edocs/ENG0223/_INDEX.HTM (accessed May 20, 2004).

Sources of Renewal: The Implementation of the Second Vatican Council. New York: Harper and Row, 1980.

Tertio Millennio Adveniente. Apostolic letter. www.vatican.va/holy_father/john_paul_ii/apost_letters/documents/hf_jp-ii_apl_10111994_tertio-millennio-adveniente_en.html (accessed June 20, 2007).

"The Transcendence of the Person in Action and Man's Self-Teleology." English translation of "Transcendencja osoby w czynie a autoteleologia człowieka." In Tymieniecka, *Analecta Husserliana,* 9:203–12.

"Transcendencja osoby w czynie a autoteleologia człowieka." In *Osoba i czyn,* 477–90. Translated into English as "The Transcendence of the Person in Action and Man's Self-Teleology," in Tymieniecka, *Analecta Husserliana,* 9:203–12.

L'uomo nel campo della responsibilità. In *Metafisica della persona.*

Ut Unum Sint. Encyclical, May 1995. www.vatican.va/edocs/ENG0221/_INDEX.HTM (accessed January 2, 2003).

Valutazione sulla possibilità di costruire l'etica cristiana sulle base del sistema di Max Scheler. In *Metafisica della persona.*

Veritatis Splendor. Encyclical. Boston: Pauline Books and Media, 1993.

"La vita cristiana come cammino verso la piena communione con Dio." General audience, August 11, 1999. www.vatican.va/holy_father/john_paul_ii/audiences/1999/documents/hf_jp-ii_aud_11081999_en.html (accessed February 3, 2010).

Works by Others

Aertsen, Jan. *Medieval Philosophy and the Transcendentals: The Case of Thomas Aquinas.* Leiden: E. J. Brill, 1996.

Allsopp, Michael E., and John J. O'Keefe, eds. Veritatis Splendor: *American Responses.* Kansas City: Sheed and Ward, 1995.

Aquinas, Thomas. *Aristotle's* De anima *in the Version of William of Moerbeke and the Commentary of St. Thomas Aquinas.* Translated by Kenelm Foster, O.P., and Silvester Humphries, O.P. New Haven: Yale University Press, 1951.

———. *Commentary on the* Metaphysics *of Aristotle.* Translated by John P. Rowan. Chicago: Henry Regnery Company, 1961.

———. *Commentary on the* Nicomachean Ethics. Translated by C. I. Litzinger, O.P. Chicago: Henry Regnery Company, 1964.

———. *De malo.* Translated by John A. and Jean T. Oesterle as *On Evil.* Notre Dame, IN: University of Notre Dame Press, 1995.

———. *De veritate.* Translated as *The Disputed Questions on Truth.* Vol. 1, translated by Robert W. Mulligan, S.J., Ph.D. Vol. 3, translated by Robert W. Schmidt, S.J., Ph.D. Chicago: Henry Regnery Company, 1952–1954.

———. *Opera omnia.* Fundación Tomás de Aquino, www.corpusthomisticum.org/iopera.html.

———. *Summa contra Gentiles.* Translated as *On the Truth of the Catholic Faith:* Summa contra Gentiles. Bk. 2, translated by James F. Anderson. Garden City, NY: Doubleday Image Books, 1956.

———. *Summa theologiae.* Translated by the English Dominican Fathers. Gervais, OR: Harmony Media, 1998.

Aristotle. *Metaphysics.* Translated by W. D. Ross. In *Great Books of the Western World*, vol. 8. Chicago: Encyclopaedia Britannica, 1952.

———. *Nicomachean Ethics.* Translated with an introduction by David Ross. Oxford: Oxford University Press, 1998.

———. *Physics.* Translated by R. P. Hardie and R. K. Gaye. In *Great Books of the Western World*, vol. 8. Chicago: Encyclopaedia Britannica, 1952.

———. *Politics.* Translated by C. D. C. Reeve. Indianapolis: Hackett Publishing Company, 1998.

Armstrong, D. M. *A Materialist Theory of the Mind.* New York: Routledge and Kegan Paul, 1968.

Auden, W. H. "September 1, 1939." In *The Major Poets: English and American*, edited by Charles M. Coffin. New York: Harcourt, Brace, and World, 1954.

Augustine. *Confessions.* Translated by John K. Ryan. Garden City, NY: Image Books, 1960.

Bacon, Francis. *Novum Organum.* In *Great Books of the Western World,* vol. 30. Chicago: Encyclopaedia Britannica, 1952.

Bell, Eric Temple. "The Prince of Mathematicians." In Newman, *World of Mathematics,* 1:295–339.

———. "The Queen of Mathematics." In Newman, *World of Mathematics,* 1:498–518.

Benedict XVI [Joseph Ratzinger]. "Christian Faith as 'the Way': An Introduction to *Veritatis Splendor.*" *Communio: International Catholic Review* 21, no. 2 (Summer 1994): 199–207.

———. Homily for Mass "Pro eligendo romano pontifice." April 18, 2005. www.vatican.va/gpII/documents/homily-pro-eligendo-pontifice_20050418_en.html (accessed September 6, 2007).

———. "Il rinnovamento della teologia morale: Prospettive del Vatican II e di *Veritatis Splendor.*" In Melina and Noriega, *Camminare nella Luce,* 35–45.

———. *Spe Salvi.* Encyclical, November 30, 2007. www.vatican.va/holy_father/benedict_xvi/encyclicals/documents/hf_ben-xvi_enc_20071130_spe-salvi_en.html (accessed January 29, 2008).

———. *Truth and Tolerance: Christian Belief and World Religions.* Translated by Henry Taylor. San Francisco: Ignatius Press, 2004.

Bentham, Jeremy. *Deontology.* In Deontology, *Together with* A Table of the Springs of Action *and* Article on Utilitarianism, edited by Amnon Goldworth. Oxford: Clarendon Press, 1983.

Berofsky, Bernard. *Determinism.* Princeton, NJ: Princeton University Press, 1971.

Buddha, Gautama. *The Dhammapada.* In *Introduction to Philosophy of Religion: Readings,* edited by James Kellenberger, 16–19. Upper Saddle River, NJ: Prentice Hall, 2007.

Burke, Ronald R. "*Veritatis Splendor*: Papal Authority and the Sovereignty of Reason." In Allsopp and O'Keefe, Veritatis Splendor: *American Responses,* 119–36.

Burkert, Walter. *Creation of the Sacred: Tracks of Biology in Early Religions.* Cambridge: Harvard University Press, 1996.

Buttiglione, Rocco. *Karol Wojtyla: The Thought of the Man Who Became Pope John Paul II.* Translated by Paolo Guietti and Francesca Murphy. Grand Rapids: Wm. B. Eerdmans, 1997.

——. *Karol Wojtyla e il pensiero europeo contemporaneo.* Bologna: CSEO Saggi, 1984.

Carlotti, Paolo. Veritatis Splendor: *Aspetti della recezione teologica.* Rome: Libraria Ateneo Salesiano, 2001.

Catechism of the Catholic Church. Ligouri, MO: Ligouri Publications, 1994.

Chakrabarti, Arindam. "Buddhist Philosophy" and "Nirvana." In Honderich, *Oxford Companion to Philosophy.* Oxford: Oxford University Press, 1995.

Clark, Stephen B. *Man and Woman in Christ.* Ann Arbor: Servant Books, 1980.

Clinton, Hillary Rodham, and Cecile Richards. "Blocking Care for Women." *New York Times,* September 19, 2008.

Constitution of the United States of America. Washington, DC: Commission on the Bicentennial of the United States Constitution, 1987.

Cooper, John M. "Contemplation and Happiness: A Reconsideration." *Synthese* 72 (1987): 187–216.

Crosby, John. "Are Being and Good Really Convertible?" *New Scholasticism* 57, no. 4 (Autumn 1983): 465–500.

———. "The Idea of Value and the Reform of the Traditional Metaphysics of *Bonum.*" *Aletheia: An International Journal of Philosophy* 1, no. 2 (1977): 231–327.

———. *The Selfhood of the Human Person.* Washington, DC: Catholic University of America Press, 1996.

Curran, Charles E. *Directions in Fundamental Moral Theology.* Notre Dame, IN: University of Notre Dame Press, 1985.

———. *The Moral Theology of Pope John Paul II.* Washington, DC: Georgetown University Press, 2005.

———. "*Veritatis Splendor*: A Revisionist Perspective." In Allsopp and O'Keefe, Veritatis Splendor: *American Responses,* 224–43.

———, ed. *Conscience.* Readings in Moral Theology 14. New York: Paulist Press, 2004.

——— and Richard A. McCormick, S.J., eds. *John Paul II and Moral Theology.* Readings in Moral Theology 10. New York: Paulist Press, 1998.

Daily Roman Missal. Chicago: Midwest Theological Forum, 2003.

Darwin, Charles. *The Descent of Man.* Princeton, NJ: Princeton University Press, 1981.

———. *The Origin of Species by Means of Natural Selection.* London: John Murray, 1884.

Dawkins, Richard. "God's Utility Function." *Scientific American,* November 1995, 80–85.

Dennett, Daniel. *Consciousness Explained.* Boston: Little, Brown, and Co., 1991.

Descartes, René. *Meditations on First Philosophy in Which the Existence of God and the Distinction of the Soul from the Body Are Demonstrated.* Translated by Donald A. Cress, 3rd ed. Indianapolis: Hackett Publishing Company, 1993.

Di Blasi, Fulvio. *God and the Natural Law: A Rereading of Thomas Aquinas.* South Bend, IN: St. Augustine's Press, 2003.

Edie, James. *Edmund Husserl's Phenomenology: A Critical Commentary.* Indianapolis and Bloomington: Indiana University Press, 1987.

Flippen, Douglas. "On Two Meanings of Good and the Foundations of Ethics in Aristotle and St. Thomas." *Proceedings of the American Catholic Philosophical Association* 57 (1984): 56.

Freud, Sigmund. *The Future of an Illusion.* Translated by W. D. Robson-Scott. Garden City, NY: Doubleday and Company, 1964.

Fuchs, Éric. *La morale selon Jean-Paul II: Réponse protestante à une encyclique.* Geneva: Labor et fides, 1994.

Fuchs, J. "Der Absolutheitscharakter sittlichen Handlungsnormen." In *Für eine menschliche Moral: Grundfragen der theologischen Ethik*, vol. 1, Freiburg, Schweiz [Fribourg, Switzerland]: Universitätsverlag, 1988.

Gaffney, James. "The Pope on Proportionalism." In Allsopp and O'Keefe, Veritatis Splendor: *American Responses*, 60–71.

Garrigou-Lagrange, Reginald, O.P. *Christian Perfection and Contemplation: According to St. Thomas Aquinas and St. John of the Cross.* Translated by Sister M. Timothea Doyle, O.P. Rockford, IL: Tan Books and Publishers, 2003.

Gould, Stephen Jay. "The Evolution of Life on Earth." *Scientific American*, October 1994, 84–91.

Groys, Boris. "Kommunismus wie im Kino: Stalin und die Allmacht des Bildes." *Süddeutsche Zeitung*, March 26–27, 1994, 17.

Gula, Richard M. "The Moral Conscience." In Curran, *Conscience*, 51–62. New York: Paulist Press, 2004.

Hare, R. M. *The Language of Morals.* New York: Oxford University Press, 1969.

Häring, Bernard, S.J. "A Distrust That Wounds." In Curran and McCormick, *John Paul II and Moral Theology*, 42–46.

Harvanek, Robert F., S.J. "The Philosophical Foundations of the Thought of John Paul II." In *The Thought of Pope John Paul II: A Collection of Essays and Studies*, edited by John J. McDermott, S.J., 1–21. Rome: Editrice Pontificia Università Gregoriana, 1993.

Honderich, Ted, ed. *The Oxford Companion to Philosophy.* Oxford: Oxford University Press, 1995.

Hume, David. *Dialogues concerning Natural Religion.* Indianapolis: Bobbs-Merrill, 1947.

———. *An Enquiry concerning the Principles of Morals.* In *Hume's Ethical Writings: Selections from David Hume*, edited by Alasdair MacIntyre. New York: Collier Books, 1965.

———. *An Inquiry concerning Human Understanding.* Indianapolis: Bobbs-Merrill, 1955.

———. *A Treatise of Human Nature.* In *Hume's Ethical Writings: Selections from David Hume*, edited by Alasdair MacIntyre. New York: Collier Books, 1965.

Husserl, Edmund. "Phenomenology." *Encyclopaedia Britannica*, 14th ed. (1932), quoted in Forrest E. Baird and Walter Kaufmann, eds., *Philosophic Classics: From Plato to Derrida*, 4th ed., 1070–77. Upper Saddle River, NJ: Prentice Hall, 2003.

Ide, Pascal. "Une théologie du don: Les occurrences de *Gaudium et spes*, no. 24, 3 chez Jean-Paul II." *Anthropotes* 17 (2001): 149–78, 313–44.

James, William. "The Dilemma of Determinism." In *Will to Believe*, 145–83.

———. *Essays in Pragmatism.* New York: Hafner Publishing Co., 1948.

———. *Pragmatism.* Buffalo: Prometheus Books, 1991.

———. "The Will to Believe." In *Will to Believe*, 1–31.

———. *The Will to Believe, Human Immortality, and Other Essays on Popular Philosophy.* New York: Dover Books, 1956.

Johnson, Luke Timothy. "A Disembodied Theology of the Body: John Paul II on Love, Sex, and Pleasure." *Commonweal*, January 26, 2001.

Kaczor, Christopher, ed. *Proportionalism: For and Against.* Milwaukee: Marquette University Press, 2000.

Kaczyński, Edward, O.P. *Verità sul bene nella morale: Alcuni temi di morale fondamentale.* Rome: Millennium Romae, 1998.

Kalinowski, Georges. "La pensée philosophique de Karol Wojtyła et la faculté de l'Université catholique de Lublin." *Aletheia: An International Journal of Philosophy* 4, Epistomology and Logic (1988): 198–216.

Kant, Immanuel. *Critique of Pure Reason.* Translated by Norman Kemp Smith. New York: St. Martin's Press, 1965.

———. *Grounding for the Metaphysics of Morals* with *On a Supposed Right to Lie because of Philanthropic Concerns*, translated by James W. Ellington, 3rd ed. Indianapolis: Hackett, 1993.

———. *Grundlegung der Metaphysik der Sitten.* In *Kant's gesammelte Schriften*, vol. 4. Berlin: Druck und Verlag von George Reimer, 1911.

———. *Kritik der praktischen Vernunft.* In *Immanuel Kants Werke*, vol. 5. Berlin: Bruno Cassirer, 1922.

———. *Kritik der reinen Vernunft.* In *Kant's gesammelte Schriften*, vol. 4. Berlin: Druck und Verlag Georg Reimer, 1911.

———. *Religion within the Limits of Reason Alone.* New York: Harper and Row, 1960.

Kierkegaard, Søren. *Philosophical Fragments.* In *Philosophical Fragments [and] Johannes Climacus*, edited and translated by Howard V. Hong and Edna H. Hong. Princeton, NJ: Princeton University Press, 1985.

Knasas, John F. X. *Being and Some Twentieth-Century Thomists.* New York: Fordham University Press, 2003.

Knauer, Peter, S.J. "The Hermeneutic Function of the Principle of Double Effect." In Kaczor, *Proportionalism*, 25–59.

———. "Teleologische als deontologische Normenbegründung." *Theologie und Philosophie* 55, no. 3 (1980): 321–60.

———. "Zu Grundbegriffen der Enzyklika '*Veritatis Splendor.*'" *Stimmen der Zeit* 212, no. 1 (January 1994): 14–26.

Kögler, Hans-Herbert, "Life-world," *The Oxford Companion to Philosophy*, edited by Ted Honderich. Oxford: Oxford University Press, 1995: 488.

Kohlberg, Lawrence. *The Philosophy of Moral Development: Moral Stages and the Idea of Justice.* San Francisco: Harper and Row, 1981.

Kupczak, Jarosław, O.P. *Destined for Liberty: The Human Person in the Philosophy of Karol Wojtyła/John Paul II.* Washington, DC: Catholic University of America Press, 2000.

Langan, John, S.J. "Beatitude and the Moral Law in St. Thomas." *Journal of Religious Ethics* 5, no. 2 (1977): 187.

LeDoux, Joseph. *Synaptic Self: How Our Brains Become Who We Are.* New York: Viking, 2002.

Lee, Patrick. "Human Beings Are Animals." In *Natural Law and Moral Inquiry: Ethics, Metaphysics, and Politics in the Work of Germain Grisez*, edited by Robert P. George, 135–51. Washington, DC: Georgetown University Press, 1998.

Lincoln, Abraham. Second inaugural address. "The Inaugural Addresses of the Presidents," the Avalon Project, Lillian Goldman Law Library, Yale University. avalon.law.yale.edu/19th_century/lincoln2.asp (accessed January 7, 2010).

Locke, John. *Second Treatise of Government.* Indianapolis: Hackett, 1980.

Lustig, A. J. "Darwin's Difficulties" in Michael Ruse and Robert J. Richards, eds., *The Cambridge Companion to the "Origin of Species".* Cambridge: Cambridge University Press, 2009.

MacIntyre, Alasdair. *After Virtue: A Study in Moral Theory.* 2nd ed. Notre Dame, IN: University of Notre Dame Press, 1984.

Marx, Karl. "Manifesto of the Communist Party." In *The Portable Karl Marx*, edited by Eugene Kamenka, 203–41. New York: Penguin Books, 1983.

McBrien, Richard P. *Catholicism.* New ed. New York: HarperCollins, 1994.

McCormick, Richard A., S.J. "Some Early Reactions to *Veritatis Splendor.*" In Curran and McCormick, *John Paul II and Moral Theology*, 5–34.

———. *The Critical Calling: Reflections on Moral Dilemmas Since Vatican II.* Washington, DC: Georgetown University Press, 1989.

McDermott, John A., S.J. "The Theology of John Paul II: A Response." In *The Thought of Pope John Paul II: A Collection of Essays and Studies*, edited by John McDermott, 55–68. Rome: Editrice Pontificia Università Gregoriana, 1993.

Melina, Livio, and José Noriega, eds. *Camminare nella Luce: Prospettive della teologia morale a partire da* Veritatis Splendor. Rome: Lateran University Press, 2004.

Mill, John Stuart. *On Liberty*. Indianapolis: Hackett Publishing Company, 1978.

———. *Utilitarianism*. Indianapolis: Hackett Publishing Company, 2001.

Monod, Jacques. *Le hasard et la nécessité: Essai sur la philosophie naturelle de la biologie moderne*. Paris: Éditions du Seuil, 1970.

Moore, G. E. *Principia Ethica*. Cambridge: Cambridge University Press, 1968.

Newman, James R. *The World of Mathematics*. Vol. 1. New York: Simon and Schuster, 1956.

Nowakowski, Piotr. "The Natural Law in Jean-Jacques Rousseau's Philosophy and Its Social and Pedagogical Consequences." Paper presented at the International Symposium on Natural Law, Catholic University of Eastern Africa (CUEA), Nairobi, Kenya, February 6–8, 2007.

O'Brien, Darcy. *The Hidden Pope*. New York: Rodale, 1998.

Odozor, Paulinus Ikechukwu, C.S.Sp. *Richard A. McCormick and the Renewal of Moral Theology*. Notre Dame: University of Notre Dame Press, 1995.

O'Keefe, John J. "No Place for Failure? Augustinian Reflections on *Veritatis Splendor*." In Allsopp and O'Keefe, Veritatis Splendor: *American Responses*, 16–37.

Oppenheim, Felix E. *Dimensions of Freedom: An Analysis*. New York: St. Martin's Press, 1961.

Ouchi, William. *Theory Z: How American Business Can Meet the Japanese Challenge*. Reading, MA: Addison-Wesley Publishing Company, 1981.

Paul VI. *Humanae Vitae*. Encyclical. Boston: Pauline Books and Media, 1968.

Peirce, Charles Sanders. *Collected Papers*. Cambridge, MA: Belknap Press, 1965.

Pew Research Center. *As Marriage and Parenthood Drift Apart, Public Is Concerned about Social Impact*. July 1, 2007. pewresearch.org/assets/social/pdf/Marriage.pdf.

Pinckaers, Servais, O.P. *Morality: The Catholic View*. Translated by Michael Sherwin, O.P. South Bend, IN: St. Augustine's Press, 2003.

———. *Pour une lecture de* Veritatis Splendor. Paris: Éditions Mame, 1995.

———. *The Sources of Christian Ethics*. Translated from the 3rd ed. by Sr. Mary Thomas Noble, O.P. Washington, DC: Catholic University of America Press, 1995.

Place, Michael D. "*Familiaris Consortio*: A Review of Its Theology." In Curran and McCormick, *John Paul II and Moral Theology*, 188.

Plato. *Apology*. In *The Collected Dialogues of Plato*, edited by E. Hamilton and H. Cairns. Princeton: Princeton University Press, 1961.

———. *Euthyphro*. In *The Collected Dialogues of Plato*, edited by E. Hamilton and H. Cairns. Princeton: Princeton University Press, 1961.

———. *Phaedo*. Translated with an introduction and notes by David Gallop. New York: Oxford University Press, 1999.

———. *Republic*. Translated by G. M. A. Grube and revised by C. D. C. Reeve. Indianapolis: Hackett Publishing Company, 1992.

Porter, Jean. "The Moral Act in *Veritatis Splendor* and in Aquinas's *Summa Theologiae*." In Allsopp and O'Keefe, eds., Veritatis Splendor: *American Responses*, 63.

———. "Moral Reasoning, Authority, and Community in *Veritatis Splendor*." *Annual of the Society of Christian Ethics* 15, no. 1 (1995): 201–19.

Preston, R. "*Veritatis Splendor*: A Comment." *Studies in Christian Ethics* 7 (1994): 40.

Rahner, Karl. *Grundkurs des Glaubens: Einführung in den Begriff des Christentums*. 3rd ed. Freiburg: Herder, 1976.

Ratzinger, Joseph. See Benedict XVI.

Rawls, John. *A Theory of Justice*. Cambridge, MA: Belknap Press, 1971.

Reimers, Adrian J. *An Analysis of the Concepts of Self-Fulfillment and Self-Realization in the Thought of Karol Wojtyła, Pope John Paul II*. Problems in Contemporary Philosophy 48. Lewiston, NY: Edwin Mellen Press, 2001.

———. "Human Suffering and John Paul II's *Theology of the Body*." *Nova et Vetera*, English ed., 2, no. 2 (Fall 2004): 445–59.

———. *The Soul of the Person: A Contemporary Philosophical Psychology*. Washington, DC: Catholic University of America Press, 2006.

———. "The Thomistic Personalism of Karol Wojtyła (Pope John Paul II)." In *Atti del IX congresso tomistico internazionale*, vol. 6, *Storia del tomismo fonti e riflessi*, 364–69. Vatican City: Pontificia Accademia di S. Tommaso, 1992.

———. "Truth and the Open-Endedness of the Natural Order." In *The Concept of Nature in Science and Theology*, edited by Niels H. Gregersen, Michael W. S. Parsons, and Christoph Wasserman, pt. 1, Geneva: Labor et fides, 1997.

———. "St. Thomas's Intentions at *De Veritate* I, 1." *Doctor Communis* 42 (1989): 175–82.

Rhonheimer, Martin. "La prospettiva della persona agente e la natura della ragione practica." In Melina and Noriega, *Camminare nella Luce*, 169–224.

Russell, Bertrand. *Selected Papers of Bertrand Russell*. New York: Random House: 1–15. [n.d.: No publication date is given for this book, but the author's introduction is dated 1927.]

Ryan, Maura Anne. "'Then Who Can Be Saved': Ethics and Ecclesiology in *Veritatis Splendor*." In Allsopp and O'Keefe, Veritatis Splendor: *American Responses*, 1–15.

Sagan, Carl. *Pale Blue Dot: A Vision of the Human Future in Space*. New York: Random House, 1994.

Sartre, Jean-Paul. *Being and Nothingness*. Translated by Hazel E. Barnes. New York: Philosophical Library, 1956.

———. "Existentialism Is a Humanism." In *Existentialism from Dostoevsky to Sartre*, edited by Walter Kaufmann, 345–69 (New York: New American Library, 1975).

———. *No Exit, and Three Other Plays*. New York: Vintage Books, 1989.

Scheler, Max. *Der Formalismus in der Ethik und die materiale Wertethik: Neuer Versuch der Grundlegung eines ethischen Personalismus*. 5th ed. Bern: Franke Verlag, 1966.

———. "On the Rehabilitation of Virtue." Translated by Eugene Kelly. *American Catholic Philosophical Society Quarterly* 79, no. 1 (Winter 2005): 21–37.

Schmitz, Kenneth L. *At the Center of the Human Drama: The Philosophical Anthropology of Karol Wojtyla/Pope John Paul II*. Washington, DC: Catholic University of America Press, 1993.

Schneider, Birgit. *Wer Gott dient, wird nicht krumm: feministische Ethik im Dialog mit Karol Wojtyla und Dietmar Mieth*. Mainz: Matthias-Grünewald-Verlag, 1997.

Searle, John R. "Consciousness, Its Irreducibility." In Honderich, *Oxford Companion to Philosophy*, 153.

———. *Minds, Brains and Science*. Cambridge: Harvard University Press, 1984.

———. *The Rediscovery of the Mind*. Cambridge, MA: MIT Press, 1992.

Seifert, Josef. *Essere e persona: Verso una fondazione fenomenologica di una metafisica classica e personalistica*. Milan: Vita e pensiero, 1989.

———. "Karol Cardinal Wojtyła (Pope John Paul II) as Philosopher and the Cracow/Lublin School of Philosophy." *Aletheia: An International Journal of Philosophy* 2 (1981): 130–99.

Shakespeare, William. *The Complete Works of Shakespeare*. Edited by W. J. Craig. New York: Oxford University Press, 1919.

Sherwin, Michael, O.P. "John Paul's Theology of Truth and Freedom: A Dissident Phenomenology in a Thomistic Anthropology." *Nova et Vetera*, English ed., 3, no. 3 (2005): 543–68.

Simpson, Peter. *On Karol Wojtyla*. Belmont, CA: Wadsworth, 2001.

Singer, Peter. *Practical Ethics*. 2nd ed. Cambridge: Cambridge University Press, 1993.

———. *Rethinking Life and Death: The Collapse of Our Traditional Ethics.* New York: St. Martin's Press, 1994.

Smart, J. J. C. *Ethics, Persuasion and Truth.* London: Routledge and Kegan Paul, 1984.

Solzhenitsyn, Aleksandr. *The Gulag Archipelago, 1918–1956: An Experiment in Literary Investigation.* Translated by Thomas P. Whitney. Vol. 2 (pts. 3 and 4). New York: Harper and Row, 1975.

Somerville, Robert. "Les encycliques du pape et l'évangile." In *Paroles de pape, paroles protestantes,* edited by André Birmelé, Jean Ansaldi, Olivier Abel, et al., 59–72. Paris: Les bergers et les mages, 1995.

Sperry, Roger Wolcoll. "Consciousness and Causality." In *The Oxford Companion to the Mind,* edited by R. L. Gregory, 164. Oxford: Oxford University Press, 1987.

Spinello, John. *The Genius of John Paul II: The Great Pope's Moral Wisdom.* Lanham: Sheed and Ward, 2007.

Spohn, William C. "Morality on the Way of Discipleship: The Use of Scripture in *Veritatis Splendor.*" In Allsopp and O'Keefe, Veritatis Splendor: *American Responses,* 83–103.

Stanford, Craig. *Significant Others: The Ape-Human Continuum and the Quest for Human Nature.* New York: Basic Books, 2001.

Styczeń, Tadeusz. "Premessa: Karol Wojtyła: Un filosofo della morale agli occhi del suo discipolo." In Wojtyła, *Metafisica della persona,* cv–cxxiv.

———. "Reply to Kalinowski: By Way of an Addendum to the Addenda." *Aletheia: An International Journal of Philosophy* 4, Epistemology and Logic (1988): 217–25.

———. "Verità, libertà e amore nell'enciclica *Veritatis Splendor.*" In Melina and Noriega, *Camminare nella Luce,* 471–77.

———. "Zur Frage einer unabhängigen Ethik." In *Der Streit um den Menschen,* by Karol Wojtyła, Andrzej Szotek, and Tadeusz Styczeń, Kevelaer: Butzon und Bercker, 1979.

Szostek, Andrzej, M.I.C. "Freiheit—Wahrheit—Gewissen." *Ethos: Vierteljahrsschrift* (Lublin), Sonderausgabe no. 1, 1993.

———. *Natur—Vernunft—Freiheit: Philosophische Analyse der Konzeption schöpferischer Vernunft in der zeitgenössichen Moraltheologie.* Frankfurt am Main: Peter Lang, 1992.

Szulc, Tad. *Pope John Paul II: The Biography.* New York: Scribner, 1995.

Tattersall, Ian. "How We Came to Be Human." *Scientific American* 16, no. 2 (2006): 66–73.

Tischner, Józef. *The Spirit of Solidarity.* Translated by Marek B. Zaleski and Benjamin Fiore, S.J. San Francisco: Harper and Row, 1984.

Tymieniecka, Anna-Teresa, ed. *Analecta Husserliana: The Yearbook of Phenomenological Research.* Vol. 7, *The Human Being in Action.* Dordrecht: D. Reidel Publishing Company, 1978.

———, ed. *Analecta Husserliana: The Yearbook of Phenomenological Research.* Vol. 9, *The Teleologies in Husserlian Phenomenology.* Dordrecht: D. Reidel Publishing Company, 1979.

———, ed. *Analecta Husserliana: The Yearbook of Phenomenological Research.* Vol. 11, *The Great Chain of Being and Italian Phenomenology.* Dordrecht: D. Reidel Publishing Company, 1981.

Van Inwagen, Peter. *Metaphysics.* Boulder: Westview Press, 1993.

———. *The Problem of Evil: The Gifford Lectures Delivered in the University of St. Andrews in 2003.* Oxford: Clarendon Press, 2006.

Vatican Council II. *Acta synodalia Sacrosancti Concilii Oecumenici Vaticani II.* Vol. 4, pts. 2–3. Vatican City: Typis Polyglottis Vaticanis, 1977.

———. *Gaudium et Spes,* Pastoral Constitution on the Church in the Modern World. Boston: Pauline Books and Media, 1965.

Von Helmholtz, Hermann. "On the Origin and Significance of Geometrical Axioms." In Newman, *World of Mathematics,* 1:647–68.

Von Hildebrand, Dietrich. *Ethics.* Chicago: Franciscan Herald Press, 1953.

Wade, Nicholas. "Is 'Do unto Others' Written into Our Genes?" *New York Times,* September 18, 2007, National Edition, D1–D7.

Waldstein, Michael. "Dietrich von Hildebrand and St. Thomas Aquinas on Goodness and Happiness." *Nova et Vetera,* English ed., 1, no. 2 (2003): 403–64.

———. "La grazia in forma paterna e il vecchio principio metafisico dell'autocommunicazione dell'essere." In Melina and Noriega, *Camminare nella Luce,* 485–89.

———. Introduction to John Paul II, *Man and Woman He Created Them,* 1–128.

Weigel, George. *God's Choice: Benedict XVI and the Future of the Catholic Church.* New York: HarperCollins, 2005.

———. *Witness to Hope: The Biography of Pope John Paul II.* New York: HarperCollins, 1999.

Williams, George. *The Mind of John Paul II: Origins of His Thought and Action.* New York: Seabury Press, 1981.

Young, Kathleen Z. "The Imperishable Virginity of Saint Maria Goretti." In "Violence against Women," special issue, *Gender and Society* 3, no. 4 (December 1989): 474–82.

Index